LEADERSHIP OF THE AMERICAN ZIONIST ORGANIZATION, 1897–1930

YONATHAN SHAPIRO

Leadership of the American Zionist Organization 1897-1930

UNIVERSITY OF ILLINOIS PRESS
URBANA · CHICAGO · LONDON

© 1971 BY THE BOARD OF TRUSTEES
OF THE UNIVERSITY OF ILLINOIS
MANUFACTURED IN THE UNITED
STATES OF AMERICA
LIBRARY OF CONGRESS CATALOG
CARD NO. 71-126521
252 00132 X

To the memory of my parents

Acknowledgment

I feel especially indebted to two of my teachers. Professor Robert K. Merton and Professor Sigmund Diamond suggested important improvements to the manuscript, but the intellectual stimulation they provided goes far beyond this specific study.

I want to thank the personnel of the libraries in which this study was researched, particularly of the American Jewish Archives in Cincinnati and the Zionist Archives in New York.

Finally, thanks to my friends who aided and encouraged me at every stage of the research and the writing of this book.

Contents

List of Abbreviations

Introduction   3
   The Purpose of the Study—Some Basic Assumptions

CHAPTER I   American Jewry in the Nineteenth
and Early Twentieth Centuries   8
   Social Composition of American Jewry
   Cultural Trends and Influences within the
      American Jewish Community
   The Zionist Ideology

CHAPTER II   The Federation of American Zionists and
Its Leadership, 1898–1914   24
   The Organization
   The Leaders of the Federation of American
      Zionists (F.A.Z.)
   The Reform Leaders
   The Conservative Leaders and the Eastern European
      Party Workers
   The Leadership of the Eastern European Intellectuals

CHAPTER III   The New Zionist Leadership   53
   The New Leaders and Why They Joined the Organization
   How Brandeis Became a Zionist Leader
   The Meaning of Zionist Ideology to Brandeis and
      to Some of His Associates

CHAPTER IV   The Fight for an American Jewish Congress,
1914–16   77
   War Relief Operations of the Zionist Organization and
      the American Jewish Committee
   The Congress Issue: The Struggle between the Zionist
      Organization and the American Jewish Committee
   The Congress Issue: Disagreements within
      the Zionist Organization
   Brandeis's Resignation and the Compromise
      on the Jewish Congress

CHAPTER V Conflicts Within the Zionist Organization, 1916–20 99

The Organization during Brandeis's Presidency
The Organization after Brandeis's Resignation
The Brandeis and Schiff Groups Attempt to Unite
Establishing the Zionist Organization of America (Z.O.A.)
The Search for a New Ideology
Anxiety and Frustration among the German-Jewish Zionist Leaders

CHAPTER VI The Struggle over Control of the World Zionist Organization 135

Sources of Friction between the American and European Leaders
The London Conference
The Dilemma of the Eastern European Party Workers
Keeping the Membership Ignorant of the Dispute
An Open Fight between the Two Sets of Leaders
Resignation of Brandeis's Supporters

CHAPTER VII Zionist Activities in the United States, 1921–26 180

The Organization's Dedication to Fund-Raising
The Brandeisists' Efforts to Develop Palestine Economically
The Zionists' Concentration on Palestinian Work and the Jewish Agency
The Success of Hadassah

CHAPTER VIII The Crisis of Leadership in the Z.O.A., 1927–30 207

Jewish Intellectuals in the Lead
Attempts to Pacify the Growing Opposition
Reentry of the Brandeis Group into Zionist Politics
Lipsky Defeats Brandeis
Efforts of the Intellectuals to Maintain Their Leadership
The Brandeis-Warburg Understanding and the Defeat of the Intellectuals
The Brandeisists in Control Again

CHAPTER IX From Zionism to Palestinianism 248

American Jewry after World War I

Contents

> *The Zionist Ideology*
> *The Zionist Organization*

CHAPTER X   A Sociological Summing-up   262

> *Acculturation, Assimilation, and Marginality*
> *The Functions of Leaders and the Legitimation*
>   *of Their Authority*
> *Types of Organized Support to Leaders' Authority*

Bibliography   277

Index   291

LIST OF ABBREVIATIONS

A.J.C.	American Jewish Committee
A.J.S.	American Journal of Sociology
A.J.R.C.	American Jewish Relief Committee
AJYB	American Jewish Year Book
A.S.R.	American Sociological Review
F.A.Z.	Federation of American Zionists
I.T.O.	International Territorialist Organization
J.D.C.	Joint Distribution Committee
J.T.S.	Jewish Theological Seminary
PAJHS	Publications of the American Jewish Historical Society
P.D.C.	Palestine Development Council
P.E.C.	Palestine Economic Corporation
P.Z.C.	Provisional Zionist Committee
U.P.A.	United Palestine Appeal
W.Z.O.	World Zionist Organization; sometimes also referred to as I.Z.O., International Zionist Organization.
Z.O.A.	Zionist Organization of America

LEADERSHIP OF THE AMERICAN ZIONIST ORGANIZATION, 1897–1930

INTRODUCTION

The Purpose of the Study— Some Basic Assumptions

This study was prompted by an interest in the problem of the survival of the Jewish community in the United States as a distinct socio-cultural group. The main concern of this work is to account for the development of an ideology in support of group survival within the American Jewish community. Previous studies have suggested that the Jews in the United States manifest stronger tendencies than other ethnic groups toward survival as a separate group.[1]

It is assumed that every ethnic group exhibits certain characteristics: a common social myth, or ideology, which justifies a separate existence; a certain degree of organization; recognized leadership. In the present case, we deal with an ethnic group that emigrated to the United States where they constituted a minority group within a dominant alien culture. This group migration to the United States was followed by a process of acculturation, the acquisition of the culture of the dominant group.

The process of acculturation requires an adjustment within the three aspects of group life we have mentioned. In an effort to maintain the loyalty of its members, the common group myth must be readjusted to minimize the conflict with the new society. At the same time, it cannot go too far in compromising its myth without undermining its own ability to survive. It will thus try to maintain enough of the myth to make membership meaningful and attractive to its members.

A certain organizational life of the minority group will have to coexist within the organizational life of the new society, which itself demands the loyalty and dedication of all members of the society. The minority group will be forced to restrict the scope of loyalty demanded from its members; otherwise they will face a conflict that will force them to choose between affiliation with the ethnic group and prime loyalty to it or affiliation with the dominant society and loyalty to it. The group must retain enough independent activity to hold its membership and to maintain their loyalty.

The type of leadership that will emerge and take control of the ethnic group will depend on developments in the two spheres and in the relationship between the dominant society and the ethnic minority. One

---

[1] For an interesting study along these lines, see C. Bezalel Sherman, *Yidden un Andere Etnishe Gruppes in die Farainigte Shtaten* (New York: Unser Veg, 1948). A shorter version of this book appeared in English titled: *The Jew within American Society* (Detroit: Wayne State University Press, 1965).

possible pattern of leadership assumes that since leadership symbolizes the wishes and aspirations of its following, the leaders of a group are expected to conform to at least some of the general standards and ideas of the society into which the minority is being acculturated. Furthermore, since the leaders of the minority group also represent it in their relations with the larger society, the minority group will seek leaders who command the respect of the dominant society. Since those leaders, deemed so valuable by the group, will also be those who will be tempted to leave the group, if accepted by the dominant society, the minority will endeavor to attract them by conferring on them all manner of honors and positions within their own group.

Another pattern, according to Pinner, Jacobs, and Selznick, is found "when a dependent, low-status constituency organizes for action vis-à-vis a dominant majority." Often a "deviant" leadership develops that does not conform to the standards and ideas of the majority and so will not be respected by it.[2]

So far we have considered the processes of acculturation and the question of group survival from the standpoint of the group, not of its individual members. The same phenomenon should be examined from the standpoint of the individual by observing the changes in the status-set and role relations of the members.[3] Thus, in our case, a Jew will have one set of patterned role relations with a fellow Jew and a different set of patterned role relations with a non-Jew. Similarly, in his status as American or Russian, he will follow one set of norms applicable to his role relations with his fellow citizens and a different set of norms with those of differing nationality.

In the case of the immigrants who came to the United States from Europe, one may expect a weakening in the power and importance of the ethnic ties as new relationships are created and new statuses acquired. The web of new statuses and role relations that immigrants acquire in their new society, whether in an occupational group, in politics, or in the social life of their residential community, has values and norms attached to them that may conflict with those of their ethnic community.

---

[2] Frank Pinner, Paul Jacobs, and Philip Selznick, *Old Age and Political Behavior* (Berkeley: University of California Press, 1959), p. 14.

[3] In the use of these sociological concepts, I am following the ideas developed by Merton. Each individual in the society occupies many statuses which together comprise his status-set and designate his position in the social structure. Each status has its distinctive patterned relations with other statuses which are themselves parts of other status-sets of other individual members of the society. Every such relationship between two statuses is called a role relationship. Robert K. Merton, *Social Theory and Social Structure*, rev. ed. (Glencoe, Ill.: The Free Press, 1957), pp. 368–70.

Introduction

The old loyalties and obligations have to yield to new ones. It is assumed that the members of the group who acquire or expect to acquire new statuses will attempt to change their status-set and role relations in such a way as to create as little conflict as possible, a rather difficult task at best.

Since our investigation focuses on problems of acculturation, the concept of acculturation should be clearly defined and distinguished from assimilation. The usefulness of this distinction was established by anthropologists long ago, although many prefer not to make it too rigid.[4]

The distinction between the two is best expressed by Melford Spiro:

> The acculturation of an ethnic group in the United States—its acquisition of the culture of the dominant group—is an exclusive function of the group's desire and capacity for acculturation; but assimilation—the disappearance of group identity through nondifferential association and exogamy (marriage outside the tribe or blood group)—is a function of both dominant and ethnic group behavior. And in some instances, even when the ethnic group desires assimilation, the dominant group prevents it.[5]

In accordance with this distinction, we assume that assimilation of the Jewish group in America lags behind the process of the acculturation. This gap is a crucial factor in the life of American Jewry. Although our study concentrates on the problem of acculturation, which is an exclusive function "of the group's desire and capacity," the relation between the process of acculturation and assimilation will have to be kept in mind constantly, since they are interdependent.

Our inquiry starts with the assumption that the American version of Zionism served the function of providing an ideology of survival for the Jewish community of the United States. We pose the question: how did Zionism come to serve this function?

To deal with this question, we must examine the developments of the Zionist idea in the United States from the end of the nineteenth century, when it was brought over from Europe, to 1930, when its present ideological formulation became dominant in the Zionist Organization of America. This development can not be adequately studied in isolation but must be related to structural changes within the Zionist Organization in America and the American Jewish community, with special reference to the national leaders of the Zionist Organization.

---

[4] Melville J. Herskovits, *Acculturation: The Study of Culture Contact* (Glouchester, Mass.: Peter Smith, 1958), p. 14.

[5] Melford E. Spiro, "The Acculturation of American Ethnic Groups," *American Anthropologist* 57 (1955): 1244.

There are several reasons for concentrating on the group of leaders of the Zionist Organization of America (Z.O.A.). (Until 1918, the Z.O.A. was known as the Federation of American Zionists, F.A.Z.) First, this is the group most directly responsible for the formulation and expression of the change that took place in the Zionist ideology. Second, there is no access to the views of the followers, in contrast to the leaders' positions, on issues of Zionism and group survival. Finally, changes and innovations in Zionist ideology, expressed by the leaders of the movement, took place at the same time as a vigorous struggle for power within the Zionist Organization. Ideological developments were thus an integral part of the power struggle. This is nothing new. As Herbert Butterfield has observed, leaders are always "the carriers of ideas as well as the repositories of vested interests."[6]

All this means that we shall have to consider a wide area of problems concerning social organization and leadership of the F.A.Z. and the Z.O.A. These problems will be related, whenever relevant, to structural and cultural developments within the American Jewish community.

We shall find that the Zionist ideology in the United States was transformed during the period under discussion from orthodox Zionism ("the Jews are and should remain a separate political and cultural entity") to Palestinianism ("all Jews should help in the upbuilding of Palestine as a national Jewish home"). This transformation is related to the transference of Zionist leadership from the foreign-born, Yiddish-speaking intellectuals to the native-born, American-educated leaders and to the transformation of Zionism from a social movement aimed at fundamental changes in the social order into an organization with limited goals. All these developments are the outcome of the process of acculturation of the American-Jewish community.

Our investigation carries us from 1898, when the Federation of American Zionists (F.A.Z.) was founded in New York, to 1930. In that year, Palestinianism became the official ideology of the American Zionist Organization and was emerging as the cornerstone of a specific American Jewish culture. The type of leaders that gained control of the Z.O.A. by 1930 continues to occupy the leadership in the organizational life of American Jewry.

The rise of Nazi Germany in the 1930's, the persecution of European Jewry, and the developments in Palestine which led to the establishment of the State of Israel only intensified the support among American Jews for a Jewish Palestine. These events were not the cause for the

---

[6] Herbert Butterfield, *George III and the Historians*, rev. ed. (New York: The Macmillan Co., 1959), p. 209.

strong Palestinian sentiment manifested by American Jewry. This book attempts to show that developments in the American Zionist Organization and its ideology during the earlier period help us understand later developments.

CHAPTER I

American Jewry in the Nineteenth and Early Twentieth Centuries

Social Composition of American Jewry

The Jewish community in the United States during the last decades of the nineteenth century and the early decades of the twentieth century comprised two distinct groups, German Jews and Eastern European Jews, which differed in various social and cultural characteristics. Most German Jews had come to the United States between 1840 and 1870. Many of them rose quickly in society, achieving high status before the Eastern Europeans started arriving in large numbers in the 1880's and before the great majority of them had arrived between 1900 and 1914.

The number of German-Jewish migrants was small, probably about 200,000, whereas about 2.5 million immigrants from Eastern Europe had entered the country by 1924.[1] Unlike the Eastern Europeans who succeeded them, the German Jews did not concentrate in a few cities but dispersed throughout the United States. In 1890, the United States Census Bureau examined a national sample of the Jewish population, the overwhelming number of whom must certainly have been German Jews. By then they already had reached a remarkably high economic level. In fact, a third of them belonged to the liberal and business professions, whereas less than a tenth of the Eastern Europeans were found in clerical jobs and the professions by 1900.[2] The rapid growth in status of the German Jews is especially remarkable because practically all German Jews arriving a generation before had started as peddlers; however, by 1890, two-thirds of them reported keeping servants.[3]

Most Eastern Europeans started their careers in the United States as laborers. Their proletarian status meant a social, though not an economic, decline, since in their homeland they were typically in lower middle-class occupations. Jacob Leschinsky, the well-known Jewish sociologist and demographer, notes that although this process of proletarianization of the Eastern European Jews had started in Russia as early as the middle of the nineteenth century, most laborers who came to the United States even after 1900 were sons of lower middle-class

---

[1] John Higham, "Social Discrimination against the Jews in America, 1830–1930," *Publications of the American Jewish Historical Society* 62 (1957–58):8.

[2] John S. Billings, *Vital Statistics of the Jews in the United States*, U.S. Census Bulletin No. 19 (Washington, D.C., Government Printing Office, 1890), p. 7; Nathan Glazer, "Social Characteristics of American Jews: 1654–1854," *American Jewish Year Book* 56 (1955): 6–7.

[3] Billings, U. S. Census Bulletin No. 19, pp. 4, 5.

parents.⁴ The importance of this social descent for understanding the Eastern European community in the United States was recognized by community leaders in the Jewish ghetto. In 1900, one of them argued that the condition of Jewish laborers was quite satisfactory, as compared with conditions in Russia and even in the United States outside the ghetto. Nevertheless, Jewish workers were dissatisfied and unhappy. They were convinced that Americans who lived outside the ghetto were better off economically than themselves. Explaining their state of mind, he wrote: "True, most of our brethren here are not wealthy though quite well off. But most of them are not really happy with what they have, especially those who had forgotten their poverty and humiliations in Russia but could never forget their decline from their status of traders to that of laborers, even though this descent is in reality an ascent for them."⁵ The resentment of the declassed Jewish laborers in the American ghetto helped motivate them to improve their economic position and to get out of the ghetto.

The economic gains of Eastern European Jews in the United States did not compensate for their loss of status. Here, in fact, is a classic example of what has come to be called relative deprivation. Judged by the values of their old country in Europe, the migrants to the United States had declined from middle-class to working-class occupations. For these immigrants, the old society provided the standards by which they evaluated themselves; it continued to be their reference group, providing the criteria by which they measured their accomplishments.

Another important social characteristic of the Eastern European Jewish immigrants was that far fewer Jews than other immigrants returned to their home countries. Also, whole families constituted a much higher percentage of Jewish immigrants from Eastern Europe than of other immigrants.⁶

---

⁴ Jacob Leschinsky, "The Social Complexion of American Jewry," *ORT Economic Review* 2 (November–December 1941): 19–22.

⁵ P. Wiernick, "Ha'hitpatchut Ha'chomrit Shell Ha'poalim Ha'yehudim Be America," *The Monthly Intelligencer* 1 (1900): 63.

⁶ C. Bezalel Sherman, *The Jews within American Society* (Detroit: Wayne State University Press, 1965), pp. 60, 61. That the Jews came here to stay is further evidenced by the figures, summarized in the following table, showing that far fewer Jews than other immigrants returned to their home countries:

Years	*Immigrants Returning from the United States*	
	Jews	All Immigrants
1908–14	7.1%	30.8%
1915–20	4.3	56.6
1921–24	0.7	25.8

Studies of immigrant groups other than the Jews show that it was the intellectuals among them who were discouraged enough to return to their old country.[7] All people are identified with the cultural traditions with which they have been brought up, and they are rarely capable of becoming fully identified with a new culture during their adult life. This is particularly true for intellectuals devoted to the "creating of new ideas or disseminating these ideas to others."[8] If immigrants in general are unable to gain a command over the new language that equals their mastery of their native tongue, intellectuals who "wield the power of the spoken and written word" are particularly handicapped in pursuing their *metier* in the new society.[9]

These difficulties, as we shall see later, were also experienced by the Jewish intellectuals. But they did not go back, since for them there was nowhere to go. Economic and social discrimination against the Jews in Eastern Europe had forced them to leave, and very few wished to return. Even intellectuals among the Russians and Poles, advocates of liberal and socialist causes, manifested strong anti-Semitic sentiments.[10] For Jewish intellectuals, there was little choice but to stay and try to adjust and find their place in the new society.

The Jewish intelligentsia was responsible for the renaissance of Jewish culture in the United States at the beginning of the twentieth century. It was the intelligentsia that created the golden age of Yiddish literature and journalism, the Yiddish theater, and the exciting intellectual life of the ghetto. In his autobiography, Lincoln Steffens, then a reporter in New York, tells the story of a dispute in the Jewish ghetto about realism in art. The argument was going on in the cafes, "where the debate was on at every table," and in the theaters, "where . . . a community of people fighting over an art question as savagely as other people fought over political or religious questions."[11]

To understand these people and their interest in "high culture," we

---

[7] On the difficulties that the intelligentsia were facing in the new society see, for example, John A. Hawgood, *The Tragedy of German-America* (New York: G. P. Putnam's Sons, 1940), *passim;* Joseph Slabey Roucek, "The Passing of the American Czechoslovaks," A.J.S. 39 (1934–40): 611–25.

[8] Raymond Aron, *The Opium of the Intellectuals* (New York: Doubleday & Co., 1957), p. 206. Aron observes in his study the identification and commitment that intellectuals in all societies feel toward their own nation. "They live their country's destiny," he writes, "in a particularly acute form," ibid., p. 217.

[9] Joseph A. Schumpeter, *Capitalism, Socialism and Democracy*, 4th ed. (London: George Allen & Unwin Ltd., 1954), p. 147.

[10] For further details see Louis Greenberg, *The Jews in Russia*, 2 vols. (New Haven, Conn.: Yale University Press, 1941).

[11] Lincoln Steffens, *The Autobiography of Lincoln Steffens* (New York: Harcourt, Brace and Company, 1931), pp. 317–18.

should note that the intelligentsia was growing rapidly in numbers and importance in continental Europe by the end of the nineteenth century. Composed of "public officials, professional men and women, teachers, trained technicians, journalists, etc.," the intelligentsia engaged in the discussion of literature, poetry, painting, music, philosophy, and, especially in Central and Eastern Europe, political issues. They helped to develop political ideologies—socialism, communism, nationalism—and built and directed the mass movements that aimed at realizing these ideologies.[12]

The emerging Jewish intelligentsia in Eastern Europe participated in these developments, and the segment of this group that came to the United States continued their literary and political activities. They provided the leadership of the Eastern European Jewish community and gave expression to the resentment felt by the Eastern Europeans against their German Jewish brethren who adopted a patronizing and condescending attitude toward the newcomers, excluding them from their social functions and social institutions and insisting that they give up their culture and traditions as a prerequisite to becoming good Americans.[13] The tension between the two groups dominated the life of the Jewish community at the time.[14] The class differences between the two communities, the different dates of their migration, and the differences in their cultures and traditions all contributed to the antagonism.

But the main cause for the exasperation of the German Jews with their Eastern European brethren seems to have been that the influx of the latecomers halted the process of assimilation of the German Jews into American society. The small and dispersed group of German Jews had hoped eventually to assimilate into American society, and some had undoubtedly succeeded in doing so. This was possible as long as the Jews were a small and dispersed group.[15] But once the Eastern European migration to the United States assumed its large proportions, the whole situation changed. Their large numbers and heavy concentration in a

---

[12] For further details on this problem see Feliks Gross, ed. *European Ideologies: A Survey of Twentieth-Century Political Ideas* (New York: Philosophical Library, 1948), especially the introductory chapter.

[13] Harold Silver, "Some Attitudes of the East European Jewish Immigrants toward Organized Jewish Charity in the United States in the Years 1890–1900," (Master's essay, New York Graduate School for Jewish Social Work, 1934), pp. 34, 275–76. Much material has been published in recent years on the friction between German Jewry and the newly arrived Eastern Europeans in the late nineteenth and early twentieth centuries. See, for example, Zosa Szajkowsky, "The Attitude of American Jews to East European Immigration, 1881–1893," *PAJHS* 40 (1950–51): 221–80.

[14] In support of this view of American Jewish history, consult Jacob Rader Marcus, "The Periodization of American Jewish History," *PAJHS* 47 (1957–58): 125–33.

[15] Glazer, "Social Characteristics of American Jews," p. 8.

few cities, and their distinct language and cultural habits forced the dominant Gentile society to recognize the group and led to the development of a stereotype of "Jew" based on the numerous and more recent Jewish immigrants rather than on the small minority of established German Jews. The anti-Semitism stimulated by this influx of immigrants, similar in quality to the anti-Semitism that existed in Europe, did not discriminate between the two communities, a fact that produced "an all-too-human resentment and anti-Semitism within the Jewish community itself."[16]

There seems to have been no escape from the fact that the road to assimilation was blocked as a result of these developments. Although this was bitterly resented by most German Jews and although the tension between the two communities continued throughout the early twentieth century, all Jews found themselves unavoidably occupying a common low-ranked status, that of Jew. Slowly a rapprochement between the two groups began. This influenced relations on the cultural and ideological levels as well as on the social and organizational levels. These later developments will be considered in later chapters.

Cultural Trends and Influences within the American Jewish Community

A most pressing problem facing the Jewish communities in the Western world after the breakdown of the ghetto walls was that of the survival of Jewry as a separate group. In response to this problem, the American Jewish community adopted a modified version of the Zionist ideology.

The roots of Zionism lay in Europe. There the Jewish communities, responsive to the challenge that modern social conditions and ideas posed for their group survival, evolved four ideologies to meet the problem, of which Zionism was one. When the European Jewish immigrants left their homes, they carried these ideologies with them as part of their spiritual luggage. In America, some were discarded and others were modified to suit the new conditions.

To understand better the solutions to the problem of group survival that occupied the American Jewish community, we must examine briefly the conditions in Europe that gave rise to them. Of the four ideologies concerned with group survival, Orthodoxy and Zionism (though religious and secular, respectively) were both particularistic. They both

---

[16] Digby E. Baltzell, "The Development of a Jewish Upper Class in Philadelphia," in *The Jews*, ed. Marshall Sklare (Glencoe, Ill.: The Free Press, 1958), pp. 282–83.

aimed at preserving the Jewish group as a separate and distinct national-cultural entity. The other two, Reform Judaism and socialism, both reflected a desire for integration with the dominant societies amidst which the group dwelt. Socialists went so far as to advocate the ultimate dissolution of the Jewish group. This was also implied in the teaching of Reform Judaism, especially in the United States in the late nineteenth and early twentieth centuries. The Reform congregations were discarding all traditional ideas and rituals that emphasized the unique and the separate among Jews. They were thus left with the one idea of their universal mission as Jews to propagate a universal truth among the nations, believing that the eventual acceptance of this truth by all civilized nations was imminent.

The adherents of Reform Judaism in the United States at the turn of the century were the Jews who migrated from Germany, not the Eastern European Jews. It had been developed in Germany at the end of the eighteenth and the beginning of the nineteenth centuries, when the emerging nationalist German society was facing the problem of Jews in its midst. Should the Jews be entitled to enjoy the civil and political rights given other German nationals and to participate fully in the political life of the German nation? This question divided German society. The liberal elements supported the emancipation of the Jews and their equal participation in the life of the German nation, on the ground that Jews in Germany were Germans by nationality who practiced a different religion; they were simply Germans of the Mosaic faith. Their opponents, the conservative nationalists, maintained that the Jews were a separate nationality and, not being part of the German nation, should not be entitled to the same civil and political rights as the Germans. Anxious to obtain civil and political equality in Germany, the Jews adopted the liberal formula that constituted the basis of Reform Judaism.[17] According to the tenets of Reform Judaism, Jews were German in Germany, French in France, English in England. Their Jewishness carried only a religious connotation. Moreover, the Jewish religion now became identified with the idea of a universal mission requiring the dispersion of Jews among different nationalities to preach their special but universal truth. This universalistic mission provided the justification for retaining a unique religious faith, which did not, however, demand any separate and particularistic loyalties from its members.

The attempts to minimize the differences between Jews and Gentiles were intensified in the United States. Here the immigrants found a so-

---

[17] Ben Halpern, *The Idea of a Jewish State* (Cambridge, Mass.: Harvard University Press, 1961), pp. 60, 79.

ciety whose peculiar spiritual heritage contained a strong philo-Semitic element, and anti-Semitic practices were rare.[18] But even in the United States, the German Jews were obsessed with the objections to their equal rights as expressed by the nationalists in Germany. This explains why they actively continued to rid their religious institutions of all Jewish nationalist and other distinctive cultural ideas in their eagerness to become part of American society. They were still reacting to the nationalist society they had left behind. And since they faced a society more receptive to their assimilation, they were encouraged to try to eliminate all that was unique to their group with even greater zeal than in Germany.

Their previous experiences in Germany also help explain their violent reaction to Zionism, which they severely attacked even at a time when the Zionist movement had only a handful of supporters and very little influence in the United States. Their fear of the accusation of dual loyalty, which still echoed in their ears, made them particularly anxious, all the more because after the 1880's the United States experienced a rise of the old-world version of anti-Semitism.[19]

The other three ideologies, Orthodoxy, socialism, and Zionism, came to the United States with the more recent and more numerous Eastern European immigrants. Eastern European Jewry was in turmoil before the migration to the United States. The ideas of the enlightenment and humanism that were influencing Eastern European thought and the advance of industrialization gave rise to movements toward adjusting their thinking and spiritual life. Within the Jewish community, these "modernistic" groups were engaged in a bitter fight against the established Orthodox leadership, with its traditional religious outlook, which for the most part was refusing all attempts to modernize religious and spiritual life and thought in the Jewish community. As a consequence of this intransigent attitude, those who eventually rebelled adopted more radical solutions to the problem. They became secularists and freethinkers. They wanted to break away completely from the stagnating Jewish society and its culture. As a result, they started a movement toward complete assimilation or, as it was called, Russification. Their reference group was composed of the more enlightened freethinking liberal elements in Russian society, who were themselves dissatisfied with the established order. They accepted the culture and values of these groups in anticipation of becoming equal members of them.

---

[18] Higham, "Anti-Semitism in the Gilded Age: A Reinterpretation," *The Mississippi Valley Historical Review* 43 (March 1957): 559–78.
[19] Higham, "Social Discrimination against the Jews in America," p. 12.

These attempts were followed by deep disappointments. Faced with rejection by many of the Russian liberals, Jews were led to realize that the barriers between Jews and Gentiles in Eastern Europe were higher than they had expected, and that a much more radical solution was needed to break them down. Many of them turned to socialism, hoping that in the new society to come Jews would find their liberation.

Some disappointed assimilationists emerged from this shattering experience with another solution, Jewish nationalism. This saved them from having to go back to the traditional religious Jewish society. It identified them instead with a distinct Jewish secular culture, a distinct language and literature, to the revival of which they now dedicated themselves. The inspiration for this nationalist solution also came from the outside. They took their cues from the nationalist movements around them that were gaining in popularity and power among the dominant ethnic groups in whose midst they lived.

The ideologies of socialism and Zionism, destined to develop into mass movements among the Jews in Eastern Europe, were both influenced by intellectual and social developments that engulfed the whole European continent in the nineteenth century. Religion was giving way to socialism and nationalism, especially among the lower classes.

Toward the end of the nineteenth century, a remarkable development took place among the Jewish socialist groups—the adoption of nationalist ideas. This was caused not only by the influence of the nationalist ideas but also by the disappointments and frustrations of the Jewish socialists in their attempts to join hands with the Russian socialists to fight together as equals for a socialist society. Socialist doctrine did not prove sufficiently strong to break down the barriers between Jews and Gentiles. As a result, although most Jewish socialists retained their belief in the ultimate destruction of the barriers between Jews and non-Jews once the victory of the new socialist society was assured, many added Jewish nationalism to their socialist ideology. This provided them with a more suitable outlook, one that enabled them to cope with the immediate failure to unite with their fellow Gentiles on a level above the merely ethnic. The Jews in Eastern Europe had been attacked as a people, had suffered as a people, and hence were reacting as a people.

In 1897, the General Jewish Workers' Union in Russia and Poland—the Bund—was established, becoming the most powerful Jewish mass movement in Europe. It accepted the idea of a separate Jewish nationalism and supported national-cultural autonomy for the Jews in their countries of residence. It was definitely and militantly anti-Zionist. This position has been recently explained by one of its leaders, who argued that "historic destiny has made the Jewish people into a stateless nation and—whether we like it or not—it is bound to remain so."[20]

What was common to both Zionism and Bundism was acceptance of Jewish secular culture. Both aimed at preserving "Jewish peoplehood and culture," and both thus "instilled in the Jewish masses a sense of pride in their destiny." In effect, both these secular ideologies accepted the principle of Jewish nationalism. They were divided only on the question of Palestine, the Zionists insisting that the revival of the Jewish nation and its culture could be achieved only in a politically independent state.

Since Jewish Orthodoxy was, in essence, an ethnic nationalist religion, the nationalist element can thus be seen as an integral part of all influential ideologies which penetrated all realms of organized life of Eastern European Jewry. In Eastern Europe, "the conception of the Jews as a nationality achieved thus emotional dominance."[21]

Turning to the American scene, we find in the Jewish socialist movement a carry-over of the conception of the Jews as a nationality by the Bund and the Zionists in the first decades of the century. This conception retained its emotional dominance within the Eastern European ghetto communities in the United States.

The most significant socio-cultural development within the Jewish ghetto in the United States was the continuous retreat of Orthodoxy. This retreat, as we have seen, started in Europe, but was much accelerated here. Orthodoxy was too institutionally rigid to adjust to the suddenly new conditions it confronted. The heavy losses suffered by Orthodoxy have been attributed, for example, to the mobility of the Jews in this country. "If mobility had been very gradual," says the sociologist Marshall Sklare, "it is conceivable that Orthodoxy might have adjusted itself."[22]

The attraction of socialism for the Jewish immigrants can also be attributed to the declassed status in which, as we have seen, so many immigrants found themselves in the United States.

When socialist activities started among the Jewish immigrants in the United States, its leaders were not Jewish nationalists. The conference of the Jewish trade unions in New York in 1890, for example, adopted

---

[20] E. Scherer, "The Bund," in *Struggle for Tomorrow*, ed. Basil J. Vlavianos and Feliks Gross (New York: Arts Incorporated, 1954), p. 171.

[21] Halpern, "Zionism and Israel," *The Jewish Journal of Sociology* 3 (December 1961): 162.

[22] Sklare, *Conservative Judaism: An American Religious Movement* (Glencoe, Ill.: The Free Press, 1955), p. 28.

the slogan: "The world is our fatherland; socialism, our religion." The ghetto did respond, however, to developments in Eastern Europe, and leaders were forced to compromise with Jewish nationalism.[23] The leaders who adopted nationalist sentiments were the ones who succeeded in establishing and maintaining their leadership. The success of the Yiddish daily, *Forward*, over its rival, the *Abendblatt*, for example, is attributed in part to its adoption of nationalist sentiments. While socialist leaders accused the paper of compromising basic socialist principles, readers were shifting to it and away from its purist rival.[24] By 1905, we are told, the chief American activity of the Jewish socialists became the establishment of Yiddish culture, journalism, literature, schools, and drama.[25]

Thus, whether it took the form of socialism or Zionism, Jewish secularism dominated the immigrant ghetto. In a way, this was peculiarly appropriate, for during this period of transition "the vast majority of immigrants . . . were interested in fostering a friendly cultural atmosphere in order to feel 'at home' in the new environment, and to assure themselves essential social and intellectual, recreational and esthetic satisfaction."[26]

Zionism could not compete with Jewish socialism in its influence on Jewish masses in the United States before World War I. As we shall see, only when it was transformed from its original European ideology did it become influential. The growing prosperity of the masses and their adjustment to the new society eventually led to their preference for a modified Zionist ideology over radical socialist ideas.

The war years were years of prosperity and were not conducive to allegiance to the mystical ideal of an American "class struggle." Instead, a concern with middle-class respectability became paramount. A quest for a new ideology served to strengthen Zionism.[27] This change will be discussed in detail in later chapters.

With the coming of prosperity, the movement out of the ghetto began, and "the commitment to Jewish culture became an impossible task." In the new American environment, as a result, Jewish secular cul-

---

[23] Bernard H. Bloom, "Yiddish-Speaking Socialists in America, 1892–1905," *American Jewish Archives* 12 (April 1960): 56.
[24] Melech Epstein, *Jewish Labor in the U.S.A.: An Industrial, Political, and Cultural History of the Jewish Labor Movement 1882–1952*, vol. 1 (New York: Trade Union Sponsoring Committee, 1950), pp. 262–72.
[25] Bloom, "Yiddish-Speaking Socialists," p. 62.
[26] Herbert Parzen, "The Passing of Jewish Secularism in the United States," *Judaism* 8 (Summer 1959): 197.
[27] Joseph Rappaport, "Jewish Immigrants and World War I: A Study of American Yiddish Press Reactions" (Ph.D. dissertation, Faculty of Political Science, Columbia University, 1951), pp. 224–25.

ture flourished only in the ghetto: "The full-flown ideology of secular Jewish culture, of Yiddishism and Hebraism, the American analogue of European ethnic autonomism, began in the immigrant ghetto, where it had a sort of natural habitat. It never really emerged from the immigrant ghetto into the real America."[28]

The Zionist Ideology

As we have seen, Eastern and Central Europe provided a fertile soil for the emergence of a nationalist ideology in the nineteenth century. The nationalist movement started in most cases as a purely cultural revival. But this was only the first step. "Before long they had worked out a philosophical justification for their claim that each nation should have the right to constitute an independent political state."[29] The source of the philosophy of nationalism was largely provided by Germany. The philosopher Herder emphasized that national consciousness rather than the political institution of the state makes the nation. Schlegel and Fichte, for their part, stressed the importance of the national language for the awakening of national consciousness. These ideas were later taken up by the various nationalities in Eastern Europe which were politically under the rule of the Russian czar and the Austrian emperor. By 1914, the most important problem occupying all areas of mixed population was the national strife of the different nationalities.

This was the soil in which Zionism grew. Though Zionism as a political movement started in Europe in the year 1897 with the convening of the first Zionist Congress in Basle by the Viennese-Jewish journalist Theodor Herzl, Zionist groups had already been active in Eastern Europe. They had been propagandizing the national idea and urging migration to the ancient homeland in Palestine. Indeed, the first group of pioneers from Russia arrived in Palestine as early as 1882, and political societies were established in various cities supporting colonization as an integral part of their political program, aimed at the creation of a Jewish state in the Holy Land.

As with other national groups, cultural revival on a national level preceded political organization. Among East European Jews, the Haskalah movement, a purely cultural movement dedicated to the revival of Jewish literature and the Hebrew language, antedated the Zionist movement.

---

[28] Halpern, *The American Jew: A Zionist Analysis* (New York: The Theodor Herzl Foundation, 1956), p. 82.
[29] C. A. Macartney, *National States and National Minorities* (London: Oxford University Press, 1934), p. 96.

Zionism embraced this cultural movement, adding to it the political philosophy adapted from the other nationalist movements. The Zionists believed that a cultural renaissance was possible only through a revival of the national consciousness of the Jewish masses, which, once achieved, would also inevitably lead them to employ their energies to secure political independence in Palestine. The colonization of Palestine was started, then, by nationally conscious Zionist groups who served as pioneers for the masses that were to follow them. Zionism was, for them, not solely a movement for the return to Palestine; it was part of the national awakening of the Jews. These early Zionists believed that full national life was impossible in the Diaspora. The Palestine movement was thus a result of the desire to make the Jews a full nation and in this way to solve the political, social, and cultural problems of Judaism. Only through the establishment of a national center in Palestine would it be possible to reach a degree of stability that would permit the development of a free national, social, cultural, and political life.[30]

However, one must not minimize the differences that existed within the Zionist movement in Europe during the first years of the movement, differences that were especially great between the Eastern European branches of the movement and the Western Jews who led it in its first years.

The Western leaders of political Zionism, who were instrumental in convening the first Zionist Congress and in establishing the World Zionist Organization, had one decisive aim. They wanted an organization that would press the European governments, through diplomatic activities, to help grant the Jews a political charter allotting them a piece of land on which to build an independent state. These governments did not sympathize with the colonization activities of the Eastern Europeans in Palestine, which they described by the derogatory term *infiltration*. Nor did they understand the cultural and literary Hebraic renaissance that was the precursor of practical and political Zionism in Eastern Europe and that was later an integral part of Zionism in that region. We must remember that this cultural revival began in Eastern Europe, where there was still a Jewish community imbued with the traditional culture.

Eastern European Jewry was also more receptive to the symbolism and ritualism of Zionism. These elements existed in all European political ideologies, and were essential to obtain the support of the masses.[31]

---

[30] Adolf Böhm, *Die Zionistische Bewegung: Eine kurze Darstellung ihrer Entwicklung* (Berlin: Welt-Verlag, 1920), pp. 229–30.
[31] Gross, *European Ideologies*, p. 37.

The symbols taken from the Jewish historical and religious tradition and employed by the Zionist movement, as well as the integration of old rituals into the new system of the nationalist ideas, are too numerous to record. The revival of the sacred and historic Hebrew language, the nationalist modern and secular content given to ancient religious holidays, the modernization of biblical stories, the idea of return to the historical homeland as the central idea of Zionism—these and many more linked tradition to the present.

All this, however, was less vital to the Zionists of Western Europe. Further removed from the Jewish tradition and in a very different social situation and intellectual climate, they developed at first a somewhat different brand of doctrine called political Zionism. The Basle Program, adopted by the first Zionist Congress in 1897, declared in its first paragraph that "the aim of Zionism is to create for the Jewish people a home in Palestine secured by public law."[32]

In the early years, the leaders primarily emphasized the diplomatic activities of the organization. Most Eastern Europeans and some Westerners represented what was called the practical school. They minimized the importance of diplomatic activities. Instead, they worked for the constant colonization of Palestine and the strengthening of the organization. According to Adolf Böhm, a noted German Zionist and the first historian of the movement, they were the "evolutionists." They wanted the movement to concentrate primarily on awakening the national consciousness of the Jewish masses, believing that once the masses became nationally conscious they would themselves mobilize their energies for the creation of a Jewish State in Palestine. The Zionist Congress of 1907 elected an executive composed of both practical and political Zionists, but by 1913 the victory of the practical Zionists was complete and no political Zionist was left on the executive.

Another issue that engaged the European Zionists and that came to plague American Zionists after World War I was the doctrine of Diaspora nationalism. According to this principle, in the Diaspora Jews were a separate nationality like Czechs, Poles, and Hungarians. They should therefore join the others in the demand for cultural autonomy and civil and political rights as a separate group within the states in which they lived.[33]

The acceptance of this doctrine and its incorporation into Zionism was a compromise of the original Zionist ideology. Zionists at first in-

---

[32] Israel Cohen, *The Zionist Movement* (New York: The Zionist Organization of America, 1946), p. 77.

[33] For a detailed discussion on the movement for national autonomy in Eastern Europe, see Macartney, *National States and National Minorities, passim.*

sisted that the only solution for the Jews was migration to Palestine. However, the recognition that such a plan could not be realized in the near future and that it could not therefore appeal to the masses who were looking for immediate solutions for their plight pushed the Zionists into accepting the idea of autonomous national rights in the Diaspora as part of the Zionist program.

Diaspora nationalism was first officially endorsed by the Eastern European Zionists in the convention of the Austrian Zionists in 1905 and later by the Federation of Russian Zionists in 1906 in its Helsingfors Program. The reasons for accepting this compromise were a mixture of tactics and ideology. For some, the aim to become a mass movement led them "to reckon with the prevailing mood of the masses and go along with them."[34] For others, it was much more a change of emphasis. They "were willing to accept the issue of Diaspora national rights as a basic principle" and "to minimize the Palestine program."[35] As time passed, Zionists became more and more committed to the idea of Diaspora nationalism and participated actively in the efforts to achieve autonomous cultural and political rights. This position was officially adopted by the World Zionist Organization in its Copenhagen Manifesto of October 1918.

The issue of Diaspora nationalism should not be confused with the question of whether the Jews are a nation like other nations or an ethnic group only. In the United States after World War I, the issue of Diaspora nationalism and the idea that the Jews are a nation became interchangeable and led to a bitter controversy within the ranks of the Zionists. Among the European Zionists, opinion was almost unanimous in regarding the Jews as a separate nationality. In Eastern Europe, this was never really questioned, while in the West, the issue was raised at one point by a prominent German Zionist and noted economist, Franz Oppenheimer, who argued that the Western Jews had an ethnic consciousness (*Stammesbewusstsein*) that was Jewish and a national consciousness (*Volksbewusstsein*) that was non-Jewish. However, the consensus among most Zionists in Western Europe was that the difference between conditions of Jews in Eastern Europe and in Western Europe were simply temporary. The Jewish problem was the same in both and so was its solution. Zionists in the East and in the West were therefore to proceed with the awakening of Jewish national consciousness and the revival of its culture and language in both regions.[36]

---

[34] Leschinsky, "Zionism," in *European Ideologies*, p. 631.
[35] Böhm, *Die Zionistische Bewegung bis zum Ende des Weltkrieges*, vol. 1 (Berlin: Judischer Verlag, 1933), p. 244.
[36] Ibid., p. 237–38.

To understand why the issue of the Jews as a separate nation became so controversial in the United States but not among Zionist circles in Germany, we must remember that Germany, unlike the English-speaking world, shared an intellectual tradition in which "nation" was not synonymous with "state," but rather denoted a people. This distinction was generally accepted in German thought, and the disagreements among political scientists, jurists, and philosophers were in most cases restricted to a concern with the position of each institution and its relative importance in human society. There were those thinkers who agreed with Hegel and Treitschke that the state should reign supreme as the manifestation of human spirit. But even Treitschke stated that "although the state is a moral community which is called upon to educate the human race by positive achievement, its ultimate object is that a nation should develop in it, a nation distinguished by real national character. . . ."[37]

It was generally agreed that nationality was a subjective psychological reality existing in the minds of the people. National consciousness was inculcated at a very young age in members of national groups. The nationalists believed that every nation had a natural right to develop its own cultural traditions and to have a state of its own. According to this view, the state should be subordinated to the nation, and its laws and institutions should express the needs and desires of the nation.[38]

One school of thought, which greatly influenced the Jewish intelligentsia in Eastern Europe, supported the idea of a "polynationality" state in which each nationality would enjoy cultural autonomy. According to this view, each nationality should have complete freedom in educating the young and should be in charge of its own school system, in which the national language would be taught. This position was adopted by the Austrian Social Democratic Party. Although members of the party were oriented toward the class struggle and argued that nationalist sentiments were being exploited by the bourgeoisie to further their own class interests, they recognized the legitimate demands of each nation to maintain its own cultural tradition.[39]

It was this doctrine that encouraged the European Zionists to endorse Diaspora nationalism, and it was no accident that the first to do so were

---

[37] Quoted in Louis L. Snyder, *The Meaning of Nationalism* (New Brunswick, N.J.: Rutgers University Press, 1954), p. 19.
[38] For a detailed discussion, see J. R. Bluntschli, *The Theory of the State* (Oxford: At the Clarendon Press, 1898), pp. 81–108.
[39] The Austrian Socialist Party position is explained in Otto Bauer, *Die Nationalitätenfrage und die Sozialdemokratie*, Marx-Studien, vol. 2 (Wien: Verlag der Volksbuchhandlung, 1924); for a more general treatment of this idea see Georg H. J. Erler, *Das Recht der nationalen Minderheiten* (Deutschland und Ausland, Heft 37/39; Münster in Westfalen, Aschendorffsche Verlagsbuchhandlung, 1931), especially Part I.

the Austrian Zionists in their convention in 1905. On the other hand, to the Zionists in the United States—where nationality also meant citizenship, and nation and state were synonymous concepts—the notion of Diaspora nationalism and the underlying idea that Jews are a separate nationality were equally embarrassing.

In addition, there were important differences in the structures of the Zionist Organizations of the two continents. Germany and other Western European countries did not have any mass Zionist movements at the time. The eccentric intellectuals in Germany could afford to remain loyal to their esoteric ideas without worry over their mass appeal and support. While they were concentrated in the intellectual centers of Berlin, Frankfort, and the old southern German universities, the mass support for their movement came from across the Oder-Neisse line. When the Eastern European Zionists leaders incorporated the doctrine of Diaspora nationalism in order to enlist mass support, the Germans, not immediately affected by this change, went along with it in the Copenhagen Manifesto of 1918.

The American situation was radically different. Although Jews in the United States came from Eastern Europe and shared the Eastern European cultural tradition, they encountered in their adopted country a cultural tradition that did not recognize a division by which the nation provided the culture and language and organized the social activities of its members, leaving it to the state to provide the police and the court system. The Zionist leaders in America who built a mass movement and desired the support of the Jewish masses had to take account of these new conditions.

The agitation for Diaspora nationalism in Eastern Europe opened the way for Zionism to become a mass movement. It provided the basis for a successful indoctrination of the masses with Jewish nationalism. Only in the face of frustrations, when their hopes for cultural autonomy and civil rights were shattered and when they were persecuted rather than granted equality, did they accept the Zionist solution. Böhm contends that the indoctrination involved in the Diaspora nationalism movement in Eastern Europe and the disappointments following this solution conditioned the Jews to accept Zionism as the only solution for their miseries. Different conditions in the United States led the Zionist movement in America to follow a different path, and the examination of this will occupy the remainder of the book.

CHAPTER II

The Federation of American Zionists and Its Leadership, 1898–1914

The Organization

The Zionist movement remained small and uninfluential in the United States until World War I. The Federation of American Zionists (the F.A.Z.), which was organized in 1898 and which remained throughout the period the central and most important Zionist organization, was at first a weak and loosely organized federation of societies.

It is impossible to estimate with any degree of assurance even the number of societies affiliated with the F.A.Z., let alone the size of its membership. By checking the number of *Shkalim* sold by the organization, one can only guess at the numerical strength of the Zionists. (A *Shekel* was a certificate that all Zionists were obligated to buy and that entitled its holder to participate in the election of delegates to the Zionist Congress.) The largest number of *Shkalim* reported sold before World War I was 12,000 in 1908; the lowest was 1,500 in 1901.

One source of the organization's weakness suggested by the evidence was the high turnover of affiliated societies, whose membership in turn seems also to have been unstable.[1] Julius Haber, one of the devoted active members of the F.A.Z., has stated that the fresh waves of immigration bringing in a steady stream of young people from Europe maintained the Zionist Organization as a going concern.[2] The core of the membership was composed of "journalists, intellectuals, shopkeepers and more or less skilled workmen."[3]

The constituent societies refused to submit to the continuous attempts of the central body to establish some degree of control over them. By vote of 74 to 48 after a bitter debate, the annual convention of 1902 resolved that constituent societies had to secure a subcharter from the federation, but the part of the resolution that required each society to report its financial activities to the center was defeated.[4] Further, it proved difficult to implement the part of the resolution that was accepted by the conven-

---

[1] Rufus Learsi [Israel Goldberg], *Fulfilment: The Epic Story of Zionism* (Cleveland: World Publishing Co., 1951), p. 15.
[2] Julius Haber, *The Odyssey of an American Zionist* (New York: Twayne Publishers, 1956), p. 125.
[3] Horace M. Kallen, *Zionism and World Politics* (New York: Doubleday, Page and Co., 1921), p. 131.
[4] "Report of the Proceedings of the Fifth Annual Convention of the Federation of American Zionists," *The Maccabean* 2 (June 1902): 331.

tion, since the societies were completely independent of the central organization, being for the most part *Landsmanschaften* whose attachment to Zionism was merely one of their many activities.[5] (*Landsmanschaften* are organizations based on common origin in European villages, towns, provinces, or countries.)

In view of the poor condition of the Zionist Organization itself, it is interesting to note that Zionism as an ideology was so hotly debated in the Jewish community and that pro-Zionist and anti-Zionist sentiments ran high. The Yiddish press gave a prominent place to the debates; Jewish organizations, the Jewish trade unions, the Conference of Reform Rabbis, and others devoted much of their energy to attacking the ideas of Zionism. All this commotion was out of proportion to the strength of the organization in the United States.

Since the F.A.Z. was an extension of the European Zionist movement, it was not surprising that many developments both in ideology and in its structure initially reflected developments in European Zionism. In Europe, the leadership of the World Zionist Organization, the W.Z.O., was in the hands of the Western European Jews in its early years. The mass support, however, came overwhelmingly from Eastern European Jewry, many of whom were committed to Zionism before the international organization was established. There was, then, a contrast between the leaders and the rank and file. The leaders were imbued with Western culture and traditions; the rank and file still lived in the ghetto, physically and spiritually.

In the United States, the national leaders of the F.A.Z. were also Western Jews, members of the established German group, while the rank and file were composed of recent immigrants from Eastern Europe. But the situation in the Zionist movement on the two continents was nevertheless different. In Europe, the Zionist Organization itself was divided along political-national lines into separate Eastern and Western European federations, while in the United States, the Jewish community was stratified along lines of Eastern and Western Jews who belonged to the same federation.

From the beginning, this situation created difficulties for the American organization. When the Western leaders organized the F.A.Z. in 1898, Eastern European groups of secularist-nationalists, and a few Orthodox Jews who accepted Zionism, refused to join and established rival organizations. One of those was the United Zionists. Clearly the different social backgrounds of the two leaderships contributed heavily to the lack of

---

[5] "Report of the Proceedings of the Ninth Annual Convention of the Fereration of American Zionists," *The Maccabean* 11 (July 1906): 20.

understanding between them and thus to the creation of the rival group.[6] However, a reconciliation and merger between the United Zionists and the F.A.Z. were effected in 1906, after a new group of German leaders, the Conservatives, had assumed control of the F.A.Z.

The Conservatives, a peculiarly American branch of neo-Orthodoxy, sprang from a group of Orthodox rabbis from the German and Sephardic communities (Jews of Spanish-Portuguese background who were settled in the United States before the German Jews had arrived) who had worked in cooperation with a few Eastern Europeans and were attempting to establish a more enlightened Jewish Orthodoxy.[7] The leading members of the group became identified with Zionism a few years later, and, as leaders of the F.A.Z. after 1904, they contributed to its reconciliation with the United Zionists. Harry Friedenwald, elected president of the F.A.Z. in 1904, was vice-president of the Orthodox Congregational Union in 1898, while Rabbi Philip Klein, president of the United Zionists, was also a member of the Orthodox Union's executive.

Unlike neo-Orthodoxy in Germany, which adopted a strong anti-Zionist stand, this group immediately declared itself in favor of the Zionist movement. In its first convention in 1898, the Orthodox Jewish Congregational Union of America declared that Zionism was not incompatible with American patriotism and urged its members to support the movement.

The pronouncements this religious group made on Zionism in 1898, which were not shared by the Zionist leaders in Europe, were also acceptable to the Conservative Zionist leaders in America in later years. The resolution on Zionism declared in part: "The desirability and the necessity of offering to those of our brethren dwelling under the rigour of oppressive laws a refuge legally assured to them cannot be questioned. . . . Furthermore, that the restoration of Zion as the legitimate aspiration of scattered Israel, in no way conflicts with our loyalty to the land in which we dwell or may dwell at any time."[8]

The homeland in Palestine was envisioned as a solution only for those Jews of Eastern Europe who were living under "the rigour of oppressive laws." This formulation of the aims of Zionism excluded American Jews from the need to migrate to Palestine and was, therefore, contrary to the position adopted by European Zionists, who considered the Zionist solution to be equally applicable to Jews in Eastern Europe facing physical

---

[6] Hyman B. Grinstein, "The Memoirs and Scrapbook of the Late Dr. Joseph Isaac Bluestone of New York City," *PAJHS* 35 (1939): 53–64; *Ha'pisgah*, March 18, 1898.
[7] *AJYB* 1 (1899–1900): 100–1.
[8] *The American Hebrew*, June 10, 1898, p. 172.

persecution and to the rest of Jewry living in those parts of the globe where people were more tolerant.

This group of religious leaders aimed not only at a religious reconciliation between Jewish traditions and modern ideas, but also at a secular one. They sought "Americanism" by way of a new interpretation of Zionism that was unknown in Europe. Unlike their counterparts in Europe, they did not question their status as Jewish Americans, which was regarded as on equal terms with Irish Americans, Italian Americans, and Russian Americans. It was the part of their status that referred to their old culture and country of origin that they wanted to clarify through the acceptance of Zionism.[9]

The endorsement of such a position by the leaders of the F.A.Z. and the United Zionists must have contributed to the alienation of a group of Eastern European Zionist intellectuals, mostly writers and journalists, who were arriving in the United States during this period. Members of this group refused to cooperate with either of the two Zionist Organizations.[10] They gravitated instead toward a third center in Chicago, which was organized as early as 1897 under the name of Knights of Zion. This organization established branches throughout the Midwest and kept its organizational independence until 1914.

Jewish intellectuals such as William Schur, the publisher of the first Hebrew magazines in the United States, *Ha'tchia* and *Ha'pisgah*, and Shmuel Deinard, a Hebrew novelist, moved from New York to Chicago to join the group. The president of the organization, who remained its active spirit throughout its existence, was Leon Zolotkoff, another Jewish intellectual. This group tried to evolve a policy in accordance with the ideas of Zionism brought over from Europe. Zolotkoff insisted, for instance, on the teaching of Jewish history in the Hebrew language rather than in English as a means of "reawakening and regeneration of the national conscience of our people."[11]

The membership and support of the Knights of Zion seem to have been concentrated among the poorer and more recent immigrants from Eastern Europe, who were attracted largely by its organizational structure.[12] The basic units of the organization were *Landsmanschaften*. These *Lands-*

---

[9] This position was restated by one of their leaders, David de Sola Pool, in "Zionism as an Expression of Jewish Patriotism," *The Maccabean* 25 (November–December 1914): 175–76.
[10] Editorial, *Ha'pisgah*, August 12, 1898; Editorial, *Ha'tchia*, June 15, 1900.
[11] "Fifth Annual Convention of the Order Knights of Zion," *The Maccabean* 4 (January 1903): 59–60.
[12] Philip Bregstone, *Chicago and Its Jews: A Cultural History* (Privately Printed, 1933), pp. 89–90.

manschaften were organized in orders that dealt with insurance and mutual aid to members, at the same time adding a peculiar social content that included initiation ceremonies, ceremonial dinners, special uniforms, and the like. The combination of *Landsmanschaften* and a fraternal order proved popular among the immigrants of the time.

The Eastern European Jewish community was what is known in sociological literature as a *Gemeinschaft* type of society, in which social relations were personal, informal, and diffuse. The big American city was a *Gesellschaft* type of society; here social relations were impersonal, formal, and specific. The new social situation, in which members could not expect the material support, social recognition, and the same concern they were accustomed to expecting from relatives, friends, and neighbors in their old environment made life very difficult. Migration to a foreign country added the strangeness of the foreign society and its culture to the shock of the transition from a *Gemeinschaft* to a *Gesellschaft* type of society. Local associations (*Landsmanschaften* in the case of the Jews in the United States) were designed to retain some of the warmth and intimacy in social contacts to which the immigrants were accustomed in the old society. Their function was to mitigate the shock of contact with the new society. In the local association, immigrants met members who had come from the old local environment and who shared their values and beliefs; it provided the immigrant, otherwise lost and helpless, with an atmosphere of familiarity, a point of contact.[13]

It is on the organizational principle that the Knights of Zion and the United Zionists are at one. The Western leaders of the F.A.Z. were political Zionists, and they tried to create an efficient organization that would achieve the single aim of securing through political pressure a charter that would recognize the right of the Jews to a land of their own. For that reason, they rejected the building of fraternal orders within the Zionist Organization. The Eastern European leaders, on the other hand, were more receptive to the needs of their followers, whose sympathy with Zionism was associated with their comforting memories of the old country, memories that the *Landsmanschaften* were fostering. The Eastern European party workers of the F.A.Z. were sensitive to their needs. They did not share the misgivings of the national leaders and so tried to attract

---

[13] Robert E. Park and Herbert A. Miller, *Old World Traits Transplanted* (New York: Harper and Brothers, 1921), pp. 119–20. One of the best analyses of the function of local organizations in the life of new immigrants in America is still to be found in William I. Thomas and Florian Znaniecki, *The Polish Peasant in Europe and America*, vol. 2 (New York: Alfred A. Knopf, 1927), p. 1518 ff. The literature on urbanization in the newly developed countries provides interesting comparative material on the development of local organizations in the new cities. See Daniel F. McCall, "Dynamics of Urbanization in Africa," *The Annals* 298 (March 1955): 151–60.

immigrants to the F.A.Z. by adding elements of the *Landsmanschaften* and of a fraternal society.[14]

When the Conservatives assumed leadership of the F.A.Z. in 1904, this became official policy. They even created an official order, Order B'nai Zion, in which the previous leaders of the United Zionists came to play a leading role.

The evidence suggests that most societies affiliated with the F.A.Z were *Landsmanschaften*, but these represented only a small fraction of the *Landsmanschaften* in the United States. The socialists were much more successful in attracting immigrants because they combined the appeal of the *Landsmanschaften*, which provided familiar associations in the new country, with attention to their immediate needs. Even those immigrants who brought a sympathetic predisposition toward Zionism from the old country were expressing only loyalty to a memory, a sentiment of empathy with the plight of their brethren. It was not apparently enough to induce most of them to make a more substantial commitment to the Zionist idea by joining the Zionist Organization.

The Knights of Zion were not persuaded to join the F.A.Z. even after the organizational principle of *Landsmanschaften* and fraternal order was accepted by the new leadership. As we have explained, they were at the time fundamentalists in American Zionism. Their separatism was supported by their concentration in the Midwest. The weakness and low national prestige of the leadership in New York also perpetuated their separatist activities. When Louis D. Brandeis succeeded to leadership, the membership at once submitted willingly to his authority. By that time, 1914, their fundamentalist position on the problems of Zionism had been greatly weakened.

The Leaders of the Federation of American Zionists (F.A.Z.)

The following question then arises: who were the national leaders of the F.A.Z. between 1898 and 1914, and why did they join the Zionist movement? As we have seen, the national leadership was composed of members of the German Jewish community. This affiliation with the Zionist movement was a deviant act since most of the German Jewish community opposed the Zionist movement. This deviant group was numerically small but organizationally significant.

The group had been active in the social and intellectual life of the Jewish community before assuming F.A.Z. leadership. Most were rabbis

---

[14] Haber, *The Odyssey of an American Zionist*, pp. 65–66.

or Judaist scholars, and the few secular professional men in the group manifested an active interest and participation in Jewish social and religious affairs. Obviously, people occupying such positions were often aware of the three cultures with which they came into contact—German, American, and Jewish—and of their marginality to each of these cultures.

Reactions to marginality differ. The marginal man is torn among two or more societies, with different values and ideas competing for his loyalties and exclusive emotional attachments. Marginal men move through a life cycle of three stages: lack of ethnic consciousness, consciousness of ethnic group membership, and adjustment to being a member of a minority within a larger society. According to sociologist Everett V. Stonequist, Zionism is a typical reaction among Jews in the second stage. This stage follows a personal crisis that often takes place when the marginal man is being rebuffed by the majority in his efforts to identify with its culture. He often achieves partial adjustment by identification with his subordinate ethnic group. "By leading his minority group the individual acquires status and self-respect."[15]

Stonequist applies this analysis to a group situation and evolves a theory of a group life cycle. At the first stage of the group life cycle, only a few members of the minority group come into close contact with the dominant culture and become marginal men. They try to identify with the dominant group. As their number grows, the marginal men become conscious of their inferior position and find that one way to overcome this position of inferiority with the dominant group, which continues to manifest attitudes of superiority, is to devote their energies to their own group's social and cultural life. As a result, the minority "begins to stir with new feelings and ideas." This renaissance attracts more of the group's marginal men, who are encouraged to abandon their desperate efforts to become fully accepted by the majority.[16]

This cycle of response, both for individual and for groups, occurs among the leaders of Zionism, as we shall see. Biographical materials suggest a reaction, often late in life, to the shock of discrimination against Jews, as was the case with the German-Jewish leaders who founded and joined the Zionist movement in its early years.

Rabbi Gustav Gottheil, the Reform rabbi of Temple Emanuel in New York, who called the first meeting that led to the creation of the F.A.Z., complained in his first pronouncement on Zionism that "gradually, but surely, we are being forced back into a physical and moral ghetto. Private

---

[15] Everett V. Stonequist, *The Marginal Man: A Study in Personality and Culture Conflict* (New York: Charles Scribner's Sons, 1937), pp. 160–62.
[16] Stonequist, "The Problem of the Marginal Man," *A.J.S.* 41 (July 1935): 12.

schools are being closed against our children one by one; we are particularly boycotted from all summer hotels—and our social life runs as far apart from those of our neighbors as it did in the worst days of our European degradation. . . . It is here he concluded that modern Zionism steps in."[17]

But it was also the Jewish group itself that began to stir "with new feelings and new ideas." The Eastern European immigrants, with their cultural life and their intellectuals, attracted converts to Zionism. Most leaders of American Zionism of German-Jewish extraction asserted in their writings that it was as a result of meeting with the proud and self-possessed Eastern European Jews, imbued with Jewish learning and traditions, that they were converted to Zionism.[18]

The writings of these leaders express a desire to be a part of the bigger Jewish community, bigger not just in numbers, but in the breadth and depth of its cultural and spiritual life. The Eastern European immigrants —especially the intellectuals among them—who were imbued with Jewish learning and knowledge of Jewish history and traditions were the only ones to whom frustrated marginal Jews could turn.

Stephen Wise, a Reform rabbi who became one of the best-known Zionist leaders, tells us that he was associated exclusively with German Jews until he went to the Zionist Congress in Europe in 1898, where "thrilled and grateful, I caught then a first glimpse of the power and the pride and the nobleness of the Jewish people, which my American upbringing and even service to New York Jewry had not in any degree given me. I was a Jew in every sense of the term. Gradually, I came to acknowledge my kinship with a great and living people. Judaism ceased to be a type of religious worship. The Jewish people became my own and I returned to my people. . . ."[19]

Likewise, Friedenwald tells us that he was converted to Zionism at the Zionist Congress in 1903, having been impressed by the Eastern European Jews, "whose Jewish interests were as wide as the dispersion," in

---

[17] Gustav Gottheil, "On Zionism," *The American Hebrew*, December 10, 1897, p. 163. A similar complaint is to be found in Rabbi Heller's pronouncement on his conversion to Zionism. See "An Interview with Heller," *The Times Democrat* (New Orleans), December 12, 1901, in the *Max Heller Papers* (Cincinnati: American Jewish Archives).

[18] See, for example, Rose Zeitlin, *Henrietta Szold: Record of a Life* (New York: The Dial Press, 1952), pp. 26–27; Norman Bentwich, *For Zion's Sake: A Biography of Judah L. Magnes, First Chancellor and First President of the Hebrew University of Jerusalem* (Philadelphia: The Jewish Publication Society of America, 1954), pp. 25–29; Harry Friedenwald, "Reminiscences," *The New Palestine*, December 29, 1944, p. 10; Stephen S. Wise, "The Beginning of American Zionism," *The Jewish Frontier* (August 1947), pp. 6–8.

[19] Wise, "The Beginning of American Zionism," p. 7.

contrast to the American Jews "of provincial outlook whose Jewish interests and activities were limited to their congregations, and their local charities . . . ."[20]

Both Wise and Friedenwald went to the Zionist Congress to meet the Jewish people and stayed to be impressed, while the religious Reform leaders who headed the German Jewish community remained within their German Jewish congregations. Since neither the Reform Rabbi Wise nor the neo-Orthodox Friedenwald could meet with the strictly Orthodox East Europeans, they adopted a broader conception of Judaism, one that they could share with the Eastern European community.

The early leaders of Zionism were also marginal in another sense. Most of their role relations were within the Jewish community, where they had achieved a certain rank. The rank of these Jewish leaders vis-à-vis the members of the majority was contingent upon their standing within the Jewish community. The source of their prestige was primarily within the Jewish community, unlike the "leaders from the periphery" that took over the Zionist Organization in 1914, whose high rank in the dominant society won leadership in Jewish organizational life.

Their status as leaders of the Jewish community also affected their decisions to join the Zionist Organization. The pro-Zionists, whether Reform or conservative rabbis or other aspirants for leadership, were those who were deliberately reacting to the structural changes taking place in the American Jewish community with the influx of the Eastern European Jews. The anti-Zionist Reform rabbis were the heads of German Jewish congregations, considered themselves leaders of the German Jewish community, and gave expression to the interests and point of view of this community. The German Jewish community considered the Eastern European Jews a threat to their standing in American society. By excluding them from their synagogues and clubs, they attempted to keep the two communities separated. One incident, widely publicized at the time, took place in Chicago in 1881 where the district grand lodge of the Independent Order of B'nai B'rith for the Midwest area refused to accept a Polish lodge. It was openly admitted that the reason for the refusal was the Eastern European origin of its members.[21]

As we have seen, the attitude of the pro-Zionist Reform rabbis and other Zionist leaders of German-Jewish background toward the Eastern European immigrants was diametrically opposite. The former wanted to incorporate their co-religionists from Eastern Europe into the American

---

[20] Friedenwald, "Reminiscences," p. 10.
[21] Harold Silver, "Some Attitudes of the East European Jewish Immigrants toward Organized Jewish Charity in the United States in the Years 1890–1900" (Master's essay, New York Graduate School for Jewish Social Work, 1934), pp. 50–52.

Jewish community under their leadership, to identify themselves with the new immigrants' cultural tradition. Though Orthodoxy and radical socialism were unacceptable to them, Zionism provided a community of interest between them and the recent Jewish immigrants, with whom they could share the love of Jewish culture, Jewish history, and the idea of a Jewish state.

Rabbi Max Heller noted that the Eastern European Jews were not attracted by Reform Judaism, but hoped that "when Reform will have been sufficiently seasoned by Zionism . . . it will become more acceptable to the Russian Jew."[22]

The top leadership of the F.A.Z. from 1898 to 1904 consisted of Reform Jews; thereafter it passed into the hands of leaders associated with the Jewish Theological Seminary, which was the source of a new branch of religious thinking to be known later as Conservative Judaism.

The Reform Leaders

It was an act of courage for a few Reform rabbis to join the Zionist Organization and assume leadership. The official position of the Reform group was militantly anti-Zionist and its literature abounded in denunciations.

As very few Eastern Europeans with whom Zionism was associated were members of Reform temples, nor were they even wanted as members, it is clear that these anti-Zionist Reform rabbis were expressing the views of German Jewry, who occupied a much higher position in American society than the newcomers from Eastern Europe. *The American Israelite*, chief organ of the Reform movement, wrote in 1904: "There is not one solitary prominent native Jewish American who is an advocate of 'Zionism.' Aside from a few young visionaries and impractical college professors, the Zionists in America are recruited entirely from the ranks of the newly arrived immigrants, and these know little of its political significance and care less."[23]

We have seen that the anti-nationalist stand of Reform Jews in Germany was a reaction to the political climate prevailing at the beginning of the nineteenth century. In part, the position taken by the Reform rabbis in America represented adherence to the stand adopted by the Reform group in Germany.[24] In part, it was also a reaction to the upsurge

---

[22] Heller, *The American Hebrew*, November 27, 1908, p. 92.

[23] *The American Israelite*, July 7, 1904, quoted in Naomi W. Cohen, "The Reaction of Reform Judaism in America to Political Zionism, 1897–1922" *PAJHS* 40 (1950–51): 368.

[24] Leo Fram, "Reform Judaism and Zionism," *Reform Judaism—Essays by H.U.C. Alumni* (Cincinnati: Hebrew Union College Press, 1949), p. 188.

of anti-Semitism in America when "nativism in the 1890's repeatedly championed the values of nationalism in a very conscious explicit way."[25] Indeed, it was being suggested that the acceptance of the ideal of Americanization led to the anti-Zionist attitudes of many Reform rabbis.[26]

Examination of the social origins of the pro-Zionist Reform rabbis shows that many of them were not, strictly speaking, German Jews. Furthermore, there are indications that the pro-Zionist Reform rabbis were deeply dissatisfied with the whole Reform system of ideas because they believed these ideas were incapable of holding the group together.[27]

Ideological developments within American religious life also contributed to the attraction of Zionism for some Reform rabbis. These rabbis were among those most influenced by the Social Gospel movement prevalent in the United States, a movement characterized "by a burning desire to bring the ethics of the church down into the factory, the street, and the market place."[28] Since the Eastern European immigrants were the poor and exploited of the Jewish community, rabbis who adhered to the Social Gospel tried to establish contact with them, and supported Zionism for that purpose.[29]

The top leaders of the F.A.Z. between 1898 and 1904 were Richard Gottheil, the son of Rabbi Gustav Gottheil of Temple Emanuel and a professor of semitics at Columbia University, and Wise, who became the first secretary of the organization. Jacob de Haas arrived from England in 1902 to be the organization's first paid official. He had been recommended by the international leader of the Zionist movement, Theodor Herzl, whose secretary he had been for a time. None of the three spoke a word of Yiddish. The activities of the central office were oriented toward English-speaking rather than Yiddish-speaking Americans, even though the latter, the overwhelming majority of the rank and file, were the party workers of the organization. The official publication of the F.A.Z., The *Maccabean*, was in English; a Yiddish supplement was discontinued in 1902 for lack of funds.[30] Most pamphlets and all convention reports were published only in English; announcements of the con-

---

[25] John Higham, *Strangers in the Land: Patterns of American Nativism, 1860-1925* (New Brunswick, N.J.: Rutgers University Press, 1955), p. 74.

[26] Naomi W. Wiener, "Reform Judaism in America and Zionism, 1897–1922" (Master's essay, Faculty of Political Science, Columbia University, 1948), p. 18.

[27] See, for example, Heller, "The Rationale of Modern Judaism," *The Maccabean* 4 (July 1903): 34.

[28] George E. Mowry, *The Era of Theodore Roosevelt, 1900–1912* (New York: Harper and Brothers Publishers, 1958), p. 29.

[29] Judd J. Teller, "America's Two Zionist Traditions," *Commentary* 20 (October 1955): 343–52.

[30] "Report of the Fifth Annual Convention of the F.A.Z.," p. 334.

vening of annual conventions were often not even published in the Yiddish press; nor did the Jewish Colonial Trust publish its announcements in the Yiddish or Hebrew press.[31] The central offices of the organization were not located in the Jewish section of the city, but on Broadway. In the light of all this, the resentment of the Yiddish-speaking majority becomes understandable. When more Zionist intellectuals from Eastern Europe arrived, the entire group's sense of being pushed aside found expression in the Yiddish press.[32]

Friction was created not only by ethnic-cultural differences between the top leaders and the Eastern Europeans, but also by class differences between the two. President Gottheil was especially upset by the Eastern European Zionists who were connected with the socialist movement. Joseph Seff, one of the first Zionists to emigrate from Europe who had attained some prominence as a Zionist leader before coming to the United States, particularly irked him. In a letter to Herzl, one of several sent on the subject, Gottheil complained that Seff was supporting the socialists who were on strike in the Sarasohn publishing house. Sarasohn himself was a member of the national executive of the F.A.Z., and his papers supported the Zionists. Gottheil explained that in supporting the strike Seff was acting against the interests of Zionism, since "the greatest gain which we made during the whole past year was the active support of just these papers, and if Mr. Seff continues his agitation we shall lose this support."[33] Gottheil also objected to de Haas coming to the United States, and among the arguments he presented was a statement that "however good a Zionist Mr. de Haas may be, he is actually not a gentleman, and I could not for a moment think of presenting him to any intellectual or fashionable audience."[34]

Gottheil's unpopularity among the Eastern Europeans is, therefore, not surprising. Furthermore, Louis Lipsky, an active member during Gottheil's presidency who a few years later became the head of the organization, testifies that Gottheil failed to attend important meetings espe-

---

[31] Editorials, *Ha'pisgah*, May 19, 1899; April 28, 1899. The Jewish Colonial Trust was constituted by the second World Zionist Congress, 1898. Its function was to organize and finance industrial and agricultural establishments in Palestine. The center of the Trust was in London, but all Zionist Federations were responsible for branches established in their respective countries. (*Stenographisches Protokoll der Verhandlungen des II. Zionisten-Congresses* [Wien, 1898], pp. 149–51.)

[32] Abraham Goldberg, "Memories of Yesterday," *The New Palestine*, June 23, 1922, p. 412.

[33] Richard Gottheil to Theodor Herzl, January 24, 1901, in the *Richard Gottheil Papers* (New York: The Zionist Archives).

[34] Gottheil to the *Actions Comité*, May 18, 1900, *Gottheil Papers*.

cially when they interfered with his vacation plans, which often coincided with the annual conventions.[35]

However, American Zionists at that time accepted a subordinate and dependent role vis-à-vis the European leadership, seeing themselves as merely a branch of the movement centered in Europe. Within this context, personal relations with the world leaders of the Zionist movement carried great weight with the delegates. Thus, because of Gottheil's personal contacts with world Zionist leaders Herzl and Max Nordau, the party workers grumblingly continued to elect him as their president year after year.

Another source of prestige and influence of the Gottheil-Wise leadership was their social contact, by virtue of their common social background, with the influential "uptown" German Jews, who had achieved positions of influence in American society. This was an important source of power. It helped sustain their leadership despite the dissatisfaction of the party workers. The group stayed in power as long as no alternative leadership with at least as close contacts with the wealthy uptown Jews came to the fore. The Eastern European intellectuals did not consider themselves possible rivals at the time.

In 1904, however, we witness the emergence of an alternative leadership that shared the social background and was in close contact with the uptown Jews. It was the Eastern European party workers of the F.A.Z. who secured the consent of Friedenwald, a physician and the son of a German Orthodox rabbi, to accept the presidency.

The prestige of the German Jews in the American Jewish community can best be illustrated by describing an incident at the 1904 convention when Gabriel Mayer, an Eastern European businessman, actually contested the presidency. Even though Mayer was one of the financial backers of the organization and a very active and devoted member, it was prestige the party workers were after, and this a businessman of the Eastern European community was unable to provide. They defeated his contestancy overwhelmingly. Apparently, they then tried to pacify Mayer by offering him a vice-presidency, but were relieved when he declined, since they could then offer it to Cyrus Sulzberger, a prominent German Jew whom "everybody wanted."[36]

Friedenwald, the new president, was connected with the Conservative movement, to which we now turn.

---

[35] Louis Lipsky, "Early Days of American Zionism, 1897–1929," *Palestine Year Book* 2 (1945–46): 450.
[36] A. N. Fromenson, "The Story of the Convention," *The Maccabean* 7 (July 1904): 26.

The Conservative Leaders and the Eastern European Party Workers

As has been noted, the top leaders of the F.A.Z. from 1904 to 1911 were closely related to the Conservative movement. The most remarkable and influential member of this group was Judah Leon Magnes, the secretary of the organization from 1905 to 1908. Born in America, he started his career as a Reform rabbi; but in the course of his studies in Germany, he came into contact with Russian Jewish intellectuals and was converted to Zionism. He eventually broke away from Reform Judaism and established an independent congregation that was Conservative in spirit.[37] Magnes was replaced as secretary by the Conservative Rabbi Joseph Jasin, 1908–10, who was followed by Henrietta Szold, 1910–11, a member of the same intellectual circle. When Friedenwald, himself a member of the board of the Jewish Theological Seminary, consented to remain as the honorary president without responsibilities, professor Israel Friedlaender of the J.T.S. faculty became chairman of the administrative committee of the F.A.Z.

One prominent member elected to the new administration of the F.A.Z. in 1904, vice-president Sulzberger, was not a member of the Conservative group, and the immediate cause for his withdrawal from the Zionist Organization the following year had to do with developments within the World Zionist Organization (W.Z.O.).

In 1903, the British government had offered the territory of Uganda as a place of refuge for the Jews, and the Western leaders of the W.Z.O. were inclined to accept the offer. The Eastern Europeans, however, considered it a betrayal of their aspirations for a Jewish state in the ancient homeland. There followed a revolt of the Eastern European federations; with the death of Herzl in 1904 and the eventual rejection of the Uganda proposal by the Zionist Congress of 1905, a new directorate of the W.Z.O., a coalition of Western and Eastern European leaders, was established.[38]

Some Western Zionist leaders, however, did not accept the resolution, withdrew from the organization, and established the International

---

[37] The Conservative movement had a peculiar development. In 1901, the Jewish Theological Seminary was established in New York; it became the center of Conservatism, from which Conservative rabbis were graduated. Only in 1913, however, was an organization of Conservative congregations established as a separate religious branch. For further details see Marshall Sklare, *Conservative Judaism: An American Religious Movement* (Glencoe, Ill.: The Free Press, 1955).

[38] "The Seventh Zionist Congress—East Africa Rejected," *The Maccabean* 9 (August 1905): 84–111; Friedenwald, "The Seventh Zionist Congress," *The Maccabean* 9 (November 1905): 239–41.

Territorialist Organization (I.T.O.).[39] Sulzberger joined the dissidents. He was a member of a wealthy and prominent German Jewish family that moved in the most influential circle of wealthy German Jews. Through their philanthrophic activities and their contacts with influential persons in the dominant American society, these wealthy Jews managed to wield great influence in the Jewish community.[40] In 1906, they established the American Jewish Committee as the leading organization of American Jewry.

The members of this organization belonged to the Reform synagogue. The Reform leaders, however, were losing their influence over the changing Jewish community and retained their influence only over German Jewry, which was now a minority within the Jewish group. These wealthy philanthropists "moved into the power vacuum created by the Union of American Hebrew Congregations [the organization of the Reform congregations] that proved ineffectual as an instrument of overall national unification."[41] Since the ideas of Reform Judaism, especially its anti-nationalism, were not popular among the new immigrants, the philanthropists did not identify too closely and openly with its leadership. Instead, they tried to assert some control over existing Jewish institutions and mass movements.

The philanthropists were also the financial backers of the Jewish Theological Seminary, which had the manifest goal of Americanizing new immigrants by supporting a more attractive middle-of-the-road religion that tried to reconcile tradition and modernism.[42] The same group supported a Yiddish socialist newspaper in the hope of diverting the Jewish masses from a more radical socialism.[43] They also supported the I.T.O. in an attempt to develop a movement that might compete with the more extreme Zionist movement. Their objections to Zionism reflected those of the Reform Jews, the idea of a Jewish nationalism propagated by the Zionists being anathema to them. It was only in the techniques and skills of leadership that the philanthropists proved more flexible and compromising than the Reform leaders. The philanthropists sup-

---

[39] *The Maccabean* 9 (September 1905): 160–61.

[40] See "Cyrus Sulzberger," *The Encyclopedia of Jewish Knowledge*, ed. Jacob de Haas (New York: Behrman's Jewish Book House, 1938). For further details on this group of Jewish philanthropists, see Cyrus Adler, *I Have Considered the Days* (Philadelphia: The Jewish Publications Society of America, 1941).

[41] Jacob Rader Marcus, "The Theme of American Jewish History," *PAJHS* 48 (1958–59): 143–44.

[42] Sklare, *Conservative Judaism*, pp. 165 ff.

[43] Bernard H. Bloom, "Yiddish-Speaking Socialists in America, 1892–1905," *American Jewish Archives* 12 (April 1960): 53.

ported the Jewish Theological Seminary, which was a hotbed of Zionists and provided much of their leadership, although at the same time they strongly objected to Zionism.

Sulzberger was the only member of this group who ever joined the Zionist Organization, but he, too, left the F.A.Z. in 1905 to join the I.T.O. Many others joined the I.T.O., and the respected leader of this group of Jewish philanthropists supported the organization financially.[44]

Of all attempts of the Jewish philanthropists to help create institutions and build organizations to attract the Eastern European masses and through these to influence the immigrants to accept more moderate and more "American" ideas and values, the one that proved most enduring was Conservative Judaism. This institution is a monument to the remarkable resourcefulness, ingenuity, and flexibility of this group in their struggle to maintain their leadership of the Jewish community. Not only did they establish and support the J.T.S. and the Conservative congregations despite their anti-Zionism, they even co-opted the Conservative leaders who led the Zionist movement into their American Jewish Committee. They appointed to its board Friedenwald, president of the F.A.Z., Magnes, its secretary, and Friedlaender, who was active in the organization and for one year the chairman of its administrative committee. This policy did pay dividends; as we shall have occasion to see later, the Zionist Organization posed no threat to the leadership of the philanthropists until after the Zionist leadership passed over to a new group of independents headed by Brandeis.

The result of all this was that although the financial backers of the Conservative movement maintained a non-Zionist position and were actually hostile to Jewish nationalism, the spiritual leaders of the movement took steps to make some sort of Jewish nationalism and Zionism part of their ideology.

Basic to an understanding of Conservative Judaism is that it catered to the Eastern European immigrants; it was in competition with the forces of traditional Orthodoxy on the one hand and of Jewish secularism on the other.

We have already discussed the nationalistic predilections of the Eastern Europeans as conditioned by their experience in the old country. To this influence we must add the moods and opinions that prevailed in the United States at the time of their arrival. When the German Jews arrived, the United States was relatively free of anti-Semitism, as is indi-

---

[44] Ben Halpern, *The Idea of a Jewish State* (Cambridge, Mass.: Harvard University Press, 1961), p. 156.

cated by John Higham, who dates the first wave of anti-Semitism in the 1880's and 1890's.[45] The emergence of Jewish nationalism as a reaction was general among immigrant members of the intelligentsia, whether they were socialists as in the Bund, secularists, or religionists like the Conservatives.[46]

Rabbi Mordecai Kaplan, one of the young leaders of the Conservative movement and a teacher in the J.T.S., described this reaction in 1909:

> . . . what does it mean to be a Jew in the Golus land? It means that . . . he must speak as the non-Jew speaks, he must think as the non-Jew thinks, he must resemble the non-Jew in dress, in manners, in ideas, in art, culture, literature, in other words give no expression to the inner forces of his life as a Jew, but simply as one of the people in whose midst he lives, and because he reads through a few prayers in a language and spirit entirely unknown to him, this constitutes a Jew. *There is a certain oddity about being ninety-nine percent Gentile and one percent Jew. The one percent Jew brings in more than fifty percent trouble into Jewish life. For that amount of trouble one feels that we want at least fifty percent Jew or not at all* [italics mine].[47]

The adoption of Zionism by the Conservative movement can also be understood when we examine its spiritual and ideological efforts. It aimed at a reconciliation between the forces of modernism and those of tradition in a way that would resolve the contradictions between the two and provide a formula for survival of the Jewish group in America. Zionism seemed to have served this purpose. It helped create a peculiar religio-nationalistic ideology that would save Conservatism from the pitfalls of assimilationist Reform Judaism and at the same time would permit the introduction of modern ideas, some change in old customs, and acceptance of biblical criticism and the use of the English language in the synagogues.[48]

The basic approach of Conservative Judaism to Zionism was in line with their general philosophy, which accepted acculturation of the Jews in American society but desired at the same time to retain some ele-

---

[45] Higham, "Anti-Semitism in the Gilded Age," *The Mississippi Valley Historical Review* 43 (March 1957): 570.

[46] The German Americans responded in similar fashion in the 1850's to the upsurge of nativism in this country. According to Hawgood, the nationalistic reaction of the Germans in America occurred largely among the German intellectuals, the forty-eighters. Though they were liberals rather than nationalists, they gave expression to feelings of German nationalism when faced by nativism and managed for a time to unite the German community behind them. John A. Hawgood, *The Tragedy of German-America* (New York: G. P. Putnam's Sons, 1940).

[47] Mordecai M. Kaplan, "Judaism and Nationality," *The Maccabean* 17 (August 1909): 63.

[48] Herbert Parzen, "Conservative Judaism and Zionism 1896–1922," *Jewish Social Studies* 23 (October 1961): 235–64.

Federation of American Zionists and Its Leadership, 1898–1914 41

ments of Jewish culture and tradition. Solomon Schechter, the spiritual leader of the Conservative movement, declared that "the problem is whether we are able to keep the immigrant with Judaism after he had become Americanized."[49] Zionism was to cement the Jewish element in the life of the American Jew, since it could provide an ideology to justify the preservation of Jewish culture in accord with modern thinking.

Once committed to Zionism, Conservatives naturally assumed leadership of the F.A.Z., which was handed to them happily by the Eastern European party workers who, lacking social contacts outside the ghetto, found an acceptable alternative to Gottheil in the Conservative leaders who mixed with the uptown Jews. In American Zionism, then, a religio-national leadership emerged that had no counterpart in Europe. Friedenwald and Magnes, the new leaders, came from the same social background as their predecessors. Both were native-born, but they were more attuned to the needs and aspirations of the Eastern Europeans even while maintaining close contacts with the wealthy philanthropists.

Jewish intellectuals from Eastern Europe, who supported Zionism and comprised the party workers of the F.A.Z., rejected the religious position of the Conservatives. In addition, their alienation from American culture and society made it impossible for them to accept the Conservative formula of Zionism. The Jewish socialists channeled their alienation into the socialist movement, the class war, and militant trade unionism, but those who joined the Zionist ranks did not fight for a new and better society in America. Instead, they adopted a more intense Zionism, committing themselves emotionally to the myth of the Jewish nation, its great past and glorious future.

Most of them brought their Zionism with them from the old country. The leading members of the group, however, were called "English-speaking" as distinct from the majority who were Yiddish-speaking, which put the latter at a disadvantage in the competition for leadership.

The English-speaking were a rather interesting group of people. Some had been born in the United States to East European parents. Others came to the United States at an early age, received part of their education in this country, and spoke English like natives. As for the problem of what brought them to Zionism, the biographical material, scanty as it is, is suggestive.

The first thing to notice is that though their Jewish upbringing and their early education influenced them greatly, they passed through the stage where they showed no consciousness of their background. Many

---

[49] Herbert Bentwich, *Solomon Schechter: A Biography* (Philadelphia: The Jewish Publication Society in America, 1938), p. 215.

of the English-speaking group started their careers apart from Jewish life and only returned to it drawn by Zionism. Lipsky tells of this early period: "The Russian Jews were emerging from their obscurity. Yiddish was giving way to English, although the influence of the Yiddish press had not diminished. The Galuth existed elsewhere. We had freedom with memory, and Zionism was the free expression of what was contained in that memory."[50]

Another member of the group, Isidor Morrison, reporting to the annual convention of the F.A.Z. as honorary secretary, declared: "We American Jews, who have the good fortune to be the citizens of a land of freedom and equal rights, have at last come to realize that our brethren living in lands of darkness and persecution are our kinsmen, bound to us by a common history, common religion and common literature. And while we are and will always remain loyal citizens of this beloved country of ours, we must and will stretch out a helping hand to our brethren across the sea."[51]

This idea of Zionism did not appeal to the Jewish intellectuals who came to this country from Eastern Europe and who had embraced Zionism while still in Russia. They refused to accept the American version promulgated by those connected with the F.A.Z. leadership. They voiced their disagreement in the Yiddish and Hebrew press, and they became more vociferous as their numbers grew.[52]

During the first decade of the twentieth century, there was a change in the ideas of the English-speaking group, many of whom were gradually accepting a more aggressive and fundamentalist point of view on Zionism in accord with the thinking of the European intellectuals more recently arrived in this country. The explanation for this change must be structural as well as ideological.

As Lipsky recalled, "the new settlers produced their own leaders, many of whom were at once at first absorbed and smothered by the A.J.C. But there were many who refused to be 'co-opted.'"[53] Instead, the English-speaking Zionists chose to become leaders of the Eastern Europeans. They secured their posts when they accepted the point of view of the newcomers.

It is not surprising that many English-speaking Zionists adopted European ideas following a period of intense ethnic consciousness stimu-

---

[50] Lipsky, "Early Days of American Zionism, 1897–1929," p. 452.
[51] "Report of the Proceedings of the Fourth Annual Convention of the Federation of American Zionists," *The Maccabean* 1 (October 1901): supplement p. xvii.
[52] Editorial, *Ha'tchia*, March 2, 1900.
[53] Lipsky, "A Revolution in American Jewry," *The Maccabean* 30 (June–July 1917): 276–77.

lated by the Russian pogroms of 1903–5, which aroused Jewish communities all over the world. These events in the Russian cities induced even newcomers who had withdrawn from Jewish affairs to join the Zionist movement. Some of the conversions were rather dramatic, as, for example, that of Joseph Barondess, a former trade union leader, who appeared at a large Zionist rally in New York and vowed his allegiance to the Jewish people, an occasion which started his active Zionist career.[54]

In anger and frustration, the English-speaking Zionists reacted by joining the more extremist Zionists and adopting the principle of the "denial of the Galuth." According to this principle, Jewish nationalism could not survive in the Diaspora, where Jews were a minority. The Jews would have to leave those lands and establish a country of their own. Lipsky wrote an article in 1907, entitled "Jewish Nationalism and American Patriotism," in support of this extremist point of view:

> The nearer Palestine is brought, the more devoted the American Zionist must become not to the Stars and Stripes, American literature, life and art, its economic welfare, but to the blue and white flag, and that land . . . . I personally cannot see how a man vitally interested in Palestinian conditions, in the revival of a national language and literature, in devoting himself to the education of himself and his children in Jewish knowledge, in the stimulation of his feelings as a Jew, and with making the word Jew a strong, impelling force in his complete life, not as a study but as a system of life, can at the same time assert that the future of the American nation, its civilization, its morality, its prophets, are vital to his existence. . . . Undoubtedly he is not actually an American.[55]

The fusion of the English-speaking group of leaders with the Yiddish-speaking intellectuals was not accomplished overnight, of course. For a time, the English-speaking group continued to support the "political" approach to Zionism which was advocated by the Western Zionist leaders in Europe. Abraham Goldberg, who came to the United States in 1901 after several years of Zionist activity in Eastern Europe, explained that "on the one hand, they were sons of Eastern Europeans, under the influence of Eastern Jewry; and on the other hand, they favored Herzl's methods, which typified the West."[56]

However, gradually the influx of Eastern European Zionist intellectuals, who stressed both the importance of maintaining Jewish culture

---

[54] Haber, *The Odyssey of an American Zionist*, p. 45.
[55] Lipsky, "Jewish Nationalism and American Patriotism," *The Maccabean* 12 (March 1907): 101.
[56] Abraham Goldberg, "American Zionism up to the Brandeis Era," in *The Avukah Annual of 1932: A Collection of Essays on Contemporary Zionist Thought, Dedicated to Louis D. Brandeis*, ed. J. S. Shubow (Boston, 1932), p. 551.

and the desirability of reviving the Hebrew language and literature, made itself felt in Zionist circles. Their ideas greatly influenced the English-speaking group, who began to accept a commitment to Jewish culture. There was now no difference between the English-speaking Zionists and the more recent arrivals.

There will be occasion to see later how Louis D. Brandeis and his associates who joined the organization in 1914 were immune to the influence of Jewish cultural tradition. The Lipsky group, on the other hand, was still close to Jewish traditions, willing and able to absorb the teachings of the Eastern European intellectuals.[57]

How did all the intellectual discussion and debates in the Zionist camp affect the adherents? How did the masses react to the ideological differences between the Conservative leadership and the Eastern European intellectuals, and to the ideological confusion within the ranks of the Jewish intellectuals themselves? The masses did not react because there was no mass movement. The Zionist Organization was small and had no power or influence in the Jewish community. The bickering and disagreement over the idea and program were typical of a small uninfluential organization on the fringes of society.

Behind all the ideological disputes and petty arguments among the Eastern European intellectuals, we can discern a single overriding aim that united them all. They were attempting to build a Jewish community that would respond to them. Without such a community, their intellectual life and activities were meaningless. This accounted for their desire to awaken Jewish consciousness, to create a cultural renaissance, to instill in the Jewish masses Jewish values and devotion to the Jewish national tradition.

The tragedy of the intellectuals was that the problem of group survival in contemporary secular culture had no immediate relevance for the Jewish masses in America, since most immigrants still lived in Jewish ghettos, where their network of social relations at work, in their neighborhood, and socially was entirely Jewish. Of those immigrants, the majority were engaged in a cruel economic struggle which made socialists—whose ideology promised a new and better society—and trade unions—which were fighting for amelioration of working conditions—more important in their lives. The *Landsmanschaften*, on the other hand, provided familiar spiritual and emotional surroundings in which old ideas and habits could be retained. Their survival as Jews became a

---

[57] Abraham Coralnik, "Babbitts in Zion," *The New Palestine*, May 18, 1928, p. 536.

problem only after World War I, when, having left the ghettos to settle in mixed neighborhoods, they were suddenly faced with the Gentile world and its institutions. But at this early period, it was mostly the Jewish intelligentsia that actually lived in two worlds but felt culturally alienated from the new one. These people found a solution in Zionism, trying to reduce their conflict by demonstrating devotion to the Jewish cultural tradition and belief in its future.

Thus, Zionism was not becoming a mass movement, and dissatisfaction among the active Eastern European members—both the English-speaking ones and the newer arrivals—was growing. They joined hands in opposing the Conservative leaders whom they considered unsuitable and inefficient.

The frustration of the Eastern Europeans in the Zionist Organization was particularly acute since, as Rabbi Herman Brodsky put it, "the leaders ignore us because they know that we cannot do without them."[58] About 1909, many of Lipsky's English-speaking followers actively joined the opposition, which became more open and vocal. The annual conventions of 1909, 1910, and 1911 were stormier than before, and the opposition was more threatening. *The Maccabean* openly joined the opposition.[59]

But the hue and cry of the Eastern Europeans about despotic and undemocratic leaders should not be taken at face value. When the despotic leaders withdrew from their positions, it was the same resentful Eastern European party workers who begged them to stay. Already in 1906, President Friedenwald announced his intention to resign his post. The party workers prevailed upon him to remain. In 1910, however, he adamantly refused the renomination, and only after considerable negotiation agreed to serve as honorary president without responsibilities. The crisis was described in *The Maccabean:* "We confess that thirty days before the convention, the Federation stood in a precarious position. . . . Its president had declined a renomination, and there was no commanding personality to take his place."[60]

Another "commanding personality" like Friedenwald was needed. Magnes, who had recently married into the family of Louis Marshall, the well-known lawyer, philanthropist, and leader of the A.J.C., and Samuel Straus, a German Jew and editor of the (New York) *Evening Globe,* who had joined the organization in the preceding year, were con-

---

[58] *Dos Yiddishe Folk,* May 7, 1909, p. 8.
[59] Editorial, *The Maccabean* 19 (September 1910): 96.
[60] Ibid.

sidered by the party workers. The two refused. In 1911, Magnes was once again considered a desirable candidate for the presidency, despite the antipathy of the Eastern Europeans after he subordinated the Jewish Kehillah, the organization of the New York Jewish community that he headed, to the control of the hated A.J.C.[61]

Whatever they said in later years, it is clear from the evidence that the Eastern Europeans did not dare to assume leadership. A person whose social contacts were not limited to the Lower East Side and who maintained contact with the uptown wealthy German Jews was preferred. Anyone in this category was considered a commanding personality. Only in 1911, after the few qualified persons withdrew from the leadership and no alternatives were available, were the Eastern Europeans forced into leadership.

The desire to devote more time and attention to other Jewish activities was given as the motive for the withdrawal of the leaders from the Zionist activities.[62] But perhaps the actual reason was that the Zionist Organization was too small and uninfluential in the Jewish community and that there was little reward in working in such an organization. It seems that at the same time other positions were open to these leaders in Jewish organizations with more prestige, and so they decided to make the change. Thus, in spite of their Zionist zeal, they reduced their activities in the Zionist Organization. Evidence for this interpretation of their action is lent by their prompt return to active duty the moment Brandeis assumed the leadership of the Zionist Organization in America. So immediate was their reaction that there can be little doubt that it was the national prominence of Brandeis that drew them back into Zionist activity.

The Leadership of the Eastern European Intellectuals

The Jewish intellectual greatly resented his inferior position in the organization. Lipsky blamed himself and fellow Zionists in a self-accusing article for the cult of personality that existed in the American Zionist Organization.[63]

Yet in the same breath, he and his followers made every effort possible to persuade Friedenwald to remain president of the organization. When all attempts failed in 1911 and his group was forced to assume

---

[61] *The Jewish Morning Journal*, June 30, 1911.
[62] "Report of the Proceedings of the Eleventh Annual Convention of the Federation of American Zionists," *The Maccabean* 15 (August 1908): 68–69.
[63] Lipsky, *Dos Yiddishe Folk*, June 17, 1910, p. 5.

leadership, Lipsky lamented that "prominence had deserted the flag of the Zionist Organization."[64]

On one hand, the German leadership was resented; on the other, the very same Zionists who were members of the A.J.C. and were accused of undemocratic practices and aloofness were urged to keep the leadership.

This paradoxical position requires an explanation. The group of Eastern European intellectuals, the party workers headed by Lipsky, was, to use Gaetano Mosca's term, the "political class" of the F.A.Z. This group provided the editors, the propagandists, and the committee members of the organization. The intellectuals refused to take over top leadership positions until the prominent people withdrew in 1911, and even then they did not think they possessed leadership abilities. The first report of the new administration to the annual convention of 1912 declared: "The Executive Committee elected at the last Tannersville convention was composed, for the most part, of men selected from the ranks of the organization. Leaders, in the sense of men with large personal followings, or capable of inspiring large masses, we had none."[65] This state of affairs resulted from the fact that

> . . . prominence had deserted the flag of the Zionist Organization—Friedenwald becoming weary; the late Israel Friedlaender refusing to desert the reference library or the lecture platform for Zionism; Leon Magnes pursuing his own plans, playing an eclectic game which might give power to his own wings; Dr. Wise imprisoned in Portland, Oregon, and returning to give exclusive attention to his rabbinical ambitions; Professor Gottheil unwilling to be around for active participation in Zionist affairs . . . .[66]

In addition to the common denominator of contact with the uptown wealthy Jews, all of these prominent men, with the exception of Friedlaender and Magnes, were of Western European parentage; and all, with the exception of Wise, were at one time or another active members of the A.J.C. Now the Zionist party workers were attacking the A.J.C. relentlessly and vehemently, calling them despots, anti-democrats, and the like. As Lipsky himself explained, "We, organizers of a free Jewish opinion, upon which Zionist success depended, felt that we

---

[64] Lipsky, "A Genius of Versatility," *Collection of Essays on the Occasion of the Fiftieth Birthday of Abraham Goldberg* (New York: Issued by the Abraham Goldberg Jubilee Committee, 1934), p. 10.

[65] "Report of the Proceedings of the Fifteenth Annual Convention of the Federation of American Zionists," *The Maccabean* 22 (July 1912): 25.

[66] Lipsky, "A Genius of Versatility," p. 10.

had to fight the American Jewish Committee or be faithless as Zionists and Americans. . . ."[67]

These were strong words from a man at the head of a group that tried to get a member of the hated A.J.C. to lead the Zionist Organization. Why were the Eastern European party workers so eager to be led by persons associated with the A.J.C.? A comparison between the conditions of the F.A.Z. under the prominent leaders between 1898 and 1911 and conditions under the non-prominent leaders between 1911 and 1914 will not reveal any significant changes in membership figures, financial position, or influence in the Jewish world. The changes in top leadership did not affect the organization for better or for worse.

The only change took place at the top, where the administrative committee was now composed of Eastern Europeans. Three of the five, including the chairman, were journalists who wrote exclusively for the immigrant press. One, the treasurer, was a small businessman, and another was a politically ambitious lawyer not yet elected or appointed to any public office. The only discernible advantage of the former leaders over this group was their connection with the group of German Jews who had attained some prominence in American society and who in education and appearance were more American than the Eastern Europeans, whose experience and activities were restricted largely to the ghetto.

These were the assets that made the old leaders more desirable in the eyes of the Eastern European Zionists, the political class of the Zionist Organization. These feelings of inferiority toward the German Jewish leaders were not shared at that time by most politically conscious members of the Eastern European Jewish community, as evidenced by their support of the socialist movement. The Jewish socialists selected their leaders with complete disregard for the relations of these men to American society, their command of the English language, or their education.[68] But the revolutionary zeal of the socialist leaders and their followers was not shared by the Zionists, who attempted to find Americanized men who had attained positions of some importance in American society to lead their organization. The most desirable leaders were, as stated before, those from the periphery who had attained positions of power and importance in American society and were willing to lead the minority group. Such leaders, however, did not associate with the Zionists before 1914. The second-best choices were German Jews, preferably

---

[67] Lipsky, *Thirty Years of American Zionism* (Nesher Publishing Co., 1927), p. 30.
[68] For further details on the leadership of the Jewish socialists see Melech Epstein, *Jewish Labor in the U.S.A.* (New York: Trade Union Sponsoring Committee, 1950), *passim*.

American-born of German-Jewish descent, who were in a position to maintain close contact with wealthy Jews in positions of power and importance in American society.

The behavior of the Eastern European Zionists is explained by the pull between the two cultures—the old one, to which they were attached by deep emotional and intellectual ties, and the new society in which they were still aliens. They vociferously attacked the established American Jews who were disloyal to their Jewish national and cultural heritage and lived like Gentiles. At the same time, however, venerating the dominant society and its culture, they desired to be led by acculturated Jews who were respected by the dominant group. They could not conceive of themselves, the aliens, as leaders of an American organization.[69]

One issue was beginning to attract the attention of Jews in the United States—the new Jewish colonies in Palestine. To the recent immigrants from Eastern Europe, who were still living in the social and intellectual climate of Eastern European ghettos, the colonization of Palestine and the creation of a Jewish state there seemed as appealing as it did to many European Jews. Though these immigrants were slowly improving their material conditions in the United States, they still felt close enough to their brethren in Europe to identify with their needs.

As early as 1900, a communal worker in the Jewish ghetto observed that "many laborers are interested in activities that have to do with general Jewish interest and support Jewish organization, and even the Zionist movement, not because they have a need for it, but because they believe that it may be of help to their brethren who are living in the oppressed lands where freedom does not prevail."[70] The pogroms in Russia intensified the feelings among American Jews in identifying themselves with their European brethren.

The growth of sentiment in favor of Palestine did not escape the attention of the Zionist leaders and party workers. The leaders were urged to concentrate on Palestinian projects. The secretary of the Zionist Council for Greater New York, for example, argued in 1909 that the only way to activate the defunct Zionist societies was to concentrate

---

[69] The reluctance of the Eastern Europeans to take over the top leadership positions in the organization was in part a consequence of their particular set of values and beliefs. Mosca analyzed the relationships between the top leaders and the political class, the officers of the organization, and concluded that " . . . in choosing its supreme leaders, a political class is in a sense the prisoner of the ideas and principles which it has adopted in regard to leadership. Those ideas and principles result from its whole history and from the level of intellectual maturity that it has attained." Gaetano Mosca, *The Ruling Class* (New York: McGraw-Hill Book Co., 1939), pp. 430-31.

[70] P. Wiernick, *The Monthly Intelligencer* 1 (1900-1): 63.

gram, the political program of the Zionist Organization, and associate membership, which did not require this pledge.[80]

The leaders did not consent, however, to make so many concessions in the case of the men's Zion Associations. They specifically declared that "it will not supplant but supplement the regular organization" and that all members must sign the Basle Program.[81] They were, however, prepared to offer the members a minimal time involvement and to restrict activities to one or two business meetings.[82]

By 1914, the Zionist Organization in America was weak, in financial distress, and with no influence in the Jewish community. A spirit of gloom and defeat engulfed the few dedicated leaders. There seemed to be no future for Zionism in America, and several leaders thought of migrating to Palestine, since this was the one place where Zionism was active and had a future.[83]

Such was the state of the Zionist Organization and the mood of its leaders and party workers. The situation was to be completely transformed with the accession to leadership of Louis D. Brandeis.

---

[80] "Report of the Proceedings of the Sixteenth Annual Convention of the Federation of American Zionists," *The Maccabean* 23 (July 1913): 203.

[81] *The Maccabean* 21 (July 1912): 29.

[82] Etzioni distinguishes between the scope of an organization and its saliency. Scope refers to the number of activities members are required to perform. Organizations whose members share many activities are broad in scope; those in which members share only few activities are narrow. The saliency of an organization refers to the importance of the members' commitment, the "relative emotional significance of participation in one organization compared to that in others." Hadassah narrowed the scope of its organization and was primarily engaged in charity work; it also maintained low saliency, since it did not require its members to sign the Basle Program. Signing the Basle Program was interpreted at the time as an acceptance of Zionism, an extreme variety of Jewish nationalism. That was an important controversial issue in Jewish quarters. The men's Zion Associations narrowed the scope of the organization to one or two business meetings a year, but by requiring their members to accept the Basle Program, they maintained high saliency. On the saliency and scope of organizations, see Amitai Etzioni, *A Comparative Analysis of Complex Organization: On Power, Involvement and Their Correlates* (Glencoe, Ill.: The Free Press, 1961), pp. 160–62.

[83] Fromenson, "Some Zionist Conventions of the Past," *The Maccabean* 30 (June–July 1917): 278.

CHAPTER III

The New Zionist Leadership

The New Leaders and Why They Joined the Organization

Early in 1914, the Zionist Organization in America was small and weak, in great financial distress, and low in morale. The situation changed overnight when in August 1914 a Provisional Zionist Committee (P.Z.C.) was formed to take care of Zionist affairs. The outbreak of World War I disrupted the World Zionist Organization, whose center was in Germany and whose national federations were located in both hostile camps. The manifest aim of this new body, constituted in the United States, a neutral country, was temporarily to carry on the activities of the W.Z.O. The president of the newly formed P.Z.C. was Louis D. Brandeis, the eminent "people's lawyer" and progressive leader. Other well-known Jewish personalities, many of whom were newcomers to any type of Jewish organizational life, joined the committee.

An examination of the new leaders suggests that it was Brandeis who drew them all into the movement and that his leadership made Zionism attractive to them. Louis Lipsky, who was the chairman of the F.A.Z. from 1911 to 1918, has said that Brandeis was the only person among the newcomers who was a devoted Zionist, that the others merely hung on to his coattails.[1] We shall have occasion to see that when Brandeis resigned his leadership in 1921, *all* those persons resigned with him, even though some were not in agreement with the particular ideas on the building of Palestine and the future of the Zionist Organization that led to his resignation.

In addition to Brandeis's attracting newcomers, all the leaders who by 1911 had left active leadership in the F.A.Z. found their way back to the Zionist movement and joined the P.Z.C. in a matter of days after Brandeis's agreement to assume control. With the exception of Harry Friedenwald, who became honorary president with the understanding that it would not entail any responsibilities on his part, none of these people held even a nominal position in the organization in 1914. The new P.Z.C. included Richard Gottheil, the first president of the F.A.Z., who had not occupied any position after 1908; Stephen S. Wise, the first secretary of the F.A.Z., who had not occupied any position after 1906; Friedenwald, Judah Magnes, Henrietta Szold, Jacob de Haas, and Israel Friedlaender. All of them were associated with the German Jewish community, but Eastern Europeans also rallied to the cause. The inde-

---

[1] Interview with the author, September 13, 1960.

pendent midwestern Zionist organization, the Knights of Zion, immediately placed itself under the command of the P.Z.C.[2] Brandeis was the effective power who encouraged them all to join and take an active part in the Zionist movement.

The list of new leaders attracted by Brandeis is impressive: Judge Julian Mack of the United States Circuit Court, a lecturer in the University of Chicago Law School and active in the movement to establish and expand the juvenile court system in the United States; Felix Frankfurter, a professor at Harvard Law School and a noted reformer; Eugene Meyer, a businessman noted for his public spirit and his interest in progressive causes, who resigned from his business in 1917 to enter government service; Mrs. Joseph Fels, widow of the famous philanthropist and a supporter of the single tax movement, who was herself active in prison reform; Elisha Friedman, another progressive, lawyer, lecturer, and author; Howard Gans, a prominent lawyer who held many appointive and elective positions in New York state and who was also active in police reform; and Louis Kirstein, the famous Boston philanthropist who supported many progressive causes.

The list indicates that the new men Brandeis attracted to the Zionist Organization were in an overwhelming majority American-born and of German-Jewish extraction. Most of them occupied positions of some prominence in American society, and all were reformers connected with different progressive causes. All were listed in *Who's Who in America*. None of the earlier Zionist leaders were listed in any similar American directory. Many, however, appeared in *Who's Who in American Jewry*, although most Jewish socialist leaders were not even listed in that.

What, apart from the Brandeis leadership, attracted all these men to Zionism at this particular time, and what attracted Brandeis himself to the movement is a little difficult to determine precisely, especially since motives cannot be analyzed in a study of this nature. Available biographies hardly tackle the problem, and especially disappointing are the biographies of Brandeis. The latest and most comprehensive one, by Alpheus T. Mason, states that Zionism was the most absorbing single interest in Brandeis's life, but makes no attempt to explain his involvement in Zionist affairs from 1914 to his death.[3]

An examination of the position of the group of new Zionists as a whole in both American society and the Jewish community indicates

---

[2] "Zionism in America before the British Mandate," *Modern Palestine: A Symposium*, ed. Jessie Sampter (published by Hadassah, The Women's Zionist Organization of America, 1933), p. 46.

[3] Alpheus Thomas Mason, *Brandeis: A Free Man's Life* (New York: The Viking Press, 1956), p. 464.

that they had achieved a degree of prominence in the dominant society and were now turning to lead their minority group. This type of leadership is sociologically described as "leadership from the periphery." As we have already mentioned, this term—first used by Kurt Lewin—designates those members of the minority who achieve some prominence in the society and, by virtue of this position outside the minority group and the prestige attached to it by the members of the minority, attain positions as leaders of the minority.[4]

Examination of leadership of other minority groups in the United States suggests that members of those groups who attained positions of prominence and renown in American society comparable to that of Brandeis and some of his associates rarely assumed leading positions within their respective ethnic minorities. Caroline F. Ware reported that "Americanization . . . has tended to draw off potential leaders who became successful in American terms, and to merge them in the general American community."[5]

This generalization, it seems, did not apply to the Jews. C. Bezalel Sherman, who made a penetrating study comparing the Jewish minority with other ethnic minorities, argues that the social barriers between the Jews and the rest of society were always higher than for other minorities who, excepting the Negroes, manage to assimilate more rapidly. Acculturation and assimilation are most pronounced among the higher classes, but it was precisely the upper-class Jews, those who attained a high socioeconomic status, who became most conscious of the barriers and found it difficult to move freely within their own social stratum. Sherman cites the Middletown and Yankee City studies, which show that in these towns the highest positions Jews achieved were in the "Upper Middle Class," in contrast to other ethnic groups, even the Irish and the Polish, some of whose members did join the "Upper Class." The wealthy Jewish businessmen and the successful members of established professions were brought face to face with a high social barrier.[6]

Historically, it was the rich Jews, those who reaped the benefits of the industrial revolution in the East, who were first faced with this problem of ethnic discrimination. One anti-Semitic incident which was nationally publicized occurred in the United States in the 1870's when

---

[4] Kurt Lewin, "The Problem of Minority Leadership," in *Studies in Leadership*, ed. Alvin Gouldner (New York: Harper and Bros., 1950), p. 193. For an interesting case study, see William Skinner, *Leadership and Power in the Chinese Community in Thailand* (Ithaca, N.Y.: Cornell University Press, 1958).

[5] "Cultural Groups in the United States," in *The Cultural Approach to History*, ed. Caroline F. Ware (New York: Columbia University Press, 1940), p. 64.

[6] C. Bezalel Sherman, *Yidden un Andere Etnishe Gruppes in die Farainigte Shtaten* (New York: Unser Veg, 1948), *passim*.

the well-known Jewish financier, James Seligman, was barred from the Grand Hotel in Saratoga Springs, New York. This incident created an uproar; anger and indignation were expressed by Jews and non-Jews throughout the country.[7] This was just one of a series of such incidents, most of which, however, were neither widely publicized nor resulted in any strong protests. Sherman commented on these experiences that although the rich Jews wished to believe that one should be "a Jew at home and a man in the street," they were the first to realize that a barrier existed between them and the non-Jewish society. "Even for them only the Jewish street was open."[8]

As a result, a group of businessmen, bankers, and wealthy lawyers engaged in business assumed active leadership of the Jewish community. The leader of the group, Jacob Schiff, was head of the famous banking firm of Kuhn, Loeb Company. In 1906, after news of the pogroms in Russia caused a furor in the Jewish communities all over the world, this group established a formal organization, the American Jewish Committee (A.J.C.), which served as a typical example of "leadership from the periphery."

Those who joined the Zionist Organization in 1914, after achieving some prominence in American society and in their respective professions, were also a case of "leadership from the periphery." Like the leaders of the A.J.C., most of them were American-born of German-Jewish extraction, but in contrast they had made their names in the liberal professions, on the bench and at the bar, and as active supporters of progressive causes; they shared with the rest of American progressives, many of whom were professionals "with claims of learning and skill . . . a common sense of humiliation and common grievances against the plutocracy."[9] The philanthropists, on the other hand, were the Jewish counterparts of the great bankers and businessmen who exercised so much influence at the end of the nineteenth century; they were associated with Big Business and the Republican party.

Brandeis was quoted as having said that he and the men of the A.J.C. were "at opposite ends of the pole" on American issues as well as on Jewish issues.[10] Members of the two groups had already clashed on American issues before 1914. Brandeis, for example, first became nationally known as a lawyer attacking the railroad companies and their policies, while the Kuhn, Loeb business interests were, of course, closely

---

[7] Ibid., pp. 327–28.
[8] Ibid., p. 329.
[9] Richard Hofstadter, *The Age of Reform: From Bryan to F.D.R.* (New York: Alfred A. Knopf, 1956), p. 149.
[10] Interview with Bernard Richards, January 25, 1961.

connected with the railways. Cyrus Adler, in his biography of Schiff, the most prominent and respected member of the A.J.C., tells us that "Schiff's most intimate and personally active business relations . . . were with the Pennsylvania, Great Northern, Illinois Central and Union Pacific railroads."[11]

But it was not until 1914 that Jewish progressives entered the Jewish community to fight the battle of progressivism against business magnates. Sherman explains that Jewish intellectuals found themselves in a predicament similar to that of the wealthy Jews. Just when they felt themselves ready to become immersed in American culture, they came across the Jewish question which formed the dividing line between them and the non-Jewish world.[12]

The association of the Jewish intellectuals with progressives, who were considered by many as radicals, did not facilitate their absorption into the American community. We mentioned earlier the growth of anti-Semitism in the United States since the end of the nineteenth century. It increased at the beginning of the twentieth century and apparently penetrated the ranks of the progressives. Some authorities, like George Mowry and Richard Hofstadter, claim that most progressives were always nativists and racists; Oscar Handlin offers as a reason for the increase of anti-Semitism in this country at the beginning of the century "the disappointment of many radicals and reformers who somehow came to blame Jews for their failure after 1900."[13]

One issue on which the progressives turned against the Jews was the problem of restriction of immigration. Since many of the immigrants at the period were Jews, the demand for restriction was seen by the American Jews as a hostile act.[14]

The United States witnessed, from 1913 to 1915, one of the most infamous outbursts of anti-Semitism of its history. Leo M. Frank, a Jew, was charged with murdering a little white Christian girl in Atlanta, Georgia. He was convicted by the jury although "outside the State the conviction was general that Frank was the victim of gross injustice." When the governor was considering the commutation of Frank's sentence, Tom Watson, twice the Populist nominee for the Presidency and

---

[11] Cyrus Adler, *Jacob Schiff: His Life and Letters* (New York: Doubleday, Doran and Company, 1928), p. 71.
[12] Sherman, *Yidden un Andere Etnishe Gruppes*, pp. 358–59.
[13] George E. Mowry, *The Era of Theodore Roosevelt, 1900–1912*. (New York: Harper and Brothers, 1958), pp. 92–93; Hofstadter, *The Age of Reform*, pp. 177 ff.; Oscar Handlin, "American Views of the Jew at the Opening of the Twentieth Century," *PAJHS* 40 (1950–51): 324.
[14] Arthur S. Link, *Woodrow Wilson and the Progressive Era, 1910–1917* (New York: Harper and Brothers, 1957), p. 60.

a resident of Atlanta, launched a series of attacks on the governor and accused the "Jewish Aristocracy" of illegal interference in due process of law. In his newspaper *The Jeffersonian*, Watson stepped up the attacks in August 1915, after the governor had commuted the death sentence. "Frank belonged to the Jewish Aristocracy," charged the paper, "and it was determined by the rich Jews that no Aristocrat of their race should die for the death of a working-class Gentile." On August 16, 1915, Frank was lynched. This act was greeted by Watson's paper with the statement: "Let Jew libertines take notice."[15]

These developments entailed more than mere social discrimination in clubs and resorts which had so upset the earlier German-Jewish Zionist leaders. The earlier hostility was now accompanied by an ideological anti-Semitism, which associated Jews with an international conspiracy to rule the world. For increasing numbers of Americans, the word *Jew* was coming to indicate a distinct status, and both American-born German Jews and recently arrived Eastern Europeans were being lumped together in an unfavorable stereotype.[16]

These higher barriers between the Jews and the rest of society were, however, concentrated mainly in the social sphere. No discrimination existed in the legal system and little in the economic, especially as compared with the existing situation in Eastern Europe. But civil and economic equality in America only increased the sensitivity of the Jew to social discrimination, so that although American Jews felt less handicapped and rejected than Eastern European Jews because of their legal and political equality and economic opportunities, the social discrimination to which they were exposed was all the more annoying.[17]

---

[15] C. Van Woodward, *Tom Watson: Agrarian Rebel* (New York: Reinhart and Co., 1938), pp. 435-49. For a more recent account of the Frank case see Leonard Dinnerstein, *The Leo Frank Case* (New York: Columbia University Press, 1968). The book describes the anxiety the affair created among prominent American Jews and their actions in trying to save Frank's life.

[16] John Higham, *Strangers in the Land* (New Brunswick, N.J.: Rutgers University Press, 1955), p. 93.

[17] Here we have a case of status inconsistency, or low degree of status crystallization—the existence of an inconsistency in the ranks of various statuses within the same status-set. Since in many social situations, several of a person's statuses are relevant, any inconsistency will prevent a clear definition of his rank and may lead to disturbances in his interactions with others. "Apparently," says Lenski, "the individual with a poorly crystallized status is a particular type of marginal man and is subjected to certain pressures by the social order which are not felt (at least to the same degree) by individuals with a more crystallized status." As a result, such individuals will try to raise their low status, which in our case is their ethnic status; a failure to accomplish this will lead to various reactions, of which two are mentioned by Lenski—withdrawal or the adoption of radical political ideologies. Gerhard E. Lenski,

Brandeis and his associates decided to establish progressive leadership in the Jewish community. Their attraction to the Zionist movement not only stemmed from the eagerness and willingness of the Zionist leaders to give them the lead, but it also resulted from the circumstance that the Zionist Organization was based on democratic principles that appealed to them as American progressives. Brandeis repeatedly emphasized that "it is democracy that Zionism represents."[18]

In our discussion of the leaders from the periphery, we noted that this turning to their own group was an attempt to seek compensation for what was often denied them outside and was frequently accompanied by at least a partial withdrawal from their activities in the larger society. It now appears, however, that their action was also often oriented toward the majority group, and so should also be interpreted as an attempt to gain esteem in the dominant society as well as to enhance the prestige of the Jewish group as a whole.

This attempt to gain esteem motivated the wealthy German Jews to build the Jewish Theological Seminary designed to educate Conservative rabbis. Reform Jews in religious affiliation, the wealthy German Jews helped create a rival organization to their own Reform Judaism, the Conservative, because of their concern with the position of the Jewish group in the United States. They therefore wanted to convert the Eastern European Jews to modern and American religious practices. They realized that "while little can be done to offset general social forces of an adverse character, within the ethnic community itself steps may be taken which it is imagined will help arrest any decline in status."[19]

Facing the same problem, the American Jewish progressives perceived the adoption of Zionism as a solution. The idea that the public image of the Jew in America was applied to all Jews and that therefore only a concerted effort by the whole community could improve the position of the group was a recurrent theme in Brandeis's speeches in 1914–15. In one of his more famous speeches he declared: "Large as this country is, no Jew can behave badly without injuring each of us in the end. Thus the Rosenthal and the white slave traffic cases, though local to New York, did incalculable harm to the standing of the Jews throughout the

---

"Status Crystallization: A Non-Vertical Dimension of Social Status," A.S.R. 19 (1954): 412.
[18] "Report of the Annual Conventions of the Zionist Organization of America," *The Maccabean* 27 (July 1915): 9.
[19] Marshall Sklare, *Conservative Judaism* (Glencoe, Ill.: The Free Press, 1955), p. 162.

country. . . . Since the act of each becomes thus the concern of all, we are perforce our brother's keepers."[20] In another speech, Brandeis declared that the Zionist ideal would help maintain the high standards of the community and thus raise its prestige in America. Zionism was to provide an ideal, a substitute for the old religious ideal which no longer had a hold on the people and which was unacceptable to Brandeis, who, along with most of his associates, was a freethinker.[21] Secularism was also an ideological tenet of the Eastern European Zionist intellectuals, so Jewish culture and nationalism as espoused by these Jewish intellectuals seemed to Brandeis an attractive substitute for the Jewish religion. It promised to give meaning and substance to Jewishness without imposing the religious aspects of Judaism.

Another element that attracted progressive leaders to Zionism was the spirit of rebellion rather than acquiescence that underlay the Zionist idea. Zionism says in effect: let us Jews take our destiny into our own hands and do something to change it. This element of protesting the existing situation and actively trying to change it fitted the progressive temperament.

Social discrimination against Jews and ideological anti-Semitism first entered the American scene in the 1880's, but John Higham tells us that the attack on Jews on both levels became more militant around 1914.[22] The Jewish reaction also changed in character and a more aggressive leadership was thus needed. The wealthy philanthropists in control of the A.J.C. reacted mildly. Their main concern was to facilitate the assimilation of their brethren.[23] They were, to use a distinction made by Gunnar Myrdal in connection with the Negro community, leaders of accommodation rather than of protest. According to Myrdal, the accommodation leaders in the Negro community were usually members of the upper classes, more acculturated, and, because of their position in society, "more interested in calming down the Negro protest than in giving it force and expression."[24]

Likewise, the wealthy leaders of the A.J.C. tried to placate the Jewish community and to secure its rights through private contacts with men in power, a method that the Eastern Europeans called derogatively *shtadlanut*. This Hebrew word denoted the patricians' policy of quiet, unpub-

---

[20] Jacob de Haas, *Louis D. Brandeis: A Biographical Sketch* (New York: Bloch Publishing Company, 1929), pp. 197–98.
[21] Ibid., p. 168.
[22] Higham, "Social Discrimination against Jews in America," *PAJHS* 43 (1957–58): 13–19.
[23] Higham, *Strangers in the Land*, p. 124.
[24] Gunnar Myrdal, *An American Dilemma* (New York: Harper and Brothers, 1944), pp. 34, 37.

lic protest to, or negotiations with, the authorities. The personal papers of such leaders as Schiff, Marshall, and Felix Warburg include endless correspondence with men in power and influence on the subject of the rights of the Jews in this country. The leaders tried, however, not to give the issue any publicity. For example, on the question of discrimination against American Jews in Russia, it was noted that although the leaders refused to discuss the issue publicly, they instigated the publication of unsigned articles in the American press demanding that the United States government intercede in the matter.[25]

How Brandeis Became a Zionist Leader

The emergence of Brandeis and his friends as Zionist leaders will be illuminated if their life history is observed along the lines of Everett V. Stonequist's life cycle of the typical marginal man.[26] Brandeis's life demonstrates the three phases of the life cycle of the marginal man's lack of ethnic consciousness, consciousness of ethnic group membership, and adjustment to being a member of a minority. His aggressive and brilliant leadership of the Zionist movement from 1914 to 1916 occurred in the second phase.

Examination of Brandeis's career along these lines is difficult because he never admitted the basic motives for his actions even in his most personal letters. This is also true of many of his close associates who, unlike the introspective and self-analytical Eastern European intellectuals, rarely acknowledged that they were motivated by any personal ambitions, attributing their behavior only to righteous principles. They never referred to a struggle for power, rarely acknowledging personal conflict. Under the circumstances, investigation of Brandeis's life history in terms of the life cycle of the marginal man can only suggest parallels.

Brandeis's phase of lack of ethnic consciousness or identification with his group is documented by his biographer, Mason, who quotes from a speech Brandeis made at a Fourth of July celebration in 1905 and repeated in an interview with the (Boston) *Jewish Advocate* in December 1910:

> There is room here for any race, of any creed, of any condition in life, but not for Protestant-Americans, or Catholic-Americans, or Jewish-Americans, nor for German-Americans, Irish-Americans, or Russian-Americans. This country demands that its sons and daughters, whatever their race, however intense or diverse their religious connections, be politically merely American citizens. Habits of living or of thought which

---

[25] Editorial, *The Maccabean* 15 (November 1908): 212.
[26] Stonequist's theories were already discussed. See chapt. II, p. 30.

tend to keep alive difference of origin or classify men according to their beliefs are inconsistent with the American ideal of brotherhood, and are disloyal.[27]

His second-in-command on the Zionist scene, Mack, appeared before a Congressional committee on immigration in December 1909 and argued on behalf of the A.J.C. that the Jews are neither a race nor a nation. He requested therefore that Jews coming to the United States should not be classified as Jews but according to the country from which they came. In reply to questions put to him by Senator Henry Cabot Lodge, Mack attributed the idea of Jewish nationalism to recent immigrants "who largely are not yet American citizens," whereas "a majority of Jews who are American citizens care nothing about the re-establishment of the Jewish nation as a nation, and therefore do not feel themselves nationally as Jews."[28]

It was only about 1910 that Brandeis became involved in American national politics. Mason tells us that the years between 1910 and 1915 "were the fullest of Brandeis's public life."[29] His national political aspirations found their first expression when, at the end of 1911, Brandeis endorsed the Republican nomination of Robert La Follette for President. In January and February of 1912, he actively campaigned in La Follette's behalf, touring the country and making speeches. Mason reports that although it was a hopeless campaign from the start, Brandeis was one of the last of La Follette's supporters to give up the fight. He conceded defeat only in May 1912. In the short respite that followed before he became involved in Woodrow Wilson's campaign, Brandeis evinced his concern and sympathy with Zionism for the first time, albeit in private conversations only.[30] When the Zionist leaders were informed about Brandeis's sympathies, apparently through de Haas, a former secretary of the F.A.Z. who had met Brandeis during that year and discussed the matter with him, they responded at once. In its annual convention in July 1912, the F.A.Z. passed a resolution thanking Brandeis "whose sympathy with our aims and methods will help to strengthen our cause."[31]

A similar resolution was passed in honor of Nathan Straus, a rich German Jew with progressive leanings. The desperate need of the Zionist

---

[27] Mason, *Brandeis*, p. 442; (Boston) *Jewish Advocate*, December 9, 1910, pp. 1, 8.
[28] "There Is No Jewish Role: The Testimony of the American Jewish Committee and the Union of American Hebrew Congregations before the Special Congressional Committee on Immigration," *The Maccabean* 18 (January 1910): 26.
[29] Mason, *Brandeis*, p. 442.
[30] De Haas, *Louis D. Brandeis*, p. 53.
[31] "Report of the Proceedings of the Fifteenth Annual Convention of the Federation of American Zionists," *The Maccabean* 22 (July 1912): 5.

Organization as a whole for men of standing in American society was always intensely felt by the Eastern European intellectuals. Contrary to some reports, however, it is clear that Brandeis did not join the Zionist Organization at the time. By August 1912, he had entered Wilson's campaign, touring and speaking vigorously.

Wilson's election in November 1912 was followed by three particularly difficult months in Brandeis's long career. Wilson was considering appointing him a member of his cabinet, first as Attorney General, then as Secretary of Commerce.[32] Certain powerful groups in the country raised objections to such an appointment. Opposition came mainly from the business community and prominent Bostonians.[33] It is difficult to ascertain the role Brandeis's Jewishness played in evoking the objections of these groups. Since anti-Semitic attitudes "clashed with the prevailing temper of American culture," such sentiments were not stated explicitly but kept covert.[34] Nonetheless, authorities agree that Brandeis's Jewishness was important in rallying the opposition to his appointment.[35] Brandeis himself was reluctant to accuse his opponents openly of being anti-Semitic, but in a private letter to a friend alluded to it by stating that the main objective to his appointment was not political.[36] Even in 1916, during the fight over his appointment to the Supreme Court, he evaded the question of anti-Semitism. In the first sentence of a memorandum submitted to the Senate Judiciary committee, he stated that objections to his nomination were due to his being "a radical and a Jew."[37] But while elaborating on his alleged radicalism, he did not return to the question of his Jewishness in this lengthy document. This seems to indicate that although he felt that his Jewishness was an important consideration in the opposition to his nomination, he was as reluctant as his opponents to make this issue public.

The support of the Jewish community to counterbalance the strong opposition inspired by anti-Semitic sentiments in the struggle over Brandeis's cabinet appointment became imperative. Instead, the powerful Jewish leaders joined the opposing forces. Their stand clearly influenced Wilson who, reluctantly, had to arrive at the decision of not appointing Brandeis. Before arriving at his final decision, however, Wilson asked

---

[32] Link, *Woodrow Wilson and the Progressive Era*, pp. 28, 30.
[33] Mason, *Brandeis*, pp. 385–97; Link, *Woodrow Wilson*, p. 31.
[34] Higham, "Anti-Semitism in the Gilded Age: A Reinterpretation," *The Mississippi Valley Historical Review* 63 (March 1957): 564.
[35] Mason, *Brandeis*, p. 387; Ray Stannard Baker, *Woodrow Wilson: Life and Letters*, vol. 3 (New York: Doubleday, Doran Co., 1931), p. 450.
[36] Quoted by Mason, *Brandeis*, p. 395.
[37] Brandeis's memorandum to the Senate Judiciary committee, March 1916, *Louis D. Brandeis Papers* (Louisville, Ky.: University of Louisville Law Library).

Norman Hapgood, a journalist, and Max Mitchell, a Boston banker, to probe the reaction of different influential persons and groups to Brandeis's appointment so as to be able to evaluate the degree of political support and the degree of opposition to this move.[38] Schiff and Louis Marshall, the heads of the A.J.C., were among those approached by Mitchell. They objected to his appointment. In reply to Mitchell's inquiries, Schiff stated: " . . . I have been asked from time to time recently whether Mr. Brandeis may be considered a representative Jew, and to this I was able to give a qualified reply only, but he is, without doubt, a representative American."[39]

This stand was adopted by these Jewish leaders not only because their general economic philosophy was opposed to that of Brandeis, but because they were only interested in promoting into positions of power Jews who were positively identified with the Jewish community.

Brandeis was fully aware that the opinion of influential Jews was being tapped, and that their support might influence the outcome of the negotiations on his cabinet appointment. He was not, however, acquainted with Jewish organizations and their leaders and could not hope to enlist their support. However, his friend de Haas, a former secretary of the F.A.Z., contacted Lipsky, chairman of the organization, and asked him to urge Jewish organizations and their leaders to send letters to Wilson supporting Brandeis's cabinet appointment.[40] But since the F.A.Z. itself had limited influence on American Jewry, only four letters were sent to Wilson through its efforts, which could not have been considered as representative of any influential segment of the Jewish community as the opinion of Schiff and his associates in the A.J.C.[41]

It is impossible from available evidence to determine how effective the refusal of these Jewish leaders to stand by Brandeis was on Wilson's final decision. Such decisions, and the consultations which preceded them, are rarely committed to writing. But from the examination of certain related events, which can be documented, we may infer that the attitude of these Jewish leaders greatly influenced the President-elect.

---

[38] Mason, *Brandeis*, pp. 388–91; entry in Colonel Edward M. House Personal Diary, January 8, 1913 (New Haven, Conn.: Yale University Library).

[39] Jacob H. Schiff to Max Mitchell, February 17, 1913. A copy of this letter was attached to a letter sent by Schiff to Brandeis in 1915 after Brandeis had become an active leader of Jewry (*Brandeis Papers*). This very carefully worded letter should be interpreted as opposition to Brandeis's appointment in view of the fact that Wilson's aides were looking for a Jew that will be a representative of the Jewish community.

[40] Bernard Rosenblatt, secretary of the F.A.Z., to Brandeis, February 14, 1913; *Brandeis Papers*.

[41] Copies of the first three letters are attached to the letter from Rosenblatt to Brandeis, February 14, 1913; Louis Lipsky to Woodrow Wilson, February 17, 1913, *Brandeis Papers*.

New Zionist Leadership 65

This inference is based on the following incidents: first, immediately following the electoral victory, Wilson's aides desired to place a Jew acceptable to Schiff and his associates in a high position in the new administration; and second, Brandeis's association with the Zionist Organization took place a few days after his rejection by Wilson. Brandeis's intimate relations with the President and with some of his closest confidants suggest that he knew what led to Wilson's decision. Brandeis's action so closely followed his political defeat that it can only be understood as a reaction to these events. It is likely that his friends in the administration, possibly the President himself, had advised him on this move. Finally, we witness the successful outcome of the fight for his appointment to the Supreme Court in 1916. Of all the groups that opposed Brandeis successfully in 1912 and 1913—Jewish businessmen, prominent Bostonians, and the business community in general—only the Jewish businessmen changed their position respecting his appointment in 1916. The events leading to his judicial appointment are revealing.

Immediately after the 1912 election, Colonel Edward M. House, Wilson's closest advisor, acknowledged the need to have a representative Jew in the administration. House urged the President to appoint Henry Morgenthau, a member of the circle of wealthy German Jews and prominently active in the A.J.C., as ambassador to Turkey.[42] This post had been occupied by Oscar S. Straus, another member of the same group, and was already becoming a "Jewish position." As long as Wilson desired to make Brandeis the representative Jew in the new administration he refused to assign him to this "Jewish position." "There ain't going to be no Turkey," he kept telling House.[43]

Once Wilson realized he could not have Brandeis in the government, he was perfectly willing to have a Jewish representative in Turkey and he offered Morgenthau the ambassadorship.[44] Morgenthau, however, refused the post, resenting the fact that the Turkish Embassy was becoming a Jewish position. Wilson attempted to enlist Schiff's support in inducing Morgenthau to accept the job, but Schiff upheld Morgenthau's stand.[45] Morgenthau's refusal prompted the administration to search for another representative Jew as ambassador to Turkey—without success.

In June, Wilson renewed his efforts to find a representative Jew whom he would appoint as ambassador to Turkey. Secretary of State William Jennings Bryan met twice with Simon Wolf, a prominent Jew who un-

---

[42] Entry on December 18, 1912, *House Diary*.
[43] Entries on December 18, 1912, and February 18, 1913, ibid.
[44] Entry on March 24, 1913, ibid.
[45] Henry Morgenthau to Woodrow Wilson, June 12, 1913, in *Woodrow Wilson Papers* (Washington, D.C.: Library of Congress).

officially represented Jewish organizations in Washington. Bryan mentioned to Wolf the names of possible candidates, and Wolf was expected to get in touch with the leading Jews in New York and get their opinions on the different candidates. Bryan, in turn, was to report to the President on the results, and Wilson was to have the last word on the matter.[46] In describing these meetings with Bryan, Wolf wrote that the Secretary of State had told him "that it was easy to get a Democrat but not so easy to get a representative of a class."[47] Schiff and his associates were willing to settle for Herman Bernstein, who was an Eastern European Jew, an active Democrat, and the editor of a Yiddish newspaper. But Wilson was not satisfied with the choice. "I should like to make a few more inquiries myself before finally deciding," he informed Bryan.[48] The reasons for Wilson's hesitation were not stated but can be easily surmised. Bernstein was not a member of the Jewish Establishment, and his appointment would not set up fruitful, stable lines of communication between them and the White House as was desired by the President. Withholding his decision on Bernstein's appointment, Wilson renewed his efforts in persuading Morgenthau to accept the ambassadorship. Inviting Wise to the White House, Wilson asked for his help in convincing Morgenthau to accept the post. Wise was successful in his mission, and Morgenthau finally agreed to go to Turkey.[49]

In the meantime, Brandeis was working to establish himself as a representative Jew. He acted swiftly. A few days after Wilson's inauguration on March 4, he made his first public appearance on a Zionist platform. At a public meeting in honor of the visiting European Zionist leader Nahum Sokolow, which took place in Boston on March 20, Brandeis acted as chairman of the welcoming committee.[50] De Haas tells us that: "... it was at the last moment prior to President Wilson's inauguration in 1913, when the whole country was gossiping about as to [sic] the possibility of Brandeis becoming Attorney General, that he [Brandeis], made his first engagement to appear on a Zionist platform. Men were looking at him as a possible member of the Cabinet whilst he was seeking the form for his first public utterance on Zionism."[51] This moment "prior to President Wilson's inauguration" was, however, precisely when Wilson dropped Brandeis from his prospective cabinet. A few days after his

---

[46] William Jennings Bryan to Woodrow Wilson, June 30 and July 1, 1913, and Wilson to Bryan, July 3, 1913, *Wilson Papers*.

[47] Simon Wolf, *The Presidents I Have Known from 1860–1918* (Washington, D.C.: Bryon S. Adams, 1918), p. 410.

[48] Wilson to Bryan, July 3, 1913, *Wilson Papers*.

[49] Wilson to Bryan, August 11, 1913, ibid.

[50] De Haas, *Louis D. Brandeis*, p. 154.

[51] Ibid., p. 53.

New Zionist Leadership

appearance at this public meeting, Brandeis enrolled in the Boston Zion Association.[52]

It is not clear how involved Brandeis wished to become in Jewish and Zionist affairs at the time of his enrollment in the Zionist Organization. In February 1914, he explained to Lipsky, chairman of the F.A.Z., how much he regretted that the pressure of other work prevented his being active in Zionist affairs.[53] He might have become an active Zionist leader immediately after his enrollment had he not been sidetracked by Wilson, who had asked him soon after the inauguration to advise the administration on matters of progressive legislation. When, shortly after he joined the organization, the Zionists offered him the presidency of the Boston Zion Association, he declined it. In his letter of refusal Brandeis explained that he was being kept busy in Washington advising the President.[54] In lieu of active leadership in the Jewish community, he was building up his power in the community by donating sums of money to various Jewish organizations. In a letter to his brother, he mentioned his donation to the Y.M.H.A. in Louisville, Kentucky, adding, "I have so much more [money] to donate to Boston Y.M.H.A. and Zionism."[55]

Elected an associate member of the executive committee of the F.A.Z., which meant membership in an advisory body that met four times a year, he never attended the meetings of this body. He always apologized profusely, pleading lack of time, and occasionally adding to his letters of apology unsolicited donations for the propaganda activities of the organization.[56] He did, however, go to New York for conferences on the establishment of an American Palestine Company and was willing to help this organization in its initial stages.[57] This organization was projected as a non-political organization that would persuade American Jews to invest in Palestine and see to it that it led to "the agricultural, industrial, and commercial development of Palestine."[58]

Suddenly on August 30, 1914, the nature of the relationship between Brandeis and the Jewish community took a new turn. On that day, Brandeis became the national leader of the whole American Zionist move-

---

[52] The exact day of Brandeis's enrollment could not be ascertained. He was not a member of the organization on the day of the public meeting on March 20, but in a letter written on April 30, he declined the offer to become the president of the Boston Zion Association. (Brandeis to Joseph Shohan, April 30, 1913, *Brandeis Papers*.) Thus, he had joined sometime between these two dates.

[53] Brandeis to Lipsky, February 2, 1914, ibid.

[54] Brandeis to Shohan, April 30, ibid.

[55] Brandeis to his brother Alfred, May 12, 1913, ibid.

[56] Brandeis to Lipsky, November 17, 1913, and February 2, 1914, ibid.

[57] Lipsky to Nahum Sokolow, November 20, 1913, in *Nahum Sokolow Papers* (Jerusalem: The Central Zionist Archives).

[58] Ibid.

ment and was elected president of the P.Z.C. which took charge of all Zionist activities for the duration of World War I. This move was stimulated by further frustration and disappointments encountered on the national political scene. Since early 1914, Brandeis witnessed the ebbing of progressive legislation in Washington. The important, though unofficial, position he occupied as an advisor to the President was becoming tenuous. During the spring, Wilson started his campaign to win back the trust of the business community. This led to friction with the progressives and came to a head on June 15 over the issue of naming businessmen to the Federal Reserve Board—an issue in which Brandeis was deeply involved. Brandeis and other progressive leaders objected to the President's candidates, who were appointed, however, in spite of the progressives' opposition.[59]

In a rather discouraged mood, Brandeis left Washington for his summer vacation, and again turned to the Jews. We are told that he decided to devote his vacation "to an intensive study of the Jewish problem."[60] Before the summer was over Brandeis had become an active Jewish leader.

There was, of course, more to Brandeis's decision to assume active leadership in a Jewish organization that political self-interest. Imagine the feelings of this man, influential in policy-making in Washington but, at the same time, barred from an official position commensurate with his responsibilities, because he was, in his words, "a radical and a Jew."[61] Then, in 1914, the decline of progressivism in the administration led to the waning of his influence; he was thus in the awkward posture of having neither unofficial influence in the administration nor an official position in the government. Brandeis's Jewish consciousness, his identity with his brethren, might well have been greatly deepened by these events. The compensatory rewards of assuming a position of power and influence in the Jewish world may also have played their part.[62]

It was this active leadership and his success in attracting influential Jews to the Zionist Organization and in building a powerful Jewish organization to rival the A.J.C. which established him as a representative Jew. This proved to be an asset when Wilson appointed him to the Supreme Court in January 1916 and during the fight for congressional approval which lasted until late May of that year.

Attempting to assess the influence of the Jewish support for the President's appointment and the Senate's confirmation of the same, we are

---

[59] Link, *Woodrow Wilson*, pp. 74–78.
[60] Mason, *Brandeis*, p. 441.
[61] Brandeis's memorandum to the Senate Judiciary committee, March 1916, *Brandeis Papers*.
[62] Mason, *Brandeis*, p. 441.

again faced with lack of written evidence on the negotiations behind the scenes and the consultations among the politicians involved. It is known, however, that the same groups who opposed Brandeis in 1912–1913—the business community and Boston's upper class—were opposing him again, with the exception of the Jewish businessmen who now actively supported him. The opposition in 1916 was open and persistent.[63] But so was the support of the whole Jewish community. Mass meetings were organized in his support; influential Jews lobbied for him and put pressure on their congressmen.[64] For example, in a countermove to the public statement against Brandeis issued by a group of prominent Bostonians headed by A. Lawrence Lowell, president of Harvard University, all Jewish lawyers in Massachusetts were approached and asked to write to the Senate Judiciary committee in support of Brandeis's appointment, and many complied with the request.[65]

Schiff endorsed Brandeis's appointment and supported him strongly during the fight over the confirmation. In an unsolicited letter to the Attorney General he declared: "It is particularly gratifying to the people from whom, like myself, Mr. Brandeis has sprung, and who now form so considerable a percentage of the population of our country, that the president has nominated one of our most eminent co-religionists to the United States Supreme Court. . . ."[66] Brandeis's status as a representative Jew could not be denied by Schiff and his associates. Brandeis, the Zionist leader, was popular with the Jewish masses, and open opposition to his nomination by the Jewish establishment would alienate it from the Jewish community and thus endanger its position of leadership. William Howard Taft shrewdly observed that "Speyer, Schiff, Kahn, Louis Marshall, all have to praise the appointment and all hate Wilson for making it."[67] Even Senator Lodge thought it politically unwise to oppose Brandeis openly, for "the Jews, especially since his taking up Zionism, take great pride in his leadership."[68] The fact that Brandeis, a recognized Jewish leader, was appointed to the Supreme Court conferred prestige on the whole community.

---

[63] A detailed account on the opposition and its activities during the debate in the Senate over Brandeis's appointment is found in Mason, *Brandeis*, pp. 465–508; see also Alden L. Todd, *Justice on Trial: The Case of Louis D. Brandeis* (New York: McGraw-Hill Book Co., 1964).
[64] Mason, *Brandeis*, p. 502.
[65] Copies of numerous letters sent by Jewish lawyers of Massachusetts to the Senate Judiciary committee are in *Brandeis Papers*.
[66] Schiff to the Attorney General, February 17, 1916, in *Jacob H. Schiff Papers* (Cincinnati: The American Jewish Archives).
[67] William Howard Taft to his brother Henry W. Taft, quoted by Todd, *Justice on Trial*, p. 80.
[68] Henry Cabot Lodge to Arthur D. Hill, ibid., p. 86.

Wise, who was himself mobilizing support for Brandeis at the time, attributed Wilson's strong public statement in support of Brandeis, made during a crucial period in the Senate's debate on Brandeis's confirmation, to Schiff's intervention.[69]

However, it was in 1914 that Brandeis first became head of the new P.Z.C. It was then deemed advisable to create a new body to which new men could be appointed by the president and who would not be bound by any constitutional procedures and elections in annual conventions. This new body was also international, and, therefore, even more attractive. In explaining its design and purposes, Richard Gottheil admitted: "we have been scheming to transfer the international organization to this country in order to place you [Brandeis] at the head."[70]

The Meaning of Zionist Ideology to Brandeis and to Some of His Associates

We have now established the "push," the rebuff on the national scene, and the "pull," the desire of the Zionists to attract Brandeis and his associates and their willingness to surrender absolute control to him, that made him the leader of the American Zionists in 1914. More light will be shed on the reasons which were behind the involvement of Brandeis and his associates in Jewish affairs and their joining the Zionist Organization when we examine what they said and what Brandeis did, as head of the organization between August 1914 and July 1916.

An aspect to consider in those years was Brandeis's serious attempt to accept Zionist ideology in its broader ramification as a cultural revival of the Jewish people, not simply as a political movement for establishing a Jewish state in Palestine. Many of his associates never reached this ideology of accepting a renaissance of Jewish culture in the United States.

In his desire to identify with his group's culture and historical traditions, Brandeis found support in the ideas prevalent at the time in some progressive circles, primarily among the workers in the Settlement House movement who were in close contact with the new immigrants. These progressives discarded earlier notions that it was necessary to Americanize the immigrants as rapidly as possible. Instead, they adopted the concept of America as a nation of nations to which all cultures should and

---

[69] Stephen S. Wise to Brandeis, May 10, 1916, *Brandeis Papers*. For Wilson's statement in support of Brandeis, see *The Public Papers of Woodrow Wilson*, ed. Ray Stannard Baker and William E. Dodd, vol. 2 (New York: Harper and Bros., 1926), pp. 160–64.
[70] Gottheil to Brandeis, February 11, 1916, *Brandeis Papers*.

could make contributions. This doctrine, according to Higham, was disseminated widely by Jane Addams and other social workers and Settlement House people after 1900.[71]

Their ideas were gradually accepted by other elements within the progressive movements.[72] One exponent of these ideas was Horace Kallen, a member of the Zionist Organization from its early days who also greatly influenced the thinking of Brandeis and some members of his circle. In earlier years, he belonged to the group of English-speaking Zionists and was an exponent of the denial of the Galuth principle, according to which the one and only solution for the Jewish problem was the migration of Jews to a country of their own.[73] In the meantime, he had received his Ph.D. from Harvard University, served as an assistant to William James, become an assistant professor at the University of Minnesota, and had begun to develop that idea of cultural pluralism which was to become influential among the new Zionists.

The essence of the idea held that America is not a nation like the European nation-states; it is a nation of nations, in which different cultures are blended. We here in America, argued Kallen, are not a "melting pot." We are rather a great cooperative commonwealth of nationalities.[74] Kallen tells us that Brandeis and Frankfurter were among the many influenced by his theory and that, in turn, they converted Mack to Zionism by presenting him with Kallen's argument for American pluralism.[75]

In such fashion, these leaders reconciled Americanism with Zionism. For them, Zionism was important because it contributed to American society, rather than because it was based on the internal developments of the Jewish people and the internal spiritual evolution of the Jewish *geist*, as the Eastern European nationalists believed. Since Mack had this broad philosophical conception of Zionism as a social movement, he conceived of it as being part of the historical evolution of the American people, not of the Jewish people. In a mass meeting of the Knights of Zion, in December 1916, he explained his outlook: ". . . but this country had large numbers of all nationalities of the world embodied in this citizenship; and these nationalities are gradually, slowly but gradually fusing together into a new nation, the American nation of which we form a part. But during the formation period, and, perhaps, after the

---

[71] Higham, *Strangers in the Land*, p. 120–22.

[72] Ibid., p. 238.

[73] Horace M. Kallen, "The Ethics of Zionism," *The Maccabean* 11 (August 1906): 69, 71.

[74] Kallen, "Democracy, Nationality and Zionism," *The Maccabean* 31 (July 1918): 187.

[75] Kallen, *Of Them Which Say They Are Jews* (New York: Bloch Publishing Company, 1959), p. 126.

completion of this fusion, each strain that goes to make up the American nation will be preserved as part of their American nationality."[76]

This difference between the new Zionist leaders and the rest of the Zionist movement can help us understand the causes of the friction that arose after the end of World War I. The position of the American leaders was "that immigrant communities, while adopting the dominant culture, retained and contributed to America a form of subculture acceptable to the general consensus."[77] The Eastern European intellectuals came into contact with American cultural traditions after being steeped in Jewish culture, and Lipsky rightly asserted that their Zionist ideas "were only slightly influenced by the early American pioneers. They received their inspiration from their own intellectual and spiritual leaders."[78]

Brandeis took the idea of cultural revival rather seriously, but was, at the same time, emotionally and intellectually a part of the American cultural tradition. Although secular Jewish culture was the only part of Judaism that appealed to Brandeis, he never became part of even this tradition. He never really resolved this paradox and was probably not fully aware of it.

In those first exciting years of Brandeis's leadership, Zionism was, for him, Jewish culture and tradition as interpreted by the Eastern European intellectuals, and since he was a stranger to Jewish culture, he made them the custodians of it.[79] He was clearly interested in the spread of this culture among his brethren. The clearest declaration of policy for the Zionist movement that embodied Brandies's Zionist principles of this period is to be found in a private letter he wrote to another new convert:

> The efforts [of the Zionists] are being directed towards establishing a publicly recognised, legally secured home for Jews in Palestine. Such a home will serve both as a haven for persecuted Jews from European countries, and also a center for Jewish ideas and Jewish culture. We must in America support the movement in two ways. Financially and culturally, and as a means to both these ends, we must develop a body of young Jewish men who thoroughly understand the aims and purposes of Zionism, and are familiar with what has been accomplished both culturally and practically in Palestine, and who can themselves become leaders of

---

[76] "Mass Meeting of the Knights of Zion Convention," *The Maccabean* 29 (December 1916): supplement, p. v.

[77] Ben Halpern, *The American Jew* (New York: The Theodor Herzl Foundation, 1956), p. 84.

[78] Louis Lipsky, *Thirty Years of American Zionism* (The Nesher Publishing Co., 1927), p. 9.

[79] Speech before the Knights of Zion, December, 1915, *Brandeis Papers*.

thought, and can, through writing, speaking, and organizing extend the Zionist movement in America.[80]

This declaration of policy was certainly in accord with Zionist thinking in Europe. A political program of this kind would have been endorsed by most Zionist leaders both in Europe and on New York's Lower East Side. Brandeis endorsed cultural activities both in Palestine and in the United States as part of the Zionist program. He named economic activities in Palestine as equal in importance to cultural activities in Palestine and the United States; he proposed appointing "leaders of thought" to perform the important functions of writing and speaking for, and organizing, the Zionist movement in America. Yet, only a few years later, he would reject all the tenets of Zionism endorsed in this letter.

It should be remembered, however, that Brandeis never immersed himself in Jewish culture, nor ever really comprehended it. In both his writings and his actions, he manifested total commitment to the American cultural tradition, and more concretely to the ideals of the American progressives. What Brandeis called Jewish ideas were in reality the basic principles of the American progressive movement, even though he claimed that these values were shared by both cultures. His exposition of the values, which he claimed were shared by both cultures, reveals his deep and absolute commitment to American ideals. In one of his more famous speeches of the period, fittingly called "Zionism and Patriotism," he argued that there was no difference between the values of American society and Jewish tradition.[81] Similarly, addressing the Zionist convention in 1915, he said: "the highest Jewish ideals are essentially American in a very important particular. It is Democracy that Zionism represents. It is Social Justice which Zionism represents, and every bit of that is the American ideals of the twentieth century."[82]

Brandeis's point of view was not shared by the Eastern European intellectuals. During the period of his leadership, however, Brandeis was partially protected from their criticism by their gratitude for his assumption of leadership.

The content of Jewish culture and traditions was rarely, if ever, discussed by the other new leaders. Nor was this neglect only a result of their ignorance or lack of interest in these matters. Even the few who struggled with the intellectual and theoretical problems of Zionism in the United States did not share the enthusiasm for Jewish culture in the

---

[80] Brandeis to Alex Cantor, November 14, 1914, ibid.
[81] Louis D. Brandeis, *The Curse of Bigness: Miscellaneous Papers of Louis D. Brandeis* (New York: The Viking Press, 1934), pp. 214–15.
[82] *The Maccabean* 23 (July 1913): 9, 34.

United States that Brandeis expressed in those early years. They were searching for a dividing line between the statuses of American and Zionist, or Jew. They were trying to define the term *Zionist* in such a way as to avoid any potential conflict with their other obligations and loyalties as Americans. Having formulated their problem in these terms, they became occupied not with Jewish culture but rather with the structural position of the Jews in American society. In his one theoretical work on Zionism, *Americanism and Zionism,* Julian Mack stated that although Jews were not a nation, they were a distinct people: "Zionism rests, as I view it, on this fundamental assumption, this basis of fact, that the Jews are a people. I purposely use the word people instead of nation or nationality because of the several connotations of these latter words."[83]

What was the purpose of such quibbling? It represented an effort to give a particular content to the status of Jew—so that it would not conflict with other statuses which Jews occupy, such as being an American—but which would not be emptied of meaning altogether. The American Jew, Mack conceded, could not give up his status as Jew. "Ask your neighbor, and let him tell you whether we are a people or not."[84] But at the same time, an excessively broad interpretation of the status of Jew, such as advocated by the Eastern Europeans, might conceivably conflict with their rights and duties as Americans. Hence the idea that Jews are a "people" but not a "nation" was an attempt to find a formula that would accommodate the two statuses.

So, although Brandeis, at least in his early writings, saw no difficulty in blending the two cultures, Mack was painfully trying to differentiate between the two statuses and the duties and obligations involved in both.

As will be seen later, this group of new Zionist leaders became increasingly concerned with the boundaries between their American and Jewish statuses. As time went on, they were inclined to give a more limited and restrictive interpretation to Zionism. The greater emphasis on their American status can be attributed in part to their structural position as leaders from the periphery. It was their position in American society that was the source of their influence and leadership in the Jewish group and the Zionist Organization. They therefore always remained part-time leaders, unable and unwilling to abandon their positions in American society. They never consented to give up posts on the bench or in the university and assume full-time leadership in the Zionist Or-

---

[83] Julian W. Mack, *Americanism and Zionism* (New York: The Federation of American Zionists, 1918), p. 3.

[84] Ibid., pp. 7–8.

ganization. This was the result not simply of attachment to American society and their position therein, but of a full realization that their position in general American society was their source of power. In 1927, for example, Brandeis, after refusing to consider resigning from the bench to assume full leadership of the Zionist movement, urged Mack to run for the presidency of the Zionist Organization. In a letter explaining his refusal to run, Mack said that "only by resigning the judgeship could I undertake such a contest. Half my influence would be gone by such resignation."[85]

The Zionism of the group associated with Brandeis, which for them was synonymous with Jewishness, contained, along with a desire to establish a Jewish state in Palestine, principles of social justice and democracy, which the group adapted as Zionist principles. Following Brandeis, these principles were reiterated time and again by the members of the group. The ideas of social justice and democracy were at that time part of the stock in trade of the progressive movement.

It was, however, the democratic principle that became the crucial issue and the central theme of American Zionism during Brandeis's active leadership. Not only was it a good American principle, but Brandeis's position in the structure of the Jewish community made it a useful one to apply to the realities of Jewish communal life in the United States. The undisputed leaders of the American Jewish community at the time were the Jewish philanthropists who established and controlled the A.J.C., an appointed rather than an elected body. Through their financial contributions, this body controlled and directed other Jewish organizations. Obviously, a leadership operating with such methods could be challenged only by a democratic mass organization of dues-paying members. Only as leaders of such an organization could the progressives challenge the leadership of the plutocracy that ruled the Jewish community.

Until 1914, only Wise, the first secretary of the F.A.Z., fought the philanthropists. In 1907, he had challenged the authority of Marshall, one of the outstanding leaders of the plutocracy. Marshall, who was chairman of the board of trustees of Temple Emanuel in New York, refused to relinquish his power to censor the activities and utterances of the rabbis at the temple. Thereupon Wise established an independent Free Synagogue and attacked the "gentry" from the pulpit. He further achieved power in American Jewry by joining the New York City reform groups who fought corruption in city and state government,

---

[85] Mack to Brandeis, December 13, 1927, *Brandeis Papers*.

and he also became a well-known and influential civic leader.[86] The real battle against the millionaires started, however, when Brandeis led the fight as head of the Zionist Organization in the United States.

---

[86] Stephen S. Wise, *Challenging Years* (New York: G. P. Putnam's Sons, 1949), *passim*.

CHAPTER IV

The Fight for an American Jewish Congress, 1914–16

War Relief Operations of the Zionist Organization and the American Jewish Committee

Louis Brandeis's struggle between 1914 and 1916 to wrest the leadership of the Jewish community from the German Jewish millionaires must be understood in the light of developments that were taking place in the community at that period. Archibald McClure, in a penetrating study of the leaderships of American minorities, published in 1916, makes two significant observations about the Jewish community which he considered relevant to the problem.

First, he contends that the trend among Jewish immigrants was away from religious beliefs and practices. They became either confirmed freethinkers or wholly indifferent to religion.[1] For most Jews, adjustment to their new life in the United States meant giving up the rigid religious observances and beliefs in which they were brought up in the old country. The process, as we have seen, had begun in Eastern Europe; but for most immigrants, this modernization and disenchantment with the old *weltanschauung* did not affect them until they settled in the United States, and it resulted in strife within the Jewish community as well as in psychological conflicts for the individual members. The immigrant Yiddish press, literature, and drama clearly reflected this crisis.[2]

McClure's second observation concerns the growth of nationalism among Jews, its acceleration after the start of World War I, and the channeling of nationalist sentiment into a collective effort in support of war-stricken Jews abroad. "They who would lead the Jewish immigrants," added McClure, "must take account of Zionism and the aroused spirit of nationalism." McClure looked on Zionism, the spirit of nationalism, and the support to war-stricken Jews in Europe as components of the same phenomenon—"the growth of the feeling of Jewish nationalism."[3]

Let us first take up McClure's observation on the growth of nationalism and the support of war-stricken Jews in Europe and examine the activities of the Zionist Organization under Brandeis.

---

[1] Archibald McClure, *Leadership of the New America: Racial and Religious* (New York: George H. Doran Co., 1916), pp. 172–76.
[2] A most interesting document of the period is Abraham Cahan, *The Rise of David Levinsky* (New York: Harper Brothers, 1917).
[3] McClure, *Leadership of the New America*, pp. 179–80.

Immediately after the eruption of hostilities in Europe, American Jewry prepared to send relief to their brethren in Europe and Palestine. The four organizations established by them represented the main groupings of the American Jewish community at the time: American Jewish Relief Committee (A.J.R.C.), organized by the A.J.C.; the Central Relief Committee, formed by Eastern European Orthodox circles; the Peoples' Relief Committee, founded by the Jewish socialists; and the Palestine Relief Fund, established by the Zionists.

The wrangles among the different agencies and their attempts to cooperate and embark on common projects make an exceedingly complicated story. The rivalry was most acute between the Zionists and the A.J.C.; each attempted to thwart the other's endeavors at domination while trying itself to dominate the scene. The struggle was another manifestation of the cleavages between the two groups of leaders.[4]

The A.J.C. was the first to start operating and the first to attempt to combine the efforts of all concerned under its leadership.[5] But in spite of these efforts, the Zionists embarked on their own independent projects at first. They tried to raise money for a ship to carry food and medicine to the Jewish community in Palestine. In the course of these preparations, however, they were forced to ask the A.J.R.C. for financial help, since they could not carry it out themselves. The latter agreed to help and in return took credit for sending the ship—which infuriated the Zionists. It was, however, becoming clear that the A.J.R.C., established by the A.J.C., was the agency that managed to collect the largest amount of money and, through its members' contacts with government agencies, was most successful in having supplies reach their destination in an orderly manner.[6] The A.J.R.C. became the leader in the relief efforts of the Jewish community. It further became clear to the Zionists

---

[4] Melech Epstein, *Jewish Labor in the U.S.A.* (New York: Trade Union Sponsoring Committee, 1950), p. 59.

[5] Marshall to Schiff, September 22, 1914, in the *Jacob H. Schiff Papers* (Cincinnati: The American Jewish Archives).

[6] Joseph C. Hyman, "Twenty-Five Years of American Aid to Jews Overseas," *AJYB* 60 (1939–40): 141–79, especially pp. 146–47; and Cyrus Adler, *I Have Considered the Days* (Philadelphia: The Jewish Publication Society of America, 1941), pp. 305–6. Both tell how the American State Department, whose help was solicited by the A.J.C., made possible the delivery of food and money to Jews in Eastern Europe and Palestine. Hyman also presents figures on the size of the relief operations of the Joint Distribution committee. The Zionist Organization itself admitted that without the help of the J.D.C., even their plan to send medical aid to Palestinian Jewry would not have materialized. Half the expense for the medical unit sent to Palestine was supplied by the J.D.C. *American Zionist Medical Unit for Palestine Maintained by the Zionist Organization of America and the Joint Distribution Committee of the American Funds for Jewish War Sufferers, June 1916–June 1919* (New York: The Zionist Organization of America, 1919), p. 8.

that, since they could not raise the necessary amounts of money, they would have to enter into negotiations with the A.J.R.C. Although they tried at first to become custodians of all relief to Palestine, this was unacceptable to the A.J.C., and the two organizations finally agreed to pool their efforts.[7]

This agreement established the Joint Distribution Committee (J.D.C.). Even though the Zionists participated in this organization, they did not occupy the top positions. Relations between the Zionists and the J.D.C. (also referred to as the Joint) remained tense all through the war, with the Zionists firmly convinced that the A.J.C. was stealing the show from them. Louis Lipsky, chairman of the F.A.Z., recalls: ". . . no sooner had we withdrawn from the administrative leadership of the relief committee than we faced in its sub-committees a stubborn resistance to our recognition as a body responsible for the work in Palestine, and the entire American Jewish Relief Committee assumed an aspect of hostility."[8]

The financial difficulties the Zionists faced were not restricted to the comparatively small sums they could collect in contrast to the funds raised by the A.J.R.C. An additional and serious limitation was the stipulation of most contributors that their contributions should be spent for relief in Palestine only and not to support any Zionist institutions either in Palestine or anywhere else. Most large donations came from people belonging to the same social circle that constituted the A.J.C. Julius Rosenwald of Chicago, for example, pledged $1,000 a month to the Zionists for the duration of the war, provided that it went only to relief work in Palestine and not for any Zionist institutions there.[9] The Zionists were thus forced to divide their efforts and to channel them separately into a relief fund for the Jewish population in Palestine and an emergency fund for all other Zionist purposes.

The Zionists, therefore, decided to abdicate the field of general relief in Palestine in favor of the J.D.C. *The Maccabean* declared that "relief work is extra work. It does not come within the scope of the original program of the Provisional Zionist Committee."[10]

From the point of view of the organization, this was apparently a wise decision. In the field of relief, they were no match for the A.J.C.,

---

[7] Agreement between the P.Z.C. and the American Jewish Relief Committee, October 27, 1915, *Louis D. Brandeis Papers* (Louisville, Ky.: University of Louisville Law Library).

[8] Louis Lipsky, "Early Days of American Zionism, 1897–1929," *Palestine Year Book*, vol. 2 (1945–46): 465.

[9] Julius Rosenwald to the Chicago representative of the executive committee of the P.Z.C., December 8, 1914, *Brandeis Papers*.

[10] Editorial, *The Maccabean* 28 (June 1916): 2.

which managed to raise huge sums of money in contrast to the meager results of Zionist attempts, when even the money collected could not go toward strengthening Zionist institutions. Brandeis and his associates shifted their energies to the problem of strengthening the organization and made great efforts to increase its membership. In his correspondence about Zionist affairs, Brandeis was concerned mainly with problems of organization. He complained incessantly of the weaknesses of the organization, maintaining that these would have to be overcome if Zionism was to emerge as a dominant force in American Jewry.

The Congress Issue: The Struggle between the Zionist Organization and the American Jewish Committee

A new issue, the creation of an American Jewish Congress, gained the support of the Jewish masses; the Zionist leaders seized upon it, adopted the issue as their own, and utilized it as a vehicle for increasing the popularity and appeal of Zionism in order to raise the enrollment of the organization.

However, much more was involved in the Congress movement; and to understand the meaning for the Eastern European community of the fight for a Jewish Congress, we must recognize one fact: that raising funds for relief of their brethren in Europe and convening an all-American Jewish Congress to help those brethren through political pressure were for them two types of action, but with one single goal. The funds were aimed at immediate relief; the Congress itself aimed at a more permanent solution. As explained by Israel Goldberg, an active member of both the Congress movement and the Zionist Organization, the Congress movement was oriented toward the international Jewish situation.[11] For the Eastern European Jews in the United States, the aims of the Congress were specifically to defend and support the civil, political, and cultural rights of the Jews in Eastern Europe as well as to support the establishment of a haven for the Jews in Palestine. This was the main issue among the Eastern Europeans and in the Yiddish press during the agitation for the Jewish Congress, and the A.J.C. strongly objected to this aspect of the projected Congress.[12] As accommodation leaders, they disapproved of any such open and public commitment by American Jews.

The idea that these efforts should be pressed by a Jewish Congress

---

[11] Interview with the author, August 25, 1960.
[12] Editorial, *The Day*, June 26, 1916; Editorial, *Dos Yiddishe Folk*, June 23, 1916, p. 6.

democratically elected by the Jewish masses made the whole project appealing to the members of the Eastern European community. The institution of free democratic elections was an aspect of American society that particularly appealed to immigrants arriving from Europe. The Congress movement was, therefore, described as an aspect of the process of Americanization of the Eastern European Jews.[13]

For the leaders of the Jewish community and for persons aspiring to leadership and power, the question of the procedure and method for selecting those leaders was of course important. The prospect of a freely elected representative body of American Jewry was a threat to the philanthropists and to their leadership. Their power and influence came from the distribution of their money to Jewish organizations and projects; free elections, on the other hand, would give power to Jewish journalists and orators.

The A.J.C. leaders excelled when social action meant the suitable middle-class activity of fund-raising. The Zionist leaders also tried their hand at fund-raising, hoping to monopolize the field of relief to Palestine, but they could not compete with the A.J.C. Supported by the "masses" rather than the "classes," the Zionists then adopted methods that had mass appeal, such as protest meetings and demonstrations, oratory, and the whole paraphernalia of social action. They gave in to the more powerful A.J.C. on fund-raising and shifted their energies to political agitation, the battlefield on which they could best challenge the leadership of the A.J.C.

On this battlefield, the Yiddish-speaking intellectuals, journalists, and writers were particularly adept. Some of the most prominent of them served on the executive committee of the F.A.Z.: Bernard Shelvin and Ephraim Caplan from *The Jewish Morning Journal,* Jacob Fishman and Abraham Goldberg from *The Day,* Gedalya Bublik from *Dos Yiddishe Folk.* They commanded powerful journals in the Jewish ghetto. Agitation was their daily bread, and they now rallied around this great cause, the Jewish Congress, to give it focus and direction.

The money magnates could not surrender on the question of free elections for a representative Jewish Congress. Unhappy as they were with the thought of an official body of American Jewry aiming at an active role in deciding the political future of the Jews of Europe and Palestine, they gradually conceded point after point of the program in order to placate the masses and their leaders. But they could not agree to democratic elections.

---

[13] Horace M. Kallen, "The Program for Tomorrow," *The Maccabean* 28 (June 1916): 129.

Other considerations did, of course, play a part in the positions adopted by both sides. The wealthy Reform Jews feared that a future with Jews as a separate nationality in America was implicit in the idea of a Jewish Congress, or might be so conceived by the rest of American society. In a letter to Bernard Richards, secretary of the Zionist-dominated Congress Organization committee, Jacob Schiff stated: "Thanks to the preaching and machinations of Jewish Nationalists we are gradually being forced into a class by ourselves and if this continues, it will not be many years before we shall be looked upon by our fellow citizens as an entirely separate class, whose interests are different than those of the grass [roots] of American people."[14] Again, in a letter to Brandeis, Schiff argued: ". . . with the actual holding of the proposed congress, the coming of political anti-Semitism into the land will be only a question of time. There is no room in the United States for any other congress upon national lines, except the American Congress."[15] Brandeis was not persuaded.

The position of the Eastern European intellectuals was clearly expressed by Bernard Richards in his several letters replying to Schiff's charges. First, he argued, Schiff's fears of the possible reaction of other Americans was unfounded. Richards also expressed the annoyance of the Eastern European nationalists with the constant worry expressed about Gentile reactions. Zionism was designed to liberate the Jews from exactly such fears and concerns, and the essence of Jewish nationalism as understood by the Eastern European intellectuals was the proud and independent action of Jews as Jews.[16] Again, in a letter to Schiff, Richards explained the need of an ideology and a popular movement of Jews in the United States that would support an autonomous cultural and social existence.[17]

The correspondence between Richards and Schiff makes clear that the two groups, the Eastern European intellectual nationalists and the German Jewish members of the A.J.C., were at cross purposes. Examination of the Congress fight and the negotiations that were going on between the A.J.C. and the Zionists shows, however, that the German Jewish leaders manifested great flexibility and were willing to compromise on points of ideology. Despite their differences of opinion, they made one concession after another.

Gunnar Myrdal has shown, in the case of the Negro minority, that

---

[14] Schiff to Bernard Richards, January 31, 1916, *Brandeis Papers*.
[15] Schiff to Brandeis, February 29, 1916, *Schiff Papers*.
[16] Richards to Schiff, February 4, 1916, ibid.
[17] Richards to Schiff, January 26, 1916, ibid.

when a protest leadership is both powerful enough and vocal, it forces the accommodation leaders into more radical positions in order to maintain their leadership. The leadership of W. E. B. Du Bois, who founded and headed the more radical N.A.A.C.P. for example, forced the moderate leader Booker T. Washington to adopt a more radical stand.[18]

This observation of Myrdal's about relations between accommodation and protest leadership can be applied to the case of leaders of the American Jewish community and their stand on the Congress issue. It was the successful agitation for a Congress carried on by protest leaders that forced the accommodation leaders to take more radical steps. At first, they agreed to convene a conference on condition that it would be attended by representatives of existing Jewish organizations, that it would have no agenda, and that it would be conducted behind closed doors. All three points were unacceptable to the protest leaders. As the agitation continued, the A.J.C. leaders made more concessions. They agreed to an open-door conference and bit by bit accepted the agenda suggested by the Zionists, including national rights for the Jews in Eastern Europe; but for a long time, they remained adamant on the question of democratic elections.[19]

As in the case of Du Bois's leadership, so Brandeis's leadership was crucial in the Jewish community. The Eastern Europeans would never have started the fight on their own, and Richards admits as much. "We may not have gone against the power, the influence and the wealth that surrounded Mr. Marshall," he recalls, "if it were not for the balancing influence and prestige of Brandeis."[20]

The awe and sense of inadequacy the Eastern European Zionists felt in relation to those who had power and prestige in American society were again demonstrated. It was Brandeis's leadership that gave them the courage to attack the A.J.C.

Brandeis's social background and his position as a leader from the periphery suggest that he would be an accommodation leader. We shall see presently that most of his associates, with the exception of Stephen Wise, did not support him in the fight against the A.J.C. for a Jewish Congress. Brandeis's particular and personal situations as a progressive in 1914 facing the hegemony of the Jewish philanthropists led him to

---

[18] Gunnar Myrdal, *An American Dilemma* (New York: Harper and Brothers, 1944), p. 743.

[19] *The Jewish Congress versus the American Jewish Committee: A Complete Statement, with the Correspondence between Louis D. Brandeis and Cyrus Adler* (New York: Jewish Congress Organization Committee, August 1915).

[20] Bernard G. Richards, "Reminiscences Recorded by the Oral History Research Office" (New York: Columbia University, 1961), p. 60.

assume leadership of the protest movement and thus to upset the balance of power in the Jewish community.

By the end of 1915, negotiations between the Zionists and the A.J.C. on the Congress issue had reached a stalemate. Though willing to retreat on purely ideological problems, neither side could compromise on the technical problem of convening the Congress or on the way the members to the body were to be selected. The A.J.C. agreed to call a preliminary conference of the different organizations, insisting on specifying the number of organizations to be invited and the number of their delegates. Realizing that such a conference might not accept the idea of a democratically elected Congress, the Zionists agreed only to call a preliminary conference empowered to arrange for a democratically elected Congress.[21]

The stalemate lasted a long time, with recriminations and insults from both camps. One incident that caused great commotion was the allegation that Schiff made derogatory remarks concerning the Yiddish language.[22] Another uproar was caused by Schiff's remarks, in a letter to Richards, that "leaders need develop and come forward by their own deservedness. Selection of leaders on a democratic basis very often brings forward demagogues and this would not unlikely be the result of such a Jewish Congress as is proposed to be held."[23] This remark, needless to say, was considered an affront to those leaders who headed the movement for the Congress, adding fuel to the fire.

The stalemate had lasted almost a year when the Zionists—or Brandeis, to be exact—decided to move. During March 26-28, 1916, a well-attended preliminary conference convened in Philadelphia and decided to call a Congress.[24] It was then the A.J.C. leaders realized, and privately acknowledged, that they had been defeated by their adversaries. In a pessimistic letter to Cyrus Adler, for example, Schiff voiced the opinion that in the face of the agitation of the Yiddish press, there was no chance of maintaining leadership.[25]

While admitting defeat, the A.J.C. tried to salvage what was left of their declining leadership. To be sure, the adoption of the democratic method in choosing the leaders of the Jewish community was detri-

---

[21] *The Maccabean* 27 (August 1915): 45-47; *The Maccabean* 27 (November 1915): 113.
[22] *The Maccabean* 28 (June 1916): 122-24.
[23] Schiff to Richards, January 31, 1916, *Brandeis Papers*.
[24] *The Maccabean* 28 (April 1916): 73-74; *The Maccabean* 28 (June 1916): 49-50.
[25] Schiff to Cyrus Adler, May 31, 1916, *Schiff Papers*.

mental to their position, but even worse was the danger of their becoming leaders of a minority party within the community. They refused to be trapped into such a position. When the disenchanted Zionist leader, Judah Magnes, who was now a member of the A.J.C., proposed a militant policy on behalf of the A.J.C. in their fight to retain leadership, his suggestion was flatly rejected.

Magnes explained to Schiff and his friends that the Yiddish paper *The Day* was in financial distress and the group could buy the paper for use in fighting the nationalists. He went on to say: "It is the Yiddish press which sets the standard of Jewish public opinion . . . if, in addition to caring for our charities, the obligation of leadership in developing the positive and spiritual side of Jewish life weighs heavy upon us, it is next to impossible to proceed unless we have within our control at least some of the organs shaping Jewish public opinion both here and elsewhere."[26]

While Schiff and his associates agreed with Magnes's diagnosis that the one cause of their declining power in the Jewish community was the Yiddish press, they did not believe that such a direct approach could be successful.[27] This, they felt, was not the battleground on which the Jewish philanthropists could fight successfully for power and influence. Schiff and his colleagues outlined instead a new tactic with emphasis on the desirability of welding *unity* within the Jewish group. They believed that only the maintenance of a united front would save their influence. In this connection, we must remember that one source of this group's power was the regard they enjoyed as "representative Jews" among those in power in the United States. Schiff was frequently invited for conferences in the White House on the Jews. He was consulted on the nomination of Jews to positions of importance in the government. Schiff's opinion had been solicited on the appointment of Brandeis to the Cabinet in 1913; and the nomination of the first Jew to the Cabinet, Oscar Straus as Secretary of Commerce in 1906, only took place after President Theodore Roosevelt had consulted him.[28] Schiff outlined the new policy in a letter to Adler, who was conducting the negotiations on behalf of the A.J.C.: ". . . if in the convention [the preliminary conference convened by the Zionists to discuss the Congress issue] there be a strong desire for the Congress, this had perhaps better be allowed to prevail

---

[26] Magnes to Schiff, December 19, 1916, ibid.
[27] Schiff to Magnes, December 22, 1916, ibid.
[28] Naomi Cohen-Wiener, "The Public Career of Oscar Straus" (Ph.D. dissertation, Faculty of Political Science, Columbia University, 1955), pp. 240 ff.

... possibly if the Congress be permitted to be held, without actually and publicly dividing the Jews of this country, the effect and the hurt will be less than if through opposition the Congress agitators and their followers be welded into a solid opposition."[29]

The Congress Issue: Disagreements within the Zionist Organization

A more detailed examination of the Zionist Organization's internal developments during the agitation that it produced for the Congress movement will shed more light on the fight for the Jewish Congress. It will also clarify the position of the different elements within the organization, as well as the peculiar position of Brandeis.

Brandeis's main concern during his presidency of the P.Z.C. was the problem of attracting new members to the organization. Most activities of the organization were geared to this goal; speeches, pamphlets, and official decisions of the governing body all reflected it. *The Maccabean*, the official organ of the F.A.Z., incessantly called for greater efforts to increase membership.[30]

Later statements by Lipsky and other leaders to the effect that at the time they were interested mainly in enlisting the sympathies of the Jewish people rather than in increasing membership do not correspond to the facts. The existing figures, which are not fully reliable, suggest that the organization membership rose from 7,000 in 1914 to 22,000 in 1917.[31] This apparent increase did not satisfy the leadership, and Brandeis, who had become obsessed with the problem of organization, was especially anxious. Horace Kallen even complained that Brandeis was so overwhelmed with problems of propaganda and organization that he failed to consider other important matters.[32]

During the height of the fight for a Jewish Congress, an episode occurred that illuminates Brandeis's continued preoccupation with increase of membership. A project was suggested to him by which many Jewish socialists might be persuaded to support the Congress movement, a project which would cost $10,000. Brandeis flatly refused, and in an angry letter declared: "We need at this time Zionists, not *stimmung* [a

---

[29] Schiff to Adler, June 12, 1916, *Schiff Papers*.
[30] Editorial, *The Maccabean* 26 (April 1915): 60; "To All Zionists," *The Maccabean* 28 (January 1916): 17.
[31] Adolf Böhm, *Die Zionistische Bewegung*, vol. 2 (Berlin: Jüdischer Verlag, 1933), p. 638; *The Jewish Communal Register of New York 1917–1918*, p. 1301.
[32] Kallen to Brandeis, February 23, 1915, *Brandeis Papers*.

favorable public sentiment]."³³ By this he meant that the socialists who would support the Congress movement would not join the Zionist Organization, and hence the investment of money would be a waste.

The Congress movement and the crucial part the Zionists played in it cannot be entirely understood without considering the desire of the Zionist leaders to increase membership and their difficulties in striving toward their ambitious goal of making the organization so strong that it would become the central factor in Jewish life in the United States.

It was the Eastern Europeans who first realized the possibilities ahead for the Zionists if they would take the lead in championing the popular cause of a Jewish congress. Lipsky recalls that the first group which was organized to propagate the idea of the Jewish Congress was not friendly to the Zionists. Once the Zionists realized the appeal this idea held for the Jewish masses, they joined the Congress movement. The first thing they did was to carry its offices away from the Lower East Side to Madison Square, and "a new lease of life" was given the committee through its removal uptown and the entrance of a number of active Zionists into the leadership.³⁴ Whether the new location of the Congress offices really gave the movement its "new lease of life" is not clear, but the fact that Lipsky, one of the most prominent and active leaders of this movement, thought that it did again indicates that the Eastern European Zionist leadership wanted to break out of the ghetto.

In a 1916 editorial, *The Maccabean* confessed that the success of Zionism in the United States resulted from the Zionists' support of the Congress movement: "Without the Congress movement—without the opportunity to prove the Jewish policy—Zionism in this great crisis was doomed to continue its existence as a minority party in a nationality which had not the strength to attempt to organize itself."³⁵

This assessment seems to correspond with the facts. Zionism was not a popular cause; it was never meaningful to the Jewish masses in the United States, only to a certain group of intellectuals. Zionism was a manifestation of cultural alienation that did not answer the needs of a community in the process of adjusting to new conditions. The Eastern European intellectuals realized that the Congress idea, because it contained the desire to help the brethren in Russia, and because it implied the principle of democracy—which fascinated all European immigrants —and evoked the strong if incoherent sentiments of Jewish nationalism

---

³³ Brandeis to de Haas, August 8, 1915, ibid.
³⁴ Lipsky, "Early Days in American Zionism," p. 467.
³⁵ Editorial, *The Maccabean* 29 (July 1916): 162.

that the Jewish masses brought with them from Eastern Europe, had a strong mass appeal.

Brandeis, however, hesitated at first and refused to commit himself to the movement. Removed from the Jewish masses and their thinking, for he neither spoke nor read Yiddish, he did not realize its popular appeal. When a mass meeting in support of the movement was called in New York early in 1915 and he was invited to speak, he refused to attend.[36] He hesitated to challenge the established leadership openly as long as he was not sure of the support of the masses. Once convinced of this support, he acted swiftly and decisively. In the annual convention of 1915, he endorsed the resolution supporting the Congress movement, although most of his associates, the members of the German Jewish community of the organization, were against it. Their opposition did not seem to affect Brandeis in the least. In an interview with *The Jewish Morning Journal* after the convention, he asserted that the Congress resolution was the most important achievement of the Zionist convention.[37] Again, in a letter to Lipsky, Brandeis explained that in his opinion the Congress movement had a potential to attract the masses to Zionism.[38]

At the time of the agitation for a Jewish Congress, the relations between Brandeis and his Eastern European lieutenants were cordial, and his letters showed a spirit of respect. The Congress movement was the one cause in which the Eastern Europeans and Brandeis cooperated wholeheartedly, but the other "American" leaders of the German Jewish group disapproved of it.

The Eastern Europeans and most of the German Jewish leaders conceived of the fight as one between the two communities existing within American Jewry. Brandeis could not conceive of it that way and insisted that he was fighting for a principle. He was trying to come to a new arrangement in the community by which leadership would be based on democratic principles. He was even convinced that it was primarily the democratic principle that attracted the masses to the movement, and advised his colleagues to stress this principle, rather than the Palestinian program, in order to get more support.[39]

The Eastern European intellectuals were fighting to annihilate the A.J.C. For years the uptown German Jews had effectively blocked their way to leadership in the Jewish community. The Congress issue was an

---

[36] Richards, "Reminiscences," p. 76.
[37] *The Jewish Morning Journal*, July 4, 1915.
[38] Brandeis to Lipsky, December 4, 1915, *Brandeis Papers*.
[39] Brandeis to Stephen Wise, August 25, 1915, ibid.

outlet for resentment for Eastern Europeans, and Brandeis's leadership gave them a good chance to win their rightful place in American Jewry. In a revealing article on the Congress fight, "A Revolution in American Jewry," Lipsky made a distinction between the Eastern Europeans who fought against the domination of the German Jews and the German Jews who supported the Congress because they accepted the principle of democracy.[40]

Most of Brandeis's associates and the German Jews in the Zionist leadership also conceived of the fight as one between the two communities, and they were unhappy with Brandeis's support of the Eastern Europeans. It testifies to Brandeis's power that only the two Conservatives on the P.Z.C. eventually resigned in protest, while all the others, though resentful and unhappy, followed the leader. This halfhearted support aroused the anger of the Eastern Europeans, who always suspected that the "English-speaking Zionists" had no desire to fight the A.J.C.[41] The German-Jewish Zionists tried throughout the struggle to dissuade Brandeis from joining the Eastern Europeans against the A.J.C. This position was most clearly expressed by Richard Gottheil in a letter to Brandeis just before the 1915 annual convention, in which he explained that "such a Congress would create a platform from which any number of light-brained enthusiasts might make pronouncements which would be exceedingly distasteful to us, if not dangerous."[42]

These sentiments were shared by the rest of the German Jews in the Zionist leadership. Most of them voiced their objections to the Congress resolution in the debate in the P.Z.C. that preceded the convention of 1915. Among those who spoke against the Congress resolution were Julian Mack, Harry Friedenwald, Israel Friedlaender, Magnes, Solis Cohen, Leon Sanders, and Samuel Lamport.[43] The last two represented a new group of Eastern Europeans who were attaining success in American society: Judge Sanders was a Tammany Hall politician who had been a member of the state legislature for some years, and Lamport was a successful businessman.

Brandeis continually was urged to stop the fight with the A.J.C. When the F.A.Z. convention was over, Mack wrote a letter to Brandeis in which he said he would refuse to have anything to do with the Con-

---

[40] Lipsky, "A Revolution in American Jewry," *The Maccabean* 30 (June–July 1917): 276–77, 304.
[41] *The Day*, July 1, 1916.
[42] Gottheil to Brandeis, May 6, 1915, *Brandeis Papers*.
[43] "The Conference of the Provisional Executive Committee," *The Maccabean* 27 (July 1915): 10–14.

gress agitation.⁴⁴ Again Mack and Friedenwald warned Brandeis that the agitators for the Congress expressed the opinion in public that all Jews would be citizens of the future Jewish state.⁴⁵ Even this did not perturb Brandeis. Although he agreed with Mack's position, he advised him not to pay too much attention, expressing surprisingly mild objections to the agitators: ". . . we have cautioned them against such utterances as they have made as being damaging to the cause and to our Palestine interests."⁴⁶ This conciliatory attitude of Brandeis to the Eastern European propagandists, his tolerance of their nationalistic position, is in sharp contrast to the vehemence with which he was to attack them and their opinions only a few years later. Also interesting for future comparison is the distinction Brandeis made in his letter to Mack between "Palestine interests" and the "cause." In this aspect, Brandeis at that period was different from his associates. He accepted the Eastern European intellectuals as the proponents of nationalist theories and Jewish culture, and he was willing to overlook possible disagreements.

Brandeis did keep insisting, however, that the fight was for the principle of democracy. This theme recurred in all his utterances on the subject of the Congress. In a letter congratulating Friedenwald on his decision to resign from the A.J.C.—which actually was not done until June 1916 and only after considerable pressure—he commented: "The action that you have taken will do much to clear the air, and bring a better understanding of the irreconcilable conflict between autocracy and democracy in Jewish life."⁴⁷

Brandeis's continual emphasis on principle rather than on the power struggle in which he was engaged should not, however, mislead us. The struggle between Brandeis and the A.J.C. was a struggle for power and influence in the Jewish community that was going to continue for the next fifteen years. Brandeis, nonetheless, never admitted the existence of such motives even in his most personal papers and letters. Faithful to the American Puritan tradition, he thought only in terms of good and evil. It was democracy against autocracy when he fought the A.J.C.; his fight with the World Zionist leaders from 1919 to 1921 was a fight for order and the rule of law against corruption; his fight against Lipsky's leadership of the Zionist Organization in the late 1920's was one of honesty against chicanery.

What was the position of the Conservatives on the Congress? In spite

---

⁴⁴ Mack to Brandeis, August 20, 1915, *Brandeis Papers*.
⁴⁵ Ibid.; Mack to Harry Friedenwald, August 21, 1915, and Friedenwald's reply August 26, 1915, in the *Harry Friedenwald Papers* (New York: Zionist Archives.)
⁴⁶ Brandeis to Mack, August 26, 1915, *Brandeis Papers*.
⁴⁷ Brandeis to Friedenwald, June 14, 1916, *Friedenwald Papers*.

of their numerical weakness at the time (they had only three members on the P.Z.C.), their influence, because of the support for Zionism by the whole Conservative movement, was of importance.[48] More important still, their position on the issue of the Congress calls attention to certain developments that might otherwise be neglected.

The two outstanding Conservative leaders on the P.Z.C. were Friedlaender and Magnes. Friedenwald also belonged to the Conservative circle. Magnes resigned from the committee in August 1915, in protest against their attitude on the Congress issue. Friedlaender resigned a few months later, whereas Friedenwald remained steadfast and resigned from the A.J.C. only in late June 1916, when the fight was almost over. Henrietta Szold, the leader of Hadassah, kept quiet throughout the period.

It is difficult to appreciate today the cleavage between secularism and religion and its importance in Jewish life in the United States in the first quarter of the century. This was a burning issue in the Jewish ghetto. For the Eastern Europeans, secularism meant an adaptation to the modern ideas of the general culture. But, as we have already seen, historical circumstances led many to accept a Jewish secular culture and the principle of Jewish nationalism, rather than Russification, which some had advocated earlier in the nineteenth century. Thus, the Eastern European intellectuals, being freethinkers and nationalists, were trying to adapt modern ideas of the secular culture and at the same time maintain them within a context of Jewish culture and traditions.

This was not the content of the secularism of Brandeis and his associates. Brandeis, however, at a certain point tried hard to meet the Europeans on the intellectual level and was even willing to make the Russian Jews the custodians of Jewish culture; only they, not the Americans, would recreate the Jewish culture in Palestine and in the United States.[49] Brandeis's associates never went so far and never really talked about the rejuvenation of Jewish culture, certainly not in the United States, and Brandeis himself was soon to undergo a thorough change of heart on the matter.

Only for the Jewish intellectuals did Zionism mean a separate cultural existence for the Jewish group in the United States. As we have seen, many were torn between their attraction to the New World and their desire to become part of it and their attachment to the cultural heritage in which they were brought up, a heritage which made it impossible for

---

[48] For an interesting recent review on this point, see Herbert Parzen, "Conservative Judaism and Zionism, 1896–1922," *Jewish Social Studies* 23 (October 1961): 235–64.
[49] Text of speech before the Knights of Zion in December, 1915, *Brandeis Papers*.

many to overcome their alienation from the new culture. Deprecation of American culture was a constant theme in the Yiddish press, though it was often mixed with admiration. This is part of the tragic experience of intellectuals uprooted from their own culture and was by no means confined to Jewish intellectuals. Joseph Roucek describes the position of the Czech intellectuals in the early 1930's:

> Very few adventurous personalities with higher education have risked the problem of emigration. . . . Most of them soon became discouraged and disgruntled in their efforts to establish a social position in the purely American environment and have drifted to the positions offered by their own nationals. Thus they cling tenaciously to positions as priests, ministers, editors, teachers of language schools. . . . They are the ones who delay the process of assimilation and insist very vociferously on the "old Ways". . . .[50]

In the Jewish community many of these people became exponents of Jewish secular culture and found refuge in the Zionist Organization. The "old ways" became involved with nationalist doctrine, the cultural renaissance, and the idea of a national revival in Palestine.

During the period from 1914 to 1916, however, the differences between the two secular cultures, the Jewish Eastern European and the progressive American, were somewhat obscured because secularism versus religion remained the central intellectual issue of the community. Unity of interests brought the two groups together and solidified them because their opponents championed the cause of Jews as a strictly religious group. The opponents equated secularism with nationalism and accused the Zionist leaders of being atheists and agnostics. Louis Marshall, in a letter to Friedenwald, stated that as a matter of principle "I should be unwilling to follow men who have no sympathy with Judaism and who are avowedly atheists or agnostics, nor can I believe that nationalism can take the place of religion.[51] Marshall was quoted, in referring to Mack, as saying: "I have been friendly with him for many years. I like him and I know his honesty and integrity. But how can I be a Zionist, if a Zionist leader is ignorant in Judaism. If Zionism is Judaism, then the first condition for a Zionist leader is to know Judaism, its sources and traditions. But if the leader knows less than I do, how can I follow him?"[52]

The A.J.C. leaders insisted that their objection to Zionism and to

---

[50] Joseph Slabey Roucek, "The Passing of American Czechoslovaks," *A.J.S.* 39 (March 1934): 616.
[51] Marshall to Friedenwald, August 2, 1915, *Brandeis Papers*.
[52] Rabbi Meir Berlin, *Me Volozhin ad Yerushalaim: Zichronot*, vol. 2 (Tel Aviv: B. Cohen, Hotzaat Yalkut, 1940), p. 204.

the Congress movement lay in the fact that these movements attempted to replace the principle of religion with that of nationalism. One leader, Judge Irving Lehman, even declared that the instant a Jewish state should be established he would without hesitation turn Unitarian.[53]

This insistence on the religious principle as the unifying force for all Jews in America was a constant threat to the secularist leaders of the Zionist Organization. The fact that the issue was kept alive in the Jewish community helped to unite the progressives and the Eastern Europeans.

Here the Conservative Zionists found themselves in a dilemma. Nationalism was the one principle that united the secular Jews, and yet the Conservatives were irritated because the secular Jews ignored the religious aspect of Judaism. A storm was created by Solomon Schechter, founder of the Conservative movement and president of the J.T.S., when shortly before his death in 1915 he openly and bitterly attacked the Zionist leadership on those very grounds.[54]

The Conservatives were middle-of-the-roaders on both the issue of tradition versus modernism and the issue of secularism and religion versus nationalism. They adhered to the Jewish religion, though encouraging the adaptation of modern forms and ideas. At the same time, they supported the idea of a separate cultural existence for the Jewish people. They believed in the Americanization of Jews, but they wanted simultaneously to retain their Jewish culture. They strongly rejected the idea held by Reform Jews that Jews are simply a religious sect, and at the same time they rejected equally strongly the idea that a separate spiritual existence of the Jews is feasible only in a Jewish state.

The Conservative leaders, however, were also caught in a dilemma on the Congress issue because of their position in the structure of the Jewish community. They were members of both the Zionist Organization and the A.J.C. The Conservative movement catered to the Eastern Europeans but was financed by the people at the head of the A.J.C. From their attitudes on the Congress issue and their attempted solution, one gains the impression that their position in the structure of the community occupied them more than the ideological problems involved in the dispute. Friedlaender, analyzing the Congress dispute, explained it as a struggle between two communities that differed not only in their ideas but also in their social and economic backgrounds. Consequently, if the Zionists supported the Congress they would have to become lead-

---

[53] Henry Hurwitz to Brandeis, September 11, 1915, *Brandeis Papers*.
[54] Solomon Schechter, *Seminary Addresses and Other Papers* (Cincinnati: Ark Publishing Company, 1915), preface, pp. xii–xiii.

ers of the masses at the price of alienating the classes. Friedlaender therefore advised the Zionist Organization to maintain its neutrality on the issue.[55] Magnes, by that time more involved than Friedlaender in the activities of the A.J.C. and also president of the New York *Kehillah*, which was financed by the A.J.C., argued that the Zionist Organization should limit itself to work for Palestine and leave other Jewish activities to other organizations, mainly to the A.J.C.[56]

Magnes resigned in August 1915, and Friedlaender decided a few months later to resign from both bodies, the A.J.C. and the P.Z.C., "saddened inexpressibly by the bitter conflict between the two bodies."[57]

Brandeis's Resignation and the Compromise on the Jewish Congress

For the leaders of the A.J.C., fighting to preserve their leadership in the Jewish community, the first encouraging sign on the horizon was Brandeis's impending withdrawal from active leadership when his nomination to the Supreme Court was approved by the Senate at the beginning of June 1916. Earlier, on February 29, in the midst of the campaign for Brandeis's nomination, which coincided with the agitation for the Jewish Congress, Schiff had sent a conciliatory letter to Brandeis. After congratulating him on his appointment, he continued: ". . . I take it, you will then no longer be able to continue as leader of the Zionist and nationalist movement in this country." Schiff then went on to suggest that Brandeis's last act on behalf of the Jewish community should be an attempt to achieve unity. For the sake of unity, Schiff explained, the agitation for the Congress must stop. He proposed that a formula for uniting Zionists and non-Zionists would be support for Jews freely settled in Palestine and their right to assume "municipal privileges whenever necessary and justified."[58]

However, Brandeis was not dissuaded at that time from heading the struggle to form a Congress. Instead, he went on with the preliminary conference, which was attended by many Jewish organizations. When, as a consequence, the A.J.C. began to have second thoughts about its position, Brandeis agreed to reopen negotiations. To the open dismay of the A.J.C. he did not resign his presidency of the P.Z.C. and of the

---

[55] Israel Friedlaender, "The Present Crisis in American Jewry: A Plan for Reconciliation," *Past and Present: A Collection of Jewish Essays* (Cincinnati: Ark Publishing Co., 1919), p. 349.
[56] *The Maccabean* 27 (July 1915): 11.
[57] Friedlaender to Wise, June 3, 1916, *Friedenwald Papers*.
[58] Schiff to Brandeis, February 29, 1916, *Schiff Papers*.

Congress committee when he assumed his post in the Supreme Court. He headed the delegation to the conference with the A.J.C. at the Astor Hotel in New York on July 16, at which time negotiations with the A.J.C. on behalf of the organizations that had participated in the preliminary conference were to be continued. The Zionists were now supported by most Jewish organizations.

Brandeis's retention of his position as head of the Zionist Organization after he began to serve as a Supreme Court Justice was, under the circumstances, an exceptionally courageous act. However, the leaders of the A.J.C. who met with him on July 16 forced him to change his mind. Though it has not been possible to find direct evidence to prove that what occurred at the meeting was shrewdly prearranged, the indirect evidence is impressive.

At the meeting, after presenting his case for a Jewish Congress, Justice Brandeis was about to leave, when the chairman, Marshall, politely asked him to remain as their guest. There followed speeches by Mayer Sulzberger and Magnes, accusing Brandeis of using his new position to force a partisan view upon the Jewish community. Magnes used sharp language, but he was not interrupted by the chairman.[59] This incident was given due publicity by the press and was followed by an editorial in *The New York Times* which repeated the same accusations. "It is evident," stated the paper, "that a good deal of feeling was aroused, and altogether the general impression will be, we fear, that Justice Brandeis might with great propriety have avoided taking part in such a controversy." In conclusion the *Times* stated: "Now that he [Brandeis] has discharged his duty as a member of the committee appointed by the Jewish Congress Organization, we venture to express the hope that he will consider that he is discharged of further obligation and will in future leave to others subjects of such controversial nature."[60]

As the leaders of the A.J.C. and the men who controlled the paper belonged to the same social circle, it can certainly be surmised that there was a link between the A.J.C. and the editorial. In any event, it was widely believed at the time that it was so.[61] Brandeis himself told Jacob de Haas that he had received letters in support of the *Times* editorial, and he felt "that these letters and the *Times* editorial and the scene itself were all premeditated."[62]

Thus, forced to resign his position as head of the Zionist Organiza-

---

[59] Editorial, *Dos Yiddishe Folk*, July 28, 1916, p. 4.
[60] Editorial, *The New York Times*, July 18, 1916.
[61] Editorial, *The Maccabean* 29 (August 1916): 2.
[62] De Haas to Lipsky, July 21, 1916, in the *Jacob de Haas Papers* (New York: Zionist Archives, microfilm).

tion, Brandeis hastened to do so, leaving himself no time to consult even his closest associates.

When we attempt to understand Brandeis's swift action, one remark he made to de Haas explaining his resignation is revealing. Although the non-Jews did not object to his retaining leadership of the Zionist Organization, he said, many Jews did. This put him in a difficult position in his relations with the other members of the Court. He felt that if he were to maintain his leadership "outwardly," it would "weaken his position" on the Court.[63] Not only did their opposition weaken his position as a "representative Jew," but it created for him what can be described, following Robert K. Merton, as a conflict in Brandeis's status-set. Their action made his status as a partisan Zionist leader conflict with his status as Supreme Court Justice.

In an attempt to resolve the status conflict, he resigned all his official positions in the Zionist Organization. However, he remained the leader de facto and continued to conduct the affairs of the Zionist Organization from Washington, maintaining full control over its activities. This mechanism to reduce the status conflict has been described as "insulation from observability."[64] Wise took over the presidency of the P.Z.C., but Brandeis did not relinquish command of the Zionist Organization. He became "the chief," who wrote scores of letters each month, giving the committee detailed instructions, receiving a stream of visitors in Washington and Boston residences, from time to time descending on New York City to take part in important meetings of the executive committee of the P.Z.C., and participating actively in the lobbies of the annual conventions. But while his control was firm, it was not visible to the other Supreme Court justices or the general American public. His influence was taken for granted, but his complete control was concealed.

The first task Brandeis undertook from Washington was to reach a compromise with the A.J.C. and force it down the throats of a disappointed organization. The decision to renew negotiations with the A.J.C. in June was received unfavorably by the party workers, since they knew that complete victory over the A.J.C. has already been achieved and that convening the Congress would seal it. This assessment was entirely correct, and the A.J.C. was already privately acknowledging defeat.

If the meeting with the A.J.C. could have been interpreted by observers as a change of tactics by Brandeis, the compromise agreed upon by the A.J.C. and Brandeis and his associates in the meetings following the

---

[63] De Haas to Lipsky, July 21, 1916, *de Haas Papers*.
[64] Robert K. Merton, *Social Theory and Social Structure*, rev. ed. (Glencoe, Ill.: The Free Press, 1957), p. 375.

Fight for an American Jewish Congress, 1914–16

Astor Hotel encounter can only be interpreted as a change of heart on his part. The terms of the compromise eventually agreed upon were: the name *Congress* was conceded, but it was not to be a permanent body, and its program was limited; democratic elections were likewise conceded, but national organizations were allowed twenty-five percent of the number of delegates; constructive relief was not to be excluded from the agenda; the phrase *group rights for Jews* was eliminated, and the Congress could discuss whatever rights Jews in affected countries asked for. The Zionists conceded a change in the phrase *Palestine as the Jewish National Home* to *a Jewish National Home*.[65]

The important concession accepted by Brandeis, a concession that almost caused a revolt within the Zionist Organization, was the agreement that the Congress would deal only with issues that concerned Jewish communities as a result of World War I and would dissolve once this task was accomplished. This meant, in effect, that no change in the methods of electing leaders in the Jewish community would take place, with the one exception of this Congress, whose task was limited to the problems arising out of the war. Autocracy gave way to democracy in this one instance, but no permanent change was accomplished. The Yiddish press was indignant; the Zionist Organization, demoralized. Wise, the president of the P.Z.C., refused to participate in the negotiations with the A.J.C. on details of the agreement.[66] As a result, the details were arranged by the people who objected to the Congress agitation from the start. The Eastern European intellectual party workers did put up a fight to prevent the agreement from taking place. The Congress Organization committee, in accord with its constitution, called for a referendum to ratify the agreement. The referendum took place on August 10; 55 of the Zionist members participating approved, and 79 rejected the agreement.[67] Even this was accomplished after pressure from "the chief." But Brandeis did not give in. A second referendum took place at the end of September, for which no figures are available, but it had been preceded by a closed meeting of the executive committee of the F.A.Z. on September 24, in which its members apparently concurred in accepting the agreement.[68] Brandeis had his way, but relations between him and his associates, on the one hand, and the Eastern

---

[65] "Fifty Years of American Zionism," mimeographed (New York: The Zionist Archives), chapt. 6, p. 9.
[66] De Haas to Brandeis, September 20, 1916, *Brandeis Papers*.
[67] *Dos Yiddishe Folk*, September 15, 1916, p. 2.
[68] *The Maccabean* 29 (October 1916): 68. This official organ of the F.A.Z. explained that details of the executive meeting were unavailable "on account of lack of space."

European party workers, on the other, were never quite the same again.

Still, the following questions remain: What led Brandeis to change his mind? Why did he abdicate the principle for which he had fought?

We may have a better idea of what lay behind the change after we carry the story of Brandeis's leadership in Zionism to the year 1921. His compromise on the Congress issue was simply a first manifestation of a radical change that led him to a new conception of Zionism, as well as an attempt to change the structure of the organization. Nothing of importance happened during these months of struggle that can explain these changes. The major event in Brandeis's life was his elevation to the Supreme Court and his attempt to reconcile his duties and obligations as a Supreme Court justice with maintenance of control over the organization. His new status and his conception of it involved him in practical as well as ideological difficulties. The effect of these pressures on his leadership and his ideas on Zionism, and the repercussion of these developments on the Zionist leadership and on the Zionist Organization, will be studied in the following chapters.

CHAPTER V

Conflicts within the Zionist Organization, 1916–20

The Organization during Brandeis's Presidency

The one person around whom all Zionist activities in the United States revolved from 1914 to 1921 was Louis Brandeis; he was the undisputed leader of the movement and the power behind all policy decisions and actions of the Zionist Organization. This is remarkable when we take into consideration that after June 1916 Brandeis was a Supreme Court justice, and after July of that year did not occupy any official decision-making position in the organization. He pursued his Zionist activities in his spare time and behind closed doors, away from the public eye. This handicap, which would have been devastating for any other leader of a mass movement, did not lead to a really serious challenge to his leadership and power before 1921, even though at times it weakened his control. The prestige this leader from the periphery brought with him into Jewish organized life was an asset that made his leadership so desirable to his followers that very little dissatisfaction or criticism was directed at him even by the generally highly critical Yiddish press.

Brandeis's official position in the Zionist Organization, until his resignation in July 1916, was president of the P.Z.C., a body formed in August 1914 with the aim of taking charge of World Zionist affairs. Its legal foundation rested on the fact that Shmarya Levin, one member of the small *Actions Comité* (the ruling body of the W.Z.O.), happened to be in the United States at the time war broke out in Europe.[1] However, after a short interim period, the main office was transferred to neutral Copenhagen, and Levin himself reported the activities of the P.Z.C. regularly to the main office. But in the United States the new body was not bound to any constitutional framework or legal limitations. It was legally and administratively separate from the F.A.Z. Several members of the executive committee of the F.A.Z., including chairman Louis Lipsky, were also members of the P.Z.C. But most members of the P.Z.C. were not elected by annual conventions. Instead, they were co-opted by

---

[1] The constitution of the W.Z.O., adopted in 1901, stipulated that all members had a right to elect delegates to a World Zionist Congress. Elections took place every two years, and each Congress met once to decide on questions of policy and ideology. The Congress elected a large *Actions Comité* that met regularly during the period between Congresses. The Congress also elected a small *Actions Comité*, the executive of the organization. (Wein: Stenographisches Protokoll der Verhandlungen des V Zionisten-Congresses, 1901, pp. 454–56.)

the president, who did not have to account for his decisions to anybody but his own committee. Furthermore, the prestige of the president led to a constant increase in the power of the P.Z.C. over the executive committee of the F.A.Z. The F.A.Z. barely retained the control over the organization that it had wielded before 1914 and was gradually becoming a subordinate body of the P.Z.C.[2]

This was an unsatisfactory situation from the point of view of the organization, and it did not satisfy the members of the executive committee and the party workers of the F.A.Z. An examination of the composition of the executive of the F.A.Z. during 1914–18 reveals a very small turnover. Its membership consisted in large part of the dedicated party workers, many of whom were also on the payroll of the organization which was growing and prospering under Brandeis's leadership. Most of the propaganda and agitation decided upon by the P.Z.C. was done through the F.A.Z. organizational machinery.

The P.Z.C. was co-opting new recruits all the time—mostly men who had made a name for themselves before joining, American-born members of the German-Jewish community who were attracted to the Zionist Organization by Brandeis's name.

The difference between the two bodies can be best illustrated by comparing the social backgrounds of the members. In Table 5.1 we singled out two variables for comparison—place of birth and occupation.

This comparison indicates the social and cultural differences between the members of the two bodies. The executive of the F.A.Z. was elected by the annual convention and was more representative of the social background of its members. The increasingly powerful P.Z.C. was composed of members co-opted by Brandeis, who was interested in people of prestige and influence.

This anomalous situation did not impair the work of the Zionists as long as Brandeis remained president of the P.Z.C. His prestige among the Eastern European party workers was very great, and the American members co-opted by him into the P.Z.C. were entirely devoted to him. The few American-born members of the Zionist Organization were either concentrated in positions of leadership on the P.Z.C. or in a few exclusive Zionist societies like the University Zionist Society. Brandeis's personality united them all. A good example of his unifying force was the Congress issue described in the previous chapter. Though many American-born members of the P.Z.C. objected to the official Zionist stand on

---

[2] "Zionism in America before the British Mandate," *Modern Palestine: A Symposium*, ed. Jessie Sampter (Published by Hadassah, The Women's Zionist Organization of America, 1933), p. 46.

TABLE 5.1 *Place of Birth and Occupation of Members on the Executive Committee of the F.A.Z. and the P.Z.C., 1917*

Place of Birth	F.A.Z[a]	P.Z.C.
United States and Western Europe	5	10
Eastern Europe	9	4
Unavailable	2	1
Total	16	15

Occupation		
Lawyers	4[b]	4[b]
Physicians	1[c]	1[c]
University professors	—	2[d]
Businessmen	—	2
Reform Rabbis	—	2
Teachers in the J.T.C.	1	—
Journalists and writers for the immigrant community	8	2[e]
Unavailable	2	2
Total	16	15

[a] The two representatives of Hadassah on the executive committee have been excluded.
[b] Of the four lawyers on the P.Z.C., two were appointed judges, one on the United States Circuit Court; of the four lawyers on the F.A.Z. executive committee, one was an elected judge and two were businessmen.
[c] The same physician served on both committees. He was honorary president of the F.A.Z. but was active in the P.Z.C.
[d] Teaching at Harvard and Columbia.
[e] One of the journalists was also the chairman of the F.A.Z., where most of his activities were concentrated.

the Congress issue, they followed him nonetheless. At the same time his relations with the bureaucrats and Congress enthusiasts were extremely cordial, and their devotion to him was unquestioned.

His associates did annoy the Eastern European party workers, and some grumbling and dissatisfaction over their increasing power in the organization was inevitable. The dissatisfaction was most openly voiced in the Yiddish press, where the Zionist journalists jealously guarded their positions of influence over the masses and disliked the English-speaking leaders who belonged to an alien culture. The grumbling and dissatisfaction with the American-born and American-educated leaders increased during the 1916 annual convention. It was alleged by the party workers that the American-born leaders were not familiar with Zionist doctrine; Zionism for them was only a part-time occupation, and most of their time and energy were spent on other unrelated things. They were obsessed with the problem of Zionism versus patriotism, and their insistence that Zionists were good Americans verged on hysteria.[3]

What was remarkable in all this grumbling and criticism was that Brandeis was immune to it. Everyone acknowledged his leadership and appreciated his efforts to bring new forces to the Zionist movement and recruit men "educated here in American ideals."[4]

We have already discussed Brandeis's preoccupation with problems of organization and enrollment of new members. He meant it literally when he declared that the goal of the Zionists was to make all Jews members of the Zionist Organization. The burden of recruiting the Eastern European masses fell on the Eastern European intellectuals, orators, and journalists. Meanwhile Brandeis, in addition to his activities in connection with the Jewish Congress, made continuous attempts to attract the members of the established German Jewish community. He wrote hundreds of letters and also met hundreds of people in an attempt to persuade them to join. In all his propaganda activities, he gave special consideration to the problem of reaching the German Jews.[5] Brandeis actively supported the establishment of such new groups as the University Zionist Society, in order to encourage German Jews to take active part in the organization.[6] He wished to recruit members of a higher-class background and American education for positions as officers in the mass organization. The men Brandeis did attract to the Zionist Organization were themselves interested in bringing in more members of their community, and they explored means for doing it successfully. In the process, some displayed more than a little antagonism toward the Eastern European intellectuals. To one new recruit, for example, those people were "idealists," inferior to the "practical" American-born Jews. In a letter to Brandeis, after explaining that the desired members would be reluctant to join societies dominated by Yiddish-speaking individuals, he complained that "there is no organization, at the present time, that can include these

---

[3] Reports of the Zionist Convention, Nachman Syrkin, *The Day*, July 8, 1916; Tchirikover, *The Day*, July 12, 1916.
[4] Bernard Shelvin, *The Jewish Morning Journal*, July 7, 1916.
[5] Brandeis to Dora Goldstein, November 1, 1915, *Louis D. Brandeis Papers* (Louisville, Ky.: University of Louisville Law Library).
[6] Brandeis to Horace M. Kallen, March 4, 1915, ibid.

people. . . . We have plenty of idealists, we need practical men. We need future millionaires."[7]

The effort to attract prominent German Jews was the main reason for Brandeis's decision to postpone the amalgamation of the P.Z.C. with the executive committee of the F.A.Z. At a meeting in 1916, he advised delaying such a reorganization, since the existing arrangement was more conducive to a successful drive for the coveted new members. The idea was to keep the door open for potential members whose position and prestige warranted their co-optation into positions of leadership without needing to go through the democratic process of election in national conventions. "Intellectuals and men of leadership" were badly needed, since "it is an unorganized and confused people that we are dealing with."[8] By "intellectuals" was meant persons in the liberal professions who had attained higher education in this country. The Eastern European intelligentsia was excluded from this group.

The attitude of the Eastern European party workers to all this should not be judged only by their vociferous complaints in the Yiddish press or their militant speeches in the conventions. Their resentment against Brandeis's nominees' taking over power was natural. Their antagonism to people imbued with a different and alien culture was understandable. But an examination of the facts reveals that their desire for these Americans to join the organization and lead them was even greater. Bernard Richards, a member of the executive committee of the F.A.Z., noted that the members on the committee encouraged and supported the usurpation of power by the P.Z.C.:

> When certain new forces came into the movement and propositions were made with regard to special efforts to win the support of some influential groups, concessions were duly made to the suggestions; every consideration was given to a policy which even involved the modification of views long entertained in connection with Zionist work. Much time and attention was devoted toward cultivating the friendship and catering to the wishes and even the whims of some prominent persons in American Jewry. Important popular activities and plans were abandoned in favor of this delicate and difficult attempt to break into society to win over certain exclusive groups.[9]

Richards makes it quite clear that in addition to the Eastern European intellectuals' ideas of a Jewish cultural renaissance and their adherence

---

[7] William Rosenblatt to Brandeis, March 18, 1915, *Richard Gottheil Papers* (New York: The Zionist Archives).

[8] Kallen to Brandeis, December 1, 1915, *Brandeis Papers*.

[9] Bernard G. Richards, "Back to First Principles," *The New Maccabean*, May 13, 1921, p. 6.

to the tenets of Zionist ideology was an overriding aspiration to "break into society." Thus the leaders with prestige and influence in this society were irresistible.

The Organization After Brandeis's Resignation

Brandeis's resignation from the presidency of the P.Z.C. in July 1916 shook the Zionist Organization, even though outwardly things remained as before. Stephen Wise became president, with Brandeis operating mostly behind the scenes. From his office in Washington, he controlled the Zionist Organization through his devoted lieutenants. Officially, his lieutenants became the top leaders of the organization, but they did not command the same respect and influence evoked by Brandeis's personality.

The result of this reshuffle in the leadership was an increasingly rebellious mood among the party workers and more strife within the organization. The conflicts were largely between the Eastern Europeans, who included most of the paid workers, and American leaders from the periphery, who represented Brandeis in the leadership but devoted only part of their energies to the organization.

An examination of the history of the Zionist Organization between 1916 and 1920 reveals a constant vocal opposition to the existing leadership and its undemocratic methods. The opposition made its first appearance in the 1917 convention and continued through all subsequent conventions. It was strongly supported by the Yiddish press. Many of the journalists, themselves members of the executive of the F.A.Z., were militant members of the group. The bureaucrats were naturally less independent in their actions than the journalists, whose livelihood was not dependent on the leaders of the F.A.Z. Although Brandeis's leadership, and that of his lieutenants, was not really challenged before the end of the World Zionist Conference in London in 1920, it became more and more of an effort for Brandeis to get his programs accepted by the executive committee and the convention, where he had to exert his influence behind the scenes to allay the clamoring opposition. He always managed to make them change their minds on the more important issues, and until 1921 the opposition was never able to rally its forces to a vote against the leadership.

The opposition became more aggressive and gained wider support in the two annual conventions of 1918 and 1919. It was aided by the Yiddish press in its demand for greater democracy within the organization.

In an extremely candid, straightforward, and resentful article in *The Jewish Morning Journal,* Bernard Shelvin, a member of the executive of the F.A.Z., reported that both Brandeis and Julian Mack, who had just been elected honorary president and president of the newly organized Zionist Organization of America, respectively, refused to be interviewed by the Yiddish press. This was the first time that Brandeis was criticized along with his lieutenants. The most severe attack was, however, reserved for Mack, who was accused by Shelvin of being completely estranged from, and uninterested in, the Yiddish press. Shelvin went on to attack the whole group of "American" leaders in the Zionist leadership with unprecedented and rather strange vehemence:

> . . . this situation will not last long. There will come a time, and the time is near, when the Yiddish press will pay more attention to its self-respect, and will not let others spit on its face, especially those who have to thank the Yiddish press for their positions, influence and reputation. There is going to come a time, and this time is near, when the leaders of a Zionist convention, that have to thank the Yiddish press for seventy-five percent of their success, will not dare to introduce special rules for the representatives of the Yiddish press and will not ever dare again to block their way from positions in Zionism.[10]

The exclusion of the Eastern Europeans from decision-making in the Zionist Organization was the main source of growing bitterness for both Shelvin and the party workers. Since July 1916, the decision-maker had been on the Supreme Court and communicated almost exclusively with a particular group of associates, regardless of their official position and contacts within the organization. These were all members of the American group. Examination of the correspondence between Brandeis and the officers of the organization reveals that most of his letters were addressed to Jacob de Haas, Mack, Felix Frankfurter, Wise, and Bernard Flexner. About 1920, Robert Szold and Ben Cohen were added. Many of these were round-robin letters; they circulated among the entire group, starting with de Haas, who was the contact man with Brandeis. Sometimes Henrietta Szold and Harry Friedenwald were added, but rarely any of the Eastern European officers. Only a few letters were addressed to Louis Lipsky throughout the five years, in spite of the fact that he was chairman of the executive of the F.A.Z. until 1918 and thereafter head of the department of organization.

The new leaders who entered the Zionist Organization with Brandeis or joined under his influence in later years were all members of a different social circle from that of the Eastern Europeans, and by virtue of this advantage had access to "the chief" and, thus, to the source of power. At the same time, they were not even interested in maintaining close

---

[10] Shelvin, *The Jewish Morning Journal*, July 2, 1918.

contacts with the Eastern Europeans. As a result, the latter were virtually excluded from a share in the power and influence in the organization.[11]

Condescension toward the Eastern European officials, the bureaucrats, on the part of the leaders from the periphery, the outsiders, was characteristic in the Zionist Organization. The leaders from the periphery at the helm of the Zionist Organization felt secure in their positions of leadership and had no comprehension that party workers, virtually unknown outside the narrow circle of the Jewish ghetto, might endanger their position of leadership.

When disagreement grew between the two groups, the American leaders' aloofness gave way first to contempt and then to hostility. Thus, they themselves closed the doors to any compromise. Mack, president of the organization and one of the most gentle, sincere, and courteous members of the American group, wrote to Brandeis a few months before they lost their leadership: "Changed Lipsky and Schweitzer (to whom I gave 11 yesterday so that they wouldn't hang over for lunch) to 11:30. Bob Szold, Ben Flexner, de Haas . . . for ten as well as lunch."[12] This was the way the bureaucrats, who were not yet uncompromising opponents, were treated.

A case illustrating the contempt of the leaders toward the Eastern European bureaucrats was that involving Abraham Goldberg, a popular speaker and writer of the Eastern European group. In the dispute that developed between the World Zionist leaders and Brandeis and his associates in 1920–1921 on the issue of the goals of the Zionist Organization, Goldberg strongly supported the administration and defended its position in the Yiddish press. He might have developed into a powerful supporter, but the leaders did not accord him any recognition. He eventually gave up his support, notifying Mack:

> . . . at no time since the London Conference, a period of nine months, was I ever consulted on anything, and even the information that came from London, which was regularly and religiously supplied to the selected few, was never sent to me, notwithstanding the fact that I was legitimately entitled to it by virtue of my election . . . as a member of the actions comité . . . it is the settled opinion in Russian-Polish Jewish circles that no matter how able and even ingenious one may be, he stands little or no chance to be treated as an equal and accepted in the good company of the leaders, if he should happen to be of Russian-Jewish parentage. . . . Well, I hate to believe it but my own sad experiences are persuading me,

---
[11] Ibid., September 13, 1919; Emanuel Neumann, "Zionist Democracy: Observation on the Chicago Convention," *The Maccabean* 32 (December 1919): 337–38.
[12] Mack to Brandeis, January 21, 1919, *Brandeis Papers.*

slowly but surely, against my own will I assure you, to accept the correctness of this strange view.[13]

As far as can be ascertained, Mack never even answered this letter. The attitude of the American leaders, ignoring the bureaucrats to the point of humiliating them even when they needed their support and could easily have won it, supports Robert Michels's analysis that the "outsiders" in the organization—those who are elected to their positions by virtue of their other high statuses in society—inevitably antagonize the bureaucrats, on whom they look "with mingled disdain and compassion."[14]

As indicated, the Eastern European bureaucrats were not passive; they tried to fight back. In 1919, they managed to abolish the administrative committee and resolved that the executive committee should get increased responsibilities and meet twice a month. They were better represented in this body than in the small administrative committee. Even more important was the decision that the districts should elect half the members of the executive committee. On this issue, they mustered 309 votes against 182.[15] They tried in this way to improve their position in the organization against the outsiders, but they did not attempt at that time to take over the power from the top leaders.

The minor constitutional changes in the organization did not affect the balance of power. The decisions continued to be made by "the chief" and his trusted lieutenants, with the national executive having no control over them. Time and again the executive committee protested this usurpation of power, with no results.[16]

An examination of the position of de Haas, secretary of the organization, and the role he played from 1916 to 1921, contributes to an understanding of the power struggle in the organization. Emanuel Neumann

---

[13] Abraham Goldberg to Mack, March 26, 1921, *de Haas Papers* (New York: The Zionist Archives).

[14] Robert Michels, *Political Parties: A Sociological Study of the Oligarchical Tendencies of Modern Democracy* (New York: Dover Publications, 1959), p. 75. The process of increased antagonism between the bureaucrats and the outsiders, as elaborated by Michels, was being repeated in the case under observation. But while the antagonism between the two groups in the Zionist Organization developed along the lines of Michels's analysis, the inevitability of the success of the bureaucrats was one element in his analysis which was not supported by our study. More than a structural analysis of the leadership of the organization was needed to explain how the American leaders maintained their power in spite of these developments and what other social forces led to their defeat in 1921.

[15] Neumann, "Zionist Democracy," p. 338.

[16] See, for example, minutes of the Executive Committee of the Z.O.A., April 17, 1920, *de Haas Papers*.

has suggested that the personal rivalry between de Haas and Lipsky was an important cause of the dispute that led to the break in 1921.[17]

It would seem, however, that there was much more than personal rivalry between the two. De Haas was born in England of Portuguese-Dutch extraction. Early in life, he came under the spell of Theodor Herzl, the founder of political Zionism, whom he served for a while as private secretary. At Herzl's request, he came to the United States to become active in the newly formed F.A.Z. A hero worshipper, he idolized Herzl, and after the latter's death he continued a lonely battle for political Zionism at a time when the Zionist movement had already abandoned the grand-style diplomacy undertaken by Herzl. De Haas returned to active leadership in the American Zionist Organization with Brandeis's accession to the position of leader of the Zionists in the United States. In Brandeis, de Haas found a new hero. The rest of de Haas's life is a story of devoted service to Brandeis by a man with an analytical mind and high intelligence who was willing to abandon independent thinking to follow the ideas of the man he adored. Inconsistent as Brandeis's views and opinions were with de Haas's previously held convictions, de Haas endorsed the ideas and wishes of the master and convinced himself of their wisdom and truth.

When Brandeis left for Washington, de Haas remained in office, as secretary of the P.Z.C., to become both the mouthpiece for Brandeis's command and the one who informed Brandeis of happenings in the office. This function, that of mediator between Brandeis and the officials of the organization, led to great resentment among the men of both groups. Brandeis's trust was complete and unshaken, a fact that increased the resentment felt against de Haas. Brandeis, understandably, found this arrangement satisfactory. The many people who used to express surprise that Brandeis maintained confidence in de Haas, in spite of the mounting criticism against him, had to remember that de Haas was the ideal contact man in the difficult task Brandeis undertook of maintaining remote control over the organization. Without de Haas's services, Brandeis's control over the organization might never have been realized.

Yet, at the same time, de Haas's role as Brandeis's mouthpiece and informant was a weak link in the control system, and this would have been the case even if de Haas had not been such a quarrelsome person and so difficult to get along with. The division between the "inner circle" of the American group and the Eastern Europeans, and the exclusion of the latter from the decision-making process, were certainly not de Haas's doing; but he was the man who carried out the policy, and not

---

[17] Interview with author, January 26, 1961.

enjoying the prestige and respect Brandeis commanded, he soon became most unpopular with the Eastern Europeans. The Yiddish press attacked him severely and leveled all kinds of accusations at him. One gets the impression that he was used as a scapegoat by the Eastern Europeans who, unable to criticize Brandeis openly, directed their vehemence against de Haas, who "has no trust in the people."[18] They found it humiliating to take orders from him: "The Jews do not want to be led by a messenger," charged Abraham Goldberg.[19]

The members of the inner circle, on the other hand, were also not happy with this arrangement. They resented the fact that de Haas was on intimate ground with Brandeis, the source of power, while they had to contact Brandeis through him. Wise complained that as a result of this arrangement, "frequently one is unable to perform one's best service because we are a little in the dark and do not quite command the confidence of the Chief."[20] In the following years, Wise was to become more and more irritated with this arrangement, and he refused to communicate with de Haas at all. Most other members felt hurt and angry at one point or another.

However, there is no indication that Brandeis ever considered any change in the arrangement in spite of all the criticism. He must have felt that since this was the only way he was able to control the organization, this was the way he would continue controlling it.

De Haas had another advantage over the rest of the members of the American group. He was the only one who had devoted his entire life, all his time and energy, to Zionism and the Zionist Organization. The others, who had only their spare time for the organization, were dependent on him. He, like Lipsky, was a party man.

There was never a clear distinction between the functions of the two men in the organization. At first, Lipsky was chairman of the executive of the F.A.Z. and de Haas secretary of the P.Z.C., and the different functions of the two positions were unspecified. Later, de Haas became secretary of the organization and Lipsky head of the organizational department, which again led to friction. The fight for control centered on the two men.

De Haas, like Lipsky and the Eastern European intellectuals, was devoted to Jewish culture and traditions. Although a Westerner, he appreciated Jewish culture and gained a deeper understanding of it than all the other members of the American group. It is interesting to note

---

[18] Jacob Fishman, *The Jewish Morning Journal*, July 1, 1918.
[19] Abraham Goldberg, *The Jewish Morning Journal*, September 14, 1919.
[20] Wise to Mack, November 19, 1918, *de Haas Papers*.

that in the Yiddish press of the period, his opponents managed always to reserve some kind words for him. So did the Eastern European leaders. Like the Eastern Europeans, he equated the Zionist movement with all that was worthwhile in Judaism, and he also shared their cultural alienation from American society. He wrote to Mack in 1927: ". . . my one hope in Jewish life is in the Zionist Organization, for it is the one idea that as a Jew has meaning to me. When its frets and fume ceases, the chances of moral urge and idealism will disappear, particularly in this country where by every means we Jews have during the last ten years put into the foreground the gospel of financial success."[21]

However, what he thought was good for Zionism and his ideas of Zionist aims were subordinated to what Brandeis thought was good and right. And though in his papers and letters we find a basic ideological agreement with the Eastern Europeans, this was entirely submerged when it came to action. Here he faithfully executed Brandeis's orders. Since he was the only full-time and paid executant of these policies, he very soon found himself in opposition to the Eastern European bureaucrats and journalists.

De Haas's first task after Brandeis left for Washington was to secure the acceptance of the compromise between the A.J.C. and the Zionist Organization on the Congress. Wise, now the president of the P.Z.C., refused even to negotiate the details of the agreement with the A.J.C. De Haas was left to mobilize the forces within the organization in support of the agreement and to press top members of the organization to accept the compromise.[22]

In the annual convention that was held in July 1916, de Haas was assigned to air the novel ideas that were to preoccupy the organization in the following years, namely, that Zionist propaganda activities should give way to practical work in Palestine; that the Zionist Organization should now be geared to this purpose; that the organization should select men of business as leaders over propagandists and agitators. This was, of course, an immediate challenge to the Yiddish-speaking journalists and writers, who comprised the party workers in the organization, and to most of the paid bureaucrats. De Haas bluntly stated in the course of his speech in the general debate:

> We must recognize that our work is not the work merely of oratory. It is no accident that hitherto whenever you selected a Zionist leader you chose someone with the power of speech, because heretofore we started out with the idea that we wanted propaganda, and we made the propa-

---

[21] De Haas to Mack, February 11, 1927, ibid.
[22] De Haas to Brandeis, August 8, 1916, *Brandeis Papers*.

gandist do the work of an editor, or anything else. Today, we have to face a new condition, that the Zionist movement must become an immense democratic guide, controlled by an honest group of workers throughout the United States. We have to understand and respect the men whose platform power is the very least of their ability; and we have to understand that every individual letter means someone's effort has been wasted; that every request that is not answered means a loss of some precious hour. . . .[23]

The nature of the relationship between de Haas and Brandeis at the time leaves no doubt that this speech was inspired by Brandeis. Brandeis himself made work in Palestine his sole interest soon after he left for Washington. On September 8, before the struggle over the Congress issue was settled, he ordered de Haas to call a special meeting of the P.Z.C. "to discuss the present conditions of the Palestinian colonies and institutions."[24] The building up of Palestine was rapidly becoming for Brandeis the sole objective of Zionism; the cultural renaissance of American Jews was forgotten. Nothing in the history of the movement or in the political developments in Palestine can explain this change. The battle for the Jewish Congress was not yet over; the drive for membership was at its height; negotiations with the British government over the future of Palestine were not yet taking place. Only Brandeis's elevation to the Supreme Court coincided with the change in his ideas about Zionism. He found it understandably more consistent for a justice of the United States Supreme Court to restrict his obligations as a Zionist and a Jew to the development of Palestine economically than to head a movement that advocated regeneration of a separate Jewish culture in America.

The Brandeis and Schiff Groups Attempt to Unite

Brandeis's thinking about the problems of Zionism was only beginning to change in July 1916. It crystalized in the following year, accelerated by developments in American society.

The year 1916 had witnessed a rise in the feelings of patriotism among the American people because of European events; this was the year of "preparedness" and military parades. In 1917, the United States entered World War I and the country experienced an upsurge of nationalistic and patriotic sentiment. The American-born and Americanized Zionists, who always felt apprehensive about the compatibility of Jewish nation-

---

[23] "Report of the Nineteenth Annual Convention of American Zionists," *The Maccabean* 29 (July 1916): 195.
[24] Brandeis to de Haas, September 8, 1916, *Brandeis Papers*.

alism and Americanism, became even more sensitive, and they tried desperately to make clear distinctions between their two statuses in an attempt to convince themselves, as well as the rest of the country, that the two were compatible and even complementary. Mack's apologia, *Americanism and Zionism*, was written during this period.

The Jews, as a group, found themselves in a particularly difficult position. The Eastern European Jews were led by their hatred for the oppressive czarist regime in Russia to sympathize with the Central Powers who fought Russia.[25] Prior to American participation in World War I, many German Jews sympathized with Germany. A great many Jews were members of, or sympathizers with, the Socialist party, which adopted an anti-war platform, and pacifists, who included a few well-known Jewish personalities like Judah Magnes.

This created great anxiety among the more respectable American Jewish groups and among the representative leaders of American Jewry, who were fearful that these actions on the part of their fellow Jews would be considered unpatriotic and reflect badly on the whole community.

The Zionists, on the whole, identified with the side of patriotism. The Hadassah organization was in disfavor in the eyes of the leaders because some of the leading women endorsed pacifism.[26] Some Zionist leaders with connections in Jewish socialist circles led the pro-war propaganda among the Jewish masses and were active in the Jewish League of American Patriots, whose purpose was "aiding in the systematic mobilization of the Jewish race in case of war . . . and to offer itself to the American nation and its government in the defense of the honor of the nation."[27] The Zionist press manifested its patriotism, and the Zionist leaders actively campaigned against Jewish anti-war socialists and pacifists.[28]

After the United States joined the Allies in the war against Germany, it was the American-born German-Jewish Zionists who were particularly apprehensive. One incident that stirred the Jewish community took place during March 1918. A delegate from the Jewish organization working for the relief of Palestinian Jews was to be appointed to represent those organizations in the Red Cross. When the candidacy of Israel Friedlaender came up, some of the German-Jewish Zionist leaders came

---

[25] Joseph Rappaport, "Jewish Immigration and World War I," (Ph.D. dissertation, Faculty of Political Science, Columbia University, 1951), *passim*.
[26] De Haas to Brandeis, September 10, 1917, *de Haas Papers*.
[27] *The Day*, March 30, 1917.
[28] Editorial, *Dos Yiddishe Folk*, April 6, 1917; editorial, *Chicago Tribune*, December 24, 1917; Melech Epstein, *Jewish Labor in the U.S.A.*, vol. 2 (New York: Trade Union Sponsoring Committee, 1950), p. 1950.

out publicly against him, accusing him of entertaining pro-German sentiments, and Richard Gottheil wrote an indignant letter to Brandeis stating that a man who shared such disloyal sentiments could not represent the American Jews.[29] None of his friends among the Jewish leaders dared rally to his support.[30]

The same state of mind prevailed among the A.J.C. leaders. When Magnes joined the pacifists, their anger and indignation knew no bounds. "What right have you," asked Louis Marshall, "to injure the Jewish people of America with whom you are so actively identified? . . . Do you believe that the American people will not attribute to the Jews generally adhesion to a policy which runs counter to that of our Government?"[31]

The sensitivity and apprehension of the leaders from the periphery to the mood of the country was naturally much greater than that of the Eastern European intellectuals. In spite of the concern of the latter, they were more alienated and isolated from the current sentiment of the dominant culture and thus were a little less apprehensive about the possible detrimental effects of their Jewish nationalism on the standing of the Jews in the American society. This difference manifested itself in the controversy within the Jewish community in October 1917 as to whether to convene the recently elected Jewish Congress. The A.J.C. people urged postponement of the Congress until the end of hostilities; Brandeis's advice from Washington urged the same course, as did all German Jewish leaders, including Congress enthusiasts like Wise. This irritated the Eastern European nationalists, who saw no connection between the Jewish Congress and the war. Wise, reporting to Brandeis on the deliberations of the committee elected to prepare the Congress, said: "I am sorry to say that all our Zionists were against us, Lipsky and Rosenblatt making strong speeches against postponement."[32] The German-Jewish Zionists were now feeling less and less comfortable in their associations and partnership with the Eastern European nationalists.

Association with Jewish nationalists became most embarrassing for Zionist leaders who took up wartime positions in the American government. Eugene Meyer became director of the War Finance Corporation; Elisha Friedman was a member of the Advisory Commission of the Coun-

---

[29] Gottheil to Brandeis, March 23, 1918, *Brandeis Papers*.
[30] For details on the Friedlaender affair, see Herbert Parzen, "Conservative Judaism and Zionism 1896–1922," *Jewish Social Studies* 23 (October 1961): 235–64.
[31] Marshall to Magnes, June 1, 1917, *Jacob H. Schiff Papers* (Cincinnati: The American Jewish Archives).
[32] Wise to Brandeis, October 5, 1917, *Brandeis Papers*.

cil of National Defense; Frankfurter was appointed Assistant Secretary of Labor; Mack was a member of the Board of Inquiry for Conscientious Objectors.

When the gulf between the German Jewish leaders—Zionists and non-Zionists—and the Eastern European Jews widened, the leaders attempted to unite their forces to maintain control over the masses. The move, if successful, might have enabled them to direct the masses away from their nationalist sympathies. Michels observed that "where there is a struggle between the leaders and the masses, the former are always victorious if only they remain united."[33]

From Washington, Friedman started negotiations with Jacob Schiff in the second half of 1917 in an attempt to unite Schiff and Brandeis and their associates on the question of Zionism. The negotiations then spread and other members took active parts. The Zionists involved were, apart from Friedman, Frankfurter, Meyer, Mack, and Brandeis. The Eastern Europeans were excluded from the negotiations, and the only other member who was kept informed, though he maintained a hostile attitude toward the negotiations, was Wise. A few officials of the P.Z.C. discussed the matter with some of the participants in the negotiations, but the leaders of the Eastern European group were kept out.

The old schism between secularists and religionists still divided the two groups and was still mentioned throughout the negotiations. It was apparent, however, that it was the idea of Jewish nationalism promulgated by the Eastern Europeans that was conceived to be a threat to both. The constant theme underlying most of the negotiations was: let us get together and lead the masses away from their misguided ideas of Jewish nationalism.[34]

The Zionists suggested drafting a declaration to be signed by Schiff and the Zionist leaders. In this declaration, Schiff was to support the Zionist movement and become a member of the organization. The rest of the negotiations dealt with the content of the document. On October 26, Schiff wrote to Friedman: ". . . anything ought to be excluded which would ask for the Jewish people independent national rights, and which, in the countries of Diaspora, could be construed as making citizens of the Jewish faith members of a separate nation, aside from the nation to which, like for instance, Jews who are American citizens—they owe their political allegiance."[35] This issue concerned both groups at the time.

---

[33] Michels, *Political Parties*, p. 157.
[34] Schiff to Elisha Friedman, July 5, 1917, *Schiff Papers*.
[35] Schiff to Friedman, October 26, 1917, ibid.

Some Eastern European enthusiasts endorsed the idea current among some Zionist circles in Europe that all Jews should consider themselves citizens of the future Jewish state. This position was never endorsed by the Zionist top leadership in Europe nor among most Eastern European Zionist leaders of the Z.O.A. But to be safe, Schiff objected to political independence for Palestine. Since the word *national* meant, in the considered opinion of Marshall, political independence, Schiff insisted that this word be taken out of the proposed document.[36]

Brandeis, while arguing that it would be politically unwise to state anything specific about the political future of Palestine while negotiations with the British were going on, agreed to remain silent on the issue of political independence. In his letter to Schiff he reassured him: ". . . and I know too, that I am but expressing the views of my colleagues, of all Zionists with whom I have personal relations, when I state that they and I neither advise nor desire an independent state; on the contrary, we should regard independent statehood, now or in the foreseeable future, as a most serious menace to the permanency of the Jewish national aspirations."[37]

This letter was sent to Schiff on the very day that the Balfour Declaration was issued in London favoring a Jewish national home in Palestine.[38] It could be argued that Brandeis's statement that he did not desire an independent state was a maneuver to get the A.J.C. to cooperate with him and join the Zionist Organization. Even if this interpretation of his action is the correct one, we are still left with a statement that expressed willingness not to press the issue of political independence for the future Jewish community in Palestine. The period of cooperation with the Eastern European nationalists was over. Their nationalistic statements and utterances made them undesirable bedfellows, and Brandeis and his associates were willing to compromise the aims of Zionism in order to achieve a united front with the same leaders to whom they referred only a few years earlier derogatively as the "monied aristocracy" of the Jewish community.

---

[36] Notes by Elisha Friedman on his meeting with Schiff and Marshall, afternoon and evening, November 8, 1917, *Brandeis Papers*.

[37] Brandeis to Schiff, November 2, 1917, ibid.

[38] The Balfour Declaration was an ambiguous document whose true meaning was open to debate in later years. However, at the time of its publication it was widely interpreted to mean support of the Jewish national aspirations for a Jewish state in Palestine. This was especially true in the United States. The belief held at the time that Brandeis played a major role in the negotiations that resulted in this declaration has been questioned by Herbert Parzen in his article, "Brandeis and the Balfour Declaration," *Herzl Year Book*, vol. 5 (1963): 309-50.

These assurances did not satisfy Schiff. What he wanted to achieve in this agreement with Brandeis was for this popular leader to use his popularity among the Jewish masses to lead them away from radical doctrines. Schiff and his friends could not now even try to influence the masses, but they were willing to strike up a partnership with Brandeis if he used his influence to carry the masses away from nationalist sentiments and channel their enthusiasm, via the Zionist Organization, to supporting only colonization of Palestine. This the American Zionists were now promising Schiff.[39] "The ideals of every movement," explained Friedman to Schiff, "are defined by the leaders and translated to the masses, who will follow trusted leadership—and Justice Brandeis is trusted whole-soully."[40]

When the negotiations were nearing a successful agreement, the document was sent to Schiff for final checking and for signature. At that point a new obstacle appeared. Schiff signed the document, adding a clause that stated that Jews are those who accept the Jewish concept of the Deity. This infuriated the freethinking Jewish progressives. They broke off the negotiations and did not publish the document. In an indignant letter to Schiff, Mack stated categorically: ". . . just as a Jew remains a Jew, notwithstanding that the weakness of flesh leads him even to commit murder, so the Jew remains a Jew, a part of our people, even though he personally rejects the biblical conception of the Deity. I personally should want to cast out the former, not the latter; you doubtless would want to reject both, but I believe both of us are impotent to do so."[41]

A careful examination of the negotiations between the two groups will strengthen the conclusion that it was not the ideological commitment to Judaism as a religion that led to Schiff's surprise move at the last moment. This issue was dropped very early in the negotiations. Furthermore, Schiff's ideas about Palestine show that he was attracted to the concept of helping build up Palestine precisely because religion had become a devisive principle in Jewry, and he hoped that helping Palestine would unite all sections. In a letter published in *The American Hebrew* in 1914, he explained his growing interest in the colonization of Palestine: "My interest became, to no small extent, further stimulated because of the prospect which here opened itself for the German, Russian and American Jew, for the Orthodox, the Reformer, the Zionist and anti-

---

[39] Friedman to Schiff, September 21, 1917, *Schiff Papers*.
[40] Notes taken by Friedman on his meeting with Schiff, October 20, 1917, *Brandeis Papers*.
[41] Mack to Schiff, December 6, 1917, ibid.

Zionist to cooperate harmoniously in the cause of cultural elevation of progress in Palestine."[42]

Why, then, this sudden religious zeal? What the Zionists asked in return for their ideological accommodation was that Schiff join their organization as it was controlled by Brandeis and his associates. We must remember that at that time Brandeis's prestige among the Jews was at its height, and for a while the A.J.C. leaders might have thought they could maintain some of their influence by joining the F.A.Z. Apparently, they had second thoughts and wondered if this act did not amount to capitulation to Brandeis, deciding as a result to demand a higher price. If the avowed atheists and agnostics would openly accept the religious clause, a principle publicly associated with Schiff and his group, Schiff's joining the Zionist Organization could be interpreted as a victory for that principle. This point was expressed by Wise, who can hardly be accused of opposing the Jewish conception of the Deity.[43]

Brandeis's power in the Jewish community rested upon his control of a mass organization. The power of the philanthropists was their money. If they joined the organization, they would acknowledge Brandeis's leadership. Now that they refused to do so, the negotiations could not go on. This became clear from de Haas's report to Brandeis shortly after negotiations broke off, in which he reported an encounter between Marshall and Mack: "Marshall had said that the time had arrived when the Zionists should call a national conference to take up the Zionist job. Mack himself answered that the organization is wide open; everybody can join us."[44] Marshall's idea of a conference to pull resources together for building Palestine was unacceptable to Brandeis, whose power lay in the Zionist Organization.

The philanthropists had one advantage over Brandeis in that the efforts of American Jewry, Zionists included, were again concentrated in the realm of fund-raising. The Zionists had just started a new drive, the Palestine Restoration Fund. This was the battleground on which the philanthropists excelled, and it seems that they decided to fight rather than submit to Brandeis.

Establishing the Zionist Organization of America (Z.O.A.)

Brandeis and his associates were now left with a Zionist Organization in which the rank and file was becoming more vocal in their insistence

---

[42] A Letter to the Editor by Jacob Schiff, *The American Hebrew*, July 3, 1914, p. 257.
[43] Wise to Mack, December 6, 1917, *Brandeis Papers*.
[44] De Haas to Brandeis, December 23, 1917, ibid.

on the Jews being a distinct nationality. This was a reaction to increased anti-Semitism in the United States. The Red Scare in the United States after the Bolshevik revolution had strong anti-Semitic overtones.[45]

Reaction to the upsurge of anti-Semitism in the United States was different in the two communities. The Americanized German Jewish community were becoming very apprehensive and insecure, continuously declaring their allegiance to the United States. The purge of the pro-German professor Friedlaender by the American Zionist leaders is evidence of their fear.

For the Eastern European immigrants, anti-Semitism was familiar, and their reaction as a group differed from that of their better-established brethren. Moreover, Europe was now in the midst of a nationalist awakening, and the Jews in Europe developed an equally intense nationalist sentiment. This influenced developments in the Jewish ghettos in the United States, which echoed the different theories and dogmas current in the Jewish ghettos in Eastern Europe. The idea of a Jewish nationality was becoming confused in the minds of the masses with other ideas exported from Europe: the notion of some measure of autonomy for all national minorities which reside in Central and Eastern Europe, including Jews, called Diaspora nationalism; the idea of a Jewish state in Palestine; and the problem of the relations between Jews in the Diaspora and the future state.

One can appreciate, under these circumstances, the difficulties of maintaining any coalition between the American Zionist leaders and the nationalist Eastern European party workers and their rank and file. An illustration of this increased tension was provided by Mrs. Nathan Straus, wife of a philanthropist who supported the Zionist movement, who wrote anxiously to Brandeis in April 1918, describing a Zionist mass meeting at which she and her husband were sharing the platform. De Haas was carried away in his speech, she said, and declared that for Zionists Zionism must come before everything else. Mr. Straus immediately asked the chairman to balance this statement by emphasizing Americanism—and this was done. "Unfortunately," continued Mrs. Straus, "they [these statements] did not meet with the same approval of the audience; while Mr. de Haas had been loudly applauded." Mrs. Straus concluded that her husband was greatly upset by the incident, and she urged Brandeis to control de Haas in the future.[46]

---

[45] John Higham, *Strangers in the Land* (New Brunswick, N.J.: Rutgers University Press, 1955), p. 262.

[46] Lina Straus to Brandeis, April 16, 1918, *Brandeis Papers*.

In the middle of 1918, Brandeis decided to move. He and his associates felt they were powerless against the nationalists sentiment of the Eastern Europeans. Thus, Brandeis's reorganization plan has to be viewed as an attack on the problem at a different level. Rather than argue against nationalism, he decided to change the organization in such a way that the task of rebuilding Palestine would remain the only goal of the organization, while all the other educational-cultural activities would be eliminated. Fund-raising and economic assistance to Palestine would remain the sole responsibilities of the Zionist Organization.

The new organization, the Zionist Organization of America (Z.O.A.), was "an American form of organization."[47] It now became, instead of a federation of societies, a centralized organization with one controlling national office and divided into geographical districts.[48]

There was great resistance to the reorganization among the delegates to the 1918 annual convention. Brandeis himself was very active in the lobbies of the convention before he could secure a majority vote in support of the new constitution.

The Eastern European party workers were split on this issue. Most local party workers, strongly backed by the journalists and writers of the independent Yiddish press, seemed to be opposed to the new constitution. The bureaucrats from the central office—Lipsky, head of the department of organization, and his associates—supported the administration on this issue.

The official publications of the Zionist Organization controlled by Lipsky and his associates, *The Maccabean* and *Dos Yiddishe Folk*, strongly supported the reorganization plan. The editorial of *The Maccabean* declared:

> The new plan of Organization involves centralization of authority, with all the safeguards of democratic administration, and the opening of doors of the Zionist Organization to all who, under the new conditions, desire to be helpful. The Zionist Organization is to be made synonymous with the organized Jewish people working for the one national aim that is visible and valuable. All who are in sympathy with the object are to be invited to join our forces, as if we were starting anew.[49]

The editorial is of particular interest for its endorsement of Palestinianism. The organization officers realized that "one national aim that is visible" was preferable from the point of view of the organization to

---

[47] Brandeis, "On Reorganization," *The Maccabean* 31 (July 1918): 193.
[48] *Constitution for the Government of the Zionist District* (n.p.: Z.O.A., 1918).
[49] Editorial, *The Maccabean* 31 (July 1918): 167.

the ambitious but amorphous ideas of cultural renaissance. In 1912, these same men established the Zion Associations in an attempt to attract new members who were unwilling to commit themselves to the Zionist ideology but were interested in devoting a small portion of their time and money to help the colonization of Palestine. Now again they were willing to reorganize the Zionist Organization along lines that would suit potential members.

For the opposition, Jacob Fishman of *The Jewish Morning Journal* explained that in the new centralized organization the old and young, the English-speaking and the Yiddish-speaking, would be put together in the same group; they would have little in common and would constitute a large army controlled by the center. As a result, the members would lose interest in the activities of the organization, which would remain the burden of the few party workers, as in the American political parties. Thus, the members would become "geographical Zionists" and would not identify themselves with the cultural and educational interests of Zionism.[50]

The organization officers around Lipsky, on the other hand, accepted the plan, recognizing that this reorganization would increase the power of the full-time party workers rather than that of the American leaders, who were preoccupied with other activities most of the time.

This division in the ranks of the Eastern Europeans—those in the central office, on the one hand, and the Yiddish journalists and local party workers, on the other—illustrated the readiness of the organization officers to deviate from the original ideology of the movement when they believed it might strengthen the organization. It was among those whose livelihood was earned in Yiddish journalism or by writing in Yiddish and Hebrew that the opposition to the new structure of the organization was concentrated. These two conflicting tendencies among the Eastern European Zionists remained, but the distinction was never as clear as during the discussions that preceded the reorganization of the Zionist Organization in 1918.

Brandeis's new plan abolished all Zionist societies committed to other special activities and established one common denominator, the signing of the Basle Program. The meaning of such a commitment was never clear, but it had to do strictly with Palestine. All other activities of the Zionist groups had to be initiated by voluntary action of the members; they ceased to be the responsibility of the organization and its central bodies.[51]

---

[50] Fishman, *The Jewish Morning Journal*, June 19, 1918.
[51] Brandeis, "On Reorganization," p. 193.

However, to understand the structural principle of the new Zionist Organization after 1918, an examination of its constitution is not sufficient. One important factor was the decision by Brandeis and his associates in the leadership to concentrate all efforts on fund-raising. This decision was taken by the Zionist leaders immediately after the publication by the British government of the Balfour Declaration in favor of the creation of a Jewish national home in Palestine. The Zionist leaders were hoping to capitalize on the enthusiasm this declaration generated among the Jews in America, and they immediately launched the Palestine Restoration Fund. Furthermore, they now demanded a greater share for Palestine of the funds collected by the Joint Distribution Committee. The J.D.C. (which was more accommodating in these first months) agreed, in February 1918, to set up a new committee of representatives of the J.D.C. and the Zionist Organization, aiming at reaching a new agreement to replace the one made in October 1915.[52] Thus, the Zionists reentered into competition with the A.J.C. and other Jewish organizations in the field of fund-raising.

When a political organization is interested in votes and popular support, it is concerned mainly with increasing membership and maintaining an efficient mass organization. When the main goal of the organization is raising funds, it will be more interested in attracting persons of wealth and influence. The leaders of the Zionist Organization from 1918 to 1920 were trying to do both—build a mass membership and attract men of wealth to contribute to economic enterprises in Palestine.

Naturally, this led to certain difficulties. The legal framework of the Z.O.A. was that of a mass movement, with members paying membership dues and democratically electing the governing bodies of the organization. But at the same time, the leaders were trying to direct all efforts of the organization to the task of fund-raising, to the neglect of other cultural and educational activities. In order to build an organization suitable and efficient for the limited task of fund-raising for Palestine, the leaders were trying to attract more influential people into the local districts and to give them positions of prominence so as to draw in men of wealth. We are told: "Men directly representing the American Headquarters [of the Z.O.A.] have travelled through the land and in no uncertain terms told district executives to quit their posts in order to make room for more influential people."[53]

---

[52] Minutes of the meeting for the Provisional Zionist Committee, February 24, 1918, *Brandeis Papers*.

[53] Harry Fram, *Primary and Basic Organization: As Affecting Zionist Endeavors in America* (Los Angeles: Privately Printed, 1922), p. 14.

The distinction made by Maurice Duverger between cadre parties and mass parties will help us understand the basic differences between these two approaches from the point of view of the organization. The cadre party, according to Duverger, is a typical middle-class party. In a cadre party quality rather than numbers is the important factor: "extent of prestige, skill in techniques, size of fortune." For the mass party, "the members are . . . the very substance of the party, the stuff of its activity." Their subscriptions secure the party's independence. These masses have first to develop a class consciousness and so the main task of the mass party is "the political education of the working class."

The mass party was a European phenomenon. It was the principle means of organization used by the socialist and nationalist movements of the nineteenth century.[54] These ideas of the function and structure of mass parties which guided the European intelligentsia who organized and led the mass socialist and nationalist parties also inspired the Jewish intelligentsia. The writings of the Eastern European intellectuals who were active in the Zionist movement both in Europe and in the United States show that they viewed the Zionist Organization as a mass movement, too, whose aim was to organize all the Jewish people, to make them politically conscious of their common interests, to select their leaders, and to make them independent of the non-Jewish majorities and the rich Jewish bankers and merchants.

The Eastern European Jewish intelligentsia in the United States shared their ideas and their cultural background with the European intelligentsia. They still addressed themselves to the "Jewish masses" and aimed at the "awakening of the Jewish consciousness," believing it to be a necessary prerequisite to involving the Jewish people in building up the Jewish homeland. Zionism, they felt, had to be a mass movement that would educate the masses for the great task.

These ideas prevailed in the United States as long as the followers of these intellectuals were recruited among the Eastern European Jewish masses who were responsive to such talk. But from the beginning, it was meaningless talk to the American Zionist leaders, to whom these intellectual traditions were alien. The different standpoints of the two groups on the problem of organization was manifested during the dispute over the existence of Zionist parties within the Zionist Organization.

Brandeis and his associates objected strongly to the existence within the Zionist Organization of parties with different ideological points of view, and they tried to eliminate them because that form of politics was

---

[54] Maurice Duverger, *Political Parties: Their Organization and Activity in the Modern State* (New York: John Wiley & Sons, 1955), pp. 63–64, 66–67, 69.

unknown in America.⁵⁵ The European political tradition, on the other hand, emphasized strongly the ideological tenets which provided the frame for their political organizations.

As disagreements prevailed on this issue between the American leaders and the world Zionist leaders in Europe, the former decided to seek the support of the American organization. In 1919, they brought before the annual convention of the Z.O.A. a resolution stating that in every country there should exist only one Zionist Organization and that different ideological groups would have no right to seek separate representation in the World Zionist Congress. This was the first major issue on which the Brandeis administration was defeated. Although the members of the opposition in this annual convention were induced by Brandeis's active intervention behind the scenes to compromise and retreat on all issues without bringing them to a vote, on this particular issue feelings among the Eastern European party workers were too strong. The Z.O.A. party workers defended the right of Zionists who fought the Z.O.A. during the elections to the World Zionist Congresses. This was therefore a clear issue over a principle rather than an interest. The Yiddish press hailed the result of the vote. *The Jewish Morning Journal* explained that from the American point of view, parties were groups who tried to gain control over a state or an organization, but that it supported the European point of view, according to which the main function of parties is to clarify the principles involved.⁵⁶

The Eastern European leaders of the Jewish masses could not conceive of an organization dedicated solely to fund-raising; the masses, they felt, would not be interested in joining. Furthermore, they worried lest without other cultural and intellectual pursuits to keep people interested in the Zionist Organization, fund-raising would suffer since there will not be enough party workers to raise funds.⁵⁷ They were evidently interested in the success of the fund-raising activities of the Zionist Organization, but, conditioned by their class environment, they believed that there was a correlation between the number of members in an organization and the amount of funds the organization was able to mobilize. They had in mind the Jewish masses and not the wealthier middle class, with whom they had little contact. Lipsky accordingly urged Brandeis to embark on a new drive for membership in 1919 "in view of the greater needs of the Palestine Restoration Fund."⁵⁸

---

⁵⁵ De Haas to Jacobson, December 25, 1917, *Brandeis Papers*.
⁵⁶ Editorial, *The Jewish Morning Journal*, September 19, 1919.
⁵⁷ Norman Weinstein, "Herzliah: A Movement for Zionist Culture," *The Maccabean* 33 (April 1920): 150.
⁵⁸ Lipsky to Brandeis, September 29, 1919, *Brandeis Papers*.

Thus, we see that another source of misunderstanding between the Eastern European and the American leaders concerned the style of action of the Zionist Organization. The first group continued to emphasize social action of the organized masses, believing that such pressure would also force the rich people of the J.D.C. to help Palestine; whereas the American leaders preferred a middle-class style of social action, such as concentrating on raising money for Palestine. By 1919, the American leaders were all busy with fund-raising and were not willing to dedicate themselves to any other activity in the organization. They were trying to attract other Jewish members of their class, the wealthier and more established German Jews, and saw this as a prerequisite to the success of their fund-raising.[59] The Eastern European leaders, on the other hand, tried to organize the masses to put pressure on organizations like the J.D.C. and the A.J.C. to contribute from their wealth to the cause of Palestine. Their approach therefore followed from their position in the social structure of American Jewry as well as from their commitment to a different culture and certain ideological principles.

These two approaches to the problems of organization, along with the vacillation of the American leaders in deciding the precise principle or organization on which to operate—that of a middle-class cadre party or a mass party—were symptomatic of the more basic problem that has been discussed. A cadre party was better for attacting the more established German Jews to join the Zionist Organization and for building an efficient fund-raising machine. But the source of power of the Brandeis group in the Jewish community was the hold they had on the Jewish masses that the A.J.C. people lacked. Giving up the leadership of a mass organization would have resulted in the weakening of their position vis-à-vis the A.J.C. leaders.

The Search for a New Ideology

The difficulties of the American Zionist leaders were accelerated by the contradiction between a mass movement and a limited specific program. A mass movement needs a broad political ideology that captures the imagination of the members and evokes their loyalty. This cannot be served by a limited and specific goal, demanding from the members restricted activity and a commitment like fund-raising.

Did the Zionist Organization provide such an ideology that could evoke "a deep feeling of common loyalty" and a "psychological identi-

---

[59] Wise to Brandeis, March 10, 1919, ibid.

fication" with the movement?[60] The ideology had originally no appeal for the Jewish masses, its influence being restricted to the Jewish intelligentsia. After 1914, its influence among the masses in the United States increased because it succeeded in evoking nationalist sentiments among the Eastern European masses through the American Jewish Congress movement. But, as we have explained, the increase of nationalist sentiment among the Eastern European masses displeased the American-born leaders, most of whom were always cool to the idea of Jewish nationalism in the United States. After 1917, this displeasure turned into an active attempt to halt the strengthening of nationalist sentiment among the masses.

The American Zionist leaders were unwilling to be associated with "the metaphysical, somewhat mystical" ideas of Jewish nationalism that inspired the members.[61] But to hold the membership of the mass organization together, they needed an inspiring ideology. So they looked for a siutable idea to substitute for the idea of Jewish nationalism and at the same time to unite all Jews, Eastern European immigrants, and Germans.

In their attempt to find a new content for Zionism that would be more acceptable to themselves, would attract the Jewish masses, and at the same time would provide Zionism with an idea to counterbalance the idea of nationalism, the American German-Jewish progressives were soon stimulated by trends and developments within the dominant society. The entrance of the United States into World War I resulted in a new lease on life for progressive ideas. The Wilson administration embarked on a scheme for economic planning, and this led to new progressive legislation. This movement, it was said, started in the latter part of 1917, gathered momentum in 1918, but came rapidly to an end the next year.[62]

This short upsurge of progressivism in the United States corresponded to the period when the American Zionist leaders, many of whom held positions of influence in the Wilson administration, were stressing the point that in Palestine, in the future Jewish commonwealth, progressive principles of economic and social order should prevail. Furthermore, they insisted that this was the essence of Zionism.

Mack, in his *Americanism and Zionism* published in 1918, defined Zionism in two possible ways: "The reasons for favoring the British Declaration, for becoming a Zionist, are various; some join the movement

---

[60] Gunnar Myrdal, *An American Dilemma* (New York: Harper and Bros., 1944), p. 713.
[61] Notes written by de Haas in June, 1921, *de Haas Papers*.
[62] Arthur M. Schlesinger, Jr., *The Crisis of the Old Order, 1919–1933* (Boston: Houghton Mifflin Co., 1957), chapt. 6.

because they believe that from its realization will come a revival and a deepening of the religious feeling of the Jews in Palestine and in other lands; others because they believe that the Jews of old set an ideal for social justice that the world has not reached and that may be attained in the Jewish commonwealth."[63]

Significantly, the nationalist interpretation of Zionism was missing. The two alternative interpretations were the religious, which might have appealed to people like Schiff and his friends, and the idea of social justice in Palestine, which appealed to the Jewish progressives. This so-called Social Zionism was a new emphasis in the Zionist doctrine.[64]

The crowning effort of the progressive leaders of the Z.O.A. was the new Zionist program that they submitted together with the reorganization plan to the annual convention in 1918. The aim of this program, known as the Pittsburgh Program, was to bring the Zionist political program up to date. The text, drafted by Brandeis and some of his close associates, is given here in full:

> We desire to affirm anew the principles which have guided the Zionist Movement since its inception and which were the foundation of the ancient Jewish state and of the living Jewish law embodied in the traditions of two thousand years of exile.
>
> First, We declare for political and civil equality irrespective of race, sex or faith of all the inhabitants of the land.
>
> Second, To insure in the Jewish national home in Palestine equality of opportunity we favor a policy which with due regard to existing rights, shall tend to establish the ownership and control by the whole people of the land, of all natural resources and of all public utilities.
>
> Third, All land, owned or controlled by the whole people should be leased on such conditions as will insure the fullest opportunity for development and continuity of possession.
>
> Fourth, The co-operative principle should be applied so far as feasible in the organization of all agricultural industrial, commercial and financial undertakings.
>
> Fifth, The system of free public instruction which is to be established should embrace all grades and departments of education.
>
> Sixth, Hebrew, the national langauge of the Jewish people, shall be the medium of public instruction.[65]

The application of these principles to the Jewish community in Palestine became the official program of the Z.O.A. The program was also an

---

[63] Julian W. Mack, *Americanism and Zionism* (New York: The Federation of American Zionists, 1918), p. 13.
[64] See Bernard A. Rosenblatt, *Social Zionism* (New York: The Public Publishing Co., 1919), with an introduction by Julian Mack, the president of the Z.O.A.
[65] "The Pittsburgh Program," *The Maccabean* 31 (August 1918): 237.

unconscious attempt to make the whole movement of those strange Eastern European enthusiasts for the regeneration of the land of Palestine and the revival of its language and culture somewhat more understandable to the leaders of the Z.O.A. This political program, however, was utterly meaningless to the Eastern European masses and their intellectuals. For them, the mystical revivalist nationalist aspect of the return from exile and the reestablishment of the ancient homeland in its historical boundaries was the essence of the Zionist idea. This the new program neglected.

The American Yiddish press of the period ignored the Pittsburgh Program. The same papers reported the proceedings of the Zionist annual convention of 1918 extensively, yet, though they noted in detail discussions of reorganization that took place at the convention, they scarcely paid any attention to the declaration of principles. Nowhere in the Yiddish press, except in the official publications of the organization, can one find the text of the Pittsburgh Program. There were at most a few passing comments. Goldberg commented a year after the issuance of the declaration that the program was written "by a few doctrinaires, but most people are not conscious of what it really meant."[66]

And so the problem of providing an ideal to motivate members and party workers and attract new recruits to the mass organization was not solved. Furthermore, the episode of the Pittsburgh Program demonstrated in no uncertain terms how utterly out of touch the American-born leaders were with their Eastern European followers.

Toward the end of 1919, the dilemma of the heads of the Z.O.A. became more acute. The growth of anti-Semitism in the United States made them anxious to dissociate themselves from Lower East Side Jewish nationalism, but their continued inability to unite their group with the wealthy Jewish philanthropists from the A.J.C. on terms acceptable to them forced them to rely on a mass organization composed of Eastern European nationalists. They were unable to come up with ideas that would both attract the Jewish masses and provide a substitute for nationalist sentiments. Frankfurter urged his colleagues to evolve an affirmative policy, but they were unable to do so.[67] Instead, they tried desperately to raise funds and to assert their position in the community through success in their endeavor. But they could not succeed so long as the established and wealthy German Jewish community refused to cooperate with them.

---

[66] Abraham Goldberg, "Organization: Essence of the Idea," *The Maccabean* 32 (December 1919): 336–37.

[67] De Haas to Brandeis, December 10, 1919, *Brandeis Papers*.

The abandon with which these leaders threw themselves into the fund-raising campaign can have been an escape from the mounting pressures of their intolerable situation. Fund-raising was also a typical social action of their class. During the period from 1914 to 1916 Brandeis managed to lead his followers away from this course after he realized that they needed other ways to attain a leading position in American Jewry. In the atmosphere of mounting nationalistic sentiments in the United States after World War I, it was Brandeis and his associates who perceived fund-raising for the colonies in Palestine to be the only activity that did not conflict with their other loyalties and obligations as Americans.

These self-imposed limitations on their status as Jews were not in accord with the needs and wishes of the Eastern European community at the time. They needed a total attachment to their Jewishness during this time of transition when they were strangers in their new land and still treasured their old culture. This attachment was strengthened by the new wave of anti-Semitism in the United States.

Thus, we see that the dispute over the structure of the Zionist Organization had a deeper meaning. The Eastern European intellectuals considered theirs and all Jews' status of over-riding importance among their various statuses. They were aiming, therefore, at a Zionist mass movement that would awaken loyalties to the group and make the members live their emotional, spiritual, and intellectual lives as Jews within the Zionist Organization. It is in this context that we have to examine their resistance to the abolition of the Zionist societies in 1918 and to their demand for cultural and educational activities within the organization, of which fund-raising for Palestine would be only one anciliary function.

Anxiety and Frustration among the German-Jewish Zionist Leaders

After 1917, and especially after the reorganization of the Z.O.A. in 1918, the American leaders threw themselves into the task of fund-raising for the building of Palestine but were unsuccessful. Although the exact figures of the funds collected by the Zionists in the United States are not available, that they declined was readily admitted.[68] De Haas maintained that between 1919 and 1920, the Z.O.A. collected less than

---

[68] De Haas to Brandeis, October 20, 1919, *de Haas Papers*.

$2.5 million, while the J.D.C., for example, during the same period, collected $27 million.[69]

More dramatic was the decline in membership. The fluctuations in membership figures between 1917 and 1920 were remarkable. From about 22,000 in 1917, membership rose to 144,235 in 1918; it went down to 56,838 in 1919, and a year later the Z.O.A. had only 21,000 members.[70]

The sudden rise in membership in 1918 was attributed to the effects of the British government's Balfour Declaration, issued in November 1917. This declaration was supported by President Wilson.

The decline in membership was also, in part, a reaction to events and moods of the larger American society. The Red Scare that prevailed in the United States during 1918 and 1919 had strong anti-Semitic overtones. Anti-Semitism spread in the United States in the following years. "Nationalism reverted in 1920 and thereafter to a racial bias."[71] In this social climate, many Jews did not wish to remain members of an international organization dedicated to the revival of the Jewish nation.

Furthermore, following the reorganization of the Z.O.A. in 1918, it was becoming a cadre party which needed only militant members who were willing to devote a substantial amount of their time and energies to fund-raising activities.

By 1919, the American-born Zionist leaders' sole concern was fund-raising for the economic development of Palestine. In the middle of 1919, they again entered negotiations with the A.J.C.

There were several reasons for the willingness of the Jewish philanthropists to unite with the Brandeis group. One was the weakening of their position as representatives of the Jews in Washington. The influence and power of the Brandeis group was manifested in their successful negotiations with the American and British governments in securing the Balfour Declaration. The philanthropists now desired to maintain their position as representatives of American Jewry in Wash-

---

[69] De Haas, *Louis D. Brandeis* (New York: Bloch Publishing Co., 1929), p. 72. These figures are presented in an attempt to demonstrate the success of the administration which was defeated in 1921. These figures are therefore the most favorable account of their activities. For the J.D.C. see: Joseph C. Hyman, *Twenty-Five Years of American Aid to Jews Overseas: A Record of the Joint Distribution Committee* (New York, 1939), p. 19.

[70] Samuel Halperin, *The Political World of American Zionism* (Detroit: Wayne State University Press, 1961), p. 327.

[71] Higham, *Strangers in the Land*, p. 262.

ington and realized that they had to take the influential Brandeis group into partnership if they wanted to succeed.[72]

The philanthropists were also willing to cooperate with the Zionists in the building up of Palestine because the American and British governments openly favored the idea of a Jewish homeland in Palestine. They felt that all Jews should insist that the settlement of Palestine be as well directed as possible. "Otherwise all Jewry, whether they were in it or not, would have to stand the blame."[73]

The main reason, however, for the desire of the A.J.C. to cooperate with Brandeis remained their belief that he alone could persuade the Jewish masses to become more moderate and give up their idea of Jewish nationalism. They hoped the Jewish masses under Brandeis's influence would restrict themselves to helping their European brethren settle in Palestine and not concern themselves with the political future of Palestine, since this might create complications for them as American citizens. It seems that Brandeis was willing to settle with the philanthropists on such terms. He now supported ideas like the stoppage of immigration to Palestine to create better and healthier conditions for immigration. His speeches in 1919 were mostly about the need to eradicate malaria as a precondition for mass immigration. Felix Warburg reported to a colleague on the negotiations with Brandeis:

> It is a matter of importance to know that Justice Brandeis is, like you and I and many others, going to recognize the fact that political Zionism for the present is dead and can in any event not be resurrected until Palestine shall in reality become a Jewish land, a prospect that cannot be realized for many a decade . . . *and since it cannot be doubted that Justice Brandeis's voice is more or less determining upon his considerable following*, what he says . . . is going to decide, to a far-reaching extent, the question whether American Jewry at least will become united on the Palestinian problem or whether it shall continue to be strongly divided in Zionist and anti-Zionist camps, as had been heretofore the case to the great detriment of the Jewish interest [italics mine].[74]

Brandeis met with Marshall on October 23, 1919, and suggested some specific economic projects for Palestine. He insisted, however, that these should be carried out by the Z.O.A., which, he explained, "ceased to be a party or a fighting organization and became a developing organization."[75]

---

[72] Felix Warburg to Max Senior, January 17, 1919, in *Felix Warburg Papers* (Cincinnati: American Jewish Archives).
[73] Quoted by Mack in a letter to Brandeis, December 8, 1919, *Brandeis Papers*.
[74] Warburg to Israel Zangwill, August 14, 1919, *Warburg Papers*.
[75] Brandeis to Mack, October 24, 1919, *Brandeis Papers*.

Conflicts within the Zionist Organization, 1916–20 131

Marshall himself was sympathetic to the specific projects recommended by Brandeis, but he wanted to build a new and special organization to carry them out. On this point, and only on this point, Brandeis disagreed. Their differences were not on goals, "some specific projects in Palestine," but on the organization that would carry them out. Brandeis insisted that it should be done by the old Zionist Organization. He was ready to enlarge it and reorganize it, but not to join with Marshall in a new organization. Consequently the negotiations between the two broke down again because of the desire of each group to gain an advantage over the other in the power struggle between them.

The pressure on the American Zionist leaders of the Z.O.A. mounted when American-born members began to defect. On December 2, Mack reported to Brandeis that two important members dropped out of the Finance committee, and soon more members left the organization because of their disagreements with the Eastern European nationalist agitation.[76]

Howard Gans, for example, left to join the J.D.C. and became one of its heads. Before his resignation, he explained his dissatisfaction as being caused by the extreme nationalism of the Jewish masses. This, he felt, was endangering the position of Jews in America as it led to an increase in anti-Semitism.[77] The association of the Z.O.A. with those radical nationalistic elements made him unhappy. As a remedy, he suggested dispensing with the mass organization. The Z.O.A. needed fewer members and more money. The organization should be less democratic and, consequently, more efficiently run.

What he suggested was, in Duverger's terms, to convert the Zionist movement from a mass organization to a cadre party without ideologies. Members would be those who could contribute money to Palestinian projects and influence enough other people to contribute. Although at the time Mack rejected the plan, a few months later he tried to reorganize the Z.O.A. along those very lines.

While the top Z.O.A. leaders were not yet willing to follow Gans's advice, Brandeis's leadership completely lost the protest quality which it had during the agitation for an American Jewish Congress. His was becoming an accommodation leadership not suitable or appealing to the agitated Eastern European masses in the post-war United States. Bran-

---
[76] Mack to Brandeis, December 2, 1919, *de Haas Papers*.
[77] Mack to Felix Frankfurter, November 14, 1919, *Brandeis Papers*.

deis's associates gained their social experience in committees, not as orators in mass meetings.[78] Among the whole group of American Zionist leaders at the head of the Z.O.A. only one, Wise, had the temperament and ability suited for a leader in a mass organization. All of those who remember Wise recall his popularity as orator in mass meetings. He was the only leader of the period to suggest using direct action to persuade the masses to give up their idea of Jewish nationalism. One such example was his suggestion to publish a Yiddish paper in order to propagate Brandeis's group ideas among the Yiddish-speaking masses.[79]

Brandeis refused to adopt this suggestion. He never specified the reasons for this refusal, and they can only be inferred. One of them seems to have been that in the nationalistic and anti-Semitic climate of opinion in the United States, the Brandeis group was afraid even to mention aloud that their associates in the Zionist Organization supported such dangerous ideas as Jewish nationalism. In the next chapter we shall see that, at the height of their struggle with the European Zionist leaders, they refused to discuss these questions for fear the American anti-Semites and the anti-Zionist German Jews would misinterpret their utterances and confuse the American public.

Instead of trying to enlist the support of the Jewish masses, they continued, notwithstanding their disappointments, to try to cooperate with the A.J.C. By the end of 1919, they wanted to unite with the Jewish philanthropists in a joint campaign for funds for Palestine. A meeting was called at Schiff's house on December 14, and a committee was elected, chaired by Judge Irving Lehman with Brandeis and Schiff as honorary vice-chairmen.[80] Some arrangements for a joint campaign were eventually made, but none of the partners was satisfied with them and nothing came out of them.

The Z.O.A. leaders continued, unsuccessfully, with their attempts to raise money and enlist the support of the German Jews. In their disappointment and frustration, they blamed the Eastern European nationalists for all their troubles and for their failure to persuade the German Jews to help Palestine. In one letter, which Mack pessimistically wrote to Brandeis in the middle of a fund-raising tour, he explained that the big obstacle to its success was the issue of Diaspora nationalism "that moves all my friends here." And Mack ended on a bitter note: "this nonsensical political nationality business."[81]

---

[78] Abraham Goldberg, "Organization: Essence of the Idea," *The Maccabean* 32 (December 1919): 336.
[79] Wise to Brandeis, April 22, 1919, *Brandeis Papers*.
[80] Mack to Schiff, December 5, 1919, *Schiff Papers*.
[81] Mack to Brandeis, March 8, 1920, *de Haas Papers*.

Conflicts within the Zionist Organization, 1916–20

Thus we see that between 1916 and 1920, the Z.O.A. witnessed an increase in the misunderstandings and antagonisms between the American-born top leaders and the Eastern European party workers. Furthermore, there existed a growing ideological split between the American-born and American-educated leaders and the recent Eastern European immigrant followers. This did not result, however, in the top leaders' losing their leadership of the Z.O.A. They were reelected by big majorities at every annual convention. Even after the 1919 annual convention, Ephraim Caplan, the Yiddish journalist, explained that the only reason the membership did not replace the leadership was that they did not have any alternative.[82] In the 1919 convention, after starting with a vigorous attack, the opposition did not even press for a vote of no confidence. Brandeis invited the opposition leaders to his hotel suite and persuaded them to withdraw their motion.[83] The annual convention of 1920 was the first in which Brandeis did not appear in the lobbies. But the mere mention of his name by the administration leaders as their head was sufficient to save them from defeat. This was the opinion of most observers. Abraham Goldberg, one of the opposition leaders, maintained that the reason the administration survived was that the members invoked the name of Brandeis, while the opposition did not have any impressive leaders as alternatives.[84] When the administration offered a vote of thanks to Brandeis for his leadership in the London Conference at which he broke with Chaim Weizmann, the world leader of Zionism, the opposition, which later supported Weizmann against Brandeis, crumbled and all voted for the resolution. Goldberg himself admitted that the opposition within the Z.O.A. would never have challenged the top leaders "had not the Brandeis group begun its campaign against the World Zionist Executive—against Weizmann and others. Brandeis numbered among his supporters most of the illustrious and wealthy Zionists, whereas the opposition was headed by men who—with few exceptions—were unknown."[85]

Thus, we witness a complete break between the top leaders—the outsiders—and the party workers and bureaucrats of the Z.O.A. The bureaucrats were in control of the organization and shared a common moral and intellectual background with the masses, while the top leaders were far removed from them and their values. Yet all this did not result in the leaders losing their place in the Zionist Organization. The political

---

[82] Ephraim Caplan, *The Jewish Morning Journal*, September 19, 1919.
[83] Interview with Neumann, January 26, 1961.
[84] Abraham Goldberg, *The Jewish Morning Journal*, December 7, 1920.
[85] Abraham Goldberg, "Zionism in America: A Chronicle of Its Development," in *Theodor Herzl: A Memorial*, ed. Meyer Weigal (New York, 1929), p. 221.

class in control of the organization and the rank and file did not attempt to replace the top leaders, the leaders from the periphery.

In the next chapter, we will examine the events that led to the defeat of Brandeis's leadership in the Z.O.A.

CHAPTER VI

The Struggle over Control of the World Zionist Organization

Sources of Friction between the American and European Leaders

The literature dealing with the power struggle between the American Zionist leadership of Louis Brandeis and the European leaders headed by Chaim Weizmann, the president of the World Zionist Organization (W.Z.O.), stresses the personalities of the two leaders as an important cause for the misunderstandings between the two groups. Differences in the temperament of both are emphasized, and the cultural backgrounds of Weizmann, the Eastern European Jew, and Brandeis, the American-born lawyer, are contrasted. These factors are important for our understanding of the struggle between the two and of their different approaches to the issues faced by the Zionist Organization after the end of World War I. Our intention in this book, however, is to take into account other important factors that have to do with the positions of the leaders in the Zionist Organization and their positions in the social structure of their respective societies. Their group affiliations, status-sets, and role relations, rather than their personality traits, will be analyzed.

We have explained that Brandeis and his associates devoted only part of their time and energies to their roles as leaders of the Zionist Organization. Their position of leadership in the Jewish community and the Zionist Organization was attained, as we have seen, by virtue of the position they had already achieved in the dominant society. As a result, one could have anticipated that they viewed their position in the dominant American society as of greater significance and importance than their position within the Jewish community. They were, moreover, ignorant of Jewish culture and tradition, bound instead to the culture of the American society into which they were born and educated and from which they had derived their values and ideas.

Most of the European Zionist leaders of Eastern European background had as their prime interest and concern their standing in the Jewish world. Even while they called themselves Russian Jews, they meant only that they shared a certain tradition with the Russian branch of the Jewish people rather than with the Russian people. Their knowledge of Russian and European culture supplemented rather than supplanted their knowledge of Jewish culture, to which they pledged their first allegiance.

One asset enjoyed by Weizmann's leadership was not shared by the Eastern European intellectuals in the United States. At the same time as Weizmann and his friends, whose first loyalty was to the Jewish people, achieved leadership within the movement, they also achieved a position of some renown in the dominant societies within which they dwelt. Weizmann was a professor in the University of Manchester and achieved a worldwide reputation as a chemist. Nahum Sokolow, his closest association, was a noted writer and journalist in Poland and Russia. Shmarya Levin, another prominent Zionist leader, had been a member of the Russian parliament. But although their reputations helped them reach and maintain their leadership in the Zionist movement, neither they nor their followers ever perceived their position outside the Jewish community as their main source of power within the Zionist movement and the Jewish community. Nor had they any doubt that their Jewish status demanded their total loyalty.

In 1918, when a Zionist Commission had to be created to represent the W.Z.O. interests in Palestine, it was natural for Weizmann to resign his post at the University of Manchester and go to Palestine as its head. Nor had he difficulty in recruiting other Eastern European leaders to join him. But when he requested that a distinguished American Zionist join them, not one such volunteer could be found.

Weizmann first wrote to Brandeis suggesting that he resign his position on the Supreme Court and join the commission; Brandeis would not think of it. Weizmann wrote again, expressed his regret, and asked Brandeis to appoint some other person as a substitute.[1] Brandeis responded by appointing Stephen Wise, the president of the P.Z.C. However, after some hesitation, Wise refused to go.

It is clear that Wise's refusal to join the commission was caused by his unwillingness to give up his other positions and activities in the United States, which he deemed of greater importance than going abroad to devote his career solely to the Zionist cause.[2] In fact, he was ready to give up "a very considerable portion" of his time to the cause, but never all of his time.[3]

This was the attitude of all the American leaders. They all devoted most of their time to other positions, which they were unwilling to give up regardless of the needs of the Zionist Organization. Julian Mack was

---

[1] Weizmann to Brandeis, January 14, 1918, *Louis D. Brandeis Papers* (Louisville, Ky.: University of Louisville Law Library).
[2] Wise to Brandeis, February 26, 1918, ibid.
[3] Wise to Heller, February 13, 1916, *Max Heller Papers* (Cincinnati: The American Jewish Archives).

another member of the leadership group who refused to serve on the commission.

Having refused to serve on the Zionist Commission for Palestine, the American Zionist leadership was at a loss where to turn.[4] Rather than consider giving this important job to any of their Eastern European lieutenants, who were certainly willing to go, they preferred not to fill the post at all. Thus, after all efforts to find a volunteer failed, Brandeis cabled Weizmann: "International situation definitely renders American membership on commission impossible."[5]

Brandeis's refusal to assume the leadership of the W.Z.O. at the Zionist Conference in London in 1920 should not have come as a surprise. Many observers both at the time and later who analyzed the reasons for his refusal maintained that Weizmann would have employed his political skills to maintain control over the executive of the W.Z.O. even if Brandeis had agreed to serve, and hence the offer was not made in good faith. This opinion is not supported by facts. Furthermore, it underestimates Brandeis's impressive political skills. But, what is most important, such considerations certainly did not play a role in his reasons for refusing the job. Brandeis himself offered many reasons for his refusal: if he went, the anti-Semites in the United States would claim that American Jews had a loyalty to their group above their loyalties to the American society; that, in his position in the Supreme Court he could render better help to the Zionist cause than if he gave it up for full time Zionist activity, etc. It seems, however, that the main reason was explained to the American delegates to the London Conference, where he stated that he "represented independently of being on the bench, in a certain sense the Liberal, Progressives . . . hope in American life."[6] Loyalty to these causes took precedence over his duty to Zionism and the Jewish people.

In this same speech, he expressed the wish to be in a position to advise the Zionist executive. It can be demonstrated that what Brandeis really desired was to control the W.Z.O. as he controlled the Z.O.A. Since he could not openly lead the W.Z.O. without abandoning the Supreme Court, he wished to control the organization behind the scenes and thus maintain his position on "the highest bench of the world," on the one hand, and direct the Zionist Organization from Washington,

---

[4] Mack to Brandeis, February 25, 1918, *Brandeis Papers*.
[5] Brandeis telegram to Weizmann, April 5, 1918, ibid.
[6] Minutes of the meeting of American delegation to the London Conference, July 14, 1920, *Jacob de Haas Papers* (New York: Zionist Archives).

on the other.⁷ It was this highly ambitious attempt that eventually also lost him his control over the Z.O.A.

Controlling the W.Z.O. and its activities in London and Palestine presented a greater challenge to Brandeis. His major weakness in this endeavor was that he had no trustworthy associates whom he could send to these areas of operation, since his lieutenants were willing to devote only part of their time to Zionist activities and refused to depart from the United States for any length of time. It was in a moment of truth that Mack wrote: ". . . until America can offer Palestine real leaders . . . we shall be at a disadvantage. Their leaders [the European Zionists] are giving their lives to the work and are ready to give them in Palestine. Ours are not yet prepared for this."⁸

We have attributed the source of the power of Brandeis's leadership in the American Zionist Organization to the high prestige Brandeis enjoyed in American society, prestige that could not be matched by any other Jewish leader in the United States. As long as no such alternative leadership emerged, his hold over the Zionist Organization remained firm in spite of his alienating the whole political class of the organization, who were blatantly kept away from the decision-making process. His self-imposed limitations as a leader, which made him silent and invisible, weakened his grip over the organization, but did not lose him control as long as there was no alternative leadership to challenge him.

It might be expected that such an alternative leadership would consist of a person or persons who enjoyed more or equal prestige among their followers. Thus, we would expect that leadership to be derived from a position of eminence in the dominant society or to have access to some other source of prestige that would be rated as high or higher in the eyes of the followers.

Let us, therefore, examine alternative leadership from 1919 to 1921 by focusing on the relations between the American leaders, Brandeis's associates, and the European Zionist leaders, and by observing how the latter managed to secure the allegiance of the Eastern European intellectuals, the political class in the Z.O.A., and the support of the Jewish masses.

Relations between the world Zionist leaders and the American heads of the Z.O.A. were strained from the start. As soon as the war was over, Zionist activities moved to London and Palestine, with London, the government seat of the power that ruled Palestine, becoming the head-

---

⁷ Ibid.
⁸ Mack to Martin Meyer, January 13, 1921, *de Haas Papers*.

quarters of the Zionist Organization. Activities were, for a time, also centered in Paris, where the Peace Conference took place in 1919. Palestine became the seat of the Zionist Commission for Palestine, which had supervised Zionist activities there since 1918.

Contacts between American and European leaders were made in Paris and later in London in 1919. The American Jewish Congress elected a committee, headed by Marshall of the A.J.C., to represent American Jewry at the Peace Conference. They were instructed by the Congress to secure autonomous civil and political rights for the Jews in Eastern European countries and the right of free immigration for the Jews to Palestine. Most members on this committee were members of the Z.O.A. It consisted of Mack, Wise, Jacob de Haas, Bernard Flexner, and Felix Frankfurter—the last two as advisers from the American leadership group—and Bernard Richards, Joseph Barondess, Bernard Levinthal, and a few others who were Eastern Europeans. The American delegation confronted the delegates from Eastern Europe, and for the first time the American Zionists came into direct contact with the Eastern European Zionists. The Zionists in control of the London office were also, by and large, of Eastern European origin. From the beginning, the two groups of Zionists, those from the United States and those from Europe, disagreed on many issues.

This cleavage became even clearer when Brandeis visited Paris and London in August 1919 and met with the European Zionist leaders to discuss and agree on a common policy. Their disagreement was on the policy to be pursued in Palestine. The Europeans insisted that the Zionist Commission should take charge of the Jewish community in Palestine and all its activities: control the schools and see to it that they were conducted in the Hebrew language; organize the community socially and politically; control and direct all colonization and reclamation of land; and take charge of immigration and its direction. The Americans felt that all these activities should be the functions of the British government and treated as internal affairs of the Palestinian Jewish community, with which Zionists were not to interfere. Zionists were not to build schools; all they were to do was help build industries—small industries (since Brandeis was not going to let Big Business take over as it had done in the United States) in order that the immigrants might maintain themselves and be economically self-sufficient as soon as possible. In their dedication to free competition they even objected to subsidizing immigration. Brandeis argued upon his return from Palestine in 1919 that even ahead of building small industries in Palestine, there was the need to eradicate malaria and to improve sanitary conditions in Palestine. This was to be done before beginning any mass immigration, and he therefore sent most of the money collected by the Z.O.A. to the American medical unit in Palestine.

The medical unit was organized by American Zionists who sent over to Palestine a medical staff and ample medical facilities. It was headed by Dr. Max Rubinow, an American M.D. and Ph.D. and a noted social worker and statistician. Funds for the project were provided by the Z.O.A., even though they had at a certain point asked help of the J.D.C., from which they received $200,000.[9]

The American leaders' position on the development of Palestine cannot be understood in terms of purely economic considerations. In the light of the problems they were facing in the United States at the time and the way they were attempting to solve them, we can understand why they should desire not to become too closely identified with a political Jewish community in Palestine and its national aspirations. Some people believed that the Diaspora Nationalism Doctrine meant political association with Jews outside the United States. This belief was the real source of trouble. De Haas felt this doctrine to be the source of the disagreements between Brandeis and Weizmann already in 1919.[10] And in the stormy debate of the national executive of the Z.O.A. on March 19–20, 1921, to which we shall return, both Frankfurter and Mack, in discussing the meetings in London and Paris in 1919, conceded that these economic questions were not really purely financial but involved the principle of Diaspora nationalism, which was the root of the conflict.[11]

The two concrete issues of disagreement, which can be understood only in the light of this more basic and underlying issue, were the creation of the Jewish Agency and control over the medical unit in Palestine.[12]

Weizmann and his associates suggested that a Jewish Agency be established with the sole aim of securing funds for the economic development of Palestine. In this agency the Zionists would be a minority, since the Jewish moneyed interests, who were largely non-Zionist, would play

---

[9] *American Zionist Medical Unit for Palestine* (New York: The Zionist Organization of America, 1919), p. 8.
[10] Memorandum on the history of Zionism written by de Haas in 1921, *de Haas Papers*.
[11] Minutes of the meeting of the national executive of the Z.O.A., March 19–20, 1921, ibid.
[12] The creation of a Jewish Agency to represent the interests of the Jewish people in Palestine was provided by the agreement that granted the mandate on Palestine to Great Britain. According to the statutes of the mandate, approved by the League of Nations, the Zionist Organization was to fulfill the functions of the Jewish Agency but was expected to invite other Jewish bodies to take part in it.

Struggle over Control of the World Zionist Organization

the leading role. The Zionist Organization would thus be free to concentrate on its main function in Palestine and in the Diaspora, the awakening of Jewish consciousness through the revival of the Hebrew language and literature. Their work, called in Zionist parlance *gegenwartsarbeit*, was considered a prerequisite for the building up of Palestine as a Jewish state by the Jewish people. Brandeis and his associates, as has been seen, disapproved of *gegenwartsarbeit*, for this meant the continuance of the nationalistic propaganda and agitation that was going on in the United States among the Eastern Europeans, and to which the American leaders were uncompromisingly opposed.

Thus, Brandeis suggested making the Zionist Organization the Jewish Agency for Palestine, to devote itself solely to the economic development of Palestine and to invite into the organization all Jews interested in contributing to the goal. This was his position with regard to the Z.O.A. in the United States, as was shown in his negotiations with Jacob Schiff in 1917, and this policy he advocated for the W.Z.O. He even hoped that by attracting Europeans, mainly British Jewish businessmen, to join the organization, they would help him persuade members of the A.J.C. to join.[13]

Friction between the two leaderships even preceded the meetings in 1919. The first member of the American leadership to meet the European leaders in their London headquarters after the war was Wise. Upon his return at the beginning of 1919, he attacked Weizmann severely for his policies in Palestine and for his autocratic style of leadership. At the meeting of the national executive of the Z.O.A., he accused Weizmann of trying to assume total control and of excluding the Americans.[14] This was a rather surprising accusation from the man who earlier refused to join the Zionist Commission. How was Weizmann to share his leadership with them? This impossible situation confronting the American leaders, arising from their desire to share responsibility for activities in Palestine while refusing to go there, plagued them continuously and led to the emergence of a solution along the lines of Brandeis's relations with the Z.O.A. The Americans desired to organize the W.Z.O. in such a way as to be able to control activities from the United States without having to leave the country for any length of time.

De Haas's task in London, where he was sent even before Wise's re-

---

[13] Mack to Brandeis, November 20, 1920, *Brandeis Papers*.
[14] Minutes of the meeting of the National Executive of the Z.O.A., February 9, 1919, *de Haas Papers*.

turn, was to negotiate with Weizmann on the issues Wise raised. In de Haas's reports to Brandeis from January to April 1919, his main concern was the unruliness of the office and the anarchic way in which business was conducted. "The term organization and system are blanks to them," de Haas complained in one report.[15] He was trying to urge Weizmann "to do things in an organized and responsible manner." He ended his report asserting, "I am determined to try to remedy the situation."[16]

In the ensuing two years, it became habitual for Brandeis and his associates to complain of the disorder, mismanagement, careless bookkeeping, and waste in the operations in London and Palestine. Such accusations were not unfounded, and it was not surprising that Brandeis, the proponent of "scientific management," was profoundly disturbed by this state of affairs. But the zeal of the American group to put things in order was intensified by their desire to facilitate their control from New York and Washington over activities abroad. For such control, more orderly bookkeeping and administrative procedures were imperative. For this same reason, the American leaders repeatedly sent qualified administrators and businessmen to look things over in London and Palestine. In the middle of 1919, Robert Kesselman, comptroller of the Z.O.A., was sent to Palestine. Brandeis took time to write to him in Jerusalem: "It will be valuable for you to write at least once a month to Judge Mack or Mr. de Haas reporting generally on things as you see them."[17] Another member of the national executive, Emanuel Mohl, a businessman, was sent on a similar mission.[18] Robert Szold, a corporation lawyer and the nephew of Henrietta Szold, started his Zionist activities by going to Palestine to put things in order. He first joined the Zionist Commission and then returned as a kind of court of inquiry upon their activities.[19]

That the Americans did not stay in Palestine infuriated the Russian Jews who had settled in Palestine and were totally committed to the

---

[15] De Haas to Brandeis, February 21, 1919, ibid.
[16] De Haas to Mack, January 22, 1919, ibid.
[17] Brandeis to Robert Kesselman, December 15, 1919, ibid.
[18] De Haas to Kesselman, November 25, 1919, ibid.
[19] In an attempt to pacify Brandeis and the American leaders, the World Zionist Executive appointed a Reorganization Commission to examine the operations of the organization in Palestine (Minutes of the meeting of the Zionist Executive, London, September 21, 1920, *de Haas Papers*). Robert Szold was asked to be a member on this commission, and he agreed to serve, provided he could return to America by the end of the year (Szold telegram to Julius Simon, London, October 7, 1920, *de Haas Papers*). A report was submitted on March 1, 1921, but the members of the commission resigned before its publication, claiming that the executive was ignoring their work. (*The New Palestine*, May 6, 1921, pp. 4–7.)

Struggle over Control of the World Zionist Organization 143

Zionist ideal. It also exasperated Brandeis, who realized full well the difficulties of controlling operations from afar. In one of his letters on the subject, he stated: "I wish we might make them [American Zionists in Palestine] take the vows to stay put when once they get there."[20]

Relations between the visiting Americans and the Russian Jews in Palestine were deteriorating rapidly. The immediate source of friction was control over the operation of the medical unit. One aspect of the conflict was the American's refusal to conduct their operations in the Hebrew language, which the European Zionists maintained was the duty of all Zionists in Palestine. The insistence of Menachem Ussishkin, the head of the Zionist Commission, that Hebrew be the official language of the medical unit angered the head of the unit, Dr. Rubinow, who complained to New York about the waste involved. He argued that his letters, which he wrote in English, were first translated in Jerusalem into Hebrew and then sent to London, where they were translated again into English for the benefit of the Zionists' London office.[21] The Russian Zionists struggled to master the strange language, sincerely believing that this was part and parcel of their task of regenerating Jews in their ancient homeland. The Americans flatly refused to accept such hardships, which they considered ridiculous and unnecessary. The Eastern European point of view was explained by Dr. Ben-Zion Mossinsohn, the headmaster of the first Hebrew-speaking high school in Palestine: ". . . [In the] American Medical Unit where all the writing was done in English . . . we had to wage a struggle for every Hebrew word, a struggle in which the threat of boycott was heard. There is no danger of Russification in Palestine. There is only the danger of the creation of an English-American-Jewish aristocracy, which will look down on the natives of Palestine Jewry."[22]

Reluctant to discuss more fundamental differences and realizing their shortage of people on the spot, the Americans wanted to assume control from New York, over the heads of the London office. They decided to send money for the medical unit to the London office, earmarked for the unit and accompanied by an order that it be distributed only by its director. Furthermore, the national executive decided in its meeting in

---

[20] Brandeis to Mack and Bernard Flexner, February 1, 1921, *de Haas Papers*.
[21] Max Rubinow to Henrietta Szold, October 17, 1919, *Brandeis Papers*.
[22] *Report of the Proceedings of the Twenty-Fourth Annual Convention of the Zionist Organization of America.* Prepared by Maurice Samuel from the official stenographic report of the National Shorthand Reporting Committee (New York: issued by the Z.O.A., August 1921), p. 131.

November 1919 to send most of its funds to the unit rather than to other Zionist projects.[23]

In late 1919, American pressure on the London executive increased, and Brandeis notified London that "it will be impossible to raise funds by the organization in America for London-Palestine account while the London-Palestine end is so persistently ignoring American interests and views and thwarting efforts via Palestine, etc."[24]

This forced the London executive to try to come to an understanding with the American leaders. They proposed to convene in London a World Zionist conference, which would not be a full-fledged congress but rather what was called in continental procedure a *jahreskonferenz*.[25] They wanted the meeting to take place at the beginning of 1920, but the Americans, hopeful that a successful fund-raising campaign would strengthen their position at the bargaining table in London, requested a postponement until summer. Emanuel Neumann, a high official of the Z.O.A., described the national executive meeting that requested this postponement: "Mr. Brandeis stated that we should come to the *jahreskonferenz* with our coffers full, and that then—I am quoting from memory but I am sure that my quotation is substantially correct—our powers of persuasion, joined with our financial power, will help us to bring our point of view to bear at the *jahreskonferenz*."[26]

The growing misunderstanding between the American leaders and the leaders in London and Palestine was not disclosed to the public, nor did the American leaders try to enlist public support for their point of view. Even when the Yiddish press became unfriendly, because some Yiddish journalists began to expose their maneuvering, they kept quiet. The leaders did nothing to answer or refute the accusations, in spite of de Haas's insistence that something be done.[27] Their efforts were concentrated instead on renewed attempts to penetrate the respectable groups of German Jews. This task received their complete attention. When Levin, the powerful Zionist orator, wanted to go on a propaganda tour, the American Zionists prevented it, because while "he would intensify Zionism in America . . . he would repel Schiff and those who had lately started to come into line.[28]

---

[23] Minutes of the meeting of the National Executive of the Z.O.A., November 1919, *Brandeis Papers*.
[24] Brandeis to Mack and de Haas, November 15, 1919, *de Haas Papers*.
[25] A *jahreskonferenz* is a body smaller than a full-fledged congress that meets only in those years in which the congress does not convene.
[26] Emanuel Neumann, "Causes of the Conflict: A Statement of Facts," *The New Maccabean*, June 1, 1921, p. 51.
[27] De Haas to Brandeis, October 27, 1919, *Brandeis Papers*.
[28] De Haas to Brandeis, February 29, 1920, *de Haas Papers*.

The London Conference

The *jahreskonferenz* in London, which opened on June 22, was attended by an impressive American delegation headed by Brandeis. Relations between the European and American Zionist leaders were tense from the start. The Americans made clear in advance their objections to the Zionist Organization's engaging in cultural and educational activities to foster Jewish nationalism in the Diaspora—*gegenwartsarbeit*, to Zionist financing of any educational or cultural institutions and activities in Palestine, and to the constitution of a Jewish Agency as a separate organization of Zionists and non-Zionists to take care of the economic development of Palestine. They also accused the Zionist Commission in Palestine and the Zionist headquarters in London of mismanagement and inefficiency.

The conference, which lasted nearly two months, was conducted under difficult circumstances. There was no common language that all delegates understood, nor was there an accepted procedure by which to conduct the meetings. Brandeis called the whole affair a "talkfest."[29]

Brandeis set the tone of the meetings by concentrating on the mismanagement in London and Palestine, in the manner and style of a progressive crusader cleaning up the mess in an American municipality. This embarrassed even de Haas, who reported on this first meeting to Mack: "Brandeis got in with an attack on Palestine administration by the Commission, compelling me to put in the details. It was a pretty nasty business, particularly Brandeis's pressure that we could not supply funds if we did not have the cause for criticism removed."[30]

The annoyance of sensitive delegates who came from poor communities not yet rehabilitated after the destruction caused by the war was not lost on Brandeis, who confided to de Haas after the meeting that "we are not liked here."[31] The Europeans did recover, however, from their first shock, and Frankfurter reported to Mack a few days later that he found among the delegates a consciousness of their defects and readiness to make the necessary adjustments.[32] At their request, Brandeis presented his plan to remedy the situation to the *Seniorem Konvent*, the ruling committee of the conference, which consisted of a small body of the more influential delegates who discussed the issues and then presented them to the larger assembly. He did so, however, with no prior

---

[29] Brandeis to Alexander Sachs, August 5, 1920, ibid.
[30] De Haas to Mack, June 22, 1920, ibid.
[31] Ibid.
[32] Felix Frankfurter to Mack, June 29, 1920, *de Haas Papers*.

consultation with the American delegates. The delegates outside the inner circle did not even know the details of the plan, a fact that infuriated them, especially as it embarrassed them in front of the European delegates.[33]

Most important in this plan was Brandeis's suggestion to appoint an executive committee of seven members, three of whom would be non-Zionist English businessmen: Lord Reading, Sir Alfred Mond, and Baron de Rothschild; the four Zionists on the executive would be Weizmann and Sokolow for the Europeans, and Flexner and himself for the Americans. Brandeis discussed the plan with the three English businessmen before presenting it to the *Seniorem Konvent*. They were willing to work for the development of Palestine, but not to submit themselves to a process of election by the conference. Brandeis agreed, therefore, that their names should not be presented to the conference. The conference would instead give a blank check to the four Zionist leaders, who would agree to co-opt these businessmen. The *Seniorem Konvent* was unhappy with a plan that would install non-Zionist members on the Zionist executive whose task it was to conduct the affairs of a Zionist Organization. However, out of deference to Brandeis, they decided to invite Mond and Rothschild to meet with them and clarify the issues involved in their becoming members of the Zionist executive. At the meeting the delegates explained the functions of the executive. The reactions of the gentlemen to these explanations were described by de Haas: "At one o'clock in the morning these two men went out, worried about being responsible for Hebrew education in Palestine and other problems which had nothing to do with the work they have been asked to do. Brandeis had talked to them about the economic upbuilding of Palestine—not the cultural program."[34]

For the European Zionists, building up Palestine economically was only one item in the Zionist program, and it was not surprising that they refused to restrict the activities of the executive to that one aspect. It is not surprising either that the non-Zionist businessmen did not wish to be responsible for the other elements of the Zionist program. To escape from the impasse, Weizmann suggested a modified plan that was acceptable to both the *Seniorem Konvent* and the non-Zionists. He offered to create an economic council headed by these financiers that would devote exclusive attention to the economic development of Palestine. The Zionist Organization would be directed by a political execu-

---

[33] Jacob Fishman, *The Jewish Morning Journal*, August 25, 1920; minutes of the meeting of the executive committee of the Z.O.A., August 29, 1920, *de Haas Papers*.

[34] Minutes of the meeting of those who resigned their posts in Z.O.A. at Hotel Cleveland, Cleveland, June 7, 1921, ibid.

tive that would take care of all other aspects of Zionist work approved by the conference. The executive would be elected by the conference, and there seems to have been a consensus among the delegates that this executive should be headed by Brandeis.

The one who was dissatisfied with this modified plan was Brandeis. He claimed that since he had already agreed with the businessmen to make them members of the executive, and since Weizmann had also agreed with him, Weizmann's new suggestions to the *Seniorem Konvent* represented a breach of promise.[35]

Brandeis's anger at the changes made in his plan, changes that even the businessmen concerned were glad to approve, can be understood only by considering what he wanted to accomplish with the plan, and when we recall the policies that Brandeis pursued in the United States.

Brandeis aimed to restrict Zionist activities to the economic development of Palestine; to achieve this change in Zionist policy, he tried first to induce non-Zionist leaders to join the Zionist Organization, to come to an agreement with them on this limited goal of Zionism, and to present the rest of the Zionist party workers with a *fait accompli*. When the non-Zionists refused to cooperate, he reorganized the Zionist Organization in a way that he hoped would eliminate all other activities of the organization, retaining only the function of fund-raising for Palestine.

This he now attempted to do in the international organization. If his one goal had been to secure the cooperation of the non-Zionist businessmen only, then Weizmann's plan achieved it. The most plausible explanation for his bitter disappointment, which led to the complete disruption of relations with the W.Z.O., was that Weizmann's plan destroyed his own. The proposed executive, consisting of the three non-Zionist businessmen, of Sokolow and Weizmann representing the Europeans, and of Flexner and himself representing the Americans, would also have given him full control over the situation. There are no indications that at any stage of the negotiations in London Brandeis considered leaving the bench and assuming active leadership of the W.Z.O.

Once Brandeis's plan was rejected, relations between Brandeis and Weizmann deteriorated rapidly. At the meeting of the American delegation on July 14, Brandeis announced his refusal to assume command of the W.Z.O. His announcement caused great disappointment among the delegates, who appealed to him to reconsider his decision. The agitated delegation met the same evening and adopted a suggestion by de Haas

---

[35] Bernard Shelvin, *The Jewish Morning Journal*, August 1, 1920; minutes of the executive committee of the Z.O.A., August 29, 1920, *de Haas Papers*.

that they try again to persuade Brandeis to change his mind. However, at the meeting of the delegation on July 16, de Haas announced that Brandeis had already appeared before the *Seniorem Konvent* and declared that he would not assume any position "in view of the unreliability of Dr. Weizmann's methods."[36] This last explanation was not given by Brandeis when he enumerated before the American delegates the reasons that led him to refuse the leadership.

The *Seniorem Konvent* asked Brandeis to become the honorary president of the organization and to nominate another American to the executive committee. At the meeting of the American delegation on July 19, Brandeis declared himself against having an American on the executive. He suggested instead that Flexner be nominated as an adviser on economic affairs but not as a member of the executive. The reason he offered for this stand was that Flexner, as one lone American against the Europeans, could not sway the vote, so his official membership on the executive would appear to give American sanction to the European decisions, whereas as an adviser he could stand apart. Brandeis's real concern was that, given the personalities on the committee and his own absence in Washington, he would have no control over the organization. At the same time, if an American would serve on the committee, he would seem to share the responsibility. The delegation overruled him for the first time and decided to place an American on the executive. However, no one dared to assume the position. When several members suggested Louis Lipsky, he declined immediately before any vote was taken.[37] It seems that the delegates themselves were paralyzed with surprise at their own daring at having opposed Brandeis's advice, and no one was elected at that meeting. The next day Brandeis again appeared at a delegation meeting and presented an ultimatum: either they would reverse their decision of the day before or he would withdraw his acceptance of the honorary presidency. The delegation reversed its decision.[38]

The American delegation was now demoralized. Brandeis went on to propose an economic plan to which Weizmann and his associates were opposed. At the same time he refused to take any responsibility for carrying out the plan, and instead insisted that Weizmann, who opposed it, should control the executive.[39] It was only now that the majority of the delegation refused to follow Brandeis any longer. Since Brandeis

---

[36] Minutes of the meeting of the American delegation to the London Conference, July 16, 1920, ibid.
[37] Ibid., July 19, 1920.
[38] Ibid., July 20, 1920.
[39] De Haas to Mack, July 27, 1920, *de Haas Papers*.

would not assume the leadership, they did not wish to support his economic plan. It is clear that it was not the economic plan to which they objected, but rather the fact that Brandeis refused the leadership. This was conceded even by Frankfurter, who reported along these lines to Mack.[40]

Brandeis's attempt to force his economic plans for Palestine upon the conference, while at the same time insisting that Weizmann and his associates were to be its executors, did not seem logical, especially since the plan could not be implemented without changing the structure of the Zionist Organization in a way unacceptable to the Europeans.

For Weizmann and his associates, it was the Jewish people who were going to build Palestine, with the organization providing its followers the proper motivation and indoctrination and recruiting the necessary manpower of high quality. Those young pioneering Zionists who came to Palestine, called *chalutzim*, were not immigrants in the same sense as were immigrants to the United States. They were not pressed into immigration by the profit motive but by a desire, aroused in them by the Zionist movement, to lay the foundations of a Jewish state with the unique culture and language of the Jews. For them, building of industries and commerce in Palestine could not be separated from the creation of Hebrew schools and universities.

Brandeis wanted to attract small businessmen and small investors, but such people were not yet emigrating to Palestine. Manpower was the real need. Weizmann explained the situation lucidly at the meeting of the national executive of the Z.O.A., a meeting, by the way, which Brandeis refused to attend: "The chalutz must know that when he builds the Ruttenberg project [the new electric power plant] or the roads, that he will build it in such a way that not a ha'peny goes into the pocket of a private person, but into the pocket of the nation."[41]

Furthermore, the Europeans argued, investors seek profits, but the investments in Palestine had to be determined by national interest; hence investments should follow a plan worked out by the Zionist Commission. One could not follow Brandeis's advice, they argued, and leave such decisions to people with wealth or to the British government. As Weizmann put it: "Supposing a gentleman from America or London would come today and invest ten million dollars in Palestine and would employ Arab labor. He may create certain things in Palestine, but the primary effect will be that he has enriched the Arabs."[42]

---

[40] Frankfurter to Mack, August 12, 1920, ibid.
[41] Minutes of the meeting of the executive committee of the Z.O.A., April 9, 1921, ibid.
[42] Ibid.

The flaw in Brandeis's plan to attract small businessmen and induce them to migrate to or invest in Palestine lay in their lack of interest to immigrate to Palestine at the time. He expected such people to migrate from the United States as well as Europe. At the same time he could not understand the Eastern European Jewish pioneers and their source of enthusiasm and was irritated by the economic waste entailed by their migration. Limited to the American experience, he believed that progressive ideals and American experience with those ideals could be transferred to Palestine. In the economic program, known in Zionist circles as the Zeeland Program, which he drew up on board ship when returning from the London Conference, he stated: "Too much aid will demoralize the people . . . our care must, therefore, be to determine in what respect aid may be given without sapping independence and preventing or destroying the prevalence of manly self-reliance on the part of the individual settlers."[43]

The socialist ideals of the pioneers and their desire to build schools even before the profits they made could support them irked him greatly. The basic principles he advocated for American society were also these he advocated for the colonization of Palestine. Brandeis's basic faith in private enterprise, which he incorporated in his progressive views and his career as a public man in the United States, also figured in his schemes for building up Palestine. Alpheus Mason, Brandeis's biographer, summarized these ideas in the following words: ". . . Brandeis believed so strongly in private property that he wanted to see it more equitably diffused among the masses of men. He valued capital so highly that he would make it more easily available to the independent entrepreneur, rather than have it monopolized and controlled by the Money Trust. . . . Indeed, he thought of private enterprise not only as an investment of gain but also as a means of raising the individual to a creative personality."[44]

The Dilemma of the Eastern European Party Workers

Brandeis's refusal to assume the leadership of World Zionism and become the head of the W.Z.O. was a new turning point in the relations between the top leaders and their political class in the Z.O.A. In the

---

[43] De Haas, *Louis D. Brandeis* (New York: Bloch Publishing Co., 1929), pp. 267–68.
[44] Alpheus Thomas Mason, *Brandeis: A Free Man's Life* (New York: The Viking Press, 1956), p. 436.

previous chapter, we saw how the Eastern European bureaucrats and party workers were kept out of power in the American organization by an inner circle of top leaders. It is, however, important to keep in mind that, in spite of their growing resentment and their dissatisfaction with this state of affairs in the Z.O.A., their opposition never threatened the leadership, whom they reelected year after year. At the London Conference, they continued with their support almost to the end before they bolted.

An examination of the attitudes of the American Eastern Europeans toward their leaders from 1919 to 1921, when the disputes between the European and American leaders were raging, helps explain their submission to their American leaders. Since the beginning of the dispute early in 1919, many of the Eastern European party workers strongly supported their American leaders. When Wise returned from Europe and accused Weizmann in the meeting of the national executive in February of ignoring the Americans, the Eastern Europeans supported his claims, being as indignant as Wise at this affront.[45]

The first confrontation between the Eastern Europeans from the United States and their brethren who had remained in Europe, which took place during the Paris Peace Conference, found the former Eastern Europeans behind their American leaders and against their former brethren on many important issues. According to reports, the opinions of Marshall and Mack on questions of minority rights and Diaspora nationalism were supported by the Americans of Eastern European extraction against the delegates from Eastern Europe. One issue that came up in the deliberation, so hotly debated that it almost broke up the conference, was the desire expressed by the nationalists from Eastern Europe for Jewish representation in the League of Nations. Marshall and Mack strongly objected to this proposal; they regarded it, commented one delegate from Eastern Europe, as "a death blow to the Jewish citizens in the Western countries."[46] To the surprise and annoyance of the Eastern European delegates, this anti-nationalist position of Mack and Marshall was strongly supported by their brethren from the American delegation. The same was the case when the conference of Jewish delegates discussed resolutions concerning recognition of Jews as a nation with political rights. Many points were disputed by the Americans, and

---

[45] Minutes of the meeting of the executive committee of the Z.O.A., February 9, 1919, *de Haas Papers*.

[46] Dr. Yoseph Tannenbaum, *Zwischen Milchama un Shalom: Yidden Oif der Shalom Konferenz Noch der ershter Welt Milchama* (Buenos Aires: Zentral Farband fun Poilishe Yidden in Argentina, 1951), p. 91.

the Americans from Eastern Europe supported their leaders.[47] The non-American Eastern Europeans were indignant and felt betrayed by their brethren, who themselves were embarrassed but nevertheless supported the westerners' point of view.[48]

This is a very telling incident. It serves to indicate the changes the Eastern European immigrants underwent in the United States. In spite of their alienation from American society and their hostility toward the American Jews who, being better established and assimilated, looked down upon them and their culture, and in spite of the added humiliation they suffered from the American-born leaders of the Z.O.A., they were acquiring their very same ideas and points of view on many problems. The Eastern Europeans in the United States who called themselves nationalists already differed from their fellow Jews who still lived in Eastern Europe in their concept of Jewish nationalism. What seemed logical and natural to the Europeans seemed utterly preposterous to the Eastern Europeans in the United States.

The differences between the two groups again came to light in the London Conference. The Eastern Europeans from the United States supported their leaders against the non-American Eastern Europeans. The whole American delegation endorsed Brandeis's position on the problem of *gegenwartsarbeit*, deciding at its meeting on July 22 that: ". . . the American delegation in the name of the Zionists in America refuses to accept any responsibility for the action of the conference in this matter, and to assume any financial obligations which would be incurred. . . ."[49] They also signed a manifesto declaring that they would never submit to a decision that would bind their organization to follow the idea of *gegenwartsarbeit* in the United States, and they even left a session of the conference in protest. For people who a few months later fought the Brandeis leadership and supported the *gegenwartsarbeit* principle, this was a strong endorsement of Brandeis's position.

When we examine the statements of the Eastern European party workers on Brandeis's economic plans for Palestine, we find acceptance of most of his ideas among some of his severest opponents in 1921. One of them was Bernard Shelvin, a Yiddish journalist and Zionist, who analyzed the situation at the London Conference in his newspaper and concluded that the economic plan submitted by Brandeis was the only sound

---

[47] Oscar Janowsky, *The Jews and Minority Rights, 1898–1919* (New York: Columbia University Press, 1933), p. 313.

[48] Tannenbaum, *Zwischen*, p. 91.

[49] Minutes of the meeting of the American delegation to the London Conference, July 22, 1920, *de Haas Papers*.

Struggle over Control of the World Zionist Organization 153

and practical one before the conference. The European leaders, he asserted, were incompetent for practical planning.[50]

Another bitter opponent of the American leaders, Jacob Fishman, supported the idea late in 1919 that all Jews should be accepted as members into the Zionist Organization to help build Palestine regardless of their ideological positions on questions of Zionism and Jewish nationalism.[51] After the London Conference, Abraham Goldberg supported Brandeis's plan in its entirety.[52]

Lipsky, who a few months later led the revolt of the bureaucrats, was ready as late as December 1920 as head of the department of organization to implement the policies of the American leadership. In his memorandum entitled "General Outlines of Zionist Work for 1921," he outlined plans for the organization in conformity with the spirit of the plans of the American leaders, abolishing all educational activities including the Hebrew bureau and publication of literature "not of direct and practical use in creating sentiment favorable to Palestine."[53]

The idea, often expressed by Brandeis's supporters, that these party workers were merely waiting for a chance to topple Brandeis's leadership and so seized upon the opportunity that presented itself when he quarreled with the international Zionist leadership, is contrary to the facts. It was some time after the dispute came out into the open before the American Eastern Europeans were willing to consider their European brethren worthy of their support, and only when the latter decided to go to the United States to fight the American leaders did the Eastern European members of the Z.O.A. support the economic and organizational plans of the European Zionists.

As we have just seen, the Eastern Europeans in the United States considered the European Zionist leaders to be impractical idealists, and they did not question the soundness of Brandeis's plans. It is likely that the Zionist offices in London and Jerusalem could have done with a better and more efficient organization. But their policies with regard to Zionist work in Palestine and the Diaspora show that they had clear ideas on which they had been advised by well-known men of affairs, some of whom occupied responsible positions in Zionist councils. For example, Isaac A. Naiditsch, a member of both the Zionist executive and the directorate of *Keren Hayesod* (the organization responsible for the

---

[50] Shelvin, *The Jewish Morning Journal*, August 11, 1920.
[51] Fishman, *The Jewish Morning Journal*, September 21, 1919.
[52] Abraham Goldberg, *The Jewish Morning Journal*, October 16, 1920.
[53] Louis Lipsky, "General Outline of Zionist Work for the Year 1921," in stencil form, *de Haas Papers*.

economic development of Palestine), was a well-known European industrialist. Another member of the directorate of *Keren Hayesod* was Dr. Arnold Barth, an attorney who received a doctorate in political economy at the University of Berlin. Dr. Arthur Ruppin, who had made a name for himself as an author of books in the fields of sociology and economics, was a member of the Zionist Commission in Palestine.[54]

Furthermore, in Europe, where after all the lion's share of Zionist work was done and the human resources for the endeavor were supplied, Brandeis and his plans seemed completely impractical and based on ignorance of the situation in Europe and Palestine. His plans for recruiting people who would themselves pay for their transportation to build small businesses in Palestine seemed completely unrealistic to the Europeans who were expected to carry them out.[55]

The Eastern Europeans in the United States were inclined from 1919 to 1921 to support Brandeis's plans for Palestine, believing them to be more realistic than those offered by the non-American Eastern Europeans. Though the dispute between the two leaderships became more bitter and more clearly stated, the Eastern European journalists and party workers in the United States failed to realize that fundamental differences of policy were involved. For them, the issue was still one of American practicality versus European impracticality.

What led to this confusion among the Eastern European Zionists in the United States, and what was the reason for their indecision over the meaning of the disagreements between the two groups of leaders and over which version to support? The confusion seems to have been symptomatic of their stage of acculturation. To Shelvin and Goldberg and their colleagues, Brandeis, the successful American, was the image of a practical leader capable of evolving and executing an efficient policy, whereas the Europeans were simply "literary critics capable of analyzing plans but not creating them." The two types of leaders symbolized the two cultures between which Shelvin and his friends were torn: the Jewish-European culture that they were in the process of abandoning, and the American culture into which they were being acculturated.

In the article quoted above, Shelvin was apologizing for the European Zionists, the impractical idealists. While acknowledging the fact that "even Zionism now needs other and more practical leaders," he pleaded

---

[54] For the positions the above persons held in the Zionist institutions, see *Der XII Zionisten-Kongress, Karlsbad, 1921: Referate, Begrüssungen, Beschlüsse* (Berlin: Jüdischer Verlag, 1922). The biographic data was taken from *The Universal Jewish Encyclopedia* (New York, 1940).

[55] Adolf Böhm, *Die Zionistische Bewegung*, vol. 2 (Berlin: Jüdischer Verlag, 1933), p. 688.

for the European leaders, saying that "one is not allowed to disregard idealism and tradition completely." Brandeis's ideas at the London Conference were right, he conceded, and his only sin was his attempt to change things in the Zionist Organization "too quickly."[56]

Caught between two different cultures and attached to both, the Eastern Europeans in the United States found it impossible to define their position in terms of any one frame of reference. It was easier for the Jewish intellectuals to follow other men and their principles than to articulate their own and to assume positions of leadership themselves. Their attachment to Brandeis was also an attachment to what he symbolized. Goldberg sent a touching letter to Brandeis in 1916 in which he confessed his admiration for him and his leadership: "I am myself mystically and religiously inclined, though I usually appear very rationalistic. And believe me, that since the Boston convention [the first Zionist annual convention in which Brandeis took part], never yet a day passed that I did not think of you, and I never went to bed without praying for your health."[57]

The Eastern European Zionists in the United States followed the leadership of the great American and did not even question the wisdom of his decisions. Lipsky, explaining his position before the London Conference, stated clearly: "I used to explain policies to the Zionists, defend them or interpret them, but never, at that time, felt myself personally responsible for these policies. We were following Mr. Brandeis's leadership. He led, and was responsible."[58]

Brandeis would have eased their conflict considerably if he had assumed the leadership of the World Zionist Organization. The great American would have become the leader of the Jewish people, a position they were convinced he certainly deserved.[59]

Brandeis, their leader, failed them in London when he refused the leadership of the Zionist movement. It was his refusal to become the head of the W.Z.O., leaving the leadership to Weizmann, that proved decisive in eventually losing him control over the Z.O.A. In the first meeting of the national executive of the Z.O.A. after the London Conference, when everyone was still in a state of shock and confusion, Morris Rothenberg, one of the leaders of the Eastern European party workers,

---

[56] Shelvin, *The Jewish Morning Journal*, August 11, 1920.
[57] Abraham Goldberg to Brandeis, March 31, 1916, *Brandeis Papers*.
[58] Lipsky, *Thirty Years of American Zionism* (The Nesher Publishing Co., 1927), pp. 74–75.
[59] Lipsky, "Early Days of American Zionism, 1897–1929," *Palestine Year Book* 2 (1945–46): 478.

declared in the name of his colleagues that had Brandeis told them openly his plan, he would have met no opposition.[60]

Thus, it was not the plans and ideas of Brandeis that they rejected but the failure to provide them with leadership. Rothenberg announced at the same meeting that they were still willing to accept Brandeis's plans for Palestine and the W.Z.O. if he would assume responsibility for carrying them out.

At the next meeting of the executive, Lipsky introduced a new note into the discussion. He declared that he always followed Brandeis even when he disagreed with his ideas, but Brandeis's refusal to assume active leadership "created a new relation to the leadership," and as a result he did not feel any obligation to follow him any longer.[61] Lipsky recalled the party workers' disappointment over Brandeis's refusal to become the leader on another occasion:

> . . . we returned from London in a defeated state. We had not played a determining part in international policy. We had not entered into international responsibility. We had made no lasting favorable impression upon our co-workers in other lands, except that arising out of our financial possibilities. They looked to us for support of the Zionist work in Palestine. . . . But we were not in harmony with the trend of Zionist events. We felt ourselves strangers to it, unable to influence it.[62]

Lipsky's last statement illustrates another aspect in his group's thinking at the time. They wanted to be led by Brandeis the American and were ready to support his policies against those of the European leaders, whom they considered impractical anyway. But at the same time they were still strongly attached to their old culture and society, which made them concerned about their position in Jewish society, not only in the United States but also in Europe. Brandeis's leadership of the W.Z.O. would have given them the standing they desired in the entire Jewish world; his refusal to lead made them "strangers to it" and "unable to influence it." Goldberg similarly expressed his disappointment with Brandeis for not trying to gain popularity in the international Zionist world where Weizmann was so successful.[63]

Their greatest disappointment was not only that Brandeis refused the leadership but that the reasons for his refusal were "not [even] related

---

[60] Minutes of the meeting of the executive committee of the Z.O.A., August 29, 1920, *de Haas Papers*.
[61] Ibid., September 29, 1920, *Brandeis Papers*.
[62] Lipsky, *Thirty Years of American Zionism*, p. 70.
[63] Minutes of the meeting of the executive committee of the Z.O.A., August 29, 1920, *de Haas Papers*.

Struggle over Control of the World Zionist Organization

to the interests of the Jewish people. They were tied up with other loyalties."[64]

Brandeis's actions upon his return from London weakened his influence over his followers even further. After the London Conference, he refused to attend any meetings of Zionists or even to come near the convention hall. Time and again his supporters implored him to come to important gatherings, explaining the importance of his appearance, but Brandeis absolutely refused. He defined his position in a letter to de Haas in September 1920, and he refused to reconsider it throughout the period of controversy. "Considering my judiciary limitations," he wrote, "I must keep out of all controversies—my hands and feet being tied as they are—and in view of this must be absent when they are likely to arise."[65]

But, as we have explained, it was not the policies that were to decide the outcome of the dispute. Brandeis's presence was needed precisely when controversies were likely to arise. De Haas answered the letter and wrote scores of pleas in the next nine months for Brandeis to come out of his seclusion and appear before his supporters, but with no result. And so the door was left open for the European Zionists to come to the United States and rally both the party workers and the Jewish masses to their support. Brandeis's followers desperately urged him to come into the open and fight. It was all of no avail. In contrast, the Europeans went from city to city throughout the United States, attended hundreds of mass meetings, and rallied the party workers behind them. The confused intellectuals then decided to follow them and adopted their point of view on all controversial issues.

It was this active and aggressive leadership on the part of the Eastern Europeans that made the issues clearer to the disoriented Eastern European intellectuals of the United States. Examination of the voluminous literature on the dispute—in the press, speeches, and pamphlets—shows that once the Europeans arrived, confusion and ambiguities with regard to all political questions disappeared, and the principles articulated by the Europeans were adopted even by those who a short while earlier had propagated exactly the opposite point of view.

The seemingly surprising action by Brandeis, risking his leadership by refusing all contacts with Zionists, will become less puzzling when we refer to our explanation of why he chose the role of invisible leader in 1916 after his partisan role in the dispute between the Zionists and the

---

[64] Lipsky, "Early Days of American Zionism," p. 478.
[65] Brandeis to de Haas, September 16, 1920, *de Haas Papers*.

A.J.C. received public notice. We explained that being a Zionist leader conflicted with his status as justice of the Supreme Court and weakened his relations with the other justices on the Court and with the American public in general. The controversy that later flared up in Jewish quarters had a similar effect and demanded even greater caution. The similarity between the two incidents was admitted by Brandeis himself when he explained to de Haas why he was not going to take part in any Zionist gathering. "I am clear that—considering my judiciary limitations—it was a mistake for me to preside in London—as it was in July, 1916 for me to appear at the conference with Marshall et al.," he wrote.[66] The anxiety that caused his hasty resignation from all his official positions in the Zionist Organization in 1916 was now repeated. Anxious for his position in the Supreme Court, he weakened and endangered his position as a Zionist leader.

But although Brandeis refused to lead the American Zionists during the period from 1920 to 1921, he still tried to force them to reject the European leadership, which would imply the severance of their connection with the European Jewry. His associates said, in effect: we, the American Jews, are different from the European Jews, and we should therefore work for Palestine and Zionism independently and through different methods. This was also the way Brandeis's policies were perceived by the party workers. In Neumann's accusations published on the eve of the annual convention of 1921, he described a meeting of the American delegation in London, in which "Mr. Justice Brandeis said to us that we should regard ourselves there as Americans; that we should forget our internal differences, as well as our differences with other American organizations, including the non-Zionists, and stand together, solidly, as against the Europeans."[67]

The Eastern Europeans in the United States were not ready to do that. It was Weizmann's appeal to their Jewish loyalty to which the Eastern European Jews in the United States responded most strongly. Caught in the United States between two worlds and two cultures, they were told by the American leaders that the other culture and its leaders, to which they were still attached, were not their own any more. Further, they were told that the Americans were better leaders and knew better but were not willing to become leaders of the Jewish people as a whole because the latter were not yet ready for American leadership. Hence, Brandeis implied, let all American Jews go it alone.

---

[66] Ibid.
[67] Neumann, *Causes of the Conflict* (New York: The New Maccabean Company, 1921), p. 12.

Struggle over Control of the World Zionist Organization

Keeping the Membership Ignorant of the Dispute

We have now to examine the struggle between the two sets of leaders after they parted company in the London Conference.

When Brandeis refused the leadership of the W.Z.O. in London, he already had a general idea of the nature of his next step in the American organization. He was going to reorganize the Z.O.A. and make it an effective organization for building up Palestine economically. Furthermore, he was not going to send money to the London office until his economic plans for the development of Palestine were accepted and until it was agreed that this task would be the sole responsibility of the Zionist Organization.[68]

After the revolt of many Eastern European members of the American delegation, he wrote to Alexander Sachs, the assistant secretary of the Z.O.A.: "I hope we may be able to commence our Second Six Years on August 30th [August 30, 1914, was the day he became the president of the P.Z.C.], by an era of solid persistence, building of and through our own organization, eliminating the sham and strengthening the worthy. Consider how best this may be done in a way worthy of the New Era."[69]

As to the form of the new organization, he laid down three basic principles:

A. It must limit organization and the like expenses to what is needed by dues or gifts especially for that purpose.
B. It must make possible full cooperation by those who do not want to build up the Zionist Organization but do want to take part in the upbuilding of Palestine.
C. We must have a large membership of those who in some way have by stockholding some stake in Palestine institutions. The goodwill of the Zionist Organization and the value of numbers must be kept constantly in mind.[70]

In response to Brandeis's request, Sachs drew up a plan in which he tried to retain the loyalty of the party workers while at the same time making room for those newcomers who were interested solely in Palestine. Hence he suggested several classes of membership. All members should be shareholders in Palestine institutions; this would be the "least

---
[68] Brandeis to Mack and Wise, July 25, 1920, *de Haas Papers*.
[69] Brandeis to Sachs, August 5, 1920, ibid.
[70] Brandeis to de Haas, September 18, 1920, ibid.

common denominator" of members. Those who in addition adhered to the Zionist political view would have the right to elect and be elected to, the governing bodies of the organization.[71] This compromise did not satisfy Brandeis, who wanted an organization of members devoted solely to economic endeavors in Palestine. This was accomplished by a reorganization committee, which brought a new plan to the annual convention at Buffalo in November 1920.

The main feature of the reorganization plan was the establishment of a Palestine Development committee that "should embrace men who have been not hitherto recognized as Zionists, men of wealth, and of ability." The work of this committee, the report added, "is the vital primary important function of the Americans for the coming year. All else is incidental and for the purpose of aiding this work."[72] As a result, all the Zionist publications were discontinued and the central office was reduced to a handful of workers. The principle of organization was becoming that of a cadre party. But an elected national executive and annual conventions were retained. All dues-paying members were to have the right to participate in the elections of officers, and the national executive was to continue its supervision over the experts, with the stipulation that "no paid employee of the Zionist Organization of America may be a member of the national executive committee."[73] All this was in line with other similar American middle-class organizations. The democratic process was retained upon Brandeis's insistence. In a letter to Mack he wrote: "I think we should plan to have ultimately a large membership. . . . The growth of membership will doubtless be slow at the start. We shall have to do much educating them—using that term in its proper sense—but that is the price we must pay for Zionism and for Democracy."[74] What this education meant and how it was to be carried out by the Zionist Organization was never made clear by Brandeis or his associates.

The Eastern European leaders were convinced that such an organization would not appeal to the Jewish masses who were not yet American or middle-class. Nor had the new organization room for the Eastern European intellectuals; in the Palestine Development committee, they were after men of wealth. The two different approaches to the concept of

---

[71] A memorandum on organization by Sachs, October 1920, ibid.
[72] "A memorandum as basis for discussion on plan to be submitted to the executive committee meeting, September 29, 1920," ibid.
[73] The resolutions adopted at the Buffalo Annual Convention, November 29, 1920, ibid.
[74] Brandeis to Mack, November 15, 1920, ibid.

Struggle over Control of the World Zionist Organization 161

organization were described by Neumann when he told the annual convention in 1921 of a conversation with Mack:

> I said: "Have certain outlines been sent out to the districts for discussion and information?" He said: "On what?" and I said: "On questions of Zionism," and then Judge Mack expressed himself substantially in this sense: He said he could not conceive of the organization in that form. He said we were over-organized. We had districts and regional organizations and things of that kind and he thought we were spending too much money on that and that there was no need for it. We should be an organization of members, individuals, each one paying so much a year, we get together, elect officers, and the officers will conduct the business of the organization. I said to him something like this: "The Hebrew Emigrant Aid Society?" He said: "Yes."[75]

What seemed so natural to Mack seemed absolutely incredible to Neumann. Neumann was convinced that the Jewish masses would never join such an organization, although Mack apparently thought that they could be educated to accept it. The differences in their cultural traditions and class backgrounds probably account for the differences of opinion. Let it be remembered, however, that this reorganization plan was accepted by the Z.O.A. at its annual convention in 1920. The opposition at this convention was completely ineffective. Brandeis's leadership was still unassailable.

Weizmann, as chairman of the W.Z.O. executive committee, and his colleagues on the committee embarked on their own program for developing Palestine and activities of the W.Z.O. in Palestine and the Diaspora after the break with Brandeis occurred in the London Conference. Following their conception of Jewish nationalism and the function of the organization, the cultural work in the Diaspora, *gegenwartsarbeit*, was approved. Overruling Brandeis's objections, they established a new fund, the *Keren Hayesod*, to collect money for the expenses of the organization in all its activities. This fund accepted both donations and investments without discrimination since, it was argued, this was the collective effort of all the Jewish people, each of whom would contribute according to his abilities. This commingling of donations and investments became the main argument of the Brandeis group's objection to its inauguration in the United States. The London Conference had resolved that the directors of the fund would disburse the money collected from the Jewish people. Actual allocation of the money was covered in general terms. Twenty per cent was for the already existing fund, *Keren*

---

[75] *Report of the Proceedings of the Twenty-Fourth Annual Convention*, p. 42.

Kayemet, for buying and reclaiming land in Palestine; of the remainder, one-third was for current expenditure like education, immigration, and social welfare, and two-thirds was to be invested in permanent national institutions or economic undertakings.

Keren Hayesod was directed toward conditions in the Diaspora rather than in Palestine. Since wealthy Jews were by and large not sympathetic to the Zionist endeavor in Palestine, the Zionist leaders decided to appeal to the masses. The resources of the masses were, of course, meager, but the Zionist leaders agreed that although efforts to enlist the financial support of rich Jews should continue, they could not afford to wait for them to respond.

This strategy was not approved by the American leaders. They considered it unbusinesslike, even though they themselves realized that "the people with little means cooperate, but not those with large means."[76] Given their middle-class American background, they would not believe that such an unsound plan could be realized in the United States. Their strongest objection to the *Keren Hayesod* seems to have been, however, their disapproval of the nationalist agitation that accompanied the fund-raising campaigns. The prospect of the continuation of such agitation horrified them. They decided to appeal instead to the "classes," in a quiet and businesslike way, rather than to the "masses." The success of both methods became apparent after June 1921, when both went into operation, one led by the Brandeis group and the other by those who remained in the Z.O.A.

The Z.O.A. annual convention in 1920 was a rather confused affair, and the confusion was deliberately encouraged by the leaders. Convention reports suggested that the delegates felt that practical work in Palestine was the only important issue and that differences in approach between the two leaderships were not important. This suited the American leaders. But the reports also indicated that the delegates felt that the ultimate authority rested with the World Zionist leadership, to which the Z.O.A. should subordinate itself. Therefore, the delegates reasoned, the resolutions approved in London, including the establishment of the *Keren Hayesod*, should be implemented by the Americans. The leadership purposely introduced a very ambiguous resolution on the issue. They flatly denied any rift between themselves and the Europeans or any intention to secede from the international organization. In the same breath they hailed Brandeis's leadership, even though Brandeis himself observed his self-imposed absenteeism.

---

[76] Wise to Brandeis, January 21, 1921, *Brandeis Papers*.

Struggle over Control of the World Zionist Organization 163

The American leaders introduced a vote of thanks to Brandeis for his handling of the London Conference and accused his critics of insulting the great leader with the charge of secession. Brandeis's name evoked so much loyalty among the delegates that this simple maneuver was sufficient to demoralize the opposition completely and led them eventually to support the vote of thanks. Shelvin, reporting these events, admitted that Brandeis remained unopposed in the Zionist Organization.[77] And another reporter, conveying the mood of the convention, asserted: "At the convention it transpired that so-called anti-Brandeis legends about his despotism, separatism and the like, were groundless, and that he is now even more than ever needed by the organization."[78]

What was the truth in the charges that the American leaders used the threat of secession in order to force the W.Z.O. to follow Brandeis's program? The correspondence between the American and the European leaders, the correspondence of the American leaders among themselves, and the proceedings of the national executive all support the accusations. The American leaders took great care to conceal these actions from the public eye. Furthermore, they took care to maintain correct formal relations with the European leaders, which made it more difficult for their opponents to accuse them publicly. The Eastern European members of the national executive of the Z.O.A. must have been aware of the design of the leaders immediately after the London Conference but, as we have already explained, could not make up their minds what to do about it for a long time. As early as the first meeting of the national executive after the London Conference, on August 29, Frankfurter had evaded a question as to whether the Z.O.A. was still a member of the W.Z.O.; when pressed for a reply, he stated only, "all I [can] say is there was an W.Z.O. up to July 20, 1920."[79] And a memorandum submitted by the administration to the national executive at its meeting on September 29 declared: "There is no thought of separation, and activity in Palestine is to be independently financed only so far as commitments require and efficiency in the upbuilding of Palestine dictates. By pressure on the Zionist Organization in London and Palestine such period is to be made as short as possible."[80]

This statement seems clear. "Efficiency" has to be understood as a label for the programs advised by the Americans, and until this was accepted by the Europeans the Americans would send the funds directly

---

[77] Shelvin, *The Jewish Morning Journal*, November 30, 1920.
[78] S. Dingol, *The Day*, November 30, 1920.
[79] Minutes of the meeting of the executive committee of the Z.O.A., August 29, 1920, *de Haas Papers*.
[80] "A memorandum as a basis for discussion . . . ," ibid.

to Palestine, ignoring the London office. The memorandum went on to suggest new arrangements for administering the work in Palestine. It recommended that the Palestine Development Council of the Z.O.A. establish committees devoted to special aspects of the work in Palestine that would also "have power to determine how funds are to be administered, [and] what reports are required as condition to advancing money." For example, "if the afforestation committee desires an American director unrestricted as to authority in his work, with full control over funds sent to him, the W.Z.O. shall appoint such person with such power."[81] They wanted to decide how the money they collected in the United States should be spent in Palestine, rather than leave the decision to the W.Z.O.

Many Eastern Europeans in the national executive were growing restless. In October, they called a meeting of the districts of greater New York and passed a resolution demanding that an American be appointed to the executive of the W.Z.O.[82] More Yiddish journalists joined the agitation, concentrating on the problem of secession and on the attempt to dictate the policies of the Zionist movement from New York or, better, from Washington.

The Americans did not take notice of the agitation, and Brandeis pursued his plans undeterred. He laid down the policy to be pursued in a number of round-robin letters that he sent to de Haas, Mack, Wise, Frankfurter, Flexner, Robert Szold, and Sachs. This policy included several points:

1. To refuse to accept the invitation by the European Zionists to go to London in February 1921 to resolve the differences. But by June, "we may have to go to London for a bout."[83]

2. To force a change in the structure of the W.Z.O. so as to make it a loose federation with great autonomy for the national federations.[84]

3. From the money collected in the United States, $35,000 was to go directly to the medical unit every month, and only if more funds were collected were they to be sent to London. This meant in effect that the London office could not count on the American federation to forward any money.

Were there plans to inform the public, or at least the party workers, of what was happening, and to enlist their support? This was not intended by the leaders. They were trying to follow the tactics, adopted at

---

[81] Ibid.
[82] *The Jewish Morning Journal*, October 11, 1920.
[83] Brandeis to Mack, Wise, et al., January 29, 1921, *de Haas Papers*.
[84] Brandeis to Mack, Wise, et al., February 6, 1921, ibid.

the Buffalo Convention, of denying the rift in the hope that the European leaders would yield to their demands before it became necessary to enlighten the public further. The correspondence between Brandeis and his associates suggests that they did not conceive of the possibility of opposition developing within the Z.O.A. that was serious enough to endanger their position. Nor were the Europeans regarded as a challenge to Brandeis.

De Haas complained afterwards that although the opposition was organizing its forces, "our leaders would not see it. They would not prepare for the consequences."[85] Most confident was Brandeis, who was furthest removed from the grass roots and who enjoyed the highest prestige in the community and also had the greatest contempt for the "mediocrities" both in New York and in London. When the Europeans announced their impending visit to the United States, Brandeis explained to his inner circle that the only way to deal with such men was by acting —which included refraining from action.[86] As late as early May, when Weizmann and the other leaders from Europe were touring the United States and being greeted enthusiastically by their supporters, Brandeis's confidence in victory remained unshaken.[87]

There was, however, another important reason for the American leaders' reluctance to bring their differences with the European leaders into the open. Added to their confidence that the masses would follow them was their worry about how an open fight would affect American anti-Semites and non-Zionist German Jews, whom they were still desperately trying to attract to Zionism. They did not want either anti-Semites or German Jews to know that their partners in the Zionist movement, with whom they were closely associated, subscribed to such dangerous doctrines as Diaspora nationalism. Thus, when the Europeans arrived in the country and it became necessary for the American leaders to state their case before the public, Mack was reluctant to utter the dangerous words. In a letter to de Haas he said:

> I have the lurking fear all along of the public danger of expressing ourselves too freely on diaspora nationalistic theories. We give the weapon not only to [Henry] Ford et al. but to [David] Philipson et al. [a famous anti-Zionist Reform Rabbi] . . . if we now publicly say or intimate that many European Zionists are imbued with it and if we define it in the sense in which they mean to the consequences may be very grave. Our failure to state what diaspora nationalism means does not in the slightest degree

---

[85] Minutes of the meeting of those who resigned their posts in the Z.O.A. at Hotel Cleveland, Cleveland, June 7, 1921, ibid.
[86] Brandeis to Mack, Wise, et al., February 6, 1921, ibid.
[87] Brandeis to Mack, May 4, 1921, ibid.

hurt us against our opponents here or in Europe. They know what it means. Our expression of it, however, can hurt us most seriously in other directions.[88]

It was thus the American anti-Semites and the wealthy Reform Jews, rather than their own constituents, who concerned the American leaders and determined their actions. The fear of these theoretical issues led them to discuss technical problems, like details of business transactions in Palestine, which could not interest their public. These self-imposed limitations in their struggle to retain leadership of the Z.O.A. stemmed from the same roots that caused Brandeis to absent himself from all public or semi-public Zionist functions after August 1920. They, too, were worried that anything they might say in connection with Diaspora nationalism in their disputations might be publicized and misinterpreted, and as a result harm them both in their status as judges, lawyers, businessmen, and public figures in the United States and in their social contacts within their German Jewish community. They constantly kept a worried eye on "Ford et al." and "Philipson et al."[89] They tried to avoid appearing at mass meetings and were very guarded, feeling secure only when they discussed their difference with the Europeans on issues such as the commingling of funds for investment with those for non-investment and the economic waste in operations in Palestine. Only in their private letters did they dare admit that the real issue was that of Diaspora nationalism. Many of their appearances at the time were among respectable German Jews, to whom they desperately appealed to invest money in Palestine and thus join their camp.

The difference between their behavior and that of Brandeis during this period was only one of degree. Being a prominent public figure in the United States and occupying a high position in American political and social life, Brandeis felt that his actions were more visible to the American public than those of his less illustrious associates; people were clearly concerned with observing the activities and behavior of men of his position on the Supreme Court. He was, therefore, more anxious to dissociate himself from the controversy that was raging in Zionist circles. He never even attended a closed session of the national executive of the Z.O.A. or of his supporters for fear that his opponents would use the same tactic used by the A.J.C. in 1916 and publicize his appearances, while his supporters, anxious to demonstrate the support of the great

---

[88] Mack to de Haas and Sachs, March 18, 1921, ibid. Henry Ford published at that time vicious anti-Semitic statements in his newspaper.
[89] Ibid.

man, would do the same. A man like Mack, who was never a controversial political figure in the United States and served only on the United States Circuit Court, found it possible to appear at small gatherings. However, even he found it expedient to avoid any mention of Diaspora nationalism, for fear of being misquoted on this dangerous issue. This attitude was demonstrated again when the group, after resigning their positions in the Z.O.A., embarked on an independent Palestine program. At that time they decided to avoid any continuation of the controversy and instead followed the maxim: "Silence in America; service in Palestine."[90]

An Open Fight between the Two Sets of Leaders

The American leaders surrounded themselves with self-imposed limitations in their fight with the Europeans and left the initiative to their opponents. Thus, it was Weizmann who at a certain point decided to visit the United States and impose the will of the world executive on the American federation. The official purpose of the visit was the inauguration of the *Keren Hayesod*, and he was determined to accomplish it with or without the approval of the American leaders. In the announcement of his visit he declared:

> The growth of the American Zionist Organization has been sudden and it has not had time to be properly adjusted to the general organization. The American Organization is also influenced somewhat by its environment and vague suggestion of the Monroe Doctrine. On us Zionists of Europe, therefore, rests the obligation to draw the American Zionists to us. . . . This will be simple enough if we only draw nearer to our people in America, who are bone of our bone and flesh of our flesh.[91]

Weizmann's strategy, therefore, was simple and clear. He was going to appeal to the Eastern European community in the United States not to dissociate itself from the rest of the Jewish nation, whose legitimate leaders were the heads of the World Zionist movement.

Only when Weizmann was about to come to the United States as the head of an impressive Zionist delegation that included most members of the Zionist executive, some of the prominent leaders of Palestine Jewry, and Albert Einstein, did the Z.O.A. leaders decide to move and make public their position on all issues on which the two leaderships

---

[90] Minutes of the meeting at Senator Straus's office in New York, June 10, 1921, ibid.
[91] Press Bureau of the Jewish Commission, January 26, 1921, *Brandeis Papers*.

disagreed. While the delegation was crossing the ocean, the Z.O.A. leaders convened the national executive and brought to a vote the following resolution:

The Zionist Organization of America stands for:

1. Concentration of the Zionist Organization's activities on Palestine as against diffusion on *gegenwartsarbeit* and Diaspora nationalism.
2. The Zionist Organization as the Jewish Agency versus the proposal made repeatedly since 1919 to substitute for the Zionist Organization a coalition composed of representatives of Zionist and non-Zionist organizations or of those elected by a general Jewish Congress.
3. Commonwealth versus Cultural Center. Primary emphasis on upbuilding and direction of activities to the economic upbuilding of Palestine, as against primary emphasis on general cultural activities. A living culture-creating and culture-radiating Israel cannot arise and endure without permanent economic foundations.
4. Separation of funds for economic development in Palestine from these destined for communal purpose as opposed to commingling of all funds. . . .
5. Budgetary system and efficiency in operations in Palestine. . . .
6. A policy of federalism promoting strong responsible federations, as opposed to a centralization imposing rigid uniformity in methods and means as well as ends.[92]

These resolutions were later published in pamphlet form with explanations by Mack. In contrast to the voluminous literature of the opponents, this was the only document published and distributed to explain the leaders' point of view. A careful examination will make the stand of the American leadership on these controversial issues quite clear.

The document is most explicit on the issue of Diaspora nationalism, which is clearly accepted as the basic motive for disagreement. It was this issue, explained the document, that caused the administration to offer an economic program for Palestine that differed from that of the Europeans.

The document makes it abundantly clear that one reason for the attempt to change the goals of the organization into goals concerned

---

[92] *Summary of the Position of the Zionist Organization of America in Conference with Dr. Weizmann and Associates. Submitted by the President of the Z.O.A. to and Adopted by the National Executive Committee at Its Meeting March 19–20, 1921* (n.p., n.d.).

On page 7 of the pamphlet, we find another document titled: *Memorandum on the Policies of the Zionist Organization of America.* It is explained in a footnote that the second document "is a personal statement of the President of the Zionist Organization of America presented to the National Executive Committee in support of the foregoing summary, but not submitted to it for any action thereof." Our analysis is also based on an earlier and somewhat more elaborate draft of the memorandum in the *de Haas Papers.*

purely with Palestinian affairs was the desire to attract non-Zionists of the type of Schiff and Marshall, whom they had tried to involve in the Zionist Organization after 1917. Since the non-Zionists supported only the economic development of Palestine, the organization had to become concerned only with Palestine, not with Zionism. The Diaspora Jews, declared Mack in the document, would not participate in the Jewish revival, but would aid Palestine and remain onlookers. Even more, "the headquarters of the Zionist Organization is to be transferred to Palestine. The work of the Zionist Organization in Palestine is to become primarily that of immigration, colonization and settlement, and the furtherance of necessary economic institutions. The Organization should not encroach on the functions of the State nor should it encroach on the functions of Palestinian Jewry."

Palestinian Jewry was thus the bearer of the Zionist idea, but the Zionist Organization had no right to interfere in their affairs. American Zionists would collect money and help develop industry and commerce in Palestine to make it more attractive for all those Jews who would like to settle there. They would have a mass organization that would be open to all Jews who were willing to participate in this enterprise. Even the Pittsburgh Program was completely forgotten; this must have been interpreted as interference in the affairs of Palestinian Jewry, as it certainly was. The only distinction that remained between Zionists and non-Zionists was that Zionists wished Palestine to become a Jewish state, while non-Zionists were not willing to see an independent Jewish state in Palestine or anywhere else.

The memorandum was discussed by the European leaders, who attacked it on all counts. Their arguments were faithfully repeated by the opposition within the ranks of the Z.O.A. When the memorandum was adopted by the national executive of the Z.O.A. a few days before the arrival in the United States of the European leaders, ten of its Eastern European members opposed it but abstained when a vote was taken.[93] A few weeks later, they joined the European leaders and set up the *Keren Hayesod* in the United States against the wishes of the Z.O.A. leaders.[94] Henceforth, they campaigned vigorously for *Keren Hayesod* and the European leaders, and against the Z.O.A. leadership.

The American leaders, on the other hand, did not exert much effort to explain their point of view; their memorandum was not even translated into the Yiddish language, which was the language of most of the Z.O.A. membership. They did not even consider the memorandum as a

---

[93] *The Jewish Morning Journal*, March 28, 1921.
[94] *The Day*, April 15, 1921.

basis for negotiations with the European visitors. Brandeis opposed any negotiations, fearful that they would result in compromise. When negotiations between the two groups of leaders were resumed at the end of April, he wrote to de Haas, "I note with apprehension the possibility of negotiations with Weizmann."[95] When the negotiations broke down soon after, he was delighted.[96]

The door was now left open to the European leaders and the opposition forces within the Z.O.A. to choose the issues they were willing to discuss. They flooded the Jewish quarters with literature and organized mass meetings in all Jewish centers to present their point of view. They made the main issue of the campaign the question of loyalty to the Jewish people and accused the American leaders of separating themselves from the rest of the nation and, what was more, of trying to dictate their will to the rest of the nation. The elected leaders of the world Zionist movement were, the opposition asserted, the representative leaders of the nation; the disobedience of the Americans made manifest their disloyalty to the nation.

The members of the national executive who joined the European leaders carried with them the bulk of the paid workers of the organization and established a competitive headquarters.[97] They called a conference of delegates representing the different districts of the Eastern part of the country, where they were strongest. The Eastern Zionist Conference issued a statement in which they declared their allegiance to the W.Z.O., support of the *Keren Hayesod,* and approval of the action of the minority members of the national executive of the Z.O.A. with reference to the international organization.[98] And thus the issue of loyalty to the world leaders, notwithstanding the substance of the other issues of controversy between them and the American leaders, publicly became the main issue.

Once the dispute was perceived along these lines, many of the American Eastern European Jews refused to join the camp of those who were being accused of disloyalty to the Jewish nation and its elected leaders. It should be remembered, however, that the crystallization of the issues along these lines of loyalty to the Jewish nation followed the arrival of Weizmann and his colleagues in the United States. Only when the European Zionist leaders, who symbolized and personified the Jewish people, arrived in the United States did the internal opposition

---

[95] Brandeis to de Haas and Mack, April 27, 1921, *de Haas Papers.*
[96] Brandeis to de Haas, April 29, 1921, ibid.
[97] Lipsky, *Thirty Years of American Zionism,* p. 75.
[98] Eastern Zionist Conference, *The New Maccabean,* May 6, 1921, p. 7.

Struggle over Control of the World Zionist Organization 171

gather its forces and come out openly in support of the world leaders and against Brandeis. But the American leaders did not react to the challenge. Their self-imposed limitations, and in particular Brandeis's invisibility, cleared the way for the victory of the Europeans.

Some observers believed that if Brandeis, with his great prestige, had entered the fight he might have defeated Weizmann. Gedalya Bublik, the noted Yiddish journalist, wrote Brandeis as late as June 1: "With you leadership is assured, without you it is impossible."[99] How much truth there was in such an assertion can, of course, be left only to speculation, though it was widely accepted by supporters as well as opponents. What is certain is that Weizmann was consciously building up the prestige of his delegation among the non-Jews in an attempt to offset the advantage Brandeis, whose standing in the Gentile world was high, hitherto held over any potential opposition.

The Zionist delegation was publicized in the Yiddish press as consisting of persons who, though leaders of the Jewish nation, commanded at the same time the respect of the non-Jewish world and its leaders. Weizmann was considered a great leader in the context of Jewish life and Jewish history, comparable to Ezra and Nehemiah. Weizmann had also appeared at the Paris Peace Conference and discussed the Jewish problem with the great leaders of the Allies, and even though Brandeis had refused to meet him he was received by President Harding. The honor given Weizmann by high officials in the United States was played up by the sympathetic Yiddish press. According to *The Day*: "It is the first time in the history of America's biggest city that a Jew is officially received by the city government. During the three hundred years of the history of New York, ninety-six persons officially received the 'keys of the city.' Dr. Chaim Weizmann, the ninety-seventh to enjoy the great honor, is the first Jew to come to New York on a mission dealing exclusively with Jewish affairs, and the first Jew ever to receive such an honor."[100]

On the following day, the paper's editorial exclaimed ecstatically:

> The official reception for Dr. Weizmann, the president of the World Zionist Organization, in City Hall as the guest of the City's Mayor, is a symbol of the political resurrection from the death of the Jewish nation . . . . It is also the first time that a prominent Jew comes to these shores as the official leader of the Jews, nay, as the political leader of the Jewish nation. . . . The whole Zionist delegation was received here in the manner only a delegation of an independent and politically recognized nation would be received. When one remembers that not long ago even

[99] Gedalya Bublik to Brandeis, June 1, 1921, *Brandeis Papers*.
[100] Editorial, *The Day*, April 4, 1921.

the liberal non-Jews regarded us as no more than a religious sect and refused to recognize the fact that we are a nation; when one remembers that even among the leading American Jews the majority did not accept until this day the fact that the Jews are a naton . . . one has to conclude that wonders occur and miracles are taking place.

The editorial concluded by urging the Jews in New York to give Weizmann a fitting welcome, implying that since Weizmann enjoyed the esteem of the non-Jewish world, American Jews should recognize him as their leader and thus raise their esteem as a group in the eyes of the majority.[101]

This asset, the esteem of the non-Jewish world, was strengthened by the inclusion in the Zionist delegation of Einstein, who had become internationally known just two years earlier. The attempts of the American leaders to dissuade Einstein from coming to the country as a member of the delegation failed. He had come to raise money for the future Hebrew University and was advised by them that he would be more successful if he did not come as an official member of the Zionist delegation. The argument did not impress him, and he appeared at the mass meetings with the delegation and sat with them at rallies. In one of the largest rallies, in which Weizmann announced the inauguration of *Keren Hayesod*, Einstein, against the wishes of the American leaders, broke his silence. His speech, made in German, a language that the Yiddish-speaking audience understood, consisted of one sentence only: "I have only one thing to tell you. Our leader and your leader, Dr. Weizmann, has rendered great service to the Jewish people. Obey him and no other."[102]

Thus "one of the most famous men in the world" used his prestige to support Weizmann against Brandeis.[103] Goldberg commented that Einstein's visit ". . . increased the prestige of Zionism in the eyes of all Americans, Jews and non-Jews."[104] This seems like a confession of a Jewish leader conscious of the low standing of his group vis-à-vis the majority and convinced that association with men who gained high prestige in the dominant culture would raise the group's standing in the eyes of the members of the minority. Whether Einstein's visit really helped the recruitment of Jews to the Zionist Organization is doubtful, but his impact on Goldberg and other members of the political class was unmistakenly great.

---

[101] Editorial, *The Day*, April 5, 1921.
[102] *The Day*, April 13, 1921.
[103] Bernard G. Richards, "Reminiscences, Recorded by the Oral History Research Office" (New York: Columbia University, 1961), p. 205.
[104] *Report of the Proceedings of the Twenty-Fourth Annual Convention*, p. 75.

Struggle over Control of the World Zionist Organization 173

Once the Europeans led the fight against the administration, the party workers and bureaucrats became bolder. Now they let loose all their grievances against the administration: the dictatorship by the leaders and control by the small inner circle of the organization, to the exclusion of all the rest; the downgrading of the Eastern Europeans by the American-born leaders; the scorn heaped upon those who spoke English with a bad accent; the contempt of the leaders for Jewish culture and the Yiddish language and their belief that "from Harvard comes the Law."[105]

The style, the vehemence, and the vindictiveness of the Eastern European journalists were reminiscent of the fight for the Jewish Congress. At that time, however, they were following Brandeis in the fight against the wealthy German Jews. Now even the progressive branch of the German Jewish community was under fire.

How did the American leaders react? Lipsky recalls that although the opposition collected money for *Keren Hayesod* and thus appeared before the public, "the administration had taken no steps to collect money for Palestine." This, he argued, "militated against them; since they did not have occasion to talk to the Zionists."[106] As a matter of fact, they did busy themselves with fund-raising, but restricted themselves to small gatherings, mostly among German Jews and away from the public eye, notwithstanding the fact that this had proved to be a thankless and unrewarding experience for the past four years.

Furthermore, their commitments to their other positions left little opportunity for exercising their leadership of the Zionist Organization at a time when they should have put their energies into the struggle to retain leadership. De Haas complained that there was nobody to fight the Eastern European leaders, since the American leaders were all up to their eyes with other activities: Brandeis and Mack on the bench, Robert Szold in his business, Frankfurter at Harvard, etc.[107] Their opponents, in contrast, were totally committed to Zionism, and many had full time for the fight.

De Haas warned that the opposition was "far more passionate in their belief, and far more willing to sacrifice."[108] This lack of total commitment explains why so many of the leaders dropped out of the struggle when it became too demanding. Flexner resigned his position on the financial committee on the Z.O.A. as early as February 1921.

---

[105] Abraham Coralnik, *The Day*, June 11, 1921.
[106] Lipsky, "Early Days of American Zionism," p. 483.
[107] De Haas to Frankfurter, February 24, 1921, *de Haas Papers*.
[108] De Haas to Brandeis, April 16, 1921, ibid.

Even Frankfurter stopped attending the meetings of the group in April. He was "below par."[109] The behavior of Wise was a little puzzling during the dispute, since he switched from a forceful struggle to maintain the group's leadership of the Z.O.A. to a withdrawal from the fight.

Wise was responsible for the maneuver in the Buffalo Convention of invoking Brandeis's name and of accusing critics of the administration of insulting him. He then introduced a vote of thanks, which rallied all the delegates behind the administration. His speech at the Cleveland Convention in 1921 was the only forceful defense of the administration and the one speech on their behalf that received loud applause from the delegates. He did not spend time on technical and economic questions, as did the other American leaders. Instead, he explained to the audience that it was Brandeis, not Weizmann, who enjoyed the high esteem of the non-Jewish world, particularly in the United States. It was in the United States, Wise argued, that the decisive actions to secure the Balfour Declaration were taken, and the success of these actions was entirely attributable to Brandeis and his influence.[110]

And yet some of Wise's other actions did not indicate a willingness to wage a strong fight against those who were trying to topple the leadership of his group in the Z.O.A. He rarely appeared at mass meetings. Instead, he continued to appear at small gatherings made up mainly of German Jews, trying unsuccessfully to persuade them to contribute money for Palestine. At one mass meeting in which he and Mack appeared on the platform with the European delegation, they both left in protest when Ussishkin, head of the Zionist Commission in Palestine, expressed himself freely on the question of Diaspora nationalism.[111]

At the root of Wise's behavior was his unhappiness over the prevalence of nationalist sentiments among the rank and file, the worry he shared with his colleagues over the possible reaction of the American public if nationalism was perceived as the prevailing sentiment among American Jews. His realization that the more militant nationalistic approach of his opponents enjoyed greater support from the masses accounted for his pessimistic and defeatist attitude all through the struggle. He therefore advised Brandeis not to go to the Cleveland Conven-

---

[109] De Haas to Brandeis, April 13, 1921, ibid.
[110] *Report of the Proceedings of the Twenty-Fourth Annual Convention*, pp. 61–62.
[111] De Haas to Brandeis, April 13, 1921, *de Haas Papers*.

Struggle over Control of the World Zionist Organization 175

tion, and explained to him that he could not obtain the leadership of the World Zionist Organization even if he tried, since "it will take years before the East Europeans will understand our point of view."[112]

At the height of the dispute, Wise wrote to Rabbi Max Heller, who supported the nationalist point of view:

> . . . I am fully in sympathy with efforts to settle colonies of Jews in Palestine who wish to go there and . . . I fully recognize the importance of the economic and industrial development of Palestine which can be most effectively brought about through Jewish immigration. What I oppose is an attempt to reproduce past history, and I have always found it surprising that you as a progressive should look backward instead of forward. Certainly the recreation of a Jewish nationality (even if it were possible) is not carrying out the ideas of prophetic Judaism. Sooner or later, I venture to predict, Zionism will have to come out definitely with a nonpolitical platform.[113]

This point of view, which the Eastern Europeans did not yet share, was the idea that the Jews in the United States were American Jews, a separate group and at the same time an integral part of the American community. In 1921, Wise was willing to leave the American Jews only two areas in which to be independent. One was in the religious sphere— "carrying out the ideas of prophetic Judaism"—and the other was in "efforts to settle colonies of Jews in Palestine."

Resignation of Brandeis's Supporters

On June 7, 1921, at the annual convention of the Z.O.A. in Cleveland, the administration's memorandum was defeated by a vote of 153 to 71. This led to the resignation of thirty-five members of the group from all official positions in the organization, including that of Brandeis from his honorary presidency of the Z.O.A.[114]

The assertion, made at the time and later, that by this vote the Jewish masses rejected Brandeis cannot be sustained. We have to remember that the membership of the organization was small; the number of members who elected the delegates to the convention cannot be determined, but the count in May 1921 gave only 17,000.[115] The evidence suggests great enthusiasm among the Jewish masses for the Zionist

---

[112] Wise to Brandeis, May 25, 1921, *Brandeis Papers*.
[113] Wise to Heller, April 16, 1921, *Heller Papers*.
[114] *Report of the Proceedings of the Twenty-Fourth Annual Convention*, pp. 120–21.
[115] De Haas to Frankfurter, May 5, 1921, *de Haas Papers*.

delegation, especially in the big centers, but they were not forced to make the actual decision of choosing between the two competing leaderships.

As for those who elected the delegates supporting Brandeis, almost a third of the convention, no accurate study of their social composition is possible. The evidence suggests, however, that almost all the American-born members supported Brandeis and that this support was centered in the provincial communities rather than in the centers like New York, where the opposition was particularly strong.[116] This will suggest that it was the more acculturated elements and those who were more in contact with the non-Jewish environment who were the source of support for Brandeis. There is also evidence that at least some of Brandeis's supporters conceived the struggle as one between loyalty to the Jewish nation and loyalty to the American people. It was the chairman of the thirtieth Zionist district of New York who declared at one meeting of the supporters of the administration: "I am an American citizen. America is first and Palestine second. That is the way I feel about it."[117] The majority of the delegates, however, declared their absolute "loyalty and allegiance to the World Zionist Organization and acknowledged the supreme authority of the Zionist Congress in all Zionist affairs." They further declared that they were "under moral and legal obligations" to support the authority of the Zionist Congress.[118]

Some idea of the nature and social composition of the two forces can be obtained from an examination of the available figures for membership of the national executive of the Z.O.A. in 1920 and 1921, and for the officers who resigned at the Cleveland Convention.

Table 6.1 indicates that all members of the national executive who were American-born or those who were born in Western Europe left with Brandeis. Table 6.2 shows that most of the Eastern Europeans who left with Brandeis were members of the liberal professions; all came to the United States at a young age and received at least an important part of their formal education in this country. As far as can be ascertained, of the eleven Eastern European businessmen who joined the national executive after Brandeis's resignation, most were small businessmen.

Another interesting group to examine is the members of the national executive in 1920–21 who, while supporting the views of one side of

---

[116] Brandeis to Mack, September 1, 1920, ibid.
[117] Minutes of the meeting of the district chairmen of Greater New York, Z.O.A., April 19, 1921, ibid.
[118] *Report of the Proceedings of the Twenty-Fourth Annual Convention*, p. 163.

Struggle over Control of the World Zionist Organization

TABLE 6.1 *Comparison of Place of Birth of Officeholders in the Z.O.A., before and after the Resignation of Brandeis*

Place of Birth	Members of the National Executive 1920–1921	Members of the National Executive 1921–1922	Officeholders Who Resigned in Cleveland
United States & Western Europe	13	1[a]	13
Eastern Europe	17	30	7
Unavailable	19	21	13
Total	49	52	33

[a] Louis Lipsky, the leader of the Eastern European group in the Z.O.A., was born in the United States.

TABLE 6.2 *Comparison of Occupation of Officeholders in the Z.O.A. Who Were Eastern European-Born between Those Who Resigned with Brandeis and Those Who Stayed*

Occupation	Officeholders Who Resigned in Cleveland	Members of the National Executive 1921–1922
Lawyers	4	2
Physicians	—	2
University professors	1	—
Reform Rabbis	1	—
Businessmen	1	11
Journalist and writers for the immigrant community	—	15
Total	7	30

the dispute, switched their support to the other when the break occurred. In fact, a certain cross-pressure seemed to have made it difficult for them to make up their minds. Out of our four known cases, three were Eastern European-born who had acquired higher education in this country and were members of the liberal professions, including Reform rabbis, who had to obtain a college degree as a prerequisite to entering their profession.

Two of the four cases were elective judges who were born in Eastern Europe and shortly before the break supported the point of view of the

American leaders. Judge Dannenbaum was a member of the "Committee of Fifty" established on May 9, 1921, to support Brandeis; later he joined the Z.O.A. national executive. Judge Bernard Rosenblatt declared in a letter to Mack on the question of Jewish nationalism that "the connection of the American Jew, who will remain in America, with the Jew who becomes part of the Palestinian state, is not a national connection but a religious one."[119] This did not prevent Rosenblatt from assuming membership of the administrative committee of the Z.O.A. at the Cleveland Convention and becoming the secretary of the organization for the next few years.

On the other hand, all three Reform rabbis on the executive committee resigned with Brandeis. Two of them, however, supported the opposition to Brandeis until very near the end. Rabbi Abba Hillel Silver, born in Lithuania and educated in this country, was associated with the opposition forces.[120] In the national executive meeting in September 1920, he introduced a resolution that, contrary to the memorandum introduced by the administration, clearly stated that "the integrity and effectiveness of the I.Z.O. [World Zionist Organization] be at all costs preserved."[121] Rabbi Heller was a convinced nationalist and supported the European point of view strongly. Both, however, resigned and stayed with Brandeis.

In the case of these cross-pressures, the decision was determined by the constituents and their sentiments. The elected judges were dependent on the votes of the Eastern Europeans and must have thought that the sentiments of the latter were with Weizmann, as did the politicians in New York City who gave Weizmann a reception at City Hall and handed him the keys of the city. The Reform rabbis, on the other hand, had to take account of the fact that almost all the members of their congregations were German Jews.

This analysis enables us to conclude that those few American-born German Jews who were willing to join with the Eastern European Jewish community in aiding the creation of a Jewish state in Palestine were only willing to do so under the direction of fellow American leaders who, like Brandeis, had made a name for themselves in American society. They refused to follow the foreign-born leaders even though the latter were the legitimate heads of the World Zionist Organization and, by virtue of this position, were acknowledged by many Jews and non-Jews as the leaders of the Jewish nation.

---

[119] Bernard Rosenblatt to Mack, January 22, 1920, *de Haas Papers*.
[120] De Haas to Brandeis, September 17, 1920, ibid.
[121] Minutes of the executive meeting of the Z.O.A., September 29, 1920, ibid.

The Eastern European immigrant community in the United States, on the other hand, supported those leaders whom they perceived as the leaders of the Jewish nation. This attachment to the idea of the Jewish nation and to their leaders was not, however, as unanimously accepted by this group as it was rejected by the former group. A division existed even among those Eastern Europeans who were active in the Zionist Organization.

The events of 1921 demonstrated that many members of the Eastern European community who were active in Jewish life, but who at the same time had received their higher education in this country and had entered the liberal professions, tended to follow the American-born leaders rather than the leaders of world Jewry. Many even withdrew from their positions in the Z.O.A. when Brandeis and his associates resigned their leadership. This must be attributed to their greater acculturation to the American society, which concurrently weakened their attachment to the World Jewish group.

Many Jewish small businessmen who shared the interest in a Jewish Palestine, and who had succeeded in improving their economic status, nevertheless maintained their attachment to the world Jewish leaders. An explanation of this group's stand will have to await our study of their role in the Zionist Organization in the 1920's, in the next two chapters.

CHAPTER VII

Zionist Activities in the United States, 1921–26

The Organization's Dedication to Fund-Raising

Observers, in assessing the progress made by the American Zionist Organization in the 1920's, often claim that the organization was enjoying increased support. But when we come to examine the facts, we find that they are not readily available. Only a sympathetic few joined the organization; others contributed to the fund-raising campaigns of the *Keren Hayesod*. There seems to be no easy way of distinguishing those Jews who sympathized with Zionism from those who were indifferent or opposed, other than by the fact that almost all supporters belonged to the Eastern European immigrant groups and not to the established German Jewish group.[1]

The same lack of information confronts us when we attempt to examine the membership of the Z.O.A. during the period under discussion. There is no accurate way of finding out what their social characteristics as a group were. But for the period after 1918, we do have overall membership figures:[2]

TABLE 7.1 *Membership of the Z.O.A., 1918–29*

Year	Number	Year	Number
1918	149,235	1924	25,934
1919	56,838	1925	27,144
1920	21,000	1926	23,784
1921	30,597	1927	21,806
1922	18,481	1928	21,539
1923	24,303	1929	18,031

These figures include, until 1921, the Hadassah membership. By the end of 1921, Hadassah gained a semi-autonomous position, at which time they had about 10,000 members.[3]

---

[1] Jacob Rader Marcus, "Zionism and the American Jew," *The American Scholar* 2 (1933): 283.
[2] Samuel Halperin, *The Political World of American Zionism* (Detroit: Wayne State University Press, 1961), p. 327.
[3] Irma Lindheim in *Hadassah Newsletter* 7 (March 1927).

Thus, between 1920 and 1929, membership figures did not fluctuate as radically as in the preceding two years. Membership rose slowly until 1925 and then decreased more rapidly until 1930. There are no reliable figures on the degree of turnover, though several active members stated that it was high. Samuel M. Melamed, who was a member of the national executive of the Z.O.A. during this period, argues that membership could be divided into two groups: the stable element, which consisted of members who accepted the ideological precepts of the Zionist doctrine; and those "with a sentiment," who paid their dues but neither knew nor cared about Zionist ideology.[4] The latter comprised the unstable element of the membership.

Throughout the period, membership of the Z.O.A. remained exceedingly low. This is explained, in part, by the fact that the Zionist Organization was associated in the public mind with the idea of a separate Jewish nationality. The departure from the Z.O.A. leadership in 1921 of Louis Brandeis and his American-born colleagues strengthened this image of the organization as the American branch of a world nationalist organization. This image held back many sympathizers of a Jewish Palestine from joining the Z.O.A.

At the same time, the organization's main activity remained that of fund-raising even after Chaim Weizmann defeated Brandeis in 1921. It will be argued in this chapter that the Jewish intellectuals, who controlled the organization from 1921 to 1930, maintained fund-raising activities as the organization's main function, to the neglect of everything else. When Brandeis's associates returned to leadership in 1930, they found an organization devoted solely to fund-raising. Jacob de Haas, who became the new head of the organization department, said in his first report to the national executive: "All the various appeals go to the same people and the personnel of all local committees is practically identical. Between demands for deficit funds, emergency funds, Jewish National Fund, Allied Jewish Campaign, etc., there is left no breathing spell for the local volunteers either to organize themselves for membership work or to provide serious local programs. Membership is thus, gradually transforming itself into a headquarters office activity—a mail order campaign."[5] Hence, membership in the Z.O.A. appealed primarily to Jews who were willing to be identified with Jewish nationalism and at the same time be actively engaged in fund-raising work.

---

[4] Samuel M. Melamed, *Dos Yiddishe Folk*, June 17, 1927, p. 4.
[5] Report of the chairman of the committee of organization to the executive committee of the Z.O.A., November 23, 1930, *Jacob de Haas Papers* (New York: Zionist Archives).

The sympathizers with the Jewish colonization of Palestine, whose members in the United States were growing in the 1920's, supported it through their contribution to the Zionist fund drives but did not become members of the Z.O.A.

A better understanding of the position of these supporters will be gained by applying a classification made by Maurice Duverger in his discussion of political parties. Duverger distinguishes between active members of a political party, whom he calls "militants," and the rest who are the party's supporters. In mass parties, the militants are the minority who follow the leaders and in turn lead the mass of members; in cadre parties, "there is no difference between militancy and membership." In such cadre parties, the party supporters are not actually included, properly, within the party structure. The supporter, explains Duverger, is the person who "makes manifest his agreement with the party; he confesses his political preference." This support "brings him into fellowship with other supporters and creates the first bond of community."[6]

In the case of the Zionist Organization, which was becoming a cadre party organization, donations to the *Keren Hayesod* were evidence of this bond. Propaganda that accompanied its campaign asserted that it was the proud obligation of each individual Jew to contribute to the great cause of Palestine. These supporters formed as important a group for the organization as voters do in a political party. As the Z.O.A. became more and more involved in fund-raising, the amount of contributions collected became the measure of success. The contributors became an influential group, and the leaders of the organization catered to their sentiments and ideas. There were thus two groups in the Zionist camp: the active members, the militants, who were totally committed to the cause, and the supporters who shared a "bond of community" through their contributions to the development of Palestine to the *Keren Hayesod*, but who did not join the organization.

One problem we must face in this chapter is to understand how a leadership that did not perceive its main function as collecting money for Palestine found itself leading an organization that was devoted almost exclusively to this function. The ready explanation embraced by those involved was a simple one: the pressing needs of Palestine, plus the difficulties in obtaining sufficient funds for the necessary work there, put the primary burden on the Zionists who resided in the richest Jewish community. But this explanation is only partly correct. It cannot ac-

---

[6] Maurice Duverger, *Political Parties* (New York: John Wiley & Sons, 1955), pp. 101, 102, 210.

count for the zeal, abandon, and resourcefulness of the American Zionist in accomplishing this one part of the Zionist program to the neglect of all the others that they promised to carry out during the struggle between Weizmann and Brandeis.

The success of the Z.O.A. leaders in fund-raising activities can be examined by comparing their achievements with those of other Jewish organizations (especially the campaign drives conducted with the support of the wealthy A.J.C.). We will then compare their success with the failure of the American leaders who resigned with Brandeis in 1921 and who were to work independently for the development of Palestine.

The comparison with the J.D.C. of the A.J.C. shows that while the *Keren Hayesod* raised $17 million between 1921 and 1930, the J.D.C. raised for the aid of Eastern and Central European Jews $63 million between 1919 and 1930.[7]

No less enlightening for our purpose would be an examination of the number of contributors to Zionist and non-Zionist funds, but there are no reliable figures. One general observation can be made: the number of contributors to all Jewish funds was increasing rapidly, even though a few large donors still dominated the field and provided a very high percentage of the amount contributed. This was also true, though less so, for the Zionist drives. Even the contributions to the *Keren Hayesod* included large donations by men like Nathan Straus, Samuel Untermeyer, and the leaders of the A.J.C., Felix Warburg and Louis Marshall. At the same time, the Zionists reached people of small means and tapped their resources. For example, the figures of the United Palestine Appeal (U.P.A.) for 1926-27 show that 180,000 persons contributed to the campaign, of whom only 60,000 gave twenty-five dollars or more.[8] On the other hand, in 1926 Marshall reported to Weizmann that as a result of the campaign of the Zionists against the J.D.C. in the New York area, the latter lost in number of contributors but doubled in contributions.[9] It is clear that throughout the 1920's the large donations were given mostly to the A.J.C. campaigns rather than to the Zionist funds. At best, the rich Jews gave to the Zionists only a small percentage of their overall contributions to philanthropic and charitable causes. At the same time, the Zionists reached new circles of Jews, like labor

---

[7] Leo W. Schwartz, "Zionism in the Postwar Era," in *Modern Palestine*, ed. Jessie Sampter (New York: Hadassah, The Women's Zionist Organization of America, 1933), p. 69.

[8] *The New Palestine*, November 11, 1927, p. 355.

[9] Charles Reznikoff, ed., *Louis Marshall: Champion of Liberty*, vol. 2 (Philadelphia: The Jewish Publication Society of America, 1957), p. 758.

groups and Jewish orders and *landsmanschaften*. In effect, rich Jews ignored Zionist funds, and the Zionist appealed to the less affluent elements of the community.

This is not to say that the Zionists appealed to the very poor. The supporters for the Zionist funds were described in 1922 by Louis Lipsky as those who were "becoming more well-to-do" and were labeled by him in 1927 as the middle class.[10]

We mentioned earlier the large number of small businessmen of Eastern European background in the new executive committee in 1921. As we shall examine later, this ruling body of the Z.O.A. included more and more businessmen; it was, in effect, a coalition between them and the Jewish intellectuals.

The Brandeisists' Efforts to Develop Palestine Economically

The group of American leaders who resigned with Brandeis in June 1921, popularly named Brandeisists, decided to work independently for the financing of efforts in Palestine. Believing that the Z.O.A. and the *Keren Hayesod* had no chance of success, they intended to implement their own schemes for building up Palestine.

Directives for the operations of the group were laid down by Brandeis at a meeting in the New York office of State Senator Nathan Straus, Jr., three days after the resignation of Brandeis and his associates in Cleveland. The group accepted Brandeis's program, which was not to secede from the Z.O.A. and not to establish a minority faction within the Z.O.A. Brandeis was reported to have said that they should do specific work that, in their judgment, ought to be done. They should act and not talk; they were not a minority party and should have nothing to do with politics. This group would deal exclusively with economic projects in Palestine and for this purpose would be headed by a Palestine Development Council (P.D.C.). Brandeis further announced that non-Zionists should be encouraged to join. The group as such would not subscribe to any specific ideology; as Brandeis stated, "anybody who wants to cooperate from the outside should be welcome without any declaration of faith." The decision was made that officers on the new Council would be appointed by the top leaders of the group, because, as Brandeis declared emphatically, democratic procedures "are proper enough for the organization which is a political organization, but they are not the way when a specific work is to be undertaken." The objec-

---

[10] Louis Lipsky, *Thirty Years of American Zionism* (The Nesher Publishing Co., 1927), pp. 78, 192.

tive was to bring together a group of people willing to invest in Palestine. No propaganda or agitation would be used in this endeavor. The leaders would personally contact all the people who desired to invest in Palestine and co-opt them into the group.[11]

It seems that the basic principle of this plan was lack of publicity. This group was even willing to depart from the principle of holding elections in order to carry out its activities unnoticed by the American public. Its officers wanted to assert their leadership in American Jewry through action in faraway Palestine.

But at the conference of the new Palestine Development Association in Pittsburgh on July 3 and 4, a number of members objected to the passivity of the new group and to their refusal to fight the new administration of the Z.O.A. and the European leaders of the W.Z.O. openly. They suggested that the group should constitute itself as a fraction and should go to the World Zionist Congress to explain its point of view.[12] However, Brandeis and his inner circle of associates would have none of it. The mere thought of going to the World Zionist Congress alarmed them. They were motivated by their fear of again bringing to public attention the issues of Diaspora nationalism and political allegiance to the future Jewish state. One observes their embarrassment when these issues cropped up during the open debate with the European leaders in which they were forced to participate. After the nationalists' victory and the successful functioning of the *Keren Hayesod*, which was directed by the hotheaded nationalist agitators, they refused to be publicly associated in any way with the Z.O.A. and the W.Z.O., even as an opposition faction. This is why they were so desperately trying to break into respectable non-Zionist circles. During the two-day debate in Pittsburgh, nobody dared mention the expression *Diaspora nationalism*; it was as though the issue had disappeared overnight. There was a conscious attempt to restrict the discussion to economic issues, to pretend that the area of disagreement with the European Zionist leaders was confined to methods of operation in Palestine. They described themselves as the group that aimed at establishing a community of self-supporting Jews in Palestine, while the Zionist leaders were committed to an erroneous, misguided, and even corrupt plan that would prevent Palestine from forming a viable economy. Stephen Wise enunciated two slogans for the future work of the group: "Silence in America,

---

[11] Minutes of the meeting at Senator Straus's office in New York, June 10, 1921, de Haas Papers.

[12] Minutes of the Palestine Development Association conference, Pittsburgh, July 3–4, 1921, ibid.

Service in Palestine" and "Non-Resistance in America, Assistance in Palestine."[13]

Thus, the new P.D.C. was a non-political organization through which the American leaders would quietly and in a businesslike manner approach potential investors for specific economic projects in consultation with the businessmen in the group and then, together, would persuade other businessmen to cooperate. Eventually, the American Jews would see their achievement, and their leadership in American Jewry would be assured. They would attain this end without endangering their positions in American society in any way, and it would enable them to continue to devote most of their time and energies to those other obligations.

This position was clearly explained by Jacob de Haas in a letter written to Max Heller in 1922 in which he admitted that they had decided on that policy *"not only because it is economically sound and really helpful, but because it also lessens the demand upon the individual.* And this policy," he added, "more in keeping with the ordinary tone of American life, will no doubt win more people, particularly of the type that you would desire to see in" [italics mine].[14]

The opposition to such a passive group attitude came from Rabbi Abba Hillel Silver, Rabbi Solomon Goldman, and Judge Hugo Pam, who claimed that it had not the power to appeal to American Jewry. Their social position depended much more on the good will and appreciation of their Jewish constituents than did Brandeis's and Frankfurter's; Pam was elected judge in a Chicago district that had many Jewish residents. Moreover, not being of national renown or involved in national politics as Brandeis, Wise, and Frankfurter were, these men were less frightened and worried about the possible reaction of the American public to their activities within the Jewish group.

When the conference of the newly established group came to define the goals of the P.D.C., a compromise had to be attained. The goal was defined as "social-economic work," with the understanding that the added "social" included enterprises like the Hebrew University.[15]

Was this plan workable? Were we to judge by the results, the answer would be negative. It was based on the erroneous assumption that there existed a large group of Jews to whom such a scheme might appeal, and

---

[13] Minutes of the meeting at Senator Straus's office, New York, June 10, 1921, ibid.

[14] De Haas to Max Heller, February 22, 1922, *Max Heller Papers* (Cincinnati: The American Jewish Archives).

[15] Minutes of the Palestine Development Association conference, Pittsburgh, July 3–4, 1921, *de Haas Papers*.

who would be willing to follow the plan and invest in Palestine. It is amazing that, having suffered previous disappointments, the group embarked on such a scheme. They persevered for quite a few years, even though they encountered one disappointment after another.

Their first step was to go back to the A.J.C. supporters and request their cooperation. Julian Mack, still the president of the Z.O.A., contacted Marshall by January 1921 and offered to establish an economic council that would invest in Palestine.[16] Details of such a plan were never worked out, but Mack reported to Brandeis that Marshall was encouraging though noncommittal. Mack then went as far as to invite the A.J.C. group to join them in their negotiations with Weizmann.[17] They politely refused, though Marshall later expressed his willingness to mediate between the two sides. That was after Weizmann himself had asked him to mediate in the dispute.[18]

It was then that the A.J.C. began to regain its power and initiative in Jewish politics, which it had almost lost to Brandeis and the Zionist Organization a few years earlier. Thus, Brandeis's fear that if he lost control over the Zionist mass organization he would also lose the power struggle against Marshall came true. With both sides of the dispute appealing to the A.J.C. for help, the position of the A.J.C. was becoming stronger. Both sides were staking their political futures on their success at fund-raising, an area in which the A.J.C. excelled because of the concentration of wealth and prestige in its ranks. From 1921 until his death in 1929, Marshall, as A.J.C. president, was to play one group against the other.

Soon after Weizmann had arrived in the United States, in early April 1921, both Marshall and Warburg went to see him, ostensibly to pay their respects to the world Zionist leader, at the same time taking great care to keep the Yiddish press informed about their visit.[19] Untermeyer, Marshall's law partner, first offered his services as a mediator in May 1921. At the same time, he promised a large sum of money to the newly established *Keren Hayesod* and was rewarded by becoming its president.[20] It has been said that Untermeyer was motivated in his action by competition with Marshall for fame and prestige within the Jewish community. Whatever his motives, this was eminently suited to Mar-

---

[16] Mack to Brandeis, January 29, 1921, *Louis Brandeis Papers* (Louisville, Ky.: University of Louisville Law Library).
[17] Mack to Brandeis, January 31, 1921, ibid.
[18] Marshall to Weizmann, May 28, 1926, *Felix Warburg Papers* (Cincinnati: The American Jewish Archives).
[19] *The Day*, April 7 and April 8, 1921.
[20] De Haas to Brandeis, June 1, 1921, *Brandeis Papers*.

shall's strategy. Marshall advised the Brandeisists that they "were committing a crime against the Cause not to arrange a peace," even if they had to make many concessions.[21] At the same time, he bolstered the *Keren Hayesod* by writing to its president that "there is no Jew, whoever he may be, who has the right to shirk the duty of assisting in giving due effect to the beneficial purposes which underlie the Balfour Declaration."[22] To these grand words he added the less grand contribution of $1,000. His actions, however, considerably harmed the position of the Brandeis group, who counted both on their success among the wealthy Jews and on the failure of the *Keren Hayesod*.

The Zionist members and sympathizers remained loyal to the Z.O.A., and the German Jews also refused to cooperate.[23] The solution seemed to be cooperation with the wealthy Eastern European Jews, who were more responsive to the needs of Palestine. "We need just this crowd of Russian Jews," wrote Mack.[24] Negotiations with such a group had been already in process since the end of 1920. At that time, a group of Eastern European businessmen headed by Samuel Lamport, who became a member of the national executive of the Z.O.A. in 1921, and the Jewish educator, Samson Benderly, were trying to establish the American Palestine Company. Mack wrote to Brandeis: "I really believe it would be valuable if you would see him [Benderly]. He said that his people had urged him to see you and Warburg and others, but he told them he would not see Warburg or any German Jew until he had raised a million dollars, and that he did not want to press himself on you."[25]

We can see here the beginning of an emerging stratum in the Jewish community, the newly rich Eastern Europeans. Some of them tried to enter the circle of the wealthy German Jews, but as their numbers grew there was friction between the *nouveaux riches* and the moneyed aristocrats. Many of the newcomers felt rebuffed, as Mack's letter insinuates. As might be expected, the alternative was a leading position in their own Eastern European community. Many associated themselves with the Zionist Organization, which was especially attractive when Brandeis was leader. The breach between the American and the Eastern European leaders was an upsetting experience for the Eastern European businessmen associated with the Zionist Organization. They tried until the last

---

[21] Mack to Brandeis et al., August 14, 1921, ibid.

[22] Marshall to Samuel Untermeyer, March 31, 1922, in *Louis Marshall Papers* (Cincinnati: The American Jewish Archives).

[23] Mack to Brandeis, June 24, 1921, *Brandeis Papers*; Mack to Brandeis, June 28, 1921, *de Haas Papers*.

[24] Mack to Brandeis, December 14, 1920, *Brandeis Papers*.

[25] Ibid.

minute to prevent a split and preserve unity. One such group organized itself into a "peace committee of nine," which was composed of eight Eastern European businessmen headed by Rabbi Mordecai Kaplan.[26] When the split occurred, they were torn between their desire to be associated with men of Brandeis's caliber and enormous prestige and their wish to be respected, recognized, and honored by the members of their own Eastern European community. So some stayed with the Z.O.A.; others associated themselves with the Brandeisists; and others at first joined hands with the Brandeisists and, at the same time, retained their seats on the national executive of the Z.O.A.

The extent of their conflict is revealed in the autobiography of one member of the group, Bernard Horwich. Horwich had arrived in this country as a boy from Eastern Europe, settled in Chicago, and by the turn of the century was a wealthy businessman. He was one of the founders of the Zionist Organization and was an active contributor to it. Though he lacked education, he confessed his respect for learning and Jewish culture. He tells of the beginning of Zionism in the Hebrew literary societies, in which he was also active, even though not proficient in the Hebrew language. "Whenever I find myself among people who are superior intellectually," he wrote, "whether I know them or not, I suffer from feeling of inferiority."[27] His respect for Jewish learning became mixed with respect for the "good manners" and civilized habits of men like the German philanthropists. Throughout his life, he was pulled between respect for the learning of the Jewish intellectuals and respect for the prestige of the wealthy German Jews.

In the 1930's, when his book was written, the latter pull became stronger. Of the crisis in the Z.O.A. he tells us: "I felt very disappointed that such men as Louis Lipsky, Abe Goldberg and Jacob Fishman (of the N.Y. *Jewish Morning Journal*) should have joined in forcing out the Brandeis group. In spite of this unexplainable action on their part, however, I consider them to be among the most able, sensible and best qualified men in the movement today." But he hastens to add: "Under the direction of men of the caliber of Brandeis and Mack, events would surely have shaped themselves differently and the Zionist Organization would have undoubtedly functioned more efficiently."[28]

In spite of this opinion, he did not back the Brandeis group in 1921. On the contrary, he arranged a large reception for Weizmann after the

---

[26] Mack to de Haas, May 31, 1921, and de Haas to Brandeis, June 1, 1921, ibid.
[27] Bernard Horwich, *My First Eighty Years* (Chicago: Argus Books, 1939), pp. 317–18.
[28] Ibid., pp. 405, 406.

convention, joined the national executive committee of the Z.O.A., and remained one of the financial backers of the organization throughout the 1920's.

A bonus he received from Weizmann as a reward for his loyalty, and one which he obviously greatly appreciated, was to be invited to meetings with Marshall and his friends. In 1923, Weizmann began to convene these conferences, to which members of the A.J.C. and the Zionists were invited, with the aim of uniting their efforts in Palestine. Horwich discussed his meetings with Marshall in detail and proudly tells us that at one such meeting, when asked by Marshall to define Zionists, he replied that "the only difference between the Zionists and the non-Zionists is that the Zionists shout louder."[29]

This group of Eastern European businessmen in the Zionist Organization was called "Bourgeois gentilhommes" by the visiting Zionist leader and sociologist, Chaim Arlozoroff. Since "they cannot," he wrote, "enter the more exclusive circles of the non-Zionists, especially the wealthy German-Jewish socialites—due to their financial conditions and their education and temperament—they look for an outlet to their social ambitions in the Zionist leadership."[30]

It was this class of people that the Brandeisists decided to rely on in carrying out their plans for the P.D.C.[31] It is interesting that the Brandeisists were hoping to involve German Jewish businessmen through their contact with Russian Jewish businessmen. Mack said to Brandeis, "by joining hands with Lamport and the group . . . we build, I believe, the bridge that will connect us with the leaders of the J.D.C., if such a connection is in any case possible."[32]

It seems, however, that the Eastern European businessmen in Brandeis's camp suffered from the same awe as their colleagues in the Z.O.A. camp. They looked up to and admired the German Jewish millionaires and philanthropists. When one of the Eastern European businessmen, Sol Rosenblum, treasurer of the P.D.C., conducted negotiations with the J.D.C., Mack sent a worried note to Brandeis that Rosenblum "seems completely captivated by those people. . . . He himself feels thoroughly competent to deal with them, but his complete trust in them made me and makes me apprehensive."[33]

---

[29] Ibid., p. 267.
[30] Chaim Arlozoroff, *Ktavim*, vol. 5 (Tel Aviv: Hotzaat A. Y. Shtible, 1935), p. 155.
[31] Lindheim to Brandeis, June 28, 1921, *Brandeis Papers*.
[32] Mack to Brandeis, June 28, 1921, ibid.
[33] Mack to Brandeis, January 28, 1922, ibid.

It was Weizmann and the Z.O.A. who gave the Eastern European businessmen prestige among the Jewish masses, for they publicized their contributions to the *Keren Hayesod*. The many conferences for Palestine gave them the desired contact with the money magnates. Brandeis, on the other hand, could only offer them his very remote association and no publicity at all in Jewish quarters. Thus, most members of this group stayed with the Z.O.A.

Discouraged by their failure to raise money (they had pinned all their hopes for success on that), the Brandeisists soon showed signs of demoralization. As early as November 1921, Mack commented sadly on "the loss of enthusiasm among every one of us, as compared with the feelings when we were in control of the Z.O.A."[34] Some members, including Rabbi Silver, objected to negotiations with the J.D.C., advocating a more aggressive policy instead. The disappointment within the group, Silver claimed, was due to the leadership's belief that money could be raised without the "propaganda and solicitation" that he advocated.[35] But the leadership refused to adopt that course. Others recommended a reconciliation with the Z.O.A., but Brandeis would have none of that, either. He was still convinced that it was possible to succeed by being silent in the United States and concentrating on economic projects in Palestine. Brandeis believed that the opportune time to negotiate with the Z.O.A. on their own terms would be when they succeeded in Palestine. He wrote to the inner circle, "I think conference with anyone representing Z.O.A. or W.Z.O. most undesirable. You know what we want to accomplish. Go straight for that."[36]

In desperation, the group decided to change their original plans and build an organization, the Palestine Development Leagues, designed to cater strictly to investors. The leagues were to consist of small branches; each league was to have no less than twenty-five members who would subscribe or secure subscriptions of no less than $5,000. Failing to achieve that goal, the league would not have a member on the Palestine Development Council. A central body was appointed that included all the prominent members of the Brandeis group.[37]

This enterprise proved to be another dismal failure, and the group rapidly disintegrated. In early 1923, members were deserting and going back to the Z.O.A., where they most often assumed positions of respon-

---

[34] Mack to Brandeis, November 2, 1921, ibid.
[35] Abba Hillel Silver to Mack, November 7, 1921, ibid.
[36] Brandeis to Mack, Wise, and de Haas, March 22, 1922, *de Haas Papers*.
[37] *Palestine Development Leagues: Tentative Constitution and By-Laws of Central Committee and Leagues* (New York, June 1923), ibid.

sibility not on the Z.O.A. executive but in the growing machinery of the *Keren Hayesod*, which was gaining in strength. Not only were the old Zionists loyal to it, but it attracted new forces in the community. De Haas reported to Brandeis in January 1923 that the people connected with the Reform movement "have given five times more to the *Keren Hayesod* than they have given to us." This was a reference to the financial backers of the Reform group, but the spiritual leaders followed the same path. "It is true that the *Keren Hayesod* is getting a good number of Reform rabbis to work for them."[38]

Two main reasons, de Haas argued, made the *Keren Hayesod* a success in the United States. One was the policy of separating the fund, which devoted itself solely to Palestine, from the Zionist Organization. "They have been trying to convince the public," de Haas contended, "that the *Keren Hayesod* has nothing to do with the Zionist Organization." This principle of separation was laid down by the European leaders who founded the *Keren Hayesod*. Rather than invite the non-Zionists into the Zionist Organization, as suggested by the American leaders in 1920, they preferred to maintain the organization's commitment to the national ideal, which it would continue to propagate among the Jews, and separately to build the *Keren Hayesod* to attract any Jews willing to help build up Palestine. In their report to the World Zionist Congress in 1923, the trustees of the *Keren Hayesod* were pleased with the results in the United States. As they explained to the delegates, ". . . its success in the United States has justified the principle of neutrality, which it has honestly tried to realize. It has succeeded in uniting Jews of all opinions; it has established working relations not only with all Zionist organizations, but also with non-Zionist groups and the leaders of the social and religious life of the Jews. . . ."[39]

The second source of the success of the *Keren Hayesod* in the United States, according to de Haas, was the agitation, propaganda, and publicity that accompanied the fund-raising and that resulted in attracting the Jewish masses. In his letter to Brandeis, Mack, and Felix Frankfurter, which might be read as a rebuff to those who advocated silence in their activities in the United States, he asserted: "There is no end to the money that can be raised, but it cannot be done quietly, nor can it be done without the machinery of jazz. There is a great amount of wealth and even a willingness to part with some of it. I think the country is fairly sold on Palestine, but it begs for excitement, as the exchange for

---

[38] De Haas to Brandeis, January 29, 1923, ibid.
[39] *Report of Keren Hayesod to the Thirteenth [Zionist] Congress, August 1923* (London: 75 Great Russell Street, 1923), p. 21.

Zionist Activities in the United States, 1921-26

its giving. I confess that in smaller towns, I can understand it; in the big cities it is a puzzle."[40]

While the Brandeisists were left wondering, trying to solve their puzzle, the Zionists were succeeding. The "machinery of jazz" was acceptable not only to the Jewish masses, to the growing Eastern European middle class, but even to some of the well-bred German Jewish millionaires who were being won over to the *Keren Hayesod*. One such case was that of Straus and his son. In June 1921, they strongly supported the Brandeisists against the *Keren Hayesod*. However, as early as April 1922 Straus was urging Brandeis to reconcile his differences with the Z.O.A.; when he failed, he became one of the largest donators to the *Keren Hayesod*.[41] Through its publicity operations, *Keren Hayesod* provided a reward the Brandeis scheme was unable to offer. Straus's prestige in the Jewish community soared with each new contribution, duly publicized by the *Keren Hayesod* and by the Yiddish press. People were more willing to donate when their donation contributed to their standing within the Jewish community. One may well suspect that those contributions, when given in the right circumstances, at mass meetings surrounded by an excitable audience, gave many the feeling of brotherhood with their fellow Jews, and that the act of donation became a "bond of community."

One of the most severe blows to the Brandeisists was the negotiation that started between Weizmann, as the head of the W.Z.O., and Marshall, the head of the A.J.C., to combine efforts in building the economy of Palestine. This was followed by several conferences that were well publicized and attended by Zionists and non-Zionists alike. The first took place in May 1923, and only Brandeisists were excluded from it. An exception was Bernard Flexner, the chairman of the committee on Palestine of the J.D.C., and as such the only *persona grata* in A.J.C. circles. As we have already seen, many American Zionists were delighted with these new contracts. This helps to explain the continuous support given by them to the idea of the constitution of a Jewish Agency in which the Marshall group and other non-Zionists would sit together with Zionists, aiming at combined efforts for Palestine. Although the European Zionists raised many objections, the project always enjoyed the support of most American Zionists.

The remnants of the Brandeis group now felt that their situation was becoming hopeless; the group had reached an impasse.[42] At that critical

---

[40] De Haas to Brandeis, May 23, 1924, *de Haas Papers*.
[41] Nathan Straus (Jr.?) to Brandeis, April 21, 1922, ibid.
[42] Mack to Brandeis, December 24, 1923, *Brandeis Papers*.

stage, Flexner came to their aid. He suggested a merger between the P.D.C. and the committee on Palestine of the J.D.C. The merger would be created by forming a new association in which both the A.J.C. and the Brandeisists would serve. It was only now that Marshall offered to cooperate with the defeated group.[43] The members of the group, overlooking their humiliation, started negotiating in spite of the fact that Brandeis declined to go along with their action.[44]

Flexner, a member of the original Brandeis group and at one time a registered Zionist, was appointed president of the new organization, the Palestine Economic Corporation (P.E.C.), and thus the bitter pill was made slightly more palatable for the Brandeisists. The two vice-presidents were Marshall and Herbert Lehman. Some of the Brandeisists, like Mack, and the Eastern European businessmen who joined the group after they had left the Z.O.A. found their place on the P.E.C. executive committee. Economically this enterprise was sounder, since it involved men of greater wealth. They decided that they were not even going to make public appeals; they had no need to raise funds "since Warburg, Marshall, and Untermeyer will give large sums of money."[45]

This was fine with the businessmen, but what about the Jewish politicians? What was their function in the new organization? Immediately after the merger was announced, Mack reported: "Naturally all over the country members of our group are getting impatient and are gradually—and I think very properly—drifting back into the Zionist Organization or *Keren Hayesod* work."[46] So did their leaders. By the end of 1925 Mack, Wise, Samuel Rosensohn, Norvin Lindheim, and Robert Szold were back in the governing bodies of the Z.O.A. and the United Palestine Appeal (U.P.A.). The U.P.A. replaced the *Keren Hayesod* in 1925.

The inevitability of the leaders' move is explained by Mack in a letter written to de Haas in 1927, in reply to de Haas's advice not to accept the position of vice-president of the U.P.A. Refusing to accept such advice, he explained that the vice-presidency was the only office from which he could exercise leadership in the Jewish community. He would have liked to devote himself strictly to economic problems in Palestine, "such as the P.E.C. is now endeavoring to do," but in this purely economic enterprise, there was no room for him. His own "best power" was in getting money, and "as the P.E.C. needed no such use of any abilities as I might have in that line for Palestine, there seemed to me no other out-

---

[43] Marshall to Max Bressler, February 26, 1925, *Marshall Papers*.
[44] Brandeis to Mack, January 4, 1924, *Brandeis Papers*.
[45] Rosalie Crohn to de Haas, October 24, 1924, *de Haas Papers*.
[46] Mack to de Haas, January 15, 1925, ibid.

let in the last two years than in helping to raise the money for the U.P.A." One may, of course, doubt his judgment of himself as being primarily a fund-raiser, especially, considering his failures in the previous years. Nevertheless, it is significant that this was what he was ready and anxious to do; it was in this sphere of activity that he was willing to remain a Jewish leader. Further, Mack explained in his letter, the vice-presidency of the U.P.A. was much more suitable than assuming responsibilities within the Z.O.A., since the latter would involve resigning from the bench, which he absolutely refused to do, and this was the reason for his not attending the annual conventions of the Z.O.A.

Mack admitted in his letter that he was unhappy that men like Lipsky led the organization, and he assured de Haas that he refrained from doing anything that paid Lipsky any personal honor. At the same time he admitted that, though Lipsky's leadership was inefficient and corrupt and his methods were wrong, the results were impressive.[47]

The Zionists' Concentration on Palestinian Work and the Jewish Agency

In this discussion there has been no mention of the issues that divided the two groups in 1921, such as Diaspora nationalism, *gegenwartsarbeit* in the United States, and the like. The issues seemed to have lost their significance in American Jewry. They were still debated among devoted Zionists, and one could find a discussion here and there in the Yiddish press or among some of the party workers. These and other ideological tenets of Zionism were still discussed in Lower East Side coffee houses by groups of intellectuals and members of the Z.O.A. But outside the closed circles, propaganda and agitation from the Zionist Organization was purely Palestinian. In the vast Zionist literature of the period and in the Yiddish press, *Zionism and anything connected with the colonization of Palestine became interchangeable terms.* To some extent, this had always been the case in the Z.O.A. and in its predecessor, the F.A.Z. However, by the end of the 1920's it was becoming the case also among the intellectual leadership and the devoted workers.

In an attempt to gain a better understanding of this phenomenon, let us return to the first period in which the same leadership was in power, 1911–14. We argued, when we evaluated their leadership, that even then they were willing to do their best to attract members to the Zionist Organization who were not necessarily conscientious Zionists, but

---

[47] Mack to de Haas, May 26, 1927, ibid.

were primarily interested in Palestine. This was why, we contended, they inaugurated the Zion Associations, members of which would be expected to attend only one or two business meetings a year, but who would contribute to Palestinian institutions. The founding of Hadassah in 1912 followed a similar line of thought. At that time, however, Palestine was in the early stages of Jewish colonization and her needs were not very great, nor was the Zionist movement expecting the Americans to share the main part of the financial burden. Lipsky, as chairman of the F.A.Z., admitted that since many members were interested primarily in Palestine, the leaders of the organization were forced to devote themselves to Palestinianism rather than Zionism. But why were the intellectuals, who led the organization and who were deeply committed to Zionist ideology, submitting so easily to the pressures of public opinion and devoting their main energies to Palestine? We concluded that the Jewish community, in the midst of the process of acculturation, could not provide the Jewish intellectuals with the prestige they could normally expect *qua* intellectuals. They then tried to assert a position of influence in the United States by associating themselves with the Zionist movement. When they realized that they could increase the power and influence of the Zionist Organization, which they now headed, by taking advantage of the sentiment for Palestine, they set out to make the best of this opportunity. They hoped it would give them their rightful place in the American Jewish community.

The situation continued to exist in the twenties, but the opportunities were even grander. The Balfour Declaration and the mandate opened Palestine to the Jews and stirred Jews everywhere. At the same time, the process of acculturation was progressing rapidly. Membership in the Zionist Organization, which was connected with an international Jewish organization and advocated Jewish nationalism, did not appeal to American Jews, particularly as the United States was going through a phase of what John Higham calls nationalistic anti-Semitism. Support for the colonization of Palestine was, however, acceptable. Eager for support, the leaders of the Z.O.A. "have developed a network of organizations devoted exclusively to fund-raising for Palestine."[48] When the *Keren Hayesod* became too closely associated with Zionists in the public's eyes, a new organization, the United Palestine Appeal (U.P.A.), was created in 1925; and every effort was made to keep it separate from the Z.O.A. and thus to increase contributions. The amount of contributions was a measure of their success.

---

[48] Schwartz, "Zionism in the Postwar Era," in *Modern Palestine*, ed. Sampter, p. 69.

A nucleus of the leaders and the devoted party workers in the early twenties was still consciously Zionist. They wanted to propagate Zionist ideals and emphasized aspects of national and cultural revival in their propaganda and educational activities. But they did not receive any hearty response. They slowly adopted the path of least resistance, some succumbing more readily and more rapidly than others. This was not accomplished, however, without internal tension and struggle among the people involved. The history of the Z.O.A. in the 1920's was largely the manifestation of these tensions and struggles. At annual conventions and other meetings, members would fervently discuss the need for cultural and educational work. From time to time, an attempt was made to fill the need, but rarely was any prolonged action taken in this direction. The members were engaged in purely Palestinian pursuits, almost exclusively fund-raising for Palestine. Members of the Z.O.A. who discussed their experiences during that period often refer to sleepless nights spent in coffeehouses and other meetingplaces, where they discussed the ideological principles of the Zionist doctrine. The impression one gets is that these were extracurricular activities of the members, conducted in their spare time after their organizational duties were completed. Their prime goal was money. They agitated for funds in rallies, on street corners, in door-to-door campaigns.

This situation was especially difficult for those who controlled the organization and were responsible for its actions. They were attempting to adjust their thinking to the existing situation. The trend away from orthodox Zionism was clear. It was left to Dr. Abraham Coralnik, one of the few pure Zionists who still occupied a place in the Z.O.A. executive, to comment sadly in 1929: "The new generation that grew up in America in the last few years never did learn the alphabet of Zionism. And since the older generation is forgetting it, there are no teachers to teach them."[49]

The difficulties encountered in studying the changes in the thinking of American Zionists in their confused and often contradictory statements are augmented by the fact that the same label, Zionism, was used so indiscriminately. Those who still professed their belief in a Jewish nation, in Diaspora nationalism and *gegenwartsarbeit*, and those who were interested exclusively in aiding the building up of Palestine called themselves Zionists. In effect, labeling aid to Palestine as Zionism facilitated the process of change. It helped many to maintain an illusion of consistency, and it made many unaware of the transformation of Zionism.

---

[49] Abraham Coralink, *The Day*, June 16, 1929.

This transformation could have been accomplished more gradually by the Eastern European intellectuals at the helm of the Z.O.A. if it had not been for the issue of the Jewish Agency. It was expected that this new organization would take away from the Z.O.A. the function of fundraising and of the development of Palestine, leaving them with no other duties.

Discussions between Weizmann and the A.J.C. concerning the organization of Zionists and non-Zionists to share responsibility for the building of Palestine had been going on since 1923. The American Zionists had to be aware of the future of their organization after the Jewish Agency took over the economic development of Palestine.

The new leadership of the Z.O.A. supported Weizmann's efforts wholeheartedly. The businessmen in the Zionist camp enjoyed their association with the wealthy philanthropists. So did the intellectuals. They followed Weizmann's leadership and adopted his explanation that the Zionist Organization had functions other than mobilizing the economic resources of all Jewry for building Palestine. After the first public conference between Weizmann and Marshall, Lipsky declared in the annual convention on the issue of the Jewish Agency: "... in the larger union, the Zionist Organization does not propose a merger or a fusion, for we have a mission still to be performed. . . . Our obligation to arouse the consciousness of the Jewish people to their duties toward nationality, the conception of life with which we have inoculated ardent souls of Jewry, we do not abandon for the sake of this alliance." Echoing the ideas of Weizmann and his associates, Lipsky went on to assert that working for Palestine would convert the non-Zionists to Zionism.[50]

Yet in the same speech, Lipsky turned to the realities within American Zionism and observed a completely different situation. One moment he echoed the conviction of the world leadership that non-Zionists through their work for Palestine would be converted to Zionism. Now, as the head of the American organization, he admitted that it was the Zionists who were being converted to Palestinianism:

> What is it that looms big on our horizon, casting into the shade, reducing in rank, all other planks of our program, all other tenets of our ideology? *It is Palestine.* Palestine is the irresistible magnet that attracts all regardless of previous conditions of intellectual or spiritual servitude. . . . Many Zionists, eager to follow intuition, disregarding logic and strategy and long vision—mindless of them—would even substitute Palestine for the whole of Zionism and aspire to make Palestine sufficient for the ful-

---

[50] Lipsky, *Thirty Years of American Zionism*, pp. 167, 188.

fillment of all their hopes. With them it is a Palestine movement, with Zionism lurking in the background, sullenly glaring at the usurper.[51]

Lipsky subscribed to and committed himself to fighting for a set of principles. He realized that his followers were moving in a different direction. He did not condemn them any more, but only admonished them, explaining that "logic and strategy" demand that Zionist ideals should be their main concern. The future of Palestine was assured if the Jews became Zionists. However, as time went by, he had to admit that "logic and strategy" had suggested a move in the opposite direction. In January 1926, the editorial of *The New Palestine*, the official organ of the Z.O.A., conceded that "we cannot today convert a man to Zionism without first winning his support for the practical upbuilding of Palestine."[52]

Some of the leaders in the group of intellectuals were already equating Zionism with Palestinianism. In 1926, Maurice Samuel, Lipsky's right-hand man, argued that there were no longer any meaningful theoretical differences between Zionists and non-Zionists, since all supported Palestine.[53] This new situation Samuel accepted without a quarrel. He argued that the only difference between Zionists and non-Zionists was in methods of leadership. The non-Zionists were rich Jews whose style of leadership was accommodating, rather than strongly open and proud. The new "poor Jews" like Lipsky provided Jewry with a leadership that was not engaged in secret negotiations with the majority, but that was open and democratic. It was for this reason that he later supported Lipsky in the organization when the latter's leadership was under severe attack.

Fresh opposition within the ranks was concentrated in the new machinery of the U.P.A., but it included members of all backgrounds, American-born and Eastern European. Many who had been staunch supporters of Weizmann in 1921 now began to show dissatisfaction with the existing leadership of both Lipsky in the United States and Weizmann in London and Palestine. Two interesting characteristics can be discerned among the members of this group. They accepted the Palestinian approach without qualms or conflict, and they were becoming increasingly unhappy about being led by Yiddish-speaking intellectuals.

Emanuel Neumann had been one of the heads of the U.P.A. since 1925. In an article published in 1926, he explained that "the political

---

[51] Ibid., pp. 177–78.
[52] Editorial, *The New Palestine*, January 8, 1926, p. 29.
[53] Maurice Samuel, "Fundamentals Regarding the Jewish Agency," *The New Palestine*, March 12, 1926, pp. 246–49.

agitation associated with Zionism was giving way to a new Zionism of economic and cultural effort in Palestine."[54] In 1921, Neumann fought for educational and cultural work in the United States as well as in Palestine. At that time, he headed the education department of the Z.O.A. Later he became fully absorbed in the fund-raising and the U.P.A. In the same article, he also expressed impatience with the Z.O.A. leaders. He and the other members of the opposition were beginning to clamor for the return of the Brandeisists: "The seceding elements [the Brandeis group] constituted the only group in the organization which represented in the public mind precisely that occidental orientation, precisely those suppositious non-Zionist qualities which were so much in demand—efficiency, administrative gifts, financial and economic ability, experience in affairs of state."[55]

Thus the group that opposed Lipsky's leadership manifested two points of view that we associate with acculturation: unqualified acceptance of Palestinianism, and the desire to have leaders with an "occidental orientation" who would fit the general standards of American society, rather than Yiddish-speaking intellectuals who lacked "experience in the affairs of state."

In 1926, it looked as if the creation of the Jewish Agency was near, and restlessness grew among the Jewish intellectuals within the organization. The opposition was clamoring for the return of Brandeis, and the leaders, in a counteroffensive, were calling for return to first principles. The leaders published "A Communication to the American Zionists," in which they abhorred the developments of the Zionist movement with its emphasis on gathering funds, and which declared: ". . . the conviction grows that upon the basis of an annual interest in Palestine, in the form of contributions to the cause, no dependable responsibility can be developed. . . . We are convinced that dependence can be placed only upon those who assume a spiritual connection with the destiny of the Zionist Organization through the acceptance of its ideals."[56]

Following this declaration of policy, the Z.O.A. dedicated their conference on May 16 to Zionist educational activities. This resulted in the inauguration of a new organization, the Jewish Cultural Association, whose officers were members of the Z.O.A. leadership group. But the life of this organization was a short one. There was no response.

---

[54] Emanuel Neumann, "What of the Agency," *The New Palestine*, January 15, 1926, p. 56.
[55] Ibid.
[56] *The New Palestine*, April 9, 1926, p. 319.

At the end of 1925, it looked as if peace had arrived at last between the Zionists and the non-Zionists of the A.J.C. Negotiations with Weizmann on the future Jewish Agency were progressing satisfactorily. In September 1925 at a conference in Philadelphia, the A.J.C. and Zionist leaders agreed that two separate campaigns should be conducted in the United States: one was to be formed by the U.P.A. for the development of Palestine; the other, by the J.D.C., to be called the Allied Jewish Campaign, for Jewish relief work. Furthermore, Marshall attended the U.P.A. conference in Baltimore and delivered an encouraging speech.

From what followed it would seem that although Weizmann and the top A.J.C. leaders were satisfied with the state of affairs, the two competing fund-raising organs were not. The issue that inflamed the two groups was the Russian government's plan to colonize Jews in the Crimea, which the J.D.C. agreed to support in their 1926 drive. At the same time Marshall, in order to forestall Zionist anger, agreed to devote 1.5 million dollars collected by the J.D.C. to Palestinian projects. He also advised against too much publicity on the Crimean project and urged the head of the campaign, David Brown, to keep the agreement with the Zionists "both for strategical reasons and because of moral obligations."[57] The bureaucrats of the J.D.C. were unhappy with these arrangements. Apparently they were beginning to feel uneasy about the increased attention given to Palestine as compared with the general relief work that was their main responsibility. Thus, the Crimean project was a godsend to them. Brown, chairman of the Allied Jewish Campaign, "forgot" to mention the contribution to Palestine in his message and instead emphasized the Crimean colonization.[58] The Zionists reacted with great hostility, and soon the situation got out of hand.

An examination of the correspondence among Marshall, Warburg, and Brown shows that the top leaders of the A.J.C. were embarrassed by the public dispute and were trying their best to restrain their own people.[59] The same cannot be said for the leaders of the Z.O.A. The fight rallied members of the organization around the leaders and relieved the mounting inner conflicts and tensions. To this, the temperament of the Zionist party workers must be added. One Yiddish journalist, usually in sympathy with the Zionists, claimed that although the non-Zionist leaders were willing to follow their agreement with the Zionists and support Palestine as well as the Crimean project, the Zionists were not willing to give similar support to both. What happened

---

[57] Telegram from Marshall to David Brown, November 14, 1925, *Marshall Papers*.
[58] *The New Palestine*, October 23, 1925, pp. 321–22.
[59] Warburg to Marshall, August 9, and a telegram, August 6, 1926, *Warburg Papers*.

was that wherever the Zionists felt they were stronger than the J.D.C., they fought them; and only where they were weak were they willing to cooperate in the fashion agreed upon by the Philadelphia conference.[60]

The oversensitivity of the Eastern Europeans in their relations with the established German Jews also played its role in this battle. Neumann, who was longing for leaders with an "occidental orientation," was yet suspicious that the German Jews did not want to associate with the Eastern European Zionists and were not eager to join in the Jewish Agency. In explaining the causes for support of Crimean colonization by the A.J.C., he wrote that one had ". . . to probe into the realm of emotions, to consider what atavistic tendencies, what inhibitions, what involuntary reactions, what socio-cultural antipathies may have been aroused from their slumbers by the startling proposal to enter into a world-wide association with Jews of the Zionist variety. . . ."[61]

Lipsky justified the fight waged by the Zionists against the J.D.C. on the issue of the Crimean project by saying that "we had to protect the one productive front of the Zionist movement at all hazards, and we were not going to let ourselves become entangled in any formal discussion or debate, no matter how interesting or illuminating, of Zionist doctrine."[62]

So it was Palestine, after all, that was "the one productive front of the Zionist movement." The leaders of the Z.O.A. pinned their hopes on the appeal of Palestine and could not bother too much with "Zionist doctrine." The storm did not subside until Weizmann returned to the United States in the middle of 1927 and restored order among his lieutenants.

Sam Z. Chinitz, in his study of the creation of the Jewish Agency, assesses the Crimean controversy and its place in the creation of the agency in his argument that "the delay in the Agency negotiations, caused by the fund-raising controversy, proved that the Zionists were not able, as yet, to place Palestine in the forefront of philanthropic endeavor in the United States."[63] The Zionists, however, managed to damage the J.D.C. campaign. Lehman, in his report to the J.D.C. executive committee in May 1926, was convinced that their campaign was harmed by Zionist agitation.[64]

---

[60] S. Dingol, *The Day*, October 8, 1926.
[61] Neumann, "What of the Agency," p. 57.
[62] Lipsky, *Thirty Years of American Zionism*, p. 197.
[63] Sam Z. Chinitz, "The Jewish Agency and the Jewish Community in the United States" (Master's essay, Faculty of Political Science, Columbia University, 1959), p. 55.
[64] Herbert Lehman's report to the executive of the J.D.C. on the Allied Jewish Campaign, May 29, 1926, *Warburg Papers*.

Due to the prestige and wealth of the A.J.C. leaders, damage to fundraising was limited; it was the aggressive propaganda of the Zionists that embarrassed them in their leadership role. When they confronted the direct action and agitation of the Zionists among the Jewish masses, they felt powerless. When the J.D.C. started a counterpropaganda campaign and used similar methods of agitation in the press, Warburg in a letter to Marshall stated that he, personally, "would not want to be the head of an organization which might be forced into a lengthy muckraking and mud-throwing contest."[65] More was involved than a desire to guard his good name and reputation in the proper circles of American society. It was a realization that once having admitted "mud-throwing," militant and aggressive elements would have the advantage over restraint. Accommodating leaders would never, therefore, be able to compete effectively. The A.J.C. could not fight such a battle in 1926 for the same reasons that Jacob Schiff had refused to fight the Zionists in the newspapers in 1916. Warburg explained that "by newspaper fighting we will only advertise the Lipsky, Neumann gang and fortify them as heroes or martyrs." And his solution was similar to the one offered by Schiff in 1916 and 1917: let us join the more respectable and moderate elements in the hope that together we will hold in check the militant and aggressive. This was one motive behind the desire of Warburg and his friends to join the Jewish Agency.[66]

This was the third time that the political class of the American Zionist Organization waged an aggressive campaign against the established element in American Jewry. The first was in their fight for a democratic American Jewish Congress from 1914 to 1916. Their opponents were the German Jewish philanthropists in control of the A.J.C., who were then accepted by American society as the leaders of the Jewish community. At that time they were led by Louis Brandeis, whose support and prestige were decisive. The second battle was fought by the Eastern European intellectuals in the Z.O.A. against Brandeis and his associates from the established German Jewry. Here the support of the world leaders of Jewry secured their success. Now they were on their own. And although they did not succeed in accomplishing their goal, they proved to all that an aggressive leadership aided by a pro-Palestine sentiment was a power to be reckoned with. On the other hand, their obvious weakness, the lack of leaders of prestige, was not overlooked by the Zionists.

The period that followed this struggle was a crisis of leadership in the

---
[65] Warburg to Marshall, August 9, 1926, ibid.
[66] Telegram from Warburg to Marshall, August 6, 1926, ibid.

Z.O.A. that ended only when the Brandeis group returned to power in 1930. Furthermore, before the struggle with the A.J.C., the number of members in the Zionist Organization increased continuously and reached its peak just before the struggle in 1925. In the year of the struggle, the Z.O.A. lost twelve per cent of its membership, and the decline continued in the following years. Although some of the members immersed themselves in their fight against the rich Jews, others thought it wiser not to associate themselves with an organization that was fighting the money magnates.

The Success of Hadassah

Although Palestine sentiment was gaining ground in American Jewry, the Z.O.A. remained a weak organization. We have attributed its weakness in part to the type of Zionist Organization that evolved; it was a cadre organization, catering only to members willing to devote a great part of their activities to the organization. We have seen also that the Jewish intellectuals who led the organization were still associated with the old ideas of Zionism as a nationalist movement and that the organization lacked leaders of prestige.

How is it, therefore, that the Hadassah Organization increased its membership between 1921 and 1930 from 10,000 to 35,000 members?[67] The Hadassah, while affiliated with the Zionist Organization, was a Palestinian organization led by American-born, college-educated women, many of whom were associated with the social-work movement in the United States. Its members were not required to adhere to the Zionist program, not even to sign the Basle Program. The goals of the organization were restricted to the building of health services and welfare institutions in Palestine. Its president, Irma Lindheim, explained in 1927: "Hadassah has a specific purpose. It has deliberately narrowed its purpose. Its great founder and leader, Henrietta Szold, applied the scientific method in organizing Hadassah and guided it through fifteen years of its development. She reduced the general Zionist idea to a particular part of its program and then proceeded to develop bit by bit the instrument with which to construct this part."[68]

In the split between Brandeis and Weizmann, Hadassah almost broke away from the W.Z.O. and the Z.O.A.; but after securing a great measure of autonomy, it stayed within the organization. The arrangement

---

[67] William Z. Spiegelman, "From Cleveland to Cleveland: American Zionism from 1921 to 1930," *The New Palestine*, June 27, 1930, pp. 402–6.

[68] Lindheim, "Hadassah: The Bond for Jewish Womanhood," *The New Palestine*, June 24, 1927, p. 572.

agreed upon was not dissimilar to the autonomy Brandeis had desired for the Z.O.A. within the international organization. According to the agreement reached with Lipsky, all money collected by Hadassah was to go into Palestine work; administrative expenses of the organization would be taken only from membership dues; the medical unit in Palestine became a special item in the *Keren Hayesod* program; Hadassah was to collect the money for the unit, which would be earmarked for its direct use; participation in *Keren Hayesod* drives was optional.[69]

To appreciate the apolitical character of the organization, its position during the renewed disputes within the Z.O.A. in 1927–28 can be taken as an illustration. In spite of increasing membership, which gave them a decisive voting power in the conventions, and despite the sympathies of the Hadassah leaders with the opposition (many women were wives and daughters of the Brandeis group), Hadassah never really succeeded in aligning with it. In 1927, although promising to support the opposition, it backed down at the last moment and supported the Lipsky leadership. In 1928, Hadassah's vote split.[70] The organization had become a purely charitable one, and the leaders were afraid to involve themselves in problems outside the narrow field of philanthropy for fear of antagonizing their following. This was explained to de Haas by the leaders who were in sympathy with the opposition in 1927. As de Haas reported to Brandeis, they told him that "only the leaders nowadays are devoted Zionists and the rank and file is only interested in health work. The leaders were therefore afraid that they are acting without consultation and understanding of followers, and so not sure about their position in a showdown."[71]

Thus it was Hadassah, led by American-born college graduates and devoted to charitable work in Palestine, which benefited greatly from the increasing popularity of Palestine among American Jewry. The political organization of the Z.O.A., affiliated with the W.Z.O., demanded that members pledge themselves to support the Basle Program. The leaders were intellectuals whose talk about the revival of Jewish consciousness and the like was losing ground in favor of increased support to Palestine.

It is not possible to conclude from the comparison that it was the Palestinianism of the Hadassah Organization and the "occidental orientation" of its leaders that explain the success of the one and the failure of the other. The membership of one organization was entirely female;

---

[69] Rachel Natelson, "The Truth in Detail: Hadassah and the Zionist Organization," *Hadassah Newsletter* 8 (April 1928): 2–4.
[70] Miriam Weinstein, *The Day*, July 3, 1928.
[71] De Haas to Brandeis, March 26, 1928, *de Haas Papers*.

the other was a male organization. But these factors enabled the leaders of Hadassah to build an organization that was a neat counterpart to American charitable organizations which were increasingly appealing to middle-class women. It was the perfect organization for the emerging Jewish gilded ghetto in the United States. The goal of Hadassah was charity, as was that of its counterparts; the leaders were middle-class and college-educated, as in the American organizations; and the activities and gatherings looked exactly like the gatherings of the Christian women's associations across the street. To this was added the Palestinian element, which gave justification and rationalization for the independent existence of an exclusively Jewish organization.

The Z.O.A., on the other hand, was not adapted to the gilded ghetto. It had difficulties in dissociating itself from the Eastern European ghetto and its atmosphere; a stigma of Jewish nationalism was attached to it; its leaders were proficient in the Yiddish language and steeped in Jewish culture. This group of intellectuals wanted to move with the changing Jewish community outside the ghetto and wanted to find their place in the new society, with the help of the Zionist Organization that they led. Their leadership, however, was hindering the success of the Z.O.A. among American Jews. The period of crisis of the organization from 1927–30 was a crisis of leadership that ended in their forced resignation.

CHAPTER VIII

The Crisis of Leadership in the Z.O.A., 1927–30

Jewish Intellectuals in the Lead

The 1927 Z.O.A. annual convention marked the beginning of a bitter struggle between the leadership of Lipsky and his associates and a group of estranged party workers who wanted to unseat them. The immediate cause was the impending creation of the Jewish Agency, which had been designed to take over the Z.O.A.'s fund-raising activities and to become the single organization to which the economic development of Palestine would be entrusted. This intention only accelerated the inevitable eruption of a conflict with the more acculturated people, who were demanding the return of leaders with an "occidental orientation." This group was strengthened by continuous defections of intellectuals and Eastern European businessmen.

Most of the Jewish intellectuals who headed the Z.O.A. were determined, however, to stay in power. Their position as leaders of a Jewish organization in the evolving Jewish community was precarious. Shmuel Margoshes, a Yiddish journalist and a member of the executive committee of the Z.O.A., provides a brilliant analysis of the situation in an article published on the eve of the 1928 convention. Attributing the continuous conflict within the Z.O.A. to the changing ideas and aspirations of an acculturating community, he says:

> [The opposition demand for] "efficiency"—is just being used as a stick with which to beat the existing Zionist leadership. What is really involved is a completely different issue, which was kept hidden during the last seven years since Brandeis's resignation. The desire to replace the leadership is not motivated by the need for better business methods in conducting the affairs of the organization—how can a mass movement be led by business methods?—but by the desire for prestige. The former administration, that of Brandeis, enjoyed prestige, hence it was a good administration. The existing administration, the one headed by Lipsky, has no prestige, therefore it is not a good administration and should be gotten rid off. . . . You can call it any name you please—prestige, the desire to buy an honor, the mania for attaining a social position; the fact remains that all America is crazy for it, and it is coveted by American society as a whole. Witness all our organizations and fund drives: which are the most successful? Those led by persons with the greatest prestige . . . what is missing in the Zionist Organization? It misses the service of prestige.

Margoshes goes on to explain that a growing number of Eastern European *nouveaux riches* desired to be associated with those members of the Jewish community who had achieved prestige in the United States, the wealthy German Jewish philanthropists, and that since prestige could be attained through association with persons who already had it, association was their goal: "Throughout the United States there are Jews who have attained wealth and established a middle-class style of life and whose most ambitious dream is to stand anywhere near the partner of Kuhn, Loeb and Company [Felix Warburg]. When they receive a letter from him they are in seventh heaven, and when they are invited to a conference with 'the great man himself!' they feel they have arrived." Such people were no longer satisfied with the leadership of Chaim Weizmann, the European Jew, and Louis Lipsky, his lieutenant in the United States. The prospering Jews looked to leaders who could confer genuine American prestige on them:

> Dr. Weizmann is only a president and a guest in the United States. And even though it is rumored that he converses with kings and prime ministers and that prominent "goyim" respect him, he is nonetheless a foreigner in this land and does not even occupy a salon on Fifth Avenue. As for Lipsky, he is just a journalist. If at least he would write in the [New York] *Times*, instead of choosing to write in *The New Palestine!* I ask you, can one see in him a person who can confer prestige on others?[1]

The struggle that started within the Z.O.A. in 1927 was not instigated by Brandeis or his associates. Contrary to current reports, the Brandeisists were encouraged to reenter the Z.O.A. political arena only after dissatisfaction and restlessness within the ranks had become clear. During the first revolt at the 1927 convention, some of the Brandeisists supported the administration. Only after the estranged party workers clamored for the return of the Brandeis leadership did they take notice.

The dominant group within the Z.O.A. consisted of Jewish intellectuals loyal to the leadership of Lipsky. They were tempted to follow the popular path of Palestinian sentiment, a direction that promised them greater support in the community, but their leadership in Zionism was handed them because they were Jewish intellectuals. Their knowledge of Jewish culture and tradition made them suitable leaders of a movement dedicated to the preservation and propagation of the cultural tradition. A Palestinian movement, on the other hand, required leaders who were administrators and businessmen, the type who surrounded Brandeis. If they were to adopt a Palestinian point of view, they would be defeating themselves; such an attitude would endanger their position. The opposition argued that Zionism was a Palestinian movement and advocated returning Brandeis to power, so the intellectuals found them-

---

[1] Shmuel Margoshes, *The Day*, May 5, 1928.

selves, often against their will, defending the cultural and educational aspects of Zionism to an unresponsive community.[2] Their confusion and the contradictions in their discussions and writings indicate the hopelessness of their situation. The stronger and more vocal the opposition became in its demand for Brandeis's return, the greater Lipsky's group became devoted to Weizmann and his ideas.[3]

Abraham Coralnik, a member of the intellectual circle that ruled the Z.O.A. in the 1920's, was one of the few American Zionists still able to articulate the tenets of the Zionist doctrine. He commented during an interview in 1928:

> It is likely that in all the discussion that has gone on about the best means for rebuilding Palestine, Zionism itself has been forgotten. . . . The ultimate purpose of Zionism is to counteract the decay of Judaism. Zionism must make the Jew feel a distinct cultural individuality; it must make him feel that he has a center of his own. Above all, the purpose of Zionism must be to give a Jew stability; it must integrate him into the life about him, whether here or in Palestine.[4]

He was, however, painfully aware that these ideas did not enjoy the support of the American Jews. He stated in 1930 that "in the last ten years, an almost new generation took over. The old have become very old and the young have no affinity for the whole thing."[5]

In his writings, Coralnik explained that the existing leadership of the Z.O.A. represented the old spirit and that the demand for a change in leadership was the result of change in the new Jewish community. In his view, "the Jew lost all respect for the Jewish intellectual, unless he is a professional, especially a judge."[6] Lipsky symbolized the intelligentsia in the Zionist movement; the opposition's demand for his resignation showed their rejection of that position.[7]

Abraham Goldberg was another diehard who, from 1927 to 1930, championed the idea that Zionism should not be restricted to the acceptance of Palestinian sentiments, although at the same time realizing that the younger generation was alien to Jewish culture.[8]

---

[2] Bernard Shelvin, *The Jewish Morning Journal*, June 23, 1927.
[3] Leo W. Schwartz, "Zionism in the Postwar Era," in *Modern Palestine*, ed. Jessie Sampter (New York: Hadassah, Women's Zionist Organization of America, 1933), pp. 62–63.
[4] "An Ideal Not a Dream: An Interview with Dr. Abraham Coralnik," *The New Palestine*, March 2, 1928, p. 282.
[5] Abraham Coralnik, *The Day*, March 7, 1930.
[6] Ibid., June 20, 1930.
[7] Ibid., May 3, 1928.
[8] Abraham Goldberg, *Dos Yiddishe Folk*, June 7, 1929, pp. 5–6 and June 17, 1927, p. 3.

The career of Goldberg, one of the most beloved leaders of the Z.O.A., illustrates the difficult position in which the Eastern European intellectuals found themselves. Goldberg was an enthusiastic follower of Louis Brandeis, whom he idolized. In 1920, Goldberg supported the Brandeis thesis that Zionism should give way to pure Palestinianism and restrict itself to building up Palestine. Later he reluctantly switched to the other side, for he resented the fact that Brandeis's people did not take him into their councils. In the twenties, he became devoted to Weizmann, whom he extolled and supported.[9]

Goldberg exemplified the struggle of the tormented Jewish intellectual, whose constant vacillation between two leaderships we have attributed to the cultural disorientation of the intellectuals. When in the late twenties Goldberg wholeheartedly supported Weizmann, he was still torn between the two cultures. In his defense of the Jewish Agency, for example, he struck a note completely missing from the European Zionist arguments, that the Zionist leaders had taken upon themselves a task of which they were not capable. They could never do as good a job as the efficient and capable Americans; the task should be left to others: "Zionist leaders should merely whip up interest in the rebuilding of Palestine. It is their function to center the attention of particular groups upon what can be achieved. However, they have undertaken to dabble in agriculture, in banks and in building projects. . . ."[10]

At the World Zionist Congress in 1929, he supported the idea of the Jewish Agency against bitter opposition, especially among delegates from Eastern Europe: "The non-Zionists [the A.J.C. leaders] will build Palestine. We can help a little but not much . . . we will be relieved of chasing pennies and of the complicated task of administering the work of Palestine."[11]

Underlying his reasoning was an argument similar to the one expressed by the Eastern European intellectuals in the Z.O.A. at the beginning of the Brandeis-Weizmann dispute; namely, that the Europeans were at their best when cultural values and spiritual ideas were concerned, while the Americans were practical and more capable of handling material issues.

This assessment of the difference between the American and European Zionist leaders was not shared by the Europeans who were anxious

---

[9] See, for example, Abraham Goldberg, *The New Palestine*, April 16, 1926, pp. 359–60; June 8, 1928, pp. 599, 611.
[10] "New Zionism for Old; An Interview with Abraham Goldberg," *The New Palestine*, February 17, 1928, p. 201.
[11] Quoted by Herbert Solow, "The Era of the Agency Begins," *The Menorah Journal* 17 (November 1929): 124.

for the creation of the Jewish Agency. Weizmann advocated creating the Jewish Agency because financial needs were greater as a result of the economic crisis in Palestine, not because the abilities of the non-Zionists were greater. When in 1927 the Z.O.A. accepted the American plan for Palestine, it was the result of the pressures of the opposition. Weizmann yielded because he needed the financial help of American Jewry, not because he thought it a superior plan or because the Americans were better administrators.[12] Necessity, not a sense of inferiority, dictated his policy, one that involved a strategic retreat but that did not lead to ideological compromise; whereas, for the Eastern European Jewish intellectuals in the United States, it involved an acceptance of American values. Another intellectual, Samuel M. Melamed, argued in 1928 that it was American civilization that had to be transplanted to Palestine. Furthermore, he contended that the Europeans were following an inferior "Jewish ghetto culture," unsatisfactory for the new country.[13]

Melamed was soon to express his delight with the return of the Brandeisists to leadership. In 1930, he argued that the Brandeisists had been right all along; it was the Eastern Europeans (in whose camp he had fought) who had been wrong, since "to them Jewish nationalism had neither reservations nor amendments, but it had to Mr. Brandeis and his associates." Now, he argued, the Jewish masses saw the light.[14] But the solution for a Jewish intellectual in the United States was not easy. The same Melamed who argued that the real goal of Zionism was to build Palestine materially also wrote elsewhere at the same time that the Z.O.A. should build Zionist centers devoted to the teaching of Zionism. "One can not study the ideology of Zionism like a catechism. One can only absorb such an ideology through Zionist circles, Zionist activities, and the like."[15] If the task of Zionism was to build Palestine materially, however, what kind of ideology did he think should be taught in such Zionist circles?

Maurice Samuel, another prominent intellectual in Lipsky's circle, adopted a completely different approach. He believed that Zionism had reached a new era, one of substituting the building up of Palestine for the previously held nationalist ideology. He thus attempted to rationalize the adoption of a pure Palestinian approach, which by now had in-

---

[12] Chaim Weizmann, *A Fratricidal War* (Privately Printed by Isidor D. Morrison, June 1928), p. 6.
[13] Samuel M. Melamed, "The Basis of Civilization," *The Reflex* 1 (January 1928): 1–10.
[14] Ibid., "The Peace of Cleveland," *The Reflex* 6 (September 1930):9.
[15] Ibid., *Dos Yiddishe Folk*, June 7, 1927, p. 4.

fected the intellectuals.¹⁶ Similarly, Margoshes believed that Jewish culture, education, and the nationalist ideology had already spread among the American Jews and all that was left for the Zionists was to keep an eye on the forthcoming Jewish Agency, to see to it that it fulfilled its task of developing Palestine.¹⁷

Lipsky still said that "we remain the only organized force dedicated to the task of transforming Jewish life in accordance with Jewish ideals, using the renaissance in Palestine to provoke renaissance in the Diaspora."¹⁸ But the policies he was carrying out as president often contradicted such statements. For example, in 1928 he embarked on a scheme according to which those who contributed to the Palestine fund, the U.P.A., would almost automatically become members of the Z.O.A. This meant bringing people into the Zionist Organization who were interested only in materially aiding Palestine.

The state of affairs in American Zionism, naturally, shocked and upset the European Zionist leaders. Chaim Arlozoroff, the European Zionist who visited the United States in 1929, expressed in his letters the state of confusion and bewilderment of the Zionist leaders. He added bitterly: "If I was for a moment ashamed of being called a Zionist, it was here in the United States."¹⁹

Arlozoroff described those at the helm of the Z.O.A. as people who felt they were the "men of yesterday." He wrote that although they ideologically supported a certain cultural program, they actually arrived at a compromise which rendered their good intentions into caricature.²⁰

Attempts to Pacify the Growing Opposition

Ideological principles were not discussed by the supporters and opponents of the administration as they had been during the struggle in 1921. Few outside the small circle of militant Zionists were interested in such principles. The members of the opposition, the Palestinians, associated Zionism with the practical problems of developing Palestine and were not concerned with other issues. They discussed personalities rather than principles and adopted the position that the existing administration was incapable of sound administrative methods of operation. The

---

[16] Maurice Samuel, "Changing Winds: The Decline of the Old Intellectual Antagonisms," *The New Palestine*, March 1, 1929, p. 158.
[17] Margoshes, *The Day*, June 29, 1929.
[18] Louis Lipsky, "Palestine Demands Jewish Unity—Not Epigrams," *The New Palestine*, June 4–11, 1929, p. 5.
[19] Chaim Arlozoroff, *Ktavim*, vol. 5 (Tel Aviv: Hotzaat A. Y. Shtible, 1935), p. 155.
[20] Ibid., p. 156.

issues were petty cash and irregularities of the administration.[21] The immediate cause of their revolt against the leaders was the decision to hand over the function of building Palestine to a new partnership—Zionist and non-Zionist businessmen in the new Jewish Agency. The intellectuals could not claim that they were capable administrators nor rely exclusively on their prestige as Jewish intellectuals for support in the community. They therefore advocated the new partnership, claimed that it was they who drew the illustrious wealthy Jews to Palestine, and called to their defense the prestige of their future partners.

It is not surprising that the revolt in 1927 was concentrated in the U.P.A. machinery, since that was the organization that was primarily affected by the new partnership.[22] Israel Goldberg, a leader of the revolt, explained that by 1927 his group, who wanted Brandeis back, realized that the victory of 1921 had been a hollow one. They needed to raise large sums of money for Palestine, and Lipsky's leadership could not do the job. The international leadership realized this but wanted to remedy the situation by creating the Jewish Agency, in which the A.J.C. group would participate. Goldberg explained that "we were alarmed by this approach," since it would destroy the Z.O.A. by removing its function. The solution of the Goldberg group was to call Brandeis back and to forestall such a development. Although Goldberg admitted that they were not sure the Brandeis group's prestige and leadership could command the necessary funds, he asserted that they were the more "capable" leaders.[23]

Still, it is a puzzling admission. The only explanation for the eagerness to have Brandeis's followers back was, to use Emanuel Neumann's words, that they "represented in the public mind precisely that occidental orientation . . . so much in demand. . . ."[24] Such leadership would raise the standing of the Z.O.A. and might prevent the transfer of its activities to a new organization. But for Lipsky's men, it meant a Z.O.A. without their leadership. There was threat in the atmosphere. Even those who wanted a compromise solution were calling for businessmen to take over the leadership from the intellectuals.[25]

Lipsky's effort was to check the attack. He made his peace with the

---

[21] Shelvin, *The Jewish Morning Journal*, June 29, 1927.

[22] Lipsky in an interview, September 13, 1960, stated that the "revolt was engineered by the bureaucrats of the U.P.A." See also editorial of *The New Palestine*, June 24, 1927, p. 3; and a letter from Norvin Lindheim to Weizmann, June 7, 1927 in *Jacob de Haas Papers* (New York: Zionist Archives).

[23] Interview with author, August 25, 1960.

[24] Emanuel Neumann, "What of the Agency," *The New Palestine*, January 15, 1926, p. 56.

[25] Margoshes, *The Day*, June 29, 1928.

A.J.C. and supported the creation of the Jewish Agency. Lipsky even invited Felix Warburg to attend the convention, promising him that "our organization will observe in all publicity connected with your coming to Atlantic City the proper respect for your known views on Zionism being concerned chiefly with Palestine aspects."[26] Although Warburg refused the invitation, he nonetheless sent an encouraging telegram of congratulation, lauding Lipsky's leadership. The telegram was given due publicity at the Zionist convention.

This explains the strong support Lipsky gave Weizmann's efforts on behalf of the Jewish Agency. Some observers state that "the driving force behind the plan [for the Jewish Agency] was the leadership of the Z.O.A."[27] Since, as Margoshes asserted, prestige was attained in the Jewish community by associating with those who already possessed it, the Jewish intellectuals were tempted, for they were in dire need of the prestige necessary for maintaining their position in the community. Their commitment to the Jewish Agency grew stronger when the opposition advocated the return of Brandeis's leadership as alternative to the creation of the Agency.

Examination of the radical Yiddish press suggests that resentment against the German Jewish philanthropists had reached its height in the fight for a Jewish Congress and was now mellowing. The Jewish community was becoming more affluent; its members were moving into mixed neighborhoods and joining with the American middle classes in the competition for status and respectability. An editorial in *The Day*, a paper that had excelled in attacking the philanthropists in previous years, said in reference to the Jewish Agency:

> We here, in America, are still used to the fact that where we see the politicians and philanthropists Marshall and Warburg together, it is there that we also find American Jewry. Obviously, such a statement needs qualification—in degree and in scope—but there is, nonetheless, a lot of truth in it. Not only are they viewed as the chosen representatives of American Jewry, but whatever they do and wherever they go, they are followed by a large and important part of this Jewry. This is true for the richest and hence the most powerful part of Jewry.[28]

This was a completely new attitude for the Yiddish press, and is to be understood against the background of the changing attitudes of the

---

[26] Telegram from Lipsky to Warburg, June 21, 1927, *Felix Warburg Papers* (Cincinnati: The American Jewish Archives).

[27] Sam Z. Chinitz, "The Jewish Agency and the Jewish Community in the United States" (Master's essay, Faculty of Political Science, Columbia University, 1959), p. 86.

[28] Editorial, *The Day*, May 26, 1928.

prospering community. Several observers of the American scene noticed similar changes in American society in the twenties when businessmen took the lead.[29] Yiddish journalists often forgot that they spoke of Zionism as propagating Jewish culture and education and in the same breath adopted a Palestinian attitude. Both Ephraim Caplan and Bernard Shelvin said before the 1927 convention that it would be a solution to all the troubles of the Zionist Organization if Brandeis would consent to assume the leadership.[30]

The leaders of the Z.O.A. felt that a bold move had to be taken. Lipsky decided to accept the plans of the opposition for more efficient methods of building Palestine, and even to give them key positions in the organization, as long as his people retained control.

At the annual convention in 1927 Lipsky, representing the Jewish intellectuals, explained the cultural and educational aspects of the movement, reiterated his belief in the Zionist doctrine, and accused the opposition of deserting these great traditions. He fiercely attacked their plans in his presidential address on the same grounds, and yet, when he reached the climactic part of the speech, it became obvious that he was accepting the criticism of the opposition. Moreover, he induced several members of the old Brandeis group to take control of the financial committee, and he promised to support them in fighting for an American plan that would insure a more efficient international administration. He stated:

> We should urge upon the [World Zionist] Congress that no further colonization be authorized until the expert commission will have made its recommendations, and steps should be taken to provide for the consolidation and the liquidation of our responsibility toward our present colonies.
> It is our duty to create such agencies as will facilitate the cooperation of private capital and enterprise, will bring about the development of private initiative, and the spirit of individual pioneering in commerce and industry. . . .[31]

Speaking like a true Brandeisist, he even agreed to drop Abraham Goldberg from the executive in an attempt to satisfy the opposition. This move, however, was accomplished only after a long struggle during which Lipsky explained that it was being done with Weizmann's approval; Goldberg himself asked the convention to accept the decision.

---

[29] William E. Leuchtenberg, *The Perils of Prosperity, 1914–1932* (Chicago: University of Chicago Press, 1958), p. 158.

[30] Ephraim Caplan, *The Jewish Morning Journal*, June 29, 1927; Shelvin, *The Jewish Morning Journal*, June 23, 1927.

[31] "Summary Report of the Proceedings of the Thirtieth Annual Convention of the Zionist Organization of America," *The New Palestine*, July 15, 1927, pp. 6–7.

The intensity of the struggle indicates that it was not the majority of the party workers who had lost confidence in the leadership of the intellectuals. It was outside the organization, among the supporters, that confidence had been shaken. Only a minority within the organization supported the opposition.

The devoted members of the Z.O.A. constituted a group that did not necessarily react to events in the same way as the supporters of the organization and the general public. Maurice Duverger tells us that in a political party, the membership constitutes "a closed circle, an exclusive world of which the reactions and the general behavior obeyed its own laws, different from those which determined the changes amongst electors, that is the variation in public opinion."[32] The majority of the active members of the Z.O.A. were the "hundred percenter" Jews, who, devoting most of their time to the organization and being totally committed to Zionism and their Jewish status, were thus devoted to the Jewish intellectuals who symbolized these loyalties.

But Lipsky had in mind the supporters, those who contributed to the funds, and certain powerful interests within the organization, notably the Hadassah members. He attempted to give a new look, an almost occidental look, to the administration. The Brandeisists were given control of the financial committee, and Goldberg was dropped from the executive. But the old leadership was to remain. An editorial in *The New Palestine* explained: "In the list [of the new administrative committee] there appeared the names of a number of new personalities and the elimination of several old names. It was agreed that in setting up the committee, indication should be given that a practically new administration under the old leadership should take control of all Zionist affairs in America."[33]

Lipsky supported the new administration and its plans in the World Zionist Congress. A business-oriented executive committee was elected by the Congress, and the labor leaders were dropped from the executive, for the Americans complained that "the funds were promoting policies of Labor Party in Palestine against Capitalist, while the money in America is collected from the Capitalist Class."[34] Weizmann and Lipsky were hoping that this would secure unity in the American Zionist camp.[35] Lindheim, one of the new Brandeisists on the financial com-

---

[32] Maurice Duverger, *Political Parties* (New York: John Wiley & Sons, 1955) p. 101.
[33] Editorial, *The New Palestine*, July 15, 1927, p. 3.
[34] Sam Rosensohn to Brandeis, October 1927, *de Haas Papers*.
[35] Weizmann, *A Fratricidal War*, p. 6.

mittee, assured Weizmann that this was "the only way in which you could secure the confidence of American Jewry in the Z.O.A."[36]

But the opposition to Lipsky within the organization in 1927 was not satisfied with compromises. Even before the 1927 convention, they contacted Jacob de Haas, Julian Mack, and eventually Brandeis himself. They wanted Brandeis back. Brandeis could have had the leadership for the asking. However, the value of his leadership lay in the publicity given to it, and the Yiddish press claimed that it was precisely this attitude that he absolutely refused to consider. The opposition leaders then offered the leadership to Mack. They were willing to make him honorary president so that he would not be overloaded with work, but he made his acceptance conditional on Robert Szold being made acting president. This the opposition leaders would not accept.[37]

From 1927 to 1930, negotiations between the Brandeis group and the Eastern European opposition came to a halt. The Eastern Europeans wanted Brandeis or Mack as a leader, but the Brandeisists offered Szold. Szold was the one member of the group willing to devote most of his time to the organization, and Brandeis endorsed him as the future head of the organization. But the party workers, anxious for Brandeis to lead the organization, absolutely refused. To them, Szold was unacceptable because he did not possess the coveted prestige. However, Szold remained, the Brandeisists' only candidate. In 1930, his leadership was accepted, together with many of Brandeis's conditions.

The issue was, therefore, not one of policy, but of leadership. While Brandeis made his "moral support" conditional on the acceptance of certain economic and financial arrangements, all agreed that the real obstacle was "that there is no leadership in the group or none sufficiently acceptable for a convention fight."[38] The other condition that was difficult for the Eastern Europeans to accept was Brandeis's absolute refusal to accept any compromise in regard to Lipsky's leadership. He stubbornly stuck to a statement made on the eve of the 1927 convention: "There can be no compromise with Lipsky or any of his ilk. All must get out, if our friends are to go in."[39] With respect to the economic aspects, he stated that a new administration should enter only after such reforms as wiping out the deficit in a prescribed way and raising a certain sum of money to make the organization viable. He re-

---
[36] Lindheim to Weizmann, July 1, 1927, *de Haas Papers*.
[37] De Haas to Brandeis, June 14, 1927, ibid.
[38] De Haas to Brandeis, June 27, 1927, ibid.
[39] Brandeis to de Haas, June 5, 1927, ibid.

fused to budge from any of those conditions, stating that his "moral support" depended on their acceptance. He was not willing to deviate "a hair's breadth" from them.[40] Brandeis's chief purpose remained as it had been in 1921: control of the Z.O.A. and, through it, control of the international organization. He expressed his designs in his correspondence with his inner circle during the preparations for the 1927 convention. The financial conditions that he stipulated were necessary for building an economically powerful American organization and "through its financial influence and otherwise to effect the indispensable house cleaning also in London and Palestine."[41] Though he absolutely refused to negotiate with Weizmann, whom he considered untrustworthy, he expected Weizmann to play the same role that had been designed for him in 1921. Brandeis said that "if our friends can control the American Organization and the money raising, I think they would [sic] have to work in the World Organization with and through Weizmann."[42] The Americans, who naturally had to remain in the United States most of the time, were willing to entrust activities outside the country to Weizmann and his associates. The latter, in turn, would be kept under control by those who headed the Z.O.A. and the fund-raising operations.

Although plans for the reorganization of the Z.O.A. were meticulously laid down by Brandeis, Lipsky's opponents suffered a crushing defeat in the convention. The Brandeisists themselves were split, and the Hadassah reached an agreement with Lipsky at the last moment. The unwillingness of Brandeis or Mack to be active leaders most probably influenced Henrietta Szold and the Hadassah women to seek a compromise with Lipsky.

Reentry of the Brandeis Group into Zionist Politics

The "new administration under the old leadership" did not satisfy the opposition, even though it had put members of the old Brandeis group in control of the economic policies of the organization. They continued their attack on Lipsky's inefficiency and mismanagement as though no change had occurred. Their behavior lends support to Margoshes's thesis that the word "efficiency" really meant "prestige."

The opposition remained displeased and did not give the new policies

---

[40] Telegram from Brandeis to de Haas, June 25, 1927, ibid.
[41] Brandeis to de Haas, June 22, 1927, ibid.
[42] Brandeis to de Haas, June 5, 1927, ibid.

a chance to prove themselves. Before long they resumed their attack on the administration with even greater bitterness, culminating in a bitter battle on the floor of the convention in 1928. The tension that had begun in 1927 and was to continue until 1930 was a naked struggle for power between the supporters of the Brandeis group and the Jewish intellectuals.

At the beginning of 1927, the Brandeisists were inconsequential as a power faction. Mack and Stephen Wise were active in the U.P.A., and Norvin Lindheim, Sam Rosensohn, and Lawrence Berenson were on the financial committee of the Z.O.A. The latter three and Wise were active members of the administrative committee.

Yet by the end of the year, the group was functioning again. After their defeat in 1927, Brandeis and his associates managed to reactivate the group for the purpose of fighting the Lipsky leadership. The fight the Brandeisists waged against the Z.O.A. administration, the methods they used, and the arguments they advanced resembled a campaign of progressive reformers determined to clean up a city government corrupted by its administration. The leaders of the Z.O.A., argued the Brandeisists, were utterly incompetent, even corrupt and immoral, and it was a moral imperative to demand their replacement by good and competent men with an understanding of practical affairs and business acumen. Their campaign was imbued with a spirit of self-righteousness; good men were fighting the rascal incumbents. Everybody in the Brandeis camp repeated the phrase he coined: the fight was against "Lipsky and his ilk."

At first, the people around Lipsky were baffled when they witnessed the renewal of attack. They had hoped that their submission on the question of economic policies in Palestine would lead to peace in the movement. After all, they argued, that was all the Brandeisists had sought to clear up Zionist finances.

Once the Eastern European leaders realized that they were not going to get rid of the opposition by accepting the American plan, they began to retreat. They withdrew their support from the plan, called it instead "misapplied Zionism," and at the first opportunity co-opted Abraham Goldberg into the administrative committee.[43] They again had been forced to rely on the "hundred percenters," those devoted members of the organization who continued to support the old leadership.

The popular clamor for the leadership of Brandeis or at least of Mack or Wise continued throughout 1927. Toward the end of that year, Bran-

---

[43] Arlozoroff, *Ktavim*, vol. 5, p. 158.

deis began to organize his followers, with the aim of resuming actual control over the Z.O.A.

The reorganization of the group was due largely to the political skills of de Haas. It was he who urged the organization of the opposition forces in order to avoid repeating the Brandeisists' performance of 1927. De Haas had to overcome many obstacles to accomplish this task, the greatest of which was the invisibility of his leader. With boundless energy, writing endless letters to all possible supporters, old and new, urging and persuading Brandeis at each step at least to write a letter, receive a supporter, or make an appearance at a closed gathering of supporters—each time having to overcome Brandeis's reluctance to expose himself as a leader of the opposition—de Haas finally managed to activate the group and in the process to add a few Eastern Europeans to it.

His first difficulty was in unifying them. Prominent members of the old Brandeis group were active in the Z.O.A. administration and had not supported the 1927 revolt; some had been actively working against them. Lindheim, who was asked to join the opposition, replied that "our job is not to wage war on Lipsky but to put the proper personnel in the administration of the Z.O.A. so that confidence may be restored."[44] A stream of letters was sent to Brandeis by de Haas explaining how the defection of his old supporters demoralized the group opposed to Lipsky, while at the same time it strengthened Lipsky himself. He urged Brandeis to use his influence to get his followers to quit the Z.O.A.[45] On November 25, Brandeis instructed de Haas to advise Wise, Lindheim, Rosensohn, and Berenson to prepare for eventual resignation from their positions in the Z.O.A.[46] This was carried out according to plan.

It was difficult even to obtain regular meetings of the group. De Haas wanted them to take place in Washington; he insisted that Brandeis's participation was essential to their success. Brandeis at first would not even agree to have the meetings in Washington and argued that "the start should be made as indicated—remote from here—so that the group may work out its independence."[47] It took considerable persuasion by de Haas to explain that without Brandeis's attendance at the Washington meetings, the whole project would end in failure. In a letter accepting the unavoidable necessity of both—the meetings in Washington and

---

[44] Lindheim to Weizmann, June 7, 1927, *de Haas Papers*.
[45] De Haas to Brandeis, November 23, 1927, ibid.
[46] Brandeis to de Haas, November 25, 1927, ibid.
[47] Brandies to de Haas, October 30, 1927, ibid.

his presence—Brandeis said: "You know my exigent limitations. I hope none of the group will come under any misapprehensions as to the limits and character of my limitations."[48]

Brandeis sent out the agenda for the first meeting, his memorandum detailing how control of the Z.O.A. was to be achieved. The letter began, "November 5 (Gunpowder plot day) is our conference day."[49] This was one of the rare occasions when Brandeis allowed himself a human and humorous touch. His dry directives were usually couched in a tone either of impatience for the lack of speed in executing his orders, or of a sense of moral self-righteousness. From his remark about the Gunpowder plot, one can imagine the old man in his office enjoying his little conspiracy to undermine the position of his opponents. It was just this type of activity, involving the invisible pulling of strings from behind the scenes, that Brandeis, like so many progressive intellectuals, enjoyed far more than the publicity that accompanied open leadership.

Two secret meetings took place in Washington, one on November 5 the other on December 17. The members of the group who served in the Z.O.A. administration were invited; and in deference to them, it was agreed that the conference should not interfere with their freedom of action. At the first meeting, all agreed that the functions of the Z.O.A. should consist of, first, the creation of a pro-Palestine *stimmung* (a favorable atmosphere) in the Jewish community through propaganda; second, raising funds for Palestine without interference from the outside (the outside included the European Zionist leaders); third, insuring "the proper expenditure of free funds" and promoting "private economic enterprises."[50]

The first item of the program expressed the most radical departure from the group's 1921 policies. It was an admission of the superior method of the operations of the *Keren Hayesod* over their abortive attempts to raise funds in a strictly businesslike fashion devoid of propaganda. The acceptance of the need to create *stimmung* meant the acceptance of the "machinery of jazz" as a necessary part of successful fund-raising. They must have learned from the experience of the *Keren Hayesod* and the U.P.A. that the propaganda that accompanied fund-raising activities could be exclusively Palestinian, without raising issues of the relations between the American Jews and Palestine and the dangerous, and for them embarrassing, doctrine of Diaspora nationalism. On the contrary, it was the Z.O.A. group that had avoided mentioning

---

[48] Brandeis to de Haas, November 2, 1927, ibid.
[49] Brandeis to de Haas, October 30, 1927, ibid.
[50] Minutes of the Washington Conference, November 5, 1927, ibid.

these problems and had even separated the administration of fund-raising from that of the Z.O.A. proper, so as not to create too obvious a connection between the Zionist Organization and the fund-raising campaigns for Palestine. The Brandeisists were also aware that the once dangerous nationalist agitators no longer antagonized the American public or the rich Jews. In fact, the non-Zionist elements in the community often supported these campaigns; and as for the anti-Semites who had worried them so much in 1921, they had become quiet after 1925.[51]

The Brandeisists' acceptance of publicity and propaganda in Zionist fund-raising was an important concession. This acceptance eliminated one of the important differences between the programs of the Brandeisists and of the leaders in control of the Z.O.A. The main source of contention was who would run the organization, Lipsky and the Jewish intellectuals or those endorsed by Brandeis. In the first meeting in Washington, it was unanimously agreed that "it was desirable to eliminate Lipsky and his 'ilk' from any connection with the management of the Z.O.A." Though the minutes state that there was unanimity on this issue, the debates indicate that at least those members who served on the administration and who had just returned from the Zionist Congress (which accepted their conditions for a balanced budget and better economy) were embarrassed. Lindheim even defended the existing situation and argued that the Brandeisists who had joined the administration did achieve their aim, a reduction of the deficit, to some extent.[52]

At the next conference, the mood was more militant. This in part reflected the mood of "the chief," who had sent out a memorandum advising the members of the group in the administration to prepare to resign. From the debates, one gains the impression that Lindheim was disgruntled, even though he followed the group decisions. At the meeting he argued that they could resign only when an issue arose that commanded public support; thus far, such an issue had not arisen. He noted also that at the convention of 1927, they could have controlled the administrative committee had not several members from their side either refused to serve or resigned shortly after the convention closed, leaving their seats to their opponents. It was their own supporters who were not willing to give their time and unstinting effort to the organization. For one of these vacated seats the administrative committee chose Abraham Goldberg, a step that infuriated the opposition.

Lindheim, supported by de Haas and Berenson, argued further that

---

[51] John Higham, *Strangers in the Land* (New Brunswick, N.J.: Rutgers University Press), pp. 329–30.

[52] Minutes of the conference in Washington, November 5, 1927, *de Haas Papers*.

Crisis of Leadership in the Z.O.A., 1927–30

their only chance of success was in supporting some commanding personalities willing to lead the organization. In the following discussion, Mack and Wise flatly refused to accept the leadership because of "other commitments."[53]

This lack of a personality with popular appeal, willing to assume leadership, was the biggest stumbling block in the group's road back to power. All of them realized that if Brandeis would accept some sort of position their victory was assured. Many, however, believed that without his open acceptance of leadership defeat was certain. Mack wrote to Brandeis that if he remained "silent and invisible except to a selected few, defeat becomes a certainty."[54]

Brandeis refused to make any public move that would associate him with the opposition. Even after the resignation of the group's members from their offices, when the fight in preparation for the 1928 convention was going on in both camps, Brandeis was only "ready to bear a generous fraction of the campaign expense." He added categorically, ". . . it must be made absolutely clear that while your group and associates have my moral and financial support, I cannot be a part of your deliberations any more than your fighting force."[55]

It seemed impossible to attain strong leadership. No one was willing to accept the responsibility at the time. At a well-attended conference in Washington, when a member announced that Mack was ready to be the next president of the Z.O.A., the latter jumped to his feet and interrupted the speaker to state that he would never be the president of the Z.O.A.[56] This incident, it was admitted by other members of the group, "has done us an enormous amount of harm."[57] In desperation, Brandeis appealed to Harry Friedenwald, the former president of the Z.O.A. and a member of the group, though not an active one. Brandeis promised him that as president "he will be relieved from duties of presiding at meetings, of speaking, of executive work and specifically of financial problems."[58] Friedenwald, however, declined the offer.[59] Thus, the group arrived at the convention in 1928 without an acceptable personality for the presidency.

This unwillingness among the leaders to devote an appreciable portion of their time to Zionist activities was characteristic. The same situa-

---

[53] Minutes of the conference in Washington, December 17, 1927, ibid.
[54] Mack to Brandeis, March 26, 1928, ibid.
[55] Brandeis to de Haas, March 25, 1928, ibid.
[56] Minutes of the conference in Washington, April 29, 1928, ibid.
[57] Julius Meyer to de Haas, May 10, 1928, ibid.
[58] Brandeis to Mack, May 8, 1928, ibid.
[59] Telegram from de Haas to Mack, May 12, 1928, ibid.

tion existed on the local level where commitment was also restricted and partial. Participation was, in fact, so limited that one member of the opposition in reply to a letter from de Haas urging the organization of a local opposition complained: "Time and again the local group had offered to step down and out, if we would step in and take hold. Time and again we have conferred and resolved over night and on the spot to overturn things. Each and every time we failed because we had neither leaders nor workers to offer."[60]

Brandeis's followers who wanted to be led by leaders with an "occidental orientation" would nevertheless make little effort of their own to secure leadership. It was the followers of the Jewish intellectuals, whose commitment to the movement was total, who were willing to give of their time generously.

Many members of Brandeis's group were restricted not only in the time they were willing to devote to Zionist activities, but also in their willingness and ability to analyze and examine the intellectual problems involved. The problems involved in Zionist doctrine seemed too remote from their experiences in the United States; their interest was limited to the plans for building up Palestine. But the Eastern European intellectuals, educated in Jewish culture and history, were still deeply involved in those issues that they felt would determine the future of the Jewish nation. De Haas shared the concern of the Eastern Europeans. His colleagues, however, were unmoved by such problems. In a letter to Mack he complained: "I was deeply distressed to discover that only some of the old Mack-Brandeis group really care enough about the movement to read, digest and try to think problems through."[61]

Since there was no leader of note to take over the Z.O.A. and no distinct ideological principles with which the members could identify, the group discussed the strategy of the coming struggle as the most important issue. Endless debates took place, but no agreement could be reached. The main question was whom to attack—Lipsky and the mismanagement of the Z.O.A., or Weizmann and the situation in Palestine and his plans for the Jewish Agency? As de Haas explained to Brandeis, a division existed between those who wanted to "hit Lipsky via Weizmann and the international situation" or "to hit Weizmann via Lipsky and the American situation."[62] Agreement could not be reached until Brandeis interfered and made the decision. Robert Szold reported to

---

[60] Maurice Avner to de Haas, November 2, 1928, ibid.
[61] De Haas to Mack, November 14, 1928, ibid.
[62] De Haas to Brandeis, October 7, 1927, ibid.

Brandeis on this crucial meeting: "After stating my own views, I said that I thought that I was articulating your views," which were to attack Lipsky and not Weizmann.[63] Within the small group of disciples and away from the public eye, Brandeis exercised strong leadership.

Available documents fail to indicate why Brandeis decided not to attack the situation in Palestine or the Jewish Agency project, to which he objected. In the following years, his group carefully refrained from attacking the Agency. It is just possible that they did not feel strong enough to attack the A.J.C. leaders or Weizmann, at whose hands they had suffered a defeat. It was Lipsky's leadership that seemed to be the weakest link.

Wise was the only active member of the group who refused to accept the decision to attack Lipsky and not Weizmann. On March 5, the group decided that Wise, Rosensohn, and Berenson should resign their posts from the Z.O.A. administrative committee (Lindheim had died a few months earlier).[64] All complied, but Wise gave Weizmann and the Jewish Agency as his reasons for resigning, thus parting company with the group.

It seemed that the more bitter and personal the fight Brandeis waged against Lipsky and his friends, the more uncomfortable Wise became. He did not share Brandeis's vindictiveness nor his hostility toward Lipsky. On the contrary, Wise came to respect those men who had unstintingly given their lives to the cause in which they believed. Brandeis's wrath against the administration rose to new heights; better, he declared, not to give money to Palestine than "that it should go through this dishonest, wicked, corrupting administration."[65] Wise, on the other hand, wrote from Europe: "I have been here long enough to face the fact that no amateurs such as you [Julian Mack] and L.D.B. [Louis D. Brandeis] and myself can exercise any influence in a movement in which all the real leaders are, using the term in the best sense, professionals—that is to say, people giving their full time, strength and energy to the movement."[66]

Wise must also have been disturbed by Brandeis's high-handed dealings with the Zionists and his intentions to control the organization from Washington surreptitiously. Mack reported that one reason Wise gave for his refusal to attack Lipsky was that "while he could sub-

---

[63] Robert Szold to Brandeis, December 1927, ibid.
[64] De Haas to Brandeis, March 5, 1928, ibid.
[65] Brandeis to Mack and Szold, March 27, 1928, ibid.
[66] Quoted by Mack in a letter to Brandeis, August 1, 1929, *Louis Brandeis Papers* (Louisville, Ky.: University of Louisville Law Library).

ordinate his views if you [Brandeis] led actively, he could not do so otherwise."[67]

When Wise attacked the Jewish Agency scheme, he was true to his opposition to the philanthropists, who intended to control Jewish affairs by virtue of their wealth. He had led a lonely battle against the new coalition of Zionists and philanthropists.

Both Rabbi Wise and Rabbi Max Heller, who were influenced by the ideas of the Social Gospel movement earlier in the century, parted company with Brandeis at this time and did not support him in his attacks on the Jewish intellectuals at the head of the Z.O.A. In 1927, Wise wrote a complimentary preface to Lipsky's collected essays, in which he stated that he welcomed Lipsky's leadership as a manifestation of devotion to the democratic ideals of the Zionist movement. "Those of us," wrote Wise, "who rejoice in the higher significance of the Zionist Movement believe that Lipsky's place in it, his . . . leadership of the Zionist Organization, is indicative of the democratic spirit that obtains throughout the movement."[68] Rabbi Heller defended the administration in the 1928 convention, accusing the opposition of opposing Judaism. Possibly the image of Brandeis as the strong man dictating the policies of the organization from Washington and fighting the devoted "poor men" did not appeal to men shaped by the teachings of the Social Gospel.

The Brandeisists, without Wise, held a national conference in Washington on April 29, 1928, in preparation for the annual convention of the Z.O.A. Although Brandeis refused to participate in the meetings, he did yield to de Haas's pressure personally to welcome several of the participants. Moreover, merely having the meeting in Washington symbolized his moral support.

Discussions at the conference were restricted to the wrongdoings of the Z.O.A. administration. An attempt made by a minority to discuss problems other than these was defeated by Mack's intervention. Emphasis was placed on the latest alleged irregularities of the administration. According to the accusations, Lipsky borrowed half a million dollars from the funds raised by the U.P.A., and without their authority loaned it to the financially floundering American Zion Commonwealth. The administration argued that Lipsky did this to maintain the good name of the Z.O.A.; for, though the American Zion Commonwealth

---

[67] Mack to Brandeis, April 14, 1928, *de Haas Papers*.
[68] Preface by Wise to Lipsky, *Thirty Years of American Zionism* (The Nesher Publishing Co., 1927), p. xiii.

was not officially linked to it, it was engaged in housing projects in Palestine. Their explanation was unacceptable to the leaders of the Brandeis group. The discussion grew heated and Mack, chairman of the meeting, did not allow it to cool off. The mood during the debate was aptly summarized by one of the participants: "American Jews have lost confidence in the movement, because American Zionism is represented not by leaders but by clerks."[69]

Lipsky Defeats Brandeis

The scene was set for the annual convention. When it opened on June 28, Lipsky's defeat seemed imminent. Weizmann, who had been visiting the United States since April, was in his last phase of negotiating for the Jewish Agency. He was embarrassed by the accusations against Lipsky concerning his irregular financial transactions and appointed a court of inquiry of five judges to investigate the allegations. On the eve of the convention the judges arrived at a verdict. Although denying that any criminal action had been committed, they nonetheless agreed that certain irregularities had taken place and that Lipsky and his associates were implicated. They recommended that ". . . no one responsible for the irregularities pointed out should be continued as an officer or as a member of any committee of the Z.O.A."[70] But in spite of this recommendation, the convention gave a vote of confidence to the outgoing administration by a majority of 398 to 159 and enthusiastically reelected Lipsky as president, ignoring the judges' recommendations.[71]

The outcome was even more remarkable when we take into account the support given by Hadassah to the opposition. Its executive board had adopted a vote of no confidence in the Z.O.A. administration just before the convention.[72] Hadassah's complaint was mismanagement in the Z.O.A. and U.P.A., not any broader issues of policy. Their gravest objection concerned the power wielded by members on the payroll of the organization. They thought that the Zionist Organization should be controlled by volunteers who gave their spare time freely, as was the

---

[69] Minutes of the conference in Washington, April 29, 1928, *de Haas Papers*.
[70] "Summary Report of the Thirty-First Annual Convention of the Zionist Organization of America," *The New Palestine*, July 13-20, 1928, p. 34.
[71] For a vivid description of the annual convention, 1928, see Solow, "The Vindication of Jewish Idealism," *The Menorah Journal* 15 (September 1928): 259-70.
[72] Lipsky, "The Zionist Controversy: Hadassah Leaders and Their Methods," *The New Palestine*, April 27, 1928, p. 451.

practice in all other American charitable organizations. The president of Hadassah even found it necessary to publish a letter on the issue in *The New York Times*.

The complaint that the organization was run by a group of officers who governed the organization by which they were employed was frequently heard. The resentment was greatest among the part-time leaders (the outsiders) who accused the bureaucrats (the insiders) of taking over control of the organization. Although the devoted and totally committed party workers were often unable to devote their time unless they were paid for it, they undoubtedly became very strong under Lipsky's leadership. The bureaucratic machinery of the Z.O.A. dominated the elective executive bodies. We are told, for example, that the publication committee for the 1927 annual convention, which was in charge of the distribution of $200,000, had all but two of its members on the payroll of the Zionist publications.[73]

Lipsky's opponents claimed that this control caused their defeat in the 1928 convention. But the claim is unacceptable, for the Z.O.A.'s support of Lipsky can be documented. In June 1929, the Brandeisists appeared on an independent list during the elections for the World Zionist Congress. They received 561 votes, against 11,990 votes for the administration's candidates.[74] Hence, even if Lipsky and his associates were losing ground in the Jewish community, his position within the organization was unchallenged.

The organization was dominated by Jewish chauvinists, "hundred percenters," and at the 1928 convention they argued for loyalty to Lipsky, the Jew, against the Americans. The "Nordic" opponents, his supporters explained, were fighting not only Lipsky and Weizmann, but Judaism itself.[75] Several incidents in the history of the Zionist Organization illustrate this quality of Jewish chauvinism in the membership. For example, Samuel Untermeyer, president of the *Keren Hayesod* and a generous donator to it, resigned his office after attending his son's marriage which had taken place in a church; Wise stayed in the U.P.A.

---

[73] Minutes of the conference in Washington, April 29, 1928, *de Haas Papers*.

[74] *Protokoll der Verhandlungen des XVI Zionisten-Kongresses* (London: Zentralbureau der Zionistischen Organisation, 1929), table II, p. xxiv.

[75] The term *Nordic* was used in reference to the German Jewish social background of Lipsky's opponents. It was meant as a hint in response to attempts made by some German Jews in the United States to dissociate themselves from Eastern European Jews who constituted part of the more recent wave of migrants from Eastern and Southern Europe. It was widely believed that the latter were culturally inferior to the earlier immigrants who had come from England and Northern Europe. Racial theories supporting ideas of the superiority of the Northern Europeans over the Eastern and Southern Europeans were also prevalent at the period.

only with great difficulty after being accused of praising Jesus in his synagogue.[76] But the best illustration was the 1928 convention itself.

The night prior to the election of the president, a story about Lipsky began circulating among the delegates. Abraham Tulin, one of the leaders of the opposition, stated that if Lipsky were reelected, he, Tulin, would ask the district attorney to investigate his personal record. It is as impossible to ascertain the accuracy of the report today as it was to do so during the convention. The delegates would not listen to any denials, since they believed it to be another illustration of what the disloyal Jews were capable of doing. In defiance they insisted that Lipsky be reelected. It is difficult to convey the atmosphere of the convention and the feelings among Lipsky's supporters. One perceptive account, written shortly after the convention, tells us that:

> Maurice Samuel . . . spoke of the inevitable, irresistible conflict between logical and biological Zionists, between Zionist by reasoned conviction and Zionist by instinct and inheritance. This conflict, this cleavage, which in specious fashion he sought to show was no sudden invention of Mr. Samuel's. It had been used in the defeat of Justice Brandeis and his associates seven years before. Its resurrection in the present controversy was simply a disingenious though highly effective political trick, in itself insignificant.
> Basically it arises from the sense of difference and consequently of distrust on the part of the emotionally Jewish masses for a Jewishness so self-conscious and so denatured [sic] as to appear alien to their inner Jewish temper and tradition . . . . The utter Jewishness of his [Lipsky's] life and interest, so complete as to have given him no standing in American life save as he achieved it through Jewish service, his faults and failings perhaps even more than his virtues and his ability, commanded him to them.[77]

The loyalty of these members had nothing to do with Zionist principles or the immediate issues that concerned the organization. Mack explained after campaigning for the Zionist Congress in 1929 that "a considerable portion of the membership are not conscious Zionists at all. They like to be thought of as being loyal."[78] It was these loyal Jews who were members of the Z.O.A. One of their idols was Samuel, who was at that period one of Lipsky's most devoted lieutenants. Samuel published two remarkable books during the period—*You Gentiles*, in 1924, and *I, the Jew*, in 1927. According to Samuel, Jewish and Gentile

---

[76] De Haas to Brandeis, December 30, 1923, *de Haas Papers*; Julius Haber, *The Odyssey of an American Zionist* (New York: Twayne Publishers, 1956), pp. 215–16.

[77] Analyticus [James Waterman Wise], *Jews Are Like That* (New York: Brentano's Publishing Co., 1928), pp. 75–76.

[78] Mack to de Haas, February 25, 1929, *de Haas Papers*.

cultures are irreconcilable, the Jewish being the superior of the two. Jews are peace-loving, Gentiles are war-mongers; Jews are serious-minded, Gentiles are dedicated to trivialities; Jews are idealists, Gentiles are materialists. In strong and militant language he wrote:

> . . . We must seem immoral to you, you to us. That is why even the lowest type of gentile despise the Jew; the lowest type of Jew, the gentile.
> We cannot assimilate; it is so humiliating to us that we become contemptible in submitting to the process; it is so exasperating to you that, even if we were willing to submit, it would avail us nothing.
> We do not say: "I am a Jew," meaning, "I am a member of this nationality"; the feeling in the Jew, even in the freethinking Jew like myself, is that to be one with his people is to be thereby admitted to the power of enjoying the infinite. I might say of ourselves: "We and God grew up together."

And, of course, all Gentiles are anti-Semites: "Here is a cult, or at least a feeling, which sits with equal grace on the grossest of your peasantry and the most refined of your aristocracy."[79]

This was a manifestation of "compensatory chauvinism," which John Higham has observed among members of minority groups in the United States during the twenties.[80] Among active members of the Z.O.A., it must have been strong.

Efforts of the Intellectuals to Maintain Their Leadership

At this point we must ask what happened between 1928, when Lipsky was reelected in spite of unfavorable circumstances, and 1930, when he resigned and was replaced by his opponents. Did the deeply ingrained loyalties dissipate in such a short time? This is highly unlikely. The evidence suggests that the rank and file of the organization was as loyal to Lipsky in 1930 as it had been in 1928.[81] But in the 1930 convention, all discussions and negotiations took place behind closed doors, and the delegates were merely passive observers who were not even asked for an opinion.[82] The forces that motivated Lipsky's resignation were not to be found within the loyal membership of the Z.O.A. in 1930.

The membership figures had shown a continuous decline since 1925, and between 1928 and 1929 there was another sharp drop. We can assume that those who left were less loyal to Lipsky, and were not happy

---

[79] Samuel, *You Gentiles* (New York, Harcourt Brace & Co., 1924), pp. 25, 74, 209.
[80] Higham, *Strangers in the Land*, p. 254.
[81] Melamed, "The Peace of Cleveland," p. 130.
[82] For a description of the 1930 annual convention, see "Summary Report of the Thirty-Third Annual Convention of the Zionist Organization of America," *The New Palestine*, July 25, 1930, pp. 4–26.

with the existing leadership. There was also a continuously growing deficit since 1926, and all attempts to reduce it by asking the support of wealthy members were of no avail. This was attributed to the loss of the financial backers' support of the organization.[83]

Lipsky's leadership was discredited by Z.O.A.'s supporters, as evidenced by the steady decline in contributions to the U.P.A., though Palestine sentiment had gained ground in the Jewish community.[84] The Jewish press reflected the rapidly deteriorating prestige of the leading Jewish intellectuals. The Yiddish press, which had once ardently supported them, now joined in the attack. The same journalists who had extolled the leaders complained about them now.[85] *The California Jewish Review*, in an editorial entitled "Zionism and Lipskyism," came out with a devastating and cruel attack on the "Right Honorable Louis Lipsky," which was, of course, a title which could have easily be applied to Brandeis rather than Lipsky. So much for irony.[86] And an editorial in *The Day* at the end of 1929 stated that the Jewish people possessed everything but leaders.[87]

If a deviant leader is defined as one "not representative of his members in social background or aspirations" and "not accepted as an entirely respectable member of the community at large," then the Jewish intellectuals became deviant leaders.[88] Coralnik, in a moving article, described how he was not recognized and his name was unfamiliar even to active Zionists, who apparently never read his articles in the Zionist and Yiddish press. The Jewish intelligentsia, he said, no longer had a place in Jewish organizations and politics in the United States.[89]

The change was observed by Louis Wirth, the noted sociologist, in his study of the Jewish ghetto. "Intellectuals can only flourish in a community that supports them and gives them status," Wirth noted, and he argued that outside the original ghetto the Talmudic scholar and

---

[83] *The Zionist Ledger: An Analysis of Income and Expenditure of the Zionist Organization of America 1921–1929. Showing how the deficit was incurred and why it is imperative that it be paid up immediately* (n.p., n.n., n.d.). "Summary Report of the Thirty-Second Annual Convention of the Zionist Organization of America," *The New Palestine*, July 19, 1929, p. 30.

[84] Solow, "The Sixteenth Congress," *The Menorah Journal* 17 (October 1929): 28.

[85] Margoshes, *The Day*, June 29, 1928; Shelvin, *The Jewish Morning Journal*, June 9, 1927.

[86] Editorial, *The California Jewish Review*, March 23, 1928, clipping, *Brandeis Papers*.

[87] Editorial, *The Day*, December 25, 1929.

[88] Frank Pinner, Paul Jacobs, and Philip Selznick, *Old Age and Political Behavior* (Berkeley: University of California Press, 1959) p. 14.

[89] Abraham Coralnik, *The Day*, June 20, 1930.

Yiddish journalist were giving way "to doctors, lawyers and politicians. . . . Probably," Wirth added, "nothing has done more to alter the attitude toward the intellectual, and to change the conception of intelligence itself, than popular secular education."[90]

In the stresses that the deviant leadership experienced, it looked as if a new source of strength had come their way to save them. This was the leadership of the A.J.C., eager to join hands with Weizmann and the Zionists in the forthcoming Jewish Agency. At the same time, Louis Marshall still considered Brandeis and his associates dangerous opponents of the A.J.C. He did everything possible to help Lipsky in his fight against them.

The prestige and influence of the philanthropists had already been utilized by Lipsky during the 1927 convention. At that time, both Irving Lehman and Warburg sent telegrams extolling Lipsky's leadership.[91] After the resignation of the Brandeisists from the administrative committee of the Z.O.A. in 1928, Nathan Straus declared that "nobody who is against Weizmann and Lipsky can be my friend. It is they who have given their whole life to the Zionist movement." That same day Warburg announced a $50,000 donation to the U.P.A.[92] Both announcements received wide publicity and captured the headlines of the Yiddish press. Warburg's donation was motivated as much by the desire to hurt Brandeis as it was to help the Zionists with whom they were negotiating the final draft of the agreement of the Jewish Agency. The strategy was further revealed in Warburg's letter to Sir Alfred Mond,

---

[90] Louis Wirth, *The Ghetto* (Chicago: University of Chicago Press, 1928), especially pp. 249–50.

A comparison with other ethnic groups and their leaders in the United States shows a similar pattern. One such study of the Czecho-Slovaks in the United States, by Kenneth D. Miller, is of particular interest since the Czechs, unlike the Slovaks, rose quickly in socio-economic status. In the earliest phase, the most powerful leaders among the Czechs were those who wrote for the immigrant press, but by 1922, when Miller's book was written, the lawyers, doctors, and businessmen had taken over. Among the Slovaks, who still belonged to the lower classes, the journalists and the priests were still very powerful.

Miller observed that this new Czech leadership was very jealous of the good name of their people in America, and this more than any other consideration induces them to provide a constructive leadership. "As most of the leaders have lived here many years, and understand the spirit of America, they are able to do much in the way of interpreting America to those who have recently arrived upon our shores." The Slovak leaders, the priests and journalists, concentrated on helping the national movement in Slovakia, and were less interested in "interpreting" America to their followers. Kenneth D. Miller, *The Czecho-Slovaks in America* (New York: George H. Doran Company, 1922).

[91] Bernard Flexner to Mack, May 8, 1928, *de Haas Papers*.

[92] *The Day*, April 2, 1928.

the British Zionist and industrialist: ". . . as his [Weizmann's] position was made difficult by some very mean and theatrical resignations from the American committee, I thought he was entitled to some encouragement by some tangible sign . . . and therefore we gave the prompt assistance."[93]

Lipsky's alleged irregularities in the U.P.A. did not seem to have disturbed the American banker, but Brandeis's opposition to the Jewish Agency irritated him. In August 1928, another large non-Zionist conference took place in New York to which many Zionist and non-Zionist leaders were invited. Only the Brandeis group was excluded. When Mack complained to Marshall of their exclusion, Marshall answered angrily: "I notice that some of your group have publicly made remarks which were indicative of an unfriendly spirit, and of a disposition to create conflict."[94]

To appreciate the importance of the philanthropists' support of Lipsky, one has to take into account the changes in the composition of the Z.O.A.'s top executive. By 1921, a number of *nouveaux riches* Eastern Europeans were in the new executive. Their number, supplemented by Eastern European lawyers, doctors, and politicians, had increased throughout the twenties. These were the men whom Arlozoroff described in 1929 as leaders eager for the creation of the Jewish Agency. Their partnership with the illustrious wealthy Jews promised "a better period for them socially."[95]

An examination of the social composition of the members of the administrative committee of the Z.O.A. illustrates the changes that took place on the Zionist leadership. The administrative committee was now the ruling body of the Z.O.A., whereas the executive committee was a large body that met infrequently to approve the policies of the former body.

Though Lipsky and the intellectuals were still in control (the party machine and workers supported them), the loyalty of the "financial backers" and the professionals was maintained primarily by the prospect of partnership with the Marshall-Warburg group. The importance of the partnership becomes clear when we witness the break-up of the coalition the moment these hopes did not materialize.

While keeping the newcomers, businessmen, and aspiring politicians reasonably content with endless campaigns for Palestine and with con-

---

[93] Warburg to Sir Alfred Mond, May 2, 1928, *Warburg Papers*.
[94] Marshall to Mack, October 23, 1928, *Louis Marshall Papers* (Cincinnati: The American Jewish Archives).
[95] Arlozoroff, *Ktavim*, vol. 5, p. 154.

TABLE 8.1 *Occupations of the Members of the Administrative Committee in the Years 1925, 1927, 1929*

Occupation	1925	1927	1929
Lawyers	4[a]	10[b]	10[c]
Physicians	—	1	3
College professors	—	—	2
Rabbis	1	2	4
Businessmen	6	4	8
Social Workers	—	1	—
Journalists and writers	7	5	4
Employees of the Z.O.A.	1	—	—
Unavailable	2	5	14
Total	21	28	45

[a] Two were engaged in politics, including one elected judge.
[b] Four were in business and four in politics, including two elected judges.
[c] Five were in business and four in politics, including three elected judges.

TABLE 8.2 *Place of Birth of Members of the Administrative Committee in the Years 1925, 1927, 1929*

Place of Birth	1925	1927	1929
United States and Western Europe	2[a]	9	8[b]
Eastern Europe	17	13	23
Unavailable	2	5	14
Total	21	27	45

[a] One was Louis Lipsky himself, and the other was Henrietta Szold, the representative of Hadassah.
[b] In March 1928, the three members of Brandeis's group resigned from the administration committee; a fourth member, Norvin Lindheim, died two months earlier.

ferences with non-Zionist wealthy Jews (aimed at partnership with them), the intellectuals decided to mend their fences. They tried to strengthen the organization by centering it on the cultural and educational aspects of Zionism. They conceived of this as the only way to secure their leadership if a Jewish Agency were created.

One significant step in that direction was the appointment of Rabbi Mordecai Kaplan as chairman of the administrative committee after the stormy convention of 1928. The choice of Kaplan was an interesting one. He was identified with the principle of the existence of the Jews in the United States as a separate cultural entity that would be continuously inspired by the existence of a Jewish state in Palestine.[96]

In the first half of 1929, more and more discussion was devoted to the problem of maintaining Jewish culture in the United States. A special supplement on this problem appeared in *The New Palestine*. Special sessions were devoted to the question in the 1929 convention in which Kaplan, Coralnik, and Abraham Goldberg were the main speakers. They agreed with Kaplan's statement that

> We Zionists are of the conviction that with the cohesive influence of Palestine and with the new Jewish values which Palestine will produce, it is possible to achieve a type of communal unity and organization in the Diaspora which will not only give wide scope for the varying religious views that obtain in Jewish life, but will also evolve new opportunities for self-expression as Jews . . . as Zionists we can be satisfied with nothing less than with a spiritual heritage which is translated into education, into art, into religion, into folkways and mores, into laws pertaining to domestic relationships.[97]

To carry out this ambitious plan, argued Kaplan, supported by Coralnik and Goldberg, one needed an organization of members who were conscious of the task ahead, who believed in its ideal. Kaplan thought optimistically that it was not the size of membership that was of importance but its conviction and enthusiasm.[98] Goldberg agreed with Kaplan. Assuming that half the members of Z.O.A. were not adherents of Zionist ideology, he recommended the retention only of those who were conscious Zionists.[99]

But the leadership of the organization did not follow the ideas of the fundamentalists and insisted on having more members. When pressed, they also admitted that they preferred leading a Palestinian organization that enjoyed a large membership and the support of the community. Samuel stated during the discussion in 1929: "There are Zionists who disclaim Diaspora Nationalism; there are Zionists without a cultural tradition. And we do not look into a man's spiritual and cultural constitution before we invite him into the Organization. We only ask him to sign the Basle Program."[100]

Lipsky mentioned repeatedly his adherence to the former fundamental-

---

[96] Mordecai Kaplan, "Our Zionist Program: An Analysis of the Functions of the Zionist Organization," *The New Palestine*, March 15, 1929, p. 219.
[97] "Summary of the Thirty-Second Annual Convention," p. 31.
[98] Kaplan, "Our Zionist Program," p. 220.
[99] *Dos Yiddishe Folk*, June 7, 1929, pp. 5–6.
[100] Samuel, "Changing Winds," *The New Palestine*, p. 158.

ist version, but in action he more often followed the latter. As head of the organization, he could not but become concerned about its survival. In 1928, the administration tried a new device to lure members into the organization. They designed a joint campaign for the U.P.A. and for membership subscription, hoping to increase the membership from among contributors to Palestine. The next year, in an attempt to rally the masses behind the Zionists, the organization asked for a roll call in which each man would pay one dollar to the organization and sign a pledge that read: "I hereby register my faith in a Jewish Palestine."[101] Not Jewish culture, but Jewish Palestine was thus the real issue. And this was sound policy, since the conflicts between the broader conception of Zionism and the Palestine approach did not even reach the masses, who were interested only in Palestine.

The Jewish intellectuals at the head of the Z.O.A. were a sorry sight in the latter part of the twenties. Confused and perplexed, they turned for help in all directions. Their official publication, *The New Palestine*, started a supplement devoted to Jewish culture in February 1929. In that issue an editorial stated: "There are Zionists, too, who are opposed to Diaspora Nationalism. The Zionist Congress refused to make it part of the Zionist articles of faith."[102] The only protest to this statement came from the European Zionist leader Arlozoroff, who wrote a letter to the editor denying this interpretation and asking for clarification, which, however, was never given.[103] Silence on so important a principle indicated their state of mind. The defenders of the Diaspora nationalism doctrine in 1921 were silent in 1929. They were too confused to express an opinion.

At the beginning of 1929, the Brandeisists were also in an unenviable position. They were out of the Z.O.A., and excluded from the negotiations in which Weizmann, American Zionists, and an increasing number of wealthy German Jews were considering the future Jewish Agency. In desperation they decided to be silent about the Jewish Agency (which was enjoying the increased support of German Jews) and concentrate on the fight against Lipsky. "Distinctly, positively and affirmatively, we are not going to wage a war on the Jewish Agency," explained de Haas to one supporter, "nor at this time on the world leadership. We are not

---

[101] Lipsky, "The National Zionist Census: A Call to the Zionists of America," *The New Palestine*, September 27–October 4, 1929, p. 224.
[102] Editorial, *The New Palestine*, February 1, 1929.
[103] *The New Palestine*, March 15, 1929, p. 228.

aligned with Wise because we do not agree with his tactics. . . . We want to fight on the incompetence, mismanagement, inefficiency and political chicanery of the American organization."[104] But silence on a vital and controversial issue is not policy, especially if the group is seeking active leadership. Their silence could only be, and was, interpreted by all as opposition to the Agency, and it did not endear them to the philanthropists.

With the readiness of their non-Zionist opponents to support the development of Palestine, they were again forced to reconsider their position as Zionists. In the early twenties, their Zionism meant readiness to help build up Palestine without interfering in the internal affairs of the Palestinian Jews, but with the understanding that the Palestinian Jews would eventually establish a Jewish state in Palestine. As Zionists they were to aid the Palestinians in achieving this aim. However, their position on this last point was not as clear in the earlier period, when during the negotiations with Schiff they were willing to compromise because Schiff did not wish to see the establishment of a politically independent Jewish state. Brandeis went so far as to state in 1917 that he "neither advise[d] nor desire[d] an independent state."[105] In the late twenties, the only difference between the Brandeisists and their bitter opponents was on this one issue. The statement that Marshall and Warburg were non-Zionists had only one meaning: they did not desire the establishment of a Jewish state in Palestine. During this period of isolation from negotiations on the Jewish Agency, the Brandeisists' convictions on the matter became firmer. During those negotiations, Mack wrote to Friedenwald that he "should have opposed the whole thing because I do not see how those who proclaim themselves to be non-Zionists can cooperate in the creation of the Jewish national home."[106] Mack remained uneasy on this point when cooperation with Warburg was established later that year, for he now felt very strongly about the political independence of the Jewish state.[107]

But their attachment to this point of view must also be attributed to their realization of the fact that it was this perspective which appealed to the American Jews. Weizmann was attacked in 1929 when he tried for tactical reasons to be silent or vague on the future of Palestine. This vagueness created some opposition in Zionist circles in Europe, but it

---

[104] De Haas to Meites, March 30, 1928, *de Haas Papers*.
[105] Brandeis to Schiff, Nobember 2, 1917, *Brandeis Papers*.
[106] Mack to Friedenwald, July 3, 1929, ibid.
[107] Mack to Brandeis, November 5, 1929, ibid.

utterly shook his supporters in the United States. The Yiddish press, papers that had been his strongest supporters, attacked him for his attitude:

> What kind of political action is this, to talk in such a way that people will not know today what their leader will say tomorrow? . . . How does this type of action fit the leader of a mass movement, a man who represents such a great national-historical responsibility? How can he follow the old maxim: the song you sing changes with the changes of your companions? . . . Did the honorable speaker really adopt such a bad political rule? If he did, we may warn him that he will not succeed in carrying it too far.[108]

For the European Zionists the creation of a Jewish state in Palestine was not the essence of the ideal but only part of it, only one aspect of the national awakening. The awakening of Jewish national consciousness among the Jewish masses was the main task; the return to the ancient homeland was to be the result of this awakening.[109]

This was not the case among Zionist members and sympathizers in the United States in the late twenties. Those American Jews and their leaders who a few years earlier had decided to subscribe to Zionism as a national-cultural movement were not capable of doing so any more. The acculturated American Jewry did not grasp Zionist ideas, and neither did their leaders. What was for Weizmann mere tactics, which had to change constantly with the changing realities of the situation, became the essence of the idea for the American Zionists and their supporters.

Sensing the similarity between their idea of Zionism and the one accepted among the Eastern Europeans in the United States, the Brandeisists began to champion Zionism as Palestinianism. They called it the "maximalist" formula, as against Weizmann's moderation. When they returned to power, the American Zionists were instrumental in forcing the resignation of Weizmann as the president of the W.Z.O.

The Brandeis-Warburg Understanding and the Defeat of the Intellectuals

In July 1929, Lipsky and his friends were still in control of the situation. The World Zionist Congress, to which the Brandeisists managed to elect only one delegate, approved the scheme of the Jewish Agency. This was done after strong support was given to it by the Americans.

The Jewish Agency came into being in August, and this was followed

---

[108] Editorial, *The Day*, December 31, 1929.
[109] Ben Halpern, "Zionism and Israel," *The Jewish Journal of Sociology* 3 (December 1961): 158.

by a series of events that led to a political crisis. The Arab riots in Palestine were followed by the issuance of the White Paper by the British government temporarily stopping immigration to Palestine. Later came the death of Marshall and the designation of Warburg as the American head of the new Jewish Agency. Since relations between Weizmann and the British government had been broken off, political activities in the United States became of crucial importance to the Zionists. Warburg issued extremely cautious and moderate statements that enraged the Zionists and their sympathizers, including the Brandeisists. Lipsky was powerless to change the situation. "On his last trip to Europe, Lipsky appealed to Weizmann to curb the rampaging Warburg, but Weizmann would do nothing."[110] Warburg, the non-Zionist, became the strong man on whom Zionist political activities were dependent. Weizmann could not exercise pressure on Warburg, since he was afraid that to do so would destroy the Jewish Agency, on which he counted for the financial support which the Zionists needed.[111]

Lipsky had no influence on Warburg and his friends, but the Brandeisists decided to establish contact with them. Utilizing their personal relations with the A.J.C. members, they arranged a meeting between Warburg and Brandeis. The idea seemed a good one since Brandeis had nothing against Warburg, such as he had against Marshall.[112] Bernard Flexner, who had been active all these years in the J.D.C., was used as the middleman, and his task was to meet with Warburg and impress upon him the idea that Brandeis and his associates were the right people with whom to be connected.[113]

The meeting between Flexner and Warburg was immensely successful. For Brandeis, in fact, it must have been too successful, since Warburg, who was not a strong leader and who was unhappy in this position and its limelight, wanted Brandeis to assume the leadership. At that meeting, Warburg suggested to Flexner that Brandeis retire from the bench and become president of the A.J.C. and head of the Zionist Organization.[114]

But the offer of the greatest position in American Jewry did not lure Brandeis away from his post on the Supreme Court. He was always ready to devote a restricted part of his time to Jewry, but not himself. His main concerns were his obligations and positions in American so-

---

[110] Zalman Yoffeh, "Peace in American Zionism," *The Menorah Journal.* 19 (October 1930): 53.
[111] Coralnik, *The Day*, January 8, 1930.
[112] De Haas to Frankfurter, October 4, 1929, *de Haas Papers*.
[113] Mack to Brandeis, September 14, 1929, *Brandeis Papers*.
[114] Mack to Brandeis, September 18, 1929, ibid.

ciety, and the fear of conflict of status made him refuse repeatedly all public positions in the Jewish community. Though he had already passed the age of seventy, he would not retire from the Supreme Court. He still believed that his prime loyalty was to the American society where he represented the liberal progressive elements.

Brandeis was still willing, however, to use his influence to defeat Lipsky and his ilk. He therefore agreed to participate in a non-Zionist conference that would discuss the economic development of Palestine and even to deliver a speech. This was the first time since the 1920 London Conference that he was willing to expose himself to the public at any kind of Jewish function connected with Palestine. The meeting was not supposed to be publicized, but news of it was to be leaked to the public by design. Brandeis was also willing to give advice, and his first sample of this was, typically, the suggestion that Warburg make de Haas his assistant, a suggestion which Warburg politely declined.[115]

The conference was carefully planned by the Brandeisists, who realized that this step might give them back their power in the Z.O.A. All the non-Zionist supporters of the Agency were invited. Mack also insisted that Eastern European businessmen be invited.[116] Brandeis agreed. "Surely, promising East Europeans should be cultivated," he answered.[117]

This was a reversal of the treatment they had received from the Zionists and Marshall. At those conferences, they were the only group not invited; now only the associates of Lipsky were dropped. This conference marked the beginning of the end of Lipsky's leadership. Once the exclusion of the Z.O.A. leaders from the conference became public knowledge, the leadership of the intellectuals and their partners began to crumble.

For a while, the Lipsky leadership tried to fight for its survival. According to the agreement on the Jewish Agency, the Z.O.A. had to transfer its fund-raising functions to the Jewish Agency. Now Lipsky decided to maintain some of the earlier functions. This led him to quarrel with Warburg, who, always threatening to resign, wrote strong letters on the matter to Weizmann.[118]

When this did not succeed, Lipsky resorted to the last and only way he could attempt to influence Warburg: enlist public support. This was the function of the roll call in which every supporter would sign the pledge, "I hereby register my faith in a Jewish Palestine." The pledge

---

[115] Brandeis to Warburg, October, 1929, ibid.
[116] Mack to Brandeis, October 2, 1929, ibid.
[117] Brandeis to Mack, October 10, 1929, ibid.
[118] Warburg to Weizmann, November 15, 1929, *Warburg Papers*.

Crisis of Leadership in the Z.O.A., 1927-30

provoked Warburg, who, with the group of non-Zionists, did not subscribe to such a statement. He again complained to Weizmann and demanded that Lipsky be stopped, since "this effort of Lipsky's, which of course has created quite a discussion among the J.D.C. people, makes my job of getting the campaign plans straightened out rather difficult."[119] Warburg apparently got his way, and the feeling among the Zionist members and supporters was that "Warburg . . . at this point is the final word in Zionist affairs."[120]

While Lipsky and his friends wanted to fight the new coalition of Warburg and the Brandeisists, many members of the administrative committee refused to go along with Lipsky. They insisted that a compromise with Brandeis be reached that would result in the return of the Brandeisists as leaders of the Z.O.A. This, they maintained, was the only way to save the position of the Z.O.A. We have no records of the deliberations within the administrative committee, but the split between the intellectuals, who were backed by the bureaucratic machine, and the businessmen and members of the liberal professions, who insisted on calling the Brandeisists back to power, was evident. The intellectuals were at first willing to fight their opponents within the organization. A militant editorial of *The New Palestine* declared:

> The very basis of the movement will be shifted. Leadership that has often risen to the top by the sheer force of money will be given a place commensurate with the intellectual standards of the movement. . . . An idealistic movement is not guided by captains of industry, except in unusual cases. . . . Intelligence must become the criterion for values in the Zionist Organization. Cultural background must be the measuring-yard by which leaders are chosen.[121]

But such a revolution was no longer possible in the Zionist Organization of America. The differences of opinion in the administrative committee paralyzed its work. Soon twelve members of the committee, described by de Haas as the "financial backers," came to see him to discuss returning Brandeis to leadership.[122] The intellectuals had to give up. On top of all else, they were losing the support of Weizmann, who was anxious to have Brandeis back in the Zionist camp.[123] The hopelessness of their situation was admitted by Coralnik in January 1930. "The Zionist party in the United States," he explained, "contains too many members of the middle-class, Jews who are psychologically closer to the

---

[119] Warburg to Weizmann, November 4, 1929, ibid.
[120] Wise to Mack, October 7, 1929, *Brandeis Papers*.
[121] Editorial, *The New Palestine*, November 29, 1929, p. 452.
[122] De Haas to Mack, January 14, 1930, *de Haas Papers*.
[123] Interview with Louis Lipsky, September 13, 1960.

Agency than to Zionism. Such a party cannot keep its fences up."[124]

The fight was soon over; all that remained to settle with the Brandeisists were the conditions of their return. In February, *The New Palestine* adopted a new tone of compromise. "Whatever is to be done in the direction of unity," it said, "must be done with the greatest tact, with a rare sensitiveness for the feelings of persons and groups, whose principles and personalities are involved."[125]

The negotiations with the Brandeis group were undertaken by a committee representing the administration of the Z.O.A., which was anxious for a settlement with Brandeis. It was headed by David Friedberger, an Eastern European lawyer and businessman, who had been connected with the Brandeisists in the early twenties but who had since devoted himself to the Z.O.A. The other members of the committee were Dr. Nathan Ratnoff, an Eastern European physician; James Heller, American-born Reform rabbi; and Israel Goldstein, American-born Conservative rabbi. Separate negotiations for unity were attempted by Wise and Emanuel Neumann. Wise became alarmed at the increased power of the heads of the A.J.C., whom he still distrusted. He was unhappy with the association between Brandeis and Warburg, and although he was pleased that Brandeis at last openly expressed his sympathies for the Palestine efforts, he added in a letter to him: "I cannot help seeing and feeling, and regretting too, that the word could not have been spoken under other auspices, auspices more nearly in accord with those ideals that you have served throughout your day."[126] Wise and Neumann were arguing that it was imperative "to get a united front on real Zionist principles and let the European understand that there are Americans, other than the present leaders of the Z.O.A., who feel strongly on the subject, so that they would have the necessary backing in their dealings with the non-Zionists."[127] Their arguments impressed Mack. From the beginning, he was genuinely disturbed by the fact that people who did not subscribe to the idea of a Jewish state could become so influential in shaping Zionist politics. Remembering his old quarrel with Schiff in 1917, he wanted it to be clear that it was not a spiritual but a national center that was to be built in Palestine. He was further disturbed to find that Warburg really believed "the Zionists had completely yielded to the non-Zionists' aim to upbuild Palestine as a country and spiritual center and care nothing about Jewish domination or num-

---

[124] Coralnik, *The Day*, January 8, 1930.
[125] Editorial, *The New Palestine*, February 14, 1930, p. 100.
[126] Wise to Brandeis, November 30, 1929, *de Haas Papers*.
[127] Mack to Brandeis, February 28, 1930, *Brandeis Papers*.

bers."[128] The fear that they might again be outsmarted by the philanthropists seemed to be prevalent among the group. As a result, they were clearly willing to compromise with Lipsky.[129]

But Brandeis could not be moved from his position, and he did not tire of repeating it: "I care for no conference of any kind or at any time with Lipsky."[130] Even when he consented to meet with the delegation of the Z.O.A., he refused to discuss any compromise on this point: Lipsky must go. To the dismay of Brandeis's associates, the negotiations broke down on this point. They tried to reason with him. De Haas told Brandeis in March: "Friedberger has been pleading with me for humanism, that somehow, somewhere, something be done for Lipsky. There is no longer any discussion as to his ability, as to his leadership, but a good deal about bread and butter and face saving."[131]

Brandeis ignored them; he fought with a single purpose and forced his will on his associates. In compliance with his wishes, they decided that "neither as a matter of principle nor as a matter of tactics was any kind of compromise desirable."[132]

This put the Z.O.A. in an awkward position. Their capitulation over Lipsky involved more than mere disloyalty to him. It was tantamount to a public confession that during the past nine years, they had been wrong and the others right.[133] They were, however, willing to go along on one condition, that Brandeis take active lead of the organization. Even though the Brandeisists were not any nearer to Zionist ideology than they had been in 1921, Ephraim Caplan stated that their leadership, recognized and publicized, "could inspire and rekindle the devotion of the party workers."[134]

This phase of the negotiations was cut short with the publication of a memorandum signed by Brandeis, Mack, Robert Szold, and de Haas. The memorandum explained that since the work of the Z.O.A. was going to be concerned with the "economic development of Palestine," and since the Z.O.A. was in such desperate condition that it was unable to carry on such an obligation, a group of "neutrals" from neither of the two quarreling groups should secure the services of "competent people" with exclusive power for six months, renewable by the neutral committee for as much as two years, to make the Z.O.A. an efficient

---

[128] Mack to Brandeis, January 19, 1930, ibid.
[129] De Haas to Brandeis, February 20, 1930, *de Haas Papers*.
[130] Brandeis to Wise, February 22, 1930, *Brandeis Papers*.
[131] De Haas to Brandeis, March 21, 1930, *de Haas Papers*.
[132] Ibid.
[133] Abraham Goldberg, *The Jewish Morning Journal*, May 27, 1930.
[134] Caplan, *The Jewish Morning Journal*, June 13, 1930.

organization. Only then would the Brandeisists be willing to take over. In return, Brandeis was ready to give his "advice" to the future administration of the Z.O.A.[135]

This memorandum, its language, and its suggestion that a group of experts should be given *carte blanche* to reorganize the Z.O.A. was a flagrant insult to the leaders. And it apparently was meant to be. The truth was, as always, that Brandeis was not ready to become an active leader. "Every one knows," wrote Jacob Fishman, "that the principal reason for the Zionist effort to establish a united front was the hope of gaining the prestige of Justice Brandeis's leadership. But it seems that the Brandeis group is again playing an invisible leadership and acting by proxy. De Haas appears as a factor once more, and Robert Szold signs the ultimatum as if he were one of the pillars of Zionism."[136]

On the eve of the annual convention, negotiations between the Brandeis group and the administration of the Z.O.A. were resumed. The difficulties of negotiating on the basis of the memorandum were acknowledged by members of the Brandeis group, but "the chief" would not listen to compromise. "I do not see how you can safely depart an iota from the substance of what is declared in our statement," he wrote Mack.[137] When de Haas reported the group's dissatisfaction with some points of the memorandum and their inclination to accept responsibility immediately, without an interim period, Brandeis immediately wired Mack: "Important no member of our group should undertake to interpret memorandum."[138] This was the way Brandeis now exercised his political leadership, a way some historians have found to be characteristic of the progressives. Such a note had been softened in an earlier period by the ethic of the Social Gospel, but it prevailed in the twenties among disillusioned progressive intellectuals.[139] Their attitude was beyond comprehension to the Eastern Europeans in the Z.O.A. who, in spite of the desperate situation in which they found themselves, could not accept the memorandum. The negotiations continued after the convention had started, but meetings were kept in suspense.

The deadlock was broken only when Brandeis consented to withdraw the memorandum, presumably influenced by the pleading of members

---

[135] "Brandeis Defines Terms," *The New Palestine*, May 30, 1930.
[136] Jacob Fishman, *The Jewish Morning Journal*, May 25, 1930, quoted in *The New Palestine*, May 30, 1930, p. 340.
[137] Brandeis to Mack, June 11, 1930, *de Haas Papers*.
[138] Telegram from Brandeis to Mack, June 27, 1930, ibid.
[139] George E. Mowry, *The Era of Theodore Roosevelt, 1900–1912* (New York: Harper and Brothers, 1958) especially pp. 87 ff.; Leuchtenberg, *The Period of Prosperity*, p. 125.

Crisis of Leadership in the Z.O.A., 1927–30   245

from his own group. In the letter read to the delegates accepting the withdrawal, he promised to give his "advice," not conditional upon the acceptance of the memorandum.[140]

Lipsky said the Brandeisists had promised as part of their deal the return of Brandeis to active leadership, and he concluded that "they fooled us." He accused not only the Brandeisists, but also Friedberger and James Heller, who conducted the negotiations on behalf of the administration, of giving him a false promise.[141] Other evidence to support this version is not available.

The compromise reached between the two groups had nothing to do with future policies, which were carefully not mentioned, at least not publicly. The new administrative committee would include twelve men from the Brandeis group and six members of the outgoing administration. It is illuminating that the Brandeisists had difficulty finding twelve of their own men willing to serve on the new committee. Thus they appointed Rabbi Abba Hillel Silver and Ratnoff, members of the outgoing administration, as their representatives on the new administrative committee. From among the eighteen members of the committee, the following were appointed to top positions: Julian Mack, honorary chairman; Louis Lipsky, honorary vice-chairman; Robert Szold, chairman; Abba Hillel Silver, vice-chairman. Robert Szold became head of the organization and was introduced by Lipsky to the convention as "a gentleman who represents the authority of Mr. Justice Brandeis."[142]

The Brandeisists in Control Again

And so the pre-1921 pattern of leadership was reestablished. Brandeis resumed complete control of the situation, while both Robert Szold and de Haas, who headed the department of organization of the Z.O.A., reported to him and consulted with him on all issues. Brandeis's letters were again circulating among the inner circle, but he himself remained invisible. After the first excitement was over, he explained to de Haas, that what little time and strength remained available after the term of court began should be devoted to necessary study and thought on Palestine matters and the few important private conferences and seeing of individuals which was unavoidable.[143]

Soon after the new administration took office, it was officially proclaimed by the chairman that the primary goal of the organization was

---
[140] "Summary Report of the Thirty-Second Annual Convention," p. 14.
[141] Interview with author, September 13, 1960.
[142] "Summary Report of the Thirty-Second Annual Convention," p. 13.
[143] Brandeis to de Haas, August 31, 1930, *de Haas Papers*.

the economic building up of Palestine. Propaganda activities on behalf of Palestine continued, however. This was in line with the decision made by the Brandeisists in 1927 that a right *stimmung* for Palestine should be created by the organization in an effort to gain public support. Once the Brandeisists returned to the helm of an organization that stressed mass membership, they were also forced to retreat from exclusive concern with purely financial problems regarding Palestine, the role Brandeis assigned to the organization. At the first meeting of the executive committee, Robert Szold announced that their program would primarily "emphasize the economic methods" of building up Palestine. But, he added, next would come the endeavor to get a better understanding on the part of the public, and following that, concern with organization: "Let us have members."[144] Some sort of participation in Jewish politics was thus unavoidable, and they were no longer afraid to engage in it. The supporters of Diaspora nationalism and the awakening of national consciousness in the United States did not trouble them. "It is freely admitted," wrote one of the Jewish intellectuals who fought Brandeis in 1921 only to regret it in 1930, "that this nationalism in the Diaspora had definite limitations and that Jewish nationalism outside Palestine is not exactly what German or French, or American or English or Italian nationalism is."[145] The Zionists were operating in a community where many of the respected Jewish leaders accepted a qualified obligation to support the colonization movement in Palestine. In the American Jewish community, a commitment to the successful colonization of Palestine was becoming the new point of reference for its members. These developments in American Jewry will be examined in the next chapter.

The exclusive concern of the Zionist Organization of America and its Americanized leadership with Palestine put them in the mainstream of the community's thought. In order to gain the support of the Jewish masses, the new leaders were emphasizing the idea that Palestine as a national home for the Jews was their goal. When, in a closed meeting of the executive of the international organization, Weizmann came out in support of a bi-national state in Palestine, the new administrative committee promptly issued a statement to the effect that the ultimate aim of the Zionist movement was and would remain a "self-governing commonwealth" in Palestine.[146]

The Jewish intellectuals remained in the organization, but forfeited

---

[144] Meeting of the executive committee of the Z.O.A., September 28, 1930, reported in *The New Palestine*, October 3, 1930, p. 97.
[145] Melamed, "The Peace of Cleveland," p. 9.
[146] "The Zionist Objective," *The New Palestine*, September 19, 1930, p. 69.

the top positions of leadership. As Coralnik explained, even though American Zionism became a philanthropic organization, it remained the only Jewish organization in the United States in which there was still room for the Jewish intelligentsia.[147] Some of them who remained and continued to devote their lives to the organization managed to wield power and influence within it. The national leadership, however, remained mostly in the hands of those representing the "occidental orientation" in American Jewry, those educated in this country on American society. They restricted their activities as Jewish leaders to the goal of helping the Palestinian Jews to create a Jewish state.

---

[147] Coralnik, *The Day*, June 20, 1930.

CHAPTER IX

From Zionism to Palestinianism

American Jewry After World War I

In previous chapters, we discussed the growth of the body of supporters of the Zionist Organization, those who contributed to various fund-raising campaigns for the development of Palestine. Our understanding of the favorable response among a growing number of American Jews to the building up of Palestine will not be complete without an examination of the changes in the social structure of the Eastern European Jewish community in the United States after World War I.

Throughout the period of our investigation, continuous upward economic and social mobility was taking place in the Eastern European community; this was followed by desertion of the ghettos and removal to new settlements on the part of the more successful members of the community. However, as long as mass immigration into this country continued, ghettos were replenished by new waves of immigrants, who in turn supported and strengthened the distinct Jewish cultural institutions of the ghetto: the Yiddish theater, its literary clubs and societies, and its independent press and political organizations.

The most important single event which changed the whole life of the Jewish community was the Immigration Act of 1924, which brought immigration of Eastern European Jews to a stop. Mass immigration of Eastern Europeans had been halted in 1914 when the war broke out. Immigration figures show that only 350,000 Eastern European Jews entered the country between 1914 and 1924, compared with the 1.5 million who arrived between 1900 and 1914.

Students of American Jewry agree that World War I marked the turning point in the life of the Eastern European community. They have observed that "areas of immigrant settlement remained stable and compact in these cities down to the end of the war."[1] The change is attributed to the cessation of mass migration from Eastern Europe, as well as to the improved economic conditions in the country, which benefited many members of the community.

The census of 1920 was the first in which the number of Jews born in the United States exceeded the number of the foreign-born. This new generation of American-born, English-speaking, and American-educated young Jews contributed to the change in character of the Eastern Eu-

---

[1] Joseph Rappaport, "Jewish Immigration and World War I" (Ph.D. dissertation, Faculty of Political Science, Columbia University, 1951), 43.

ropean community in the United States and accelerated its rate of acculturation.

Even though the Eastern European community experienced a constant improvement in economic status, an especially great advance occurred during and immediately after the war. We are told in C. Bezalel Sherman's study of American Jewry that "one can talk of an increased proletarianization of the American Jews only till about the First World War. Since then, a process of deproletarianization can be detected, which at first led to a decrease in the number of Jewish industrial workers relative to the Jewish population and later on to an absolute decrease."[2] The changes in the economic standards of American Jews can be appreciated only when we also consider the increase of earnings of those who stayed in the factories as workers.[3]

According to the figures presented by Leo Grebler in his study of New York's Lower East Side, the biggest exodus of Jews from that area took place between 1925 and 1930, after the Immigration Act had been passed, when the number of Jews living in this compact neighborhood was cut in half.[4] Furthermore, "the later immigrants had a tendency to stay on the Lower East Side area over much shorter periods than did the earlier immigrants."[5] The same pattern was observed in the other big Jewish ghettos in the United States. The number of Russian-born immigrants in the Chicago ghetto, for example, was more than halved between 1914 and 1920.[6]

Grebler also conducted a survey among the members of the Amalgamated Clothing Workers in New York in an attempt to discover what caused them to move. The two most common reasons were the desire to find better housing and the wish to find a better environment for the children. Grebler suggests that the immigrants' awareness of the differences in housing quality in and out of the ghetto and their desire to improve the childrens' environment by moving out of it, was in itself a result of acculturation and adaptation to the new world. And once they moved to mixed neighborhoods, the inevitable process of acculturation was accelerated. It was the children, many of them American-born and

---

[2] C. Bezalel Sherman, *Yidden un Andere Etnishe Gruppes, in die Farainigte Shtaten* (New York: Unser Veg, 1948), p. 284. See also Nathan Goldberg, *Occupational Pattern of American Jewry* (New York: Jewish Theological Seminary and Peoples' University Press, 1947).

[3] Leo Grebler, *Housing Market Behavior in a Declining Area* (New York: Columbia University Press, 1952), p. 118.

[4] Ibid., p. 254.

[5] Ibid., p. 123.

[6] Nathan Glazer, "Social Characteristics of American Jews, 1654–1954" *AJYB* 56 (1955): 17.

educated, who caused more and more Jewish families to escape from the isolated and separatist Jewish atmosphere that prevailed in the ghetto, leaving behind mostly "the poor, the Orthodox, and the servers of cultural needs."[7]

It was at this point that the Eastern European community was beginning to realize that advancement did not lead automatically to the disappearance of discrimination, and that barriers between Jews and Gentiles existed also in the United States. The widely accepted stereotype of the Jew in American society was scarcely complimentary. The status of Jew ranked pretty low in society, in comparison with other groups. A study made by Emory Bogardus in 1926 on the ranking of ethnic status in the United States places the Eastern European Jews twenty-eighth in a list of forty groups.[8] The inconsistency between the Jew's increasingly high economic position and his educational attainments, on the one hand, and his low status as a Jew, which being an ascribed status could not be changed, on the other, added to his frustrations. This new reality hit the Eastern European Jews as they were moving out of the ghettos into mixed neighborhoods.

Inconsistency in the status set of the growing number of middle-class Jews was a common experience shared by both German Jews and Eastern Europeans Jews. In Bogardus' study, there was only a slight difference in the ranking of German and Eastern European Jews, the first being the twenty-sixth on the list, the second, the twenty-eighth.[9] Thus, the common denominator was not German, or Eastern European, but Jew—and this common experience, coupled with the intense anti-Semitism prevalent in the United States in the early 1920's, led to the emergence of a certain group solidarity among the American Jews that transcended earlier distinctions between them. American Jewry was organizing for common action vis-à-vis the dominant society.[10]

One of the new activities, which was a manifestation of the group's new solidarity, was the development of a network of Jewish organizations to serve the social needs of the members of the community, who found American organizations and social clubs closed to them. Another was the emergence of group voting behavior; all classes of Jews gradually shifted toward the Democratic party.

This loyalty of Jews to the Democratic party has its roots in the

---

[7] Grebler, *Housing Market Behavior*, p. 143.
[8] Emory S. Bogardus, *Immigration and Race Attitudes* (New York: D. C. Heath & Co., 1928), p. 25.
[9] Ibid., p. 25.
[10] Oscar Handlin, *Adventure in Freedom* (New York: McGraw-Hill Book Co., 1954), pp. 210–11.

1920's. Oscar Handlin attributes the shift to "solidarity with the underprivileged."[11] The Jewish masses were deserting the Socialist ticket, and in 1928 a very heavy Jewish vote was registered for Al Smith.[12] The German Jews, who at first resented any group vote, and whose leaders were mostly connected with the Republicans, were now joining the larger group. It was as if their group loyalty transcended their class loyalty. Support for the Socialists was viewed as a protest vote of an alien group, but support for the Democratic party was a positive group action for recognition by the larger society. This interpretation is supported by Robert Lane in his analysis of the political activities of minorities in the United States:

> As contact with the larger society increases for groups losing their language and custom differences, the ethnic group looks outward and becomes an embattled social group, enormously sensitive to reflections on group status and eager to advance group interests by all available means. Under these circumstances, under-evaluation by society produces, not acceptance of low esteem but doubts and anxiety about the self and group, which may be resolved by individual or group achievement.[13]

Thus their acculturation increased the conflict experienced by American Jewish groups and led to group action. But it was not a separatist movement; it was rather a collective attempt to raise its status in society in the way accepted and approved by American social institutions.

The Zionist Ideology

In our study, we singled out one type of action by which American Jews reacted to the growth of anti-Semitism and to their low ethnic status in the United States—i.e., support of Zionism. This choice was motivated by our observation that it was a modified version of Zionism, the principle of Palestinianism, that provided an ideology of survival for the American Jewish group. Palestinianism stated that all Jews should help build up Palestine as a Jewish national home. It served to justify the separate existence of the Jewish community in the United States and provided the ethnic status with a self-respect denied the group by the dominant society and its culture. At the same time, we have explained, Palestinianism did not conflict with the duties and obligations of Jews as Americans.

The increase of support for Palestine among American Jews in the

---

[11] Ibid., p. 212.
[12] Lawrence H. Fuchs, *Political Behavior of American Jews* (Glencoe, Ill.: The Free Press, 1956), pp. 66–67.
[13] Robert E. Lane, *Political Life* (Glencoe, Ill.: The Free Press, 1959), p. 252.

1920's meant that Palestinianism was emerging as a cornerstone of what we might call the American Jewish marginal culture. When a large number of people share a common position of marginality, they often develop a "marginal culture," which serves to define their relations to the majority, rather than have them remain in a constant state of tension and frustration.[14] The foundations of the emotional dominance that Palestinianism gained among American Jews in later years are to be found in the developments of the 1920's. Events in Europe and in Palestine from 1933 to 1945 only accelerated these developments in the United States and intensified the Palestinian sentiments in American Jewry. Understanding of events in the earlier period helps explain later developments.

Our investigation dealt with the leaders of the Z.O.A. Two sets of leaders, who joined the organization as a reaction to their marginality in American society, stood out in our analysis. One group, headed by Louis Brandeis, consisted of American-born and American-educated German Jews; the other was a group of Jewish intellectuals who immigrated from Eastern Europe. We saw that the two groups, following a short period of cooperation, became bitterly opposed to each other. They differed in their cultural background, in the degree of their acculturation, and in their position in the American social structure. The American leaders had achieved high rank in all important statuses but the ethnic, while the Eastern European intellectuals, associated with the ghetto and its culture, remained outsiders to American society. As a result, within the framework of Zionist ideology and the Zionist Organization, the two groups differed in their proposed solutions to their marginality.

It was Brandeis and his associates who promulgated Palestinianism, while the intellectuals adhered to orthodox Zionism and desired the awakening of the national consciousness of Jews everywhere and the revival of a distinct culture. Brandeis's conversion from Zionism to Palestinianism after 1916 was attributed to the status conflict in which he found himself after his elevation to the Supreme Court, a conflict aggravated by the upsurge of nationalistic anti-Semitism in the United States.

The spread of Palestinianism in the Jewish community during the 1920's should not be attributed to Brandeis's influence. It was a result of the fact that more and more American Jews came to occupy positions

---

[14] Milton M. Goldberg, "A Qualification of the Marginal Man Theory," A.S.R. 6 (1941): 52–58.

in the American social structure similar to that of Brandeis and his associates and were experiencing similar conflicts. It coincided with the exodus of more and more Jews from the ghettos, with their improved economic conditions, and the growing number of American-born and American-educated members in the community. The pervasiveness of anti-Semitic feelings in American society and the low status ascribed to the Jew kept American Jews on the defensive.

Palestinianism was not only suitable for the growing number of marginal Jews, but for the entire Jewish group in the United States. Facing the anti-Semitism of the dominant society, the whole group was under attack and felt the need to fight back. As we explained in the introduction, any viable ethnic group must have a certain degree of organization, a common social myth or ideology, and a recognized leadership. Although a network of exclusively Jewish organizations was emerging, the group lacked a common ideology to help unite its forces.

The community was losing its cultural distinctiveness and was hopelessly divided between religionists and secularists, as well as within those two groups. This was described succinctly by Rabbi Max Kadushin, a noted leader of the Conservative movement in the United States, who wrote in 1926: "Today, our conception of God is vague, and what is worse for our group consciousness, lacking its core, is powerless . . . the chaos of the various parties in Jewry is the result of groping attempts to find a new point of reference for the group's culture."[15]

It was at this point that Palestinianism was slowly emerging as a suitable ideology, or point of reference, for diverse Jewish groups and organizations. Palestinianism was an expression of Jewish nationalism. Nationalism is the typical reaction of members of groups who "have been made to feel inferior and as not privileged enough to enjoy a respectable status. . . . Their wounded self-feelings and their desire to re-establish self-respect" led them to nationalism.[16] But acculturated Jews felt that acceptance of the Zionist version of Jewish nationalism would cut them off from the country to which they now belonged. Jews in Eastern Europe did not consider themselves Poles or Russians. The situation of American Jews was different; they considered themselves Americans though their belonging to America was never free of doubts. The well-known social psychologist Kurt Lewin asserted that it was this

---

[15] Quoted by Marshall Sklare, *Conservative Judaism* (Glencoe, Ill.: The Free Press, 1955), pp. 274–75.

[16] Herbert Blumer, "Collective Behavior," in *New Outlines of the Principles of Sociology*, ed, Alfred McClung Lee, 2nd ed. rev. (New York: Barnes and Noble Inc., 1951), p. 219.

uncertainty about belonging which plagued the Jews in the Western world.[17]

Palestinianism was the solution to this conflict of loyalty, since, while an expression of Jewish nationalism, it was interpreted by the majority as being congruous with loyalty to the American nation. This interpretation was sanctioned by many American leaders who expressed sympathy with Jewish aspirations in Palestine. It was such pro-Palestine sentiments of non-Jewish American leaders which encouraged many Jews to adopt Palestinianism.

Non-Jewish American politicians were the first to sense that they could utilize the sentiments for Palestine prevailing among Eastern European Jews to gain the support of Jewish constituents. Even in the pre-Zionism days, in the year 1881, President Garfield appointed Simon Wolf as Consul General in Egypt. Wolf was a prominent Jewish leader who acted as the representative of certain Jewish organizations in Washington. Palestine was at the time under Egyptian control, and the President told Wolf: "I hope you will . . . find the land of your forefathers all that you expect."[18]

In 1887, when Palestine was again directly controlled by the Turkish government, Oscar Straus was appointed Minister to Turkey. When he resigned in 1890, President Harrison invited Wolf to the White House and told him of his desire "to appoint a representative American citizen of Jewish faith to Turkey." Wolf recommended a wealthy Jewish merchant, Solomon Hirsch, who was subsequently appointed.[19] After 1909, and as long as Turkey controlled Palestine, all American ambassadors to Turkey were Jews.

The strong American support for the Balfour Declaration and the international recognition given to Zionist aspirations in Palestine after 1917 persuaded many Jews in the United States to abandon their anti-Zionist stand. Most of them refused to attend an anti-Zionist conference that Rabbi David Philipson wanted to convene in 1918, and their refusal led to the cancellation of the conference. Straus explained in his refusal that

> In view of the fact that Great Britain, France and other allied nations, through their highest officials, have given assurances for the welfare of the Jews in Palestine, regardless of the fact whether one is a Zionist or not, to

---

[17] Kurt Lewin, *Resolving Social Conflicts* (New York: Harper & Brothers, 1948), p. 180.

[18] Simon Wolf, *The Presidents I Have Known from 1860–1918* (Washington, D.C.: Byron S. Adams, 1918), p. 111.

[19] Ibid., p. 115.

From Zionism to Palestinianism

oppose such a beneficent purpose on the part of a section of our people can only be hurtful and show a lack not only of unanimity but of appreciation for those welcome assurances which should receive the gratitude not only of Jews as such but as Americans. . . .[20]

When the Jewish socialists started their campaign for Jewish trade unions in Palestine, they argued along the same line. Since the international labor movement was supporting Palestine, they said, Jewish socialists could not lag behind.[21]

During the 1920's, more and more Jewish organizations were committing themselves to the support of Jewish efforts in Palestine. This provided the acculturated Jewish community a rationale for maintaining the separate existence of exclusively Jewish organizations since in all other aspects, in form as well as in content, these Jewish organizations only duplicated similar non-Jewish organizations.

The *Landsmanschaften*, for example, were becoming more concerned with Palestine during the 1920's. N. Blachman, in his historical analysis of the Jewish *Landsmanschaften* in the United States, divides its history into three distinct periods. In the first, which ended in 1914, the main activity was to help relatives to immigrate to the United States. In the second, which lasted until 1924, they were mostly engaged in sending relief in an organized way to their brethren in Europe. The third period was stimulated by the Immigration Act of 1924, when it became apparent to all that the solution to the plight of their brethren had to be on a national scale, and when activities of the *Landsmanschaften* shifted to the aid of colonization of Palestine. In that year, a Committee of Jewish Organizations for Palestine was created that provided the central organization for *Landsmanschaften* interested in supporting Palestine.[22]

The traditionally anti-Zionist Jewish labor movement in the United States was also moving in the same direction. In 1923, a new organization came into being, the National Labor Committee for Organized Jewish Labor in Palestine, the *Gewerkschaften*, engaged in campaigns for the collection of money for Jewish trade unions in Palestine. In 1926, as many as 158 organizations joined the yearly campaign.[23]

---

[20] *Correspondence on the Advisability of Calling a Conference for the Purpose of Combatting Zionism* (New York: The Zionist Organization of America, 1918), p. 4.
[21] Hyman J. Fliegel, *The Life and Times of Max Pine* (New York: Privately Printed, 1959), pp. 20, 31.
[22] N. Blachman, "Die Landsmanschaften un die Centrale Organizatzies," in *Die Yiddishe Landsmanshaften fun New York* (New York: Peretz Shreiber Farein, 1938), pp. 33–42.
[23] Fliegel, *The Life and Times of Max Pine*, p. 25.

Even the anti-Zionist Reform synagogue, the most important organization of the German Jews, was shifting its position. The first move was made by Hebrew Union College when in 1928 it conferred a Doctor of Hebrew Letters on Chaim Weizmann, the president of the W.Z.O. Next, the president of Hebrew Union College, Rabbi Julian Morgenstern, took part in the deliberations of the 1929 annual convention of the Z.O.A. At that convention he declared: "To me [Judaism] is primarily a religion. But a religion not fully comprehensible, apart from the consciousness of Israel as a unique people in the world; and I am sure that when I say that you will see that, as I understand it, Reform Judaism has advanced, too, from its established position of our great honored pioneers and reformers of the nineteenth century."[24]

Finally, Jewish philanthropists were moving in the same direction and in 1929 joined the enlarged Jewish Agency for Palestine as non-Zionist members, strictly interested in the economic development of Palestine.

The duty of Jews to support the development of a Jewish Palestine was thus accepted by a growing number of American Jews and their organizations. It was being institutionalized as a basic value of American Jewish marginal culture.

The Zionist Organization

When the Zionist Organization in the United States gave in to the prevailing Palestinian sentiments and limited its goal to aiding the building of Palestine, it ceased to be a spearhead of a social movement aimed at bringing about "fundamental changes in the social order" and became instead an organization aiming at "a partial reform in the social order."[25] It is, however, not an easy task to determine when exactly this change took place.

In 1918, the newly established Z.O.A. became officially dedicated to the development of Palestine, excluding all cultural and educational activities. This decision was reversed in 1921 and reimposed in 1930. But, as we have shown, during the 1920's the organization was almost exclusively engaged in Palestinian activities. Moreover, Louis Lipsky, the chairman of the F.A.Z., admitted as early as 1914 that many members of the organization were interested only in Palestine; the educational

---

[24] "Summary Report of the Thirty-Second Annual Convention of the Zionist Organization of America," *The New Palestine*, July 19, 1929.

[25] Rudolf Heberle, *Social Movements: An Introduction to Political Sociology* (New York: Appleton-Century-Crofts, 1951), pp. 6–7.

and cultural activities were even at that early date less vigorously pursued than the fund drives.[26]

We also examined the structural changes of the Zionist Organization and explained that only a mass party with dues-paying members and the broad ideological principles that are the basis for political education of the members can provide the spearhead for a social movement aimed at effecting a fundamental change in the life of its members. After 1918, the Z.O.A. made a major effort to attract influential people who would merely aid the fund-raising operations of the organization. But attracting those who would only contribute money to Palestine had already begun with the establishment of the Zion Associations in 1912. Members of these associations were required only to contribute to Palestine institutions and attend one or two business meetings a year.[27]

Whatever the manifest goals of the organization and its structure, many of its active members were the "hundred percenter" Jews, totally dedicated to the organization and to Jewish nationalism. Maurice Duverger observes that militant members often "take their task so much to heart and show such a liking for politics that these gradually absorb their whole life; for these enthusiasts the restricted party becomes totalitarian in character."[28] For the militants in the Z.O.A. Zionism remained a social movement, as it did not for most supporters of Zionism in the United States, who were interested only in aiding Palestine.

The key to an understanding of the nature of American Zionism lies in the relationship between the Zionist Organization and its supporters. Any social movement consists of "one or more formally organized cores or nuclei surrounded by a mass of less formally and less intensively attached supporters."[29] The supporters are potential members of the organization; but in the case of the Z.O.A., the increase in the number of supporters was not reflected in an increase in membership. The supporters, anxious to avoid any possible conflict with their American status, did not join the Z.O.A. because of the stigma of Jewish nationalism attached to it.

To get their support, the Zionists had to build a network of organizations devoted almost exclusively to fund-raising for Palestine, such as the *Keren Hayesod*, the United Palestine Appeal, and the Jewish

---

[26] Louis Lipsky, "What Is Wrong with the Zionist Organization in America," *The Maccabean* 24 (May 1914): 141.
[27] "Report of the Fifteenth Annual Convention of the Federation of American Zionists," *The Maccabean* 22 (July 1912): 29.
[28] Maurice Duverger, *Political Parties* (New York: John Wiley & Sons, 1955), p. 119.
[29] Heberle, *Social Movements*, p. 279.

Agency for Palestine. To attract support to these organizations, the Zionists made them independent of the Z.O.A. It was the principle of neutrality that was believed to have greatly contributed to the success of the *Keren Hayesod* and the United Palestine Appeal.[30]

The inability of the Zionists to communicate with their supporters on any level other than fund-raising for Palestine was demonstrated in their failure in the field of Jewish education. Even in the 1930's, when the Jewish community became concerned with Jewish education, the members of the community entrusted it to religious organizations rather than to the Zionists. The Z.O.A.'s almost exclusive concern with fund-raising for Palestine was a result of receiving a favorable response from supporters in this one field.

The attitude of caution on behalf of supporters who were interested strictly in Palestine was also, in part, the result of the militant type of membership that comprised the Z.O.A. As we have explained, many were the "hundred percenters," including immigrants dedicated to the old ways. The few young American-born members in the Z.O.A. were those recruited during that phase in their lives when they were reacting to discrimination. Stonequist, in his sociological study of the marginal man, described the act of joining the Zionist Organization as a typical reaction during the second phase in the life cycle of the marginal man, that of consciousness of ethnic group membership. "When I felt the race problem most," says one of Stonequist's interviewees, "I joined a group of Zionists." This period was described by the joiner as a period of intense Jewish nationalism.[31] The supporters, on the other hand, refused to carry their nationalism beyond financial donations to the development of Palestine, and they kept away from the Z.O.A.

But there was one other group of members, mostly American-educated and interested solely in Palestine who, wishing to be leaders in the community, joined the organization. Most of Brandeis's associates belonged to this group.

The Brandeis group in the Z.O.A., which we have examined in detail, had much in common with the supporters of the organization. Many of the supporters of the Z.O.A. in the 1920's and 1930's were born in the United States or at least educated in this country; many attained high positions in business or the professions, and lived in middle-class, mixed neighborhoods. Reacting to anti-Semitism and their low ethnic status,

---

[30] *Report of the Keren Hayesod to the Thirteenth Congress, August 1923* (London: 75 Great Russell Street, 1923), p. 21.

[31] Everett V. Stonequist, *The Marginal Man* (New York: Charles Scribner's Sons, 1937), pp. 123–29.

they became oriented to Palestine, since this, they felt, did not conflict with their status as Americans.

But while the supporters made their adjustment by contributing funds for Palestine and remaining outside the organizations, the Brandeisists, who wished to remain Jewish leaders, could not stay outside. They needed an organization through which to reach the supporters and exercise their leadership. It was their status as Jewish leaders that kept them in the organization. Within the organization, they tried to dissociate themselves from Jewish nationalism and dedicate themselves as Zionists and Jews strictly to Palestine. Rather than support Palestinian activities from the outside, they tried to reorganize the Z.O.A. in such a way that it would become solely Palestinian. Their various reorganization plans were designed to attract the supporters, who were only interested in Palestine, into the organization. Instead, it was the totally committed "hundred percenters" who remained, while most Jews with restricted commitment to Palestine and their status as Jews stayed out.[32]

The reinstatement of Brandeis's supporters to Z.O.A. leadership in 1930 was an attempt to attract both members and supporters who were deserting the organization. Brandeis's supporters were identified with Palestinianism and had also achieved prestige in the dominant society. By contrast, the Jewish intellectuals who ruled the organization until 1930 were identified in the public eye with Jewish nationalism and had "not yet become adept in American manners and mannerism."[33]

The prestige of the Jewish leaders in the dominant society became of great concern to many American Jews because the growing Jewish com-

---

[32] Samuel Halperin, in his study on American Zionism from 1929 to 1948, defines all Jews who wished to see the establishment of a Jewish state in Palestine as Zionists. No distinction is made either between affiliated members of Zionist organizations and sympathizers who remained outside the organizations, or between nationalists and mere Palestinians. On the other hand, Jews who actively aided and contributed to the development of Palestine but did not wish to see a politically independent Jewish state in Palestine are defined as non-Zionists.

Halperin describes how most of these non-Zionists agreed, during the 1930's and 1940's, to support the Zionist leaders in their efforts to secure Palestine as a Jewish state. Our analysis is concerned with the development of an attachment to Palestine by American Jewry. The caution of many Jewish leaders who worked for the development of Palestine supports our contention that many American Jews, especially those who attained a position of prominence in the dominant society, worried lest their work for Palestine would be interpreted as support to nationalism. They therefore called themselves non-Zionists and opposed the establishment of a Jewish state. See Halperin, *The Political World of American Zionism* (Detroit: Wayne State University Press, 1961), *passim*.

[33] Jacob Rader Marcus, "Zionism and the American Jew," *The American Scholar* 2 (1933): 283.

munity outside the original ghetto erected a gilded ghetto, a network of organizations which resembled in form and content the non-Jewish organizations. These new organizations penetrated all spheres of life. The growth of Conservative Judaism, for example, was attributed by one of its leaders "not . . . so much to a desire to improve the content of Jewish life as . . . to establish organizations that should be similar in form to those of their wealthier fellow Jews or their Gentile friends."[34]

In such organizations, leaders from the periphery were desired, since they had achieved success in American society and could confer prestige on the organizations they were leading. It was believed that the lack of just such leadership caused the deterioration of the Z.O.A. which was losing members and contributors.

Under the new leadership, the deficit of the organization was reduced, and contributions to Palestine increased somewhat, despite the depression. Membership figures, however, continued to decline. In later years, even though membership figures increased, they remained low in comparison to the successes of the fund drives.[35]

Hence, while pro-Palestine sentiments were achieving emotional dominance among American Jews and penetrating Jewish-organized religious and secular life, the Z.O.A. leaders, who subscribed to Palestinianism, did not achieve the dominant position in the Jewish community to which they aspired.

Since the Z.O.A. was a branch of the W.Z.O., an international Jewish organization dedicated to the revival of the Jewish nation, and since it provided in the United States a refuge for those who were identified with the nationalist ideas promulgated by European and Palestinian Zionists, most supporters in the United States carefully kept away from the organization. They expressed their sympathies with Palestinianism through their contributions and did not join the Z.O.A.

This explanation for the Z.O.A.'s weakness in the American Jewish community, based on our examination of its history up to 1930, holds nonetheless true to this day.

For a number of years, however, between 1944 and 1948, the Z.O.A. and its leadership temporarily escaped their predicament. Those were the days when the news of massacre of European Jewry shook the world—the years of agitation for the right of the surviving Jewish refugees to enter Palestine, and the struggle for the creation of a Jewish state. During this period, we witness a rapid increase in membership of

---

[34] Quoted by Sklare, *Conservative Judaism*, p. 118.
[35] Halperin, *The Political World of American Zionism*, appendices IV and V.

the Z.O.A. and Zionist leaders playing a major role in mobilizing American Jewry to the struggle for a Jewish Palestine.

But immediately after 1948, the old pattern reemerged. Z.O.A. membership dwindled as rapidly as during the years 1919–1920—American Jews again refused to be members of a nationalist Jewish organization. And only those Zionists who held prominent positions in American organizations others than the Z.O.A. maintained leading positions in the American Jewish community after the Z.O.A.'s decline.

CHAPTER X

A Sociological Summing-up

The work presented in this book is a study in the field of historical sociology. Viewed as history, it describes and analyzes developments in the American Zionist movement from 1897 to 1930 and examines changes in its ideology, its organization, and its national leadership throughout this period. Methods of historical research were employed and canons of historical investigation were followed. In this historical study, however, our knowledge of sociological theories aided us in selecting the problems to be examined, in posing the questions to be answered by the data collected, and in interpreting our findings. Hence we considered the Jewish community in the United States during the period under examination a minority group in a process of being acculturated into a dominant society; we analyzed the function of Zionist ideology for the survival of the Jewish group as a distinct socio-cultural entity; we classified Zionist leaders into types of leadership, and utilized sociological concepts in studying the structural changes which the Zionist organization underwent.

As a work in sociology, the American Zionist organization and its leadership were treated in this book as one case, the study of which increased our knowledge on a number of important sociological problems —acculturation, marginality, political leadership, formal organizations, the relation between ideology and social position. These sociological findings, hitherto interspersed in our historical narrative, will be summarized in this chapter.

Acculturation, Assimilation, and Marginality

Acculturation is a process by which one group acquires the cultural values and norms of another group. This is likely to take place whenever there exists "some approximation between two cultures."[1]

As the process of acculturation continues, it may reach a point at which members of the acculturating group begin to evaluate themselves in accordance with the standards of the new culture. This constitutes a new phase in the process of acculturation since it involves a gradual weakening of the membership group as the reference group providing criteria for the beliefs and standards of behavior of its own members. If

---

[1] A. L. Kroeber, *Anthropology: Culture Pattern and Processes* (New York: Harcourt, Brace and World, n.d.), p. 236.

A Sociological Summing-up

acculturation proceeds uninterrupted, the new group becomes the dominant point of reference for the acculturating group.

Such a development forces, sooner or later, changes in the social structure of the subordinate group; the status-sets of its members have to be adjusted to the newly accepted cultural standards.[2] Certain statuses are not recognized by the new culture and have to be abandoned, while new statuses are acquired and the boundaries of still others are rearranged.

This distinction between the acquisition of new values and the changes in the status-sets of those acquiring them is an analytical distinction; empirically, the two processes can hardly be separated. However, a distinction between the two becomes discernible whenever the changes of values and statuses lead to acute conflicts. Conflicts during this change are, of course, inevitable; but the greater the contradictions between the values of the old and the new cultures, the greater the personal and group conflicts such transformation produces.

Several examples of such conflicts have been demonstrated in this study. For example, the different interpretations of the concepts of state and nation in Eastern Europe and the United States resulted in confusion and constraints among the Jews who immigrated from Eastern Europe. In the United States, the two concepts were synonymous, while in Eastern Europe the nation and not the state was the source of the group's language, history and cultural traditions. In order to adjust to the American culture, the status "Jew" had to be restricted. A new status, that of "American," took over many of the rights and duties which belonged to the Jewish status in the old country.

This example introduces an important mechanism used to reduce conflict during the period of transition from one culture to the other. Those involved in the process of acculturation often conform in their behavior to the new standards, abandoning some statuses and rearranging the boundaries of others, but at the same time persistently denying that they have given up their old values and ideas. The abandonment of Zionism for Palestinianism, discussed at length, illustrates this point. Although this ideological change entailed the abandonment of the idea of the Jews as a separate nation whose duty it was to retain its distinct culture and language, there was a refusal to admit that basic tenets of the Zionist ideology were being abandoned. The new Palestinian ideology, restricted to aiding Jews to build a Jewish homeland in Palestine, was persistently called Zionism, and the proponents of the new doctrine claimed that no compromise of the Zionist ideology had taken place.

---

[2] For an explanation of the concept *status-set* see, Introduction, footnote 3, p. 4.

An incidental product of acculturation is "the marginal man" who is attached to two or more competing groups and their cultures, using them as reference groups for his beliefs and standards of behavior.[3] Groups in this situation are marginal groups. Acculturation may eventually lead to full assimilation which is achieved when acquisition of the new culture results in the acculturating group's losing its distinct identity and accepting a common identity with the group whose culture it had adopted.[4]

It is, however, conceivable that acculturation does not lead to assimilation. This book is concerned with one type of situation in which the acculturating group was refused full membership by the dominant group and did not assimilate. When a group reaches a phase in its acculturation at which it adopts the dominant group as a normative reference group—that is, with the intention of gaining admittance into it— and is then refused full membership, its marginality ceases to be a transitory state of affairs. It is this type of marginality which concerns us in this work.

Most illustrations in the sociological literature on marginality describe a situation in which entry to the dominant group is not clearly proscribed. It must be assumed that when a clear proscription does exist, the acculturating group has no hope of getting admittance and does not adopt the dominant group as a normative reference group. It may adopt the dominant group as a comparative reference group, however, using its values as a point of reference in making evaluations of themselves and others, without seeking acceptance.[5]

Our study suggests that groups who become marginal are often those trapped into believing they might gain acceptance into the dominant group and assimilate into it, only to realize later that a special social mechanism has been erected by the dominant group which bars their entrance. This mechanism, detectable only by those who have already gained an intimate knowledge of the new culture, consists of the fol-

---

[3] Robert Parks' introduction to Everett Stonequist, *The Marginal Man* (New York: Charles Scribner's Sons, 1937), p. xviii.

[4] Kroeber, *Anthropology*, pp. 233–40.

[5] A comparative reference group is a group whose values and standards are used by others as a reference point in making evaluations of themselves and others. A normative reference group is a group into which persons are motivated to gain or maintain acceptance. In the second type, the members seeking acceptance by the group will conform to what they perceive to be the consensus among the group members. For a more detailed explanation of the distinction between a comparative and a normative reference group, see Harold H. Kelley, "Attitudes and Judgements as Influenced by Reference Group," *Readings in Social Psychology*, ed. Guy E. Swanson, Theodore M. Newcomb, and Eugene L. Hartley, rev. ed. (New York: Henry Holt & Company, 1952), pp. 410–14.

lowing: a) low status is assigned to the group which tries to gain admittance, and, b) there are no prescribed norms to enable members of the subordinate group to abandon their ties with their old group.

In a social situation in which both values are in existence, the barriers are very effective. In some situations, only the first value operates, as, for example, in the case of lower-class Americans attempting to gain acceptance into middle-class society. For a number of ethnic groups in the United States, including the American Jewish group we have examined, both values are in operation.

One type of reaction, but not necessarily the only one, of the acculturating group when it realizes its predicament is to reject those values of the dominant group which assign low status to their own. Some sort of group solidarity emerges, accompanied by an ideology whose function it is to reject the low status attributed to the group and to substitute a more favorable evaluation. The socialist ideology, for example, might be interpreted as the ideology developed by the working classes in reaction to the low status ascribed their class by the dominant middle classes.

Nationalism is the ideology developed by ethnic groups on whom low status was conferred according to standards of the society of which they had hoped to be equal members. As the number of marginal men within the ethnic minority grows, some decide to devote themselves to the group's social and cultural life and begin to shape its own nationalist ideology. Their accomplishments attract more of the marginal members of the group who are encouraged to abandon their desperate efforts to become fully accepted by the dominant group and to identify themselves instead with their rising group.

In its extreme form, nationalism advocates the abandonment of the dominant group as a reference group and the strengthening of the ethnic group's own culture which should provide an attractive reference group for its members. Where, however, the subordinate group is enmeshed in the economic, political, and cultural institutions of the dominant society, and is unable to achieve political and economic independence—as in the case of American Jewry—this extreme version of nationalism is utopian. Under such circumstances, the nationalist ideology most likely to be adopted by the group rejects those values of the dominant group's culture which relate to the subordinate group's low esteem, and a marginal subculture tends to emerge within the overall dominant culture which is restricted to ideas explaining and justifying the existence of the ethnic group within the larger society. This has been demonstrated in this book.

The version of nationalist ideology an ethnic group adopts in reaction to its marginality and humiliation by the dominant culture varies according to:

1. The degree of its acculturation to the dominant society, i,e., the strength of the dominant group as a reference group relative to the strength of the old membership group as a reference group;
2. The degree of integration of its members in the social structure of the dominant society or, correlatively, the degree of their independence of the dominant group's structure.

One important variable that can measure the degree of integration into the structure of the dominant society is the rank the members of the subordinate group have achieved in it by virtue of statuses other than ethnic. The rank achieved in the dominant social structure and the rate of acculturation are interdependent variables. It was observed that the higher the social position of the subordinate group members in the dominant society, the greater their acculturation.[6] This study has shown that the higher the rank reached by Jews in American social structure, the greater their concern for the avoiding of engagements in activities that might be interpreted as contrary to American values.

Two types of marginal men were distinguished in our study:

1. Members of the subordinate group who attained a high degree of acculturation and a high rank in the dominant society;
2. Members of the subordinate group who attained a low degree of acculturation and a high rank in the dominant society.

Both types of marginal men rejected the values that assigned low rank to their ethnicity. However, the group of the more acculturated marginal men adopted Palestinianism, a milder version of nationalist ideology. In addition, this group wished to reduce the conflict created by their low-ranking ethnic status among their highly ranked statuses by way of restricting both the scope of the low-ranking ethnic status, i.e., the number of activities required from the occupants of this status, and its saliency, i.e., its importance compared to their other statuses. The less acculturated marginal men, still committed to the old society as its reference group, adhered to some of the old values and were concerned with their social standing within their old society. That group, the Jewish intellectuals, retained their orthodox Zionist ideology and refused to restrict the scope and saliency of their Jewish status to the extent desired by the first group, the American-born Zionist leaders.

The members of the former group of marginal men, who had attained

---

[6] S. Alexander Weinstock, "Role Elements: A Link between Acculturation and Occupational Status," *B.J.S.* 14 (June 1963): 144–49.

a high rank in the dominant culture in all their statuses but one, were caught in a typical situation of status inconsistency. Gerhard Lenski showed that such people tend to adhere to liberal political ideas, and explained this tendency as their protest "against the social order which produced such unpleasant experiences in their lives."[7] Moreover, this tendency, according to Lenski, was especially strong among those whose only low status was ethnic.[8] Since most of Lenski's examples used to prove his last point were American Jews, this may be explained by the fact, already mentioned, that they had no normative way of abandoning their low ethnic status.

In our sample, most marginal men with a status inconsistency accepted liberal political beliefs, but their further frustration, resulting from their marginal position in the American society, added the nationalist element to their protest. In addition, their efforts to restrict the scope and saliency of their low status suggests another form of reaction typical among people in a position of status inconsistency.

Both types of marginal men felt their marginality acutely and tended to develop a marginal culture, which rejected the low status ascribed to their ethnicity by the dominant culture and justified a separate existence. But the highly acculturated group whose members achieved high positions in the dominant society were unwilling, as well as unable, to attach themselves to any values which did not receive the sanction of the dominant system of beliefs, while the other group, still attached to the old culture, wished to maintain some aspects of it. Palestinianism became the content of the marginal culture of the first group since it catered to its self-respect, justified separate activities on behalf of American Jews, and at the same time was in accord with the dominant culture which expected Jews to be attached to their ancient homeland.

Many of the marginal men with low acculturation and low status in the new society were caught between two cultures, the old and the new, using both as their reference groups. They found themselves unable to operate within one frame of reference where new ideas could be formed, and they were unable to develop their own ideology which could explain and justify their position.

The diehards among the second group, the Jewish intellectuals who insisted on maintaining allegiance to the old society, were those who could not accept the standards of the new one without loss of prestige. They were being acculturated to the new society, but the adjustment

---

[7] Gerhard E. Lenski, "Status Crystallization: A Non-Vertical Dimension of Social Status," A.S.R. 19 (1954): 412.
[8] Ibid.

of their status-set to the new standards was painful, since it involved a loss in rank. On the other hand, they felt strongly committed to the new society and hence were unable to reduce the conflict. Thus, the hopelessness of their situation made their marginality most difficult.

The Functions of Leaders and the Legitimation of Their Authority

The leader, says Alvin Gouldner, is "an individual who, in some situations, has the right to issue kinds of stimuli which tend to be accepted by others in the group as obligations."[9] Leadership status is secured when it is accepted by followers, and the position is sustained by continuous acceptance of the leaders' authority.

In defining the concept of leader, this work excluded the category of officers, i.e., those who achieve their leadership "mainly from their position in the organization."[10] We further restricted ourselves to the problem of normative authority of the leaders and did not deal with the problem of power, coercive or economic, which leaders frequently utilize to gain and maintain their positions.

Sociological literature on leadership stresses the importance of the functions leaders perform for the group as an attribute that explains their acceptance as leaders. The usefulness of the function for the group explains the group's choice of its leaders.

Philip Selznick defines leadership as "a kind of work done to meet the needs of a social situation."[11] He goes on to say that different leadership skills are needed by groups in different social situations, but he does not specify the type of skills needed by groups in different types of social situations. Two broad types of leadership skills are classified by Talcott Parsons as administrative roles and representative roles.[12]

Gaetano Mosca, who examined at length the problem of the function of leaders, or the "attribute" which enable them to fulfill this function, makes several useful comments. First, he says, this attribute can be either "real or apparent." Second, it has to be believed to be of importance by its followers, and this is possible only if all participants, leaders and followers, share "moral and intellectual backgrounds which

---

[9] Alvin W. Gouldner, ed., *Studies in Leadership* (New York: Harper and Bros., 1950), p. 19.
[10] Amitai Etzioni, *A Comparative Analysis of Complex Organizations* (Glencoe Ill.: The Free Press, 1961), p. 90.
[11] Philip Selznick, *Leadership in Administration: A Sociological Interpretation* (New York: Row, Peterson & Co. 1957), p. 27.
[12] Parsons, *The Social System*, p. 135.

A Sociological Summing-up

are not dissimilar."[13] Thus, the shared ideology has to indicate what are the important and esteemed attributes that will make their holders acceptable as leaders.

Max Weber stressed another element in the leaders-followers relationship, namely that such a relationship has to be legitimized before it can achieve stability; an ideology which explains and justifies the right of leaders to lead and the duty of the followers to obey must be accepted by both leaders and followers. Legitimation of leaders' authority helps avoid constant struggles for leadership. In the absence of such legitimation, it is likely that the continuous social and economic changes any group undergoes, with the resulting shifts in social structure, may constantly bring to the fore members who can claim the right to be obeyed.

For an understanding of leader-follower relations, one has to bear in mind that in all groups other than small face-to-face groups, there exist groups of lower-ranking leaders who function as intermediaries between the top leaders and the rank and file.

Certain functions of the top leaders might be considered important for the lower-ranking leaders and not for the rank and file, and vice versa. Moreover, in complex groups, different segments share specific interests not shared by the rest of the group.

The number of intermediary leaderships varies among different social structures. In this study, however, we adopted Mosca's model, as developed in his work on political societies, and assumed the existence of just one such intermediary leadership occupying a distinct position in the authority structure. Mosca divides the political society between the ruling class and the ruled; the ruling class itself is then further divided between top leaders and the lower ranking leadership which he calls the political class.

It is the top leaders, says Mosca, who are in possession of "some attribute, real or apparent, which is highly esteemed and very influential in the society in which they live."[14] The political class has to be persuaded to follow the top leaders. Their decision will be affirmative only if it conforms with their own ideas and interests. Once the political class accepts the top leaders, it is their task to convince the masses to accept the dominance of the ruling class. Mosca then explains that the masses are themselves unable to formulate opinions on these issues, and this, together with their propagation among the masses, is left to the

---

[13] Gaetano Mosca, *The Ruling Class* (New York: McGraw-Hill Book Co., 1939), p. 115.
[14] Ibid., p. 62.

political class. This political class of editors, journalists, party workers, public orators, and pamphleteers molds public opinion.

Mosca does not assume that once the political class has made up its mind and goes into action, the ruled automatically accept its decision. The political class is effective only as long as the masses share with the leaders a common system of beliefs. The right to exercise authority is not granted if there exists "too noticeable a difference in beliefs and education" between the rank and file and the proposed leaders.

This last observation points to an important latent function of the leaders for their followers. Only if the leaders share with their followers a common belief system can they symbolize and personify for the masses their abstract beliefs. The rank and file wishes to identify itself with these abstract ideas through its attachment to the leaders.

In this book, this latent function of leaders was clearly demonstrated. We examined the Eastern European Jews in the United States in a period of transition—the traditional values of the Eastern European Jewish society were breaking down and the new American values were not yet firmly established. This accounts for their vacillation in 1921 between the two alternative leaderships presented to them: that of Chaim Weizmann and his associates, leaders of the Jewish people, or Louis Brandeis and his associates, the American leaders. In 1921, many Eastern Europeans sympathized with Weizmann, while the American-born German Jews and the more acculturated Eastern Europeans supported Brandeis. During the 1920's, following an accelerated acculturation of the Eastern European Jewish community in the United States, we witness a change in their choice of leaders, a choice which gave preference for the American-born leaders. The political class of the Zionist organization, the Eastern European intellectuals, found it expedient consequently to rely more and more on the support of leaders like Louis Marshall and Felix Warburg, the heads of the A.J.C. who held high positions in the American society and who could symbolize American values to the acculturating group. As we have demonstrated, when the political class of the Zionist Organization lost the support of these American leaders, they were forced to withdraw from the positions they had held in the Zionist Organization.

The struggle between the European leaders and the American-born leaders in 1921 exemplifies an important aspect of the leader's function as symbols of the group's values and beliefs. The difficulties experienced in 1921 by active Zionists in deciding which of the two competing leaderships to support was attributed to their more basic conflict between the two cultures symbolized by the competing leaders. Many resolved their conflict in favor of the Europeans after the latter decided to come

A Sociological Summing-up

to the United States and openly challenge the American leaders. The visibility of the Europeans who attended endless public meetings in the United States contrasted with the nonvisibility of the Americans who refused to make public appearances. Brandeis went so far as to refuse to attend meetings, or even see his supporters privately, for fear of publicity. This difference between the two leaderships at a crucial period tipped the balance in favor of the Europeans. An object can function as a symbol for a group of people only if it can be observed. The symbolic quality of leadership for their followers who wish to identify through them with their society and its culture makes it essential that leaders be visible to their followers.

The need of the followers to observe their leaders is related to another function of the leaders—that of conferring prestige upon their followers. Prestige is acquired through association with people who possess it. For the conferring of prestige to be of value in social relations, this association has to be observable to others in their role relations. This function of the leaders is most important for the political class in its relations with the rank and file. The position of such an intermediary leadership group depends on the prestige it acquires through proximity to the leaders and its visibility to the followers. The ability of top leaders to confer prestige upon their associates is an important element in establishing their authority over the political class.

Top leaders might bring the political class into line by appealing to the masses directly and thus threaten the position of the intermediary leadership. This was done by the European leaders in 1921 with the aid of one segment of the political class. The American leaders, on the other hand, absented themselves, thus weakening the position of the low-ranking leaders who supported the American leadership. Rather than endanger their position among their followers, many switched and openly supported the Europeans.

The problem to be discussed next is that of the legitimation of authority, the existence of an ideology which justifies the right of certain leaders to exercise leadership and the duty of members of the group to obey them. Such an ideology should contain at least the following elements: a) a statement of what are, or should be, the group's goals; and b) an indication of the desired attributes that qualify members to lead the group in accomplishing the goals. Unless such an ideology is accepted by the group, its authority structure will lack stability.

Even if a group limits the choice of leaders to those who can function as symbols of the group and its culture, a great number of people are still eligible for leadership positions. The masses can be persuaded to choose among a great number of possibilities as long as the proposed leaders can be highly esteemed and "have been trained to intellectual and moral background that are not dissimilar."[15] Mosca believed that the masses have no clearer opinions on the goals of the group nor better guidelines as to who are the most suitable leaders.

The political class, on the other hand, has definite opinions on the goals of the group and on the qualification of the leaders who are to carry them out. Their choice is shaped, said Mosca, by "the ideas and principles which it has adopted in regard to leadership."[16] Their concern with the question of leadership is great, since their social positions as lower-ranking leaders depend on the top leaders and the prestige those leaders are able to confer upon them.

The ideology whose function it is to stabilize the authority system cannot, however, merely suit the political class. It has to appeal and be acceptable to the rank and file. The masses do have to make up their minds and reach a decision whenever alternative ideologies and alternative leaderships are presented to them by the political class. Whenever the leadership of a group is being contested, the contesting top leaders and their political classes try to present the mass with an ideology which serves to legitimate their right to be leaders. We illustrated this when we observed two competing leaderships in the Zionist Organization advancing two alternative ideologies on the goals of Zionism and American Jewry. The American-born Zionist leaders stated that the building up of Palestine economically should be the goal of American Jews, and that they, as successful men of affairs, were best suited to achieve it. The Jewish intellectuals contended that the cultural revival of the Jewish nation should be the main goal of American Jewry and that they, as experts in Jewish culture and its historical traditions, were most suited to lead the community.

Types of Organized Support to Leaders' Authority

It has been explained that those who wish to attain and maintain leadership should symbolize the values and ideas of their followers, enjoy high prestige, and have the members of the society accept an ideology which establishes their right to lead the society. But such an authority relationship has to be organized; a distinct structure with a set of norms and role relationships has to exist to enable the leaders to exercise their leadership.

---

[15] Ibid., p. 115.
[16] Ibid., p. 430.

A Sociological Summing-up

The basic problem of the structure of authority concerns the ways used by the leadership to mobilize and organize the support of low-ranking leaders and the masses. Two possible methods were discerned in this study—a direct and an indirect leadership.

An indirect leadership organizes a network of formal and informal organizations—committees, conferences, charities, social clubs, and the like—headed and controlled by the top leaders and staffed by lower-ranking leaders, the political class. The indirect leaders examined in this book, the wealthy German Jewish leaders, established such institutions in the Jewish community to which they lent their prestige and whose activities they helped to finance. Through these ramified institutions, the top leaders controlled as many of the community's activities as possible. Ambitious members of the community, who rose from the ranks and were seeking a leadership role, were co-opted into the network of organizations and through the prestige and influence thus gained, became low-ranking leaders in the Jewish community.

The underlying assumption of this type of leadership is the passivity of the masses. The task of steering them in the direction desired by the top leaders is left to the political class which runs the community's activities. If the masses, or some fragments of them, are getting restive, the political class is expected to bring them into line. The low-ranking leaders might be able to muster some following, and it might become a source of independent prestige and authority. Their independence can, most likely, be checked by the top leaders through their control of the community's activities and through their manipulation of their prestige and allocation of funds which help finance the group's activities.

In our study, the position of the indirect leaders was at a certain period somewhat weaker than it would have been under ordinary circumstances; the differences in beliefs and education between the German Jewish philanthropists and the Eastern European masses were too noticeable. Operating within different belief systems, the prestigious German Jewish millionaires who conformed to the values of the American culture were not sufficiently effective among the alien Eastern European masses as symbols of their cultures and conferrers of prestige. As anticipated by Mosca, under such circumstances the masses created and followed a new class of leaders, and to such a class belonged many of the leaders of the Jewish socialist and anarchist groups. But these groups were not examined in our study.

Those low-ranking leaders of Eastern European backgrounds who cooperated with the German Jewish leaders gained in importance in the indirect authority structure. They provided a link between the two cultures which separated the top leaders from the masses and which gave an opportunity to some lower-ranking leaders to secure a measure of independent authority. Their independence was tolerated by the top leaders as long as the latter found the lower-ranking leaders instrumental in maintaining some control and direction over the masses.

This observation was illustrated by the spiritual leaders of the Conservative movement. Although their organization was founded and financed by the German Jewish top leaders, they became active Zionists and led the Zionist organization in spite of opposition from the top leaders. The top leaders continued nonetheless to support the Conservative movement, believing that the Conservative leaders were fulfilling an important function in Americanizing the masses and in turning them away from irresponsible radical activities. This support was at the same time a restraining influence on the Conservative leaders in their Zionist activities. Furthermore, when the hegemony of the indirect top leadership was challenged by independent leaders who gained control over the Zionist Organization, the Conservatives upheld the authority of their indirect leaders.

A real challenge to an indirect leadership can be effected by leaders who can arouse the masses from their passivity and enroll them into an active mass organization. In an indirect leadership structure, the rank and file plays no active role; no self-respecting positions or functions are allotted them in the authority structure. A direct leadership, on the other hand, builds mass organizations in which an attempt is made to give all members a feeling of belonging and importance. All mass organizations establish democratic procedures; the members elect delegates to congresses which are convened periodically to discuss and decide upon policies and elect the leaders. This gives the members a feeling of participating in policy-making and in the choice of leadership.

Mass organizations were developed by socialist and nationalist leaders in nineteenth-century Europe. According to Duverger, these leaders built mass parties in order to activate the masses and mobilize them to wrest control from the indirect leaders and their associates, who controlled political life with the help of a network of committees and caucuses. The conflict was between mass parties and cadre parties. The mass parties adopted democratic procedures and developed ideology designed to raise the self-esteem of the masses who, upon becoming conscious of their power, would abandon their passive attitude toward politics. This ideology designated the masses as the decisive social force in human history. The leader was only the mouthpiece of the masses; it was not his task to impose his will on the masses, but only to awaken

A Sociological Summing-up

their class consciousness or their *Volksgeist*; the masses were the masters on their own destiny.[17]

It is the Eastern European Jewish intellectuals, who comprised the majority of the political class of the American Zionist Organization and who shared the European socialist-populist tradition, who promulgated these ideas. On the other hand, the German Jewish millionaires, the indirect leaders of American Jewry, refused to be subjected to democratic elections. "Leaders need to develop and come forward by their own deservedness," wrote Jacob Schiff. "Selection of leaders on a democratic basis very often brings forward demagogues."[18] The American-born direct leaders, Brandeis and his associates who headed the Zionist Organization, adopted a mediary position between the two opposing concepts. They shared with other American progressives an elitist attitude and believed they deserved to lead the masses because of their superior education and ability. At the same time, they were committed to the idea of democracy and acknowledged the right of the masses to elect their leaders. "We must not fall into the same error of which we constantly complain against the Europeans, namely, to worry what the masses think," wrote Felix Frankfurter on one occasion, "instead of making up our minds what ought to be done, putting it candidly to the masses and then facing whatever the consequences may be."[19]

The different ideas the three groups held toward the obligations and rights of leadership are related to the organizational structure of authority they preferred. The indirect leaders preferred what we termed, following Duverger, a cadre party. A cadre party needed no dues-paying mass membership; instead, the leaders created a network of committees and organizations to fulfill specific and restricted functions. These committees were run by persons of influence or by those endowed with a special skill needed for any specific purpose. The two other groups wished to activate their followers through a mass membership organization. In a mass organization, the top leaders head the organization, the political class provides the officers and militants, and the masses comprise the rank and file. This leadership is, therefore, active and direct. The range of membership activities the leader can influence, however, depends on the nature of the mass organization.

---

[17] Maurice Duverger, *Political Parties* (New York: John Wiley & Sons, 1955), *passim*.
[18] Schiff to Richards, January 31, 1916, *Louis Brandeis Papers* (Louisville Ky.: University of Louisville Law Library).
[19] Frankfurter to Mack, August 14, 1920, *Jacob de Hass Papers* (New York: The Zionist Archives).

One cannot conclude, on the basis of this study, that a direct leadership is more attuned to the wishes of the masses than an indirect leadership. They only differ in the methods employed to secure acceptance to their authority. The study does lend support, however, to the contention that a direct leadership in control of a mass organization, if it is united and carries out its duties effectively, can greatly influence the members and their activities.

Bibliography

UNPUBLISHED MATERIAL

COLLECTIONS OF PRIVATE PAPERS

Brandeis, Louis D. University of Louisville, Law Library, Louisville, Kentucky. A copy of the material relating to Zionism is on microfilm in the American Jewish Archives, Cincinnati, Ohio.
De Haas, Jacob. Microfilm in the Zionist Archives, New York.
Friedenwald, Harry. Microfilm in the Zionist Archives, New York.
Gottheil, Richard. Photostats in the Zionist Archives, New York.
Heller, Max. The American Jewish Archives, Cincinnati, Ohio.
House, Colonel Henry M. Personal Diary in Yale University Library, New Haven, Connecticut.
Marshall, Louis. The American Jewish Archives, Cincinnati, Ohio.
Schiff, Jacob H. The American Jewish Archives, Cincinnati, Ohio.
Sokolow, Nahum. The Central Zionist Archives, Jerusalem.
Warburg, Felix. The American Jewish Archives, Cincinnati, Ohio.
Wilson, Woodrow. The Library of Congress, Washington, D.C.

PERSONAL INTERVIEWS

Goldberg, Israel. August 25, 1960.
Lipsky, Louis. September 13, 1960.
Neumann, Emanuel. January 26, 1961.
Richards, Bernard G. January 25, 1961.
Szold, Robert. February 20, 1961.

DISSERTATIONS AND MASTER'S ESSAYS

Chinitz, Sam Z. "The Jewish Agency and the Jewish Community in the United States." Master's essay, Faculty of Political Science, Columbia University, 1959.
Cohen-Wiener, Naomi W. "The Public Career of Oscar Straus." Ph.D. dissertation, Faculty of Political Science, Columbia University, 1955.
Rappaport, Joseph. "Jewish Immigration and World War I: A Study of American Yiddish Press Reactions." Ph.D. dissertation, Faculty of Political Science, Columbia University, 1951.
Silver, Harold. "Some Attitudes of the East European Jewish Immigrants toward Organized Jewish Charity in the United States in the Years 1890–1900." Master's essay, New York Graduate School of Jewish Social Work, 1934.
Wiener, Naomi W. "Reform Judaism in American and Zionism, 1897–1922." Master's essay, Faculty of Political Science, Columbia University, 1948.

OTHER MANUSCRIPTS

"Fifty Years of American Zionism." Mimeographed, New York: Zionist Archives.

PUBLISHED MATERIAL

NEWSPAPERS AND MAGAZINES

The Day (Yiddish). 1914–30.
Dos Yiddishe Folk (Yiddish). 1909–29.
Ha'pisgah (Hebrew). 1898–99.
Ha'tchia (Hebrew). 1899–1901.
The Jewish Morning Journal (Yiddish). 1906–30.
The Maccabean. 1901–21.
The Monthly Intelligencer (Hebrew). 1900–1.
The New Maccabean. 1921.
The New Palestine. 1921–30.

BOOKS

Jewish and Zionist

Adler, Cyrus. *Jacob H. Schiff: His Life and Letters.* New York: Doubleday, Doran & Co., 1928.
———. *I Have Considered the Days.* Philadelphia: The Jewish Publication Society of America, 1941.
American Zionist Medical Unit for Palestine Maintained by the Zionist Organization of America and the Joint Distribution Committee of the American Funds for Jewish War Sufferers, June 1916–June 1919. New York: The Zionist Organization of America, 1919.
Analyticus [Wise, James Waterman]. *Jews Are Like That.* New York: Brentano's Publishing Co., 1928.
Arlozoroff, Chaim. *Ktavim.* 7 vols. Tel Aviv: Hotzaat A. Y. Shtible, 1935.
Association for the Reorganization of the Z.O.A. New York Conference, October 14, 1928. New York, November 1928.

Bentwich, Herbert. *Solomon Schechter: A Biography.* Philadelphia: The Jewish Publication Society of America, 1938.
Bentwich, Norman. *For Zion's Sake: A Biography of Judah L. Magnes, First Chancellor and First President of the Hebrew University of*

Bibliography

Jerusalem. Philadelphia: The Jewish Publication Society of America, 1954.
Berlin, Meir. *Me Volozhin ad Yerushalaim: Zichronot.* 2 vols. Tel Aviv: B. Cohen, Hotzaat Yalkut, 1940.
Billings, John S. *Vital Statistics of the Jews in the United States.* Census Bulletin No. 19. Washington, D.C.: Government Printing Office, December 30, 1890.
Böhm, Adolf. *Die Zionistische Bewegung. Eine kurze Darstellung ihrer Entwicklung.* Berlin: Welt-Verlag, 1920.
──────. *Die Zionistische Bewegung.* 2 vols. Berlin: Jüdischer Verlag, 1933.
Brandeis, Louis D. *Zionism and Patriotism.* New York: The Federation of American Zionists, 1915.
Bregstone, Philip. *Chicago and Its Jews: A Cultural History.* Privately Printed, 1933.

Cahan, Abraham. *The Rise of David Levinsky.* New York: Harper Brothers, 1917.
Cohen, Israel. *The Zionist Movement.* New York: The Zionist Organization of America, 1946.
Collection of Essays on the Occasion of the Fiftieth Birthday of Abraham Goldberg. New York: The Abraham Goldberg Jubilee Committee, 1934.
Constitution for the Government of the Zionist Districts. The Zionist Organization of America, 1918.
Correspondence on the Advisability of Calling a Conference for the Purpose of Combatting Zionism. New York: The Zionist Organization of America, 1918.

De Haas, Jacob. *Louis D. Brandeis: A Biographical Sketch.* New York: Bloch Publishing Co., 1929.
──────, ed. *The Encyclopedia of Jewish Knowledge.* New York: Behrman's Jewish Book House, 1938.
Dinin, Samuel. *Zionist Education in the United States: A Survey.* New York: The Zionist Organization of America, 1944.

Epstein, Melech. *Jewish Labor in the U.S.A.: An Industrial, Political, and Cultural History of the Jewish Labor Movement, 1882–1952.* 2 vols. New York: Trade Union Sponsoring Committee, 1950.

Fliegel, Hyman J. *The Life and Times of Max Pine.* New York: Privately Printed, 1959.
Fram, Harry. *Primary and Basic Organization: As Affecting Zionist Endeavors in America.* Los Angeles: Privately Printed, 1922.

Friedlaender, Israel. *Past and Present: A Collection of Jewish Essays*. Cincinnati: Ark Publishing Co., 1919.
Friedman, Elisha M. *Survival or Extinction: Sociological Aspects of the Jewish Question*. New York: Thomas Seltzer, 1924.
Fuchs, Lawrence H. *Political Behavior of American Jews*. Glencoe, Ill.: The Free Press, 1956.

Glazer, Nathan. *American Judaism*. Chicago: University of Chicago Press, 1957.
Goldberg, Nathan. *Occupational Patterns of American Jewry*. New York: Jewish Theological Seminary and Peoples' University Press, 1947.
Goldstein, Herbert S. *Forty Years for a Principle: A Biography of Harry Fischel*. New York: Bloch Publishing Co., 1928.
Gordon, Benjamin L. *Between Two Worlds: The Memories of a Physician*. New York: Bookman Association, 1952.
Grebler, Leo. *Housing Market Behavior in a Declining Area*. New York: Columbia University Press, 1952.
Greenberg, Louis. *The Jews in Russia*. 2 vols. New Haven, Conn.: Yale University Press, 1941–43.

Haber, Julius. *The Odyssey of an American Zionist*. New York: Twayne Publishers, 1956.
Halperin, Samuel. *The Political World of American Zionism*. Detroit: Wayne State University Press, 1961.
Halpern, Ben. *The American Jew: A Zionist Analysis*. New York: The Theodor Herzl Foundation, 1956.
———. *The Idea of the Jewish State*. Cambridge, Mass.: Harvard University Press, 1961.
Handlin, Oscar. *Adventure in Freedom: Three Hundred Years of Jewish Life in America*. New York: McGraw-Hill Book Co., 1954.
Hertzberg, Arthur, ed. *The Zionist Idea: A Historical Analysis and Reader*. New York: Doubleday & Co., and The Herzl Press, 1959.
Horwich, Bernard. *My First Eighty Years*. Chicago: Argus Books, 1939.
Hyman, Joseph C. *Twenty-Five Years of American Aid to Jews Overseas: A Record of the Joint Distribution Committee*. New York, 1939.

Janowsky, Oscar. *The Jews and Minority Rights, 1898–1919*. New York: Columbia University Press, 1933.
The Jewish Congress Versus the American Jewish Committee: A Complete Statement with the Correspondence between Louis D. Brandeis and Cyrus Adler. New York: Jewish Congress Organization Committee, August 1915.

Kallen, Horace M. *Zionism and World Politics*. New York: Doubleday, Page and Co., 1921.
———. *Of Them Which Say They Are Jews*. New York: Bloch Publishing Co., 1959.

Learsi, Rufus [Goldberg, Israel]. *Fulfilment: The Epic Story of Zionism*. Cleveland: World Publishing Co., 1951.
———. *The Jews in America: A History*. Cleveland: World Publishing Co., 1954.
Lewisohn, Ludwig. *Up Stream: An American Chronicle*. New York: Boni & Liveright, 1922.
Linefield, Harry. *The Communal Organization of the Jews in the United States*. New York: The American Jewish Committee, 1930.
Lipsky, Louis. *Thirty Years of American Zionism*. The Nesher Publishing Co. for the Louis Lipsky Jubilee Committee, 1927.
———. *A Gallery of Zionist Profiles*. New York: Farrar, Straus & Cudahy, 1956.

Mack, Julian W. *Americanism and Zionism*. New York: The Federation of American Zionists, 1918.
Mason, Alpheus Thomas. *Brandeis: A Free Man's Life*. New York: The Viking Press, 1956.
Meyer, Isidor S., ed. *Early History of Zionism in America*. New York: The American Jewish Historical Society and The Theodor Herzl Foundation, 1958.

Neumann, Emanuel. *Causes of the Conflict*. New York: The New Maccabean Co., 1921.

Report of Keren Hayesod to the Thirteenth Congress, August 1923. London, 75 Great Russell Street, 1923.
Report of Keren Hayesod to the Sixteenth Congress, 1929. Jerusalem: The International Zionist Organization, 1929.
Report of the Proceedings of the Twenty-Fourth Annual Convention of the Zionist Organization of America. New York: The Zionist Organization of America, August 1921.
Reports of the Proceedings of the International Zionist Congresses for the Years 1897–1929, published by the Central Office of the International Zionist Organization (in German).
Reznikoff, Charles, ed. *Louis Marshall, Champion of Liberty. Selected Papers and Addresses*. 2 vols. Philadelphia: The Jewish Publication Society of America, 1957.
Richards, Bernard G. Reminiscences, Recorded by the Oral History Research Office. New York: Columbia University, 1961.

Rosenblatt, Bernard A. *Social Zionism.* New York: The Public Publishing Co., 1919.

Sampter, Jessie, ed. *Modern Palestine: A Symposium.* New York: Hadassah, The Women's Zionist Organization of America, 1933.
Samuel, Maurice. *You Gentiles.* New York: Harcourt, Brace & Co., 1924.
———. *I, the Jew.* New York: Harcourt, Brace & Co., 1927.
Schachner, Nathan. *The Prize of Liberty: A History of the American Jewish Committee.* New York: The American Jewish Committee, 1948.
Schechter, Solomon. *Zionism: A Statement.* The Federation of American Zionists, n.d.
———. *Seminary Addresses and Other Papers.* Cincinnati: Ark Publishing Co., 1915.
Sherman, C. Bezalel. *Yidden un Andere Etnishe Gruppes in die Farainigte Shtaten.* New York: Unser Veg, 1948.
———. *The Jew within American Society: A Study in Ethnic Individuality.* Detroit: Wayne State University Press, 1961.
Sklare, Marshall. *Conservative Judaism: An American Religious Movement.* Glencoe, Ill.: The Free Press, 1955.
Summary of the Position of the Zionist Organization of America in Conference with Dr. Weizmann and Associates. Submitted by the President of the Zionist Organization of America to and adopted by the National Executive Committee at the meeting March 19–20, 1921, n.p., n.d.

Tannebaum, Yoseph. *Zwischen Milchama un Shalom: Yidden Oif der Shalom Konferenz Noch der ershter Welt Milchama.* Buenos Aires: Zentral Farband fun Poilishe Yidden in Argentina, 1951.

Waldman, Morris D. *Nor by Power.* New York: International Universities Press, 1953.
Weizmann, Chaim. *A Fratricidal War.* Privately Printed by Isidor D. Morrison, June 1928.
Wirth, Louis. *The Ghetto.* Chicago: University of Chicago Press, 1928.
Wise, Stephen S. *Challenging Years.* New York: G. P. Putnam's Sons, 1949.
Wolf, Simon. *The Presidents I Have Known from 1860–1918.* Washington, D.C.: Byron S. Adams, 1918.

Zeitlin, Rose. *Henrietta Szold: Record of a Life.* New York: The Dial Press, 1952.
*The Zionist Awakening: A Summary Report of the Washington Con-

ference Held April 29, 1928. New York: Issued by the Committee for Z.O.A. Reorganization, 1928.

The Zionist Ledger: An Analysis of Income and Expenditure of the Zionist Organization of America, 1921–1929. Showing how the deficit was incurred and why it is imperative that it be paid up immediately, n.p., n.d.

General

Aron, Raymond. *The Opium of the Intellectuals*. New York: Doubleday & Co., 1957.

Baker, Ray Stannard. *Woodrow Wilson: Life and Letters*. 8 vols. New York: Doubleday, Doran & Co., 1927–39.
Baker, Ray Stannard, and Dodd, William E. *The Public Papers of Woodrow Wilson*. 6 vols. New York: Harper & Brothers, 1926.
Bauer, Otto. *Die Nationalitätenfrage und die Sozialdemokratie*. Marx-Studien, vol. 2. Wien: Verlag der Volksbuchhandlung, 1924.
Bluntschli, J. R. *The Theory of the State*. Oxford: At the Clarendon Press, 1898.
Bogardus, Emory S. *Immigration and Race Attitudes*. New York: D. C. Heath & Co., 1928.
Butterfield, Herbert. *George III and the Historians*, rev. ed. New York: The Macmillan Co., 1959.

Capek, Thomas. *The Czechs in America*. Boston: Houghton Mifflin Co., 1920.
Carpenter, Niles, and Katz, Daniel. *A Study of Acculturation in the Polish Group in Buffalo, 1926–1928*. Buffalo, N.Y.: University of Buffalo Studies, vol. 7, June 1929.

Duverger, Maurice. *Political Parties: Their Organization and Activity in the Modern State*. New York: John Wiley & Sons, 1955.

Erler, Georg H. J. *Das Recht der nationalen Minderheiten*. Deutschland und Ausland, Heft 37/39. Münster in Westfalen, Aschendorffsche Verlagsbuchhandlung, 1931.
Etzioni, Amitai. *A Comparative Analysis of Complex Organization: On Power, Involvement and Their Correlates*. Glencoe, Ill.: The Free Press, 1961.

Gross, Feliks, ed. *European Ideologies: A Survey of Twentieth-Century Political Ideas*. New York: Philosophical Library, 1948.

Handlin, Oscar. *Race and Nationality in American Life.* Boston: Little, Brown & Co., 1958.
Hawgood, John A. *The Tragedy of German-America.* New York: G. P. Putnam's Sons, 1940.
Heberle, Rudolf. *Social Movements: An Introduction to Political Sociology.* New York: Appleton-Century-Crofts, 1951.
Hertzler, J. O. *American Social Institutions: A Sociological Analysis.* Boston: Allyn and Bacon Inc., 1961.
Higham, John. *Strangers in the Land: Patterns of American Nativism, 1860–1925.* New Brunswick, N.J.: Rutgers University Press, 1955.
Hofstadter, Richard. *The Age of Reform: From Bryan to F.D.R.* New York: Alfred A. Knopf, 1956.

Lane, Robert E. *Political Life.* Glencoe, Ill.: The Free Press, 1959.
Leuchtenberg, William E. *The Perils of Prosperity, 1914–1932.* Chicago: University of Chicago Press, 1958.
Lewin, Kurt. *Resolving Social Conflicts.* New York: Harper and Brothers, 1948.
Link, Arthur S. *Woodrow Wilson and the Progressive Era, 1910–1917.* New York: Harper and Brothers, 1957.

Macartney, C. A. *National States and National Minorities.* London: Oxford University Press, 1934.
McClure, Archibald. *Leadership of the New America: Racial and Religious.* New York: George H. Doran Co., 1916.
Merton, Robert K. *Social Theory and Social Structure,* rev. ed. Glencoe, Ill.: The Free Press, 1957.
Michels, Robert. *Political Parties: A Sociological Study of the Oligarchical Tendencies of Modern Democracy.* New York: Dover Publications, 1959.
Miller, Kenneth D. *The Czecho-Slovaks in America.* New York: George H. Doran Co., 1922.
Mosca, Gaetano. *The Ruling Class.* New York: McGraw-Hill Book Co., 1939.
Mowry, George E. *The Era of Theodore Roosevelt, 1900–1912.* New York: Harper and Brothers, 1958.
Myrdal, Gunnar. *An American Dilemma: The Negro Problem and Modern Democracy.* New York: Harper and Brothers, 1944.

Park, Robert E., and Miller, Herbert A. *Old World Traits Transplanted.* New York: Harper and Brothers, 1921.
Pinner, Frank; Jacobs, Paul; and Selznick, Philip. *Old Age and Political Behavior.* Berkeley: University of California Press, 1959.

Schlesinger, Arthur M., Jr. *The Crisis of the Old Order, 1919–1933.* Boston: Houghton Mifflin Co., 1957.
Schumpeter, Joseph A. *Capitalism, Socialism and Democracy.* 4th ed. London: George Allen & Unwin, Ltd., 1954.
Skinner, William. *Leadership and Power in the Chinese Community of Thailand.* Ithaca, N.Y.: Cornell University Press, 1958.
Snyder, Louis L. *The Meaning of Nationalism.* New Brunswick, N.J.: Rutgers University Press, 1954.
Steffens, Lincoln. *The Autobiography of Lincoln Steffens.* New York: Harcourt, Brace & Co., 1931.
Stonequist, Everett V. *The Marginal Man: A Study of Personality and Culture Conflict.* New York: Charles Scribner's Sons, 1937.

Thomas, William I., and Znaniecki, Florian. *The Polish Peasant in Europe and America.* 2 vols. New York: Alfred A. Knopf, 1927.

Ware, Caroline F., ed. *The Cultural Approach to History.* New York: Columbia University Press, 1940.
Warner, Lloyd W., and Srole, Leo. *The Social System of American Ethnic Groups.* New Haven, Conn.: Yale University Press, 1945.
Woodward, C. Vann. *Tom Watson: Agrarian Rebel.* New York: Reinhart and Co., 1955.

ARTICLES

Jewish and Zionist

Baltzell, Digby E. "The Development of a Jewish Upper Class in Philadelphia, 1782–1940," in *The Jews.* Edited by Marshall Sklare, pp. 271–81. Glencoe, Ill.: The Free Press, 1958.
Blachman, N. "Die Landsmanschaften un die Centrale Organizatzies," in *Die Yiddishe Landsmanschaften fun New York,* pp. 33–42. New York: Peretz Shreiber Farein, 1938.
Bloom, Bernard H. "Yiddish-Speaking Socialists in America, 1892–1905," *American Jewish Archives* 12 (April 1960): 34–68.

Cohen, Naomi W. "The Reaction of Reform Judaism in America to Political Zionism, 1897–1922," *PAJHS* 40 (1950–51): 361–99.
———. "The Maccabean Message," *Jewish Social Studies* 18 (1956): 163–79.

Fram, Leo. "Reform Judaism and Zionism," in *Reform Judaism—Essays by H.U.C. Alumni,* pp. 174–95. Cincinnati: Hebrew Union College Press, 1949.

Friedenwald, Harry. "Reminiscences," *The New Palestine* (December 29, 1944), p. 10.

Glazer, Nathan. "Social Characteristics of American Jews, 1654–1954," *AJYB* 56 (1955): 3–41.

Goldberg, Abraham. "Zionism in America," in *Theodor Herzl: A Memorial*. Edited by Meyer W. Weisgal, pp. 211–22. New York, 1929.

———. "American Zionism up to the Brandeis Era," in *The Avukah Annual of 1932: A Collection of Essays on Contemporary Zionist Thought Dedicated to Justice Louis D. Brandeis*. Edited by J. S. Shubow, pp. 549–68. Boston, 1932.

Gottheil, Gustav. "The Position of the Jews in America," *North American Review* 126 (March–April 1878): 293–308.

———. "On Zionism," *The American Hebrew* (December 10, 1897), p. 163.

Grinstein, Hyman B. "The Memories and Scrapbooks of the Late Dr. Joseph Isaac Bluestone of New York City," *PAJHS* 35 (1939): 53–64.

Halpern, Ben. "The American Jewish Committee," *The Jewish Frontier* 10 (December 1943): 13–16.

———. "Zionism and Israel," *The Jewish Journal of Sociology* 3 (December 1961): 155–73.

Handlin, Oscar. "American Views of the Jew at the Opening of the Twentieth Century," *PAJHS* 40 (1950–51): 323–44.

Heller, Max. "Letter to the Editor," *The American Hebrew* (November 27, 1908) p. 92.

Herberg, Will. "Socialism, Zionism and Messianic Passion," *Midstream* 2 (Summer 1956): 65–74.

Higham, John. "Anti-Semitism in the Gilded Age: A Reinterpretation," *The Mississippi Valley Historical Review* 43 (March 1957): 559–78.

———. "Social Discrimination against Jews in America, 1830–1930," *PAJHS* 47 (1957–58): 3–33.

Isaacs, Abram S. "The Jews of the United States," *AJYB* 1 (1899–1900): 14–20.

Leschinsky, Jacob. "Die Entwicklung fun Yiddishen Folk far die Letzte Hundred Yahr," *Shriften Far Economic un Statistic*, vol. 1, pp. 1–64. Berlin, 1928.

———. "The Social Complexion of American Jewry," *ORT Economic Review* 2 (November–December 1941): 11–22.

Lipsky, Louis. "Early Days of American Zionism, 1897-1929," *Palestine Year Book* 2 (1945-46): 447-88.

Marcus, Jacob Rader. "Zionism and the American Jew," *The American Scholar* 2 (1933): 279-92.
———. "The Periodization of American Jewish History," *PAJHS* 47 (1957-58): 125-33.
———. "The Theme of American Jewish History," *PAJHS* 48 (1958-59): 141-46.
Melamed, Samuel M. "The Basis of Civilization," *The Reflex* 1 (January 1928): 1-10.
———. "L. D. Brandeis and Chaim Weizmann," *The Reflex* 2 (May 1928): 1-10.
———. "The Peace of Cleveland," *The Reflex* 6 (September 1930): 3-14.
Miller, Norman. "The Jewish Leadership of Lakeport," in *Studies in Leadership*. Edited by Alvin Gouldner, pp. 195-227. New York: Harper and Brothers, 1950.
———. "Pattern of Leadership in the Jewish Community," *Jewish Social Studies* 17 (1955): 179-84.

Natelson, Rachel. "The Truth in Detail: Hadassah and the Zionist Organization," *Hadassah News Letter* 8 (April 1928): 2-4. The *New York Times*, Editorial, July 18, 1916.

Parzen, Herbert. "The Passing of Jewish Secularism in the United States," *Judaism* 8 (Summer 1959): 195-205.
———. "Conservative Judaism and Zionism, 1896-1922," *Jewish Social Studies* 23 (October 1961): 235-64.

Rantch, Y. A. "Der Itztiger Matzav fun die Landsmanschaften," in *Die Yiddishe Landsmanschaften fun New York*, pp. 9-23. New York: Peretz Shreiber Farein, 1938.

Scherer, E. "The Bund," in *Struggle for Tomorrow*. Edited by Basil J. Vlavianos and Feliks Gross, pp. 135-96. New York: Arts Incorporated, 1954.
Schiff, Jacob H. "Letter to the Editor," *The American Hebrew* (July 3, 1914), p. 257.
Solow, Herbert. "The Vindication of Jewish Idealism," *The Menorah Journal* 15 (September 1928): 259-70.
———. "The Sixteenth Zionist Congress," *The Menorah Journal* 17 (October 1929): 23-40.
———. "The Era of the Agency Begins," *The Menorah Journal* 17 (November 1929): 111-25.

Srole, Leo. "Impact of Anti-Semitism," *Jewish Social Studies* 17 (July 1955): 275–79.

Szajkowsky, Zosa. "The Attitude of American Jews to East European Jewish Immigration, 1881–1893," *PAJHS* 40 (1950–51): 221–80.

Teller, Judd J. "America's Two Zionist Traditions: Brandeis and Weizmann," *Commentary* 20 (1955): 343–52.

Wise, Stephen S. "The Beginning of American Zionism," *The Jewish Frontier* (August 1947), pp. 6–8.

Yoffeh, Zalman. "Peace in American Zionism," *The Menorah Journal* 19 (October 1930): 52–62.

General

Antonovsky, Aaron. "Toward a Refinement of the Marginal Man Concept," *Social Forces* 35 (1956): 57–62.

Blumer, Herbert. "Collective Behavior," in *New Outlines of the Principles of Sociology*. Edited by Alfred McClung Lee, pp. 167–222. New York: Barnes and Noble, 1951.

Glazer, Nathan. "Ethnic Groups in America: From National Culture to Ideology," in *Freedom and Control in Modern Society*. Edited by Monroe Berger, Theodore Abel, and Charles H. Page, pp. 158–73. New York: D. Van Nostrand Co., 1954.

———. "America's Ethnic Pattern," *Perspectives U.S.A.* 9 (1954): 137–52.

Goldberg, Milton M. "A Qualification of the Marginal Man Theory," A.S.R. 6 (1941): 52–58.

Green, Arnold W. "A Reexamination of the Marginal Man Concept," *Social Forces* 26 (1947): 167–71.

Kelly, Harold H. "Attitudes and Judgements as Influenced by Reference Group," in *Readings in Social Psychology*. Edited by Guy E. Swanson, Theodore M. Newcomb, and Eugene L. Hartley, pp. 410–14. New York: Henry Holt & Co., 1952.

Lenski, Gerhald E. "Status Crystallization: A Non-Vertical Dimension of Social Status," A.S.R. 19 (1954): 405–13.

McCall, Daniel. "Dynamics of Urbanization in Africa," *The Annals* 298 (March 1955): 151–60.

Park, Robert E. "Human Migration and the Marginal Man," *A.J.S.* 33 (1928): 881–93.

Roucek, Joseph Slabey. "The Passing of the American Czechoslovaks," *A.J.S.* 39 (1934): 611–25.

Spiro, Melford E. "The Acculturation of American Ethnic Groups," *American Anthropologist* 57 (1955): 1240–52.

Stonequist, Everett V. "The Problem of the Marginal Man," *A.J.S.* 41 (1935): 1–12.

Index

Acculturation, 3–5 passim, 154, 251–53 passim, 262–67
Addams, Jane, 71
Adler, Cyrus, 57, 84
American Jewish Committee (A.J.-C.), 38, 42, 46–48, 56, 58, 62, 64; and an American Jewish Congress, 80–86, 90, 94–97, 110, 113; relief to Jews abroad, 78–79; negotiations with Brandeis, 114–17, 129–32; negotiations with Weizmann, 193, 201; relations with the Z.O.A., 201–4, 239, 241
American Jewish Congress, 80–98, 110–13
American Medical Unit in Palestine, 139, 140, 143
American Progressives, 56–60 passim, 125, 244. See also Progressive Movement
American Zion Commonwealth, 227
Anti-Semitism, 10, 12, 14, 34, 39–40, 55–60 passim, 63, 82, 118, 129, 132, 137, 165–66, 230, 251–52, 258
Anti-Zionism, 32, 33, 132, 254
Arlozoroff, Chaim, 190, 212, 233, 236
Assimilation, 5, 11, 12, 60, 262–64

Balfour Declaration, 115, 121, 129, 174, 188, 196, 254
Barondess, Joseph, 43, 139
Basle Program, 20, 51–52, 120, 204, 205, 235
Berenson, Lawrence, 219, 222, 225
Berenstein, Herman, 66
Bogardus, Emory, 250
Böhm, Adolf, 20
Brandeis, Louis D: before becoming a Zionist, 61–65; active Zionist before becoming leader, 66–67; position as Jewish leader, 68–70 passim; fight for the Supreme Court, 68–70; on Zionist ideology, 59–60, 72–73, 252; and the A.J.C., 56, 75–76, 83–84, 90, 94–98, 114–17, 130–32, 239–40; and the American Jewish Congress, 83–84, 88, 90, 94–98, 113; organizational problems of American Zionist Organization, 53–54, 80, 86–87, 99–100, 102, 119–23, 141, 159–61, 163–64, 168–69; and Hadassah 204–5; and the Knights of Zion, 29; plans for building Palestine, 149–50, 154, 169, 184–85; dispute with Weizmann and the W.Z.O., 135–38, 140, 142–45, 156–76, 185, 191, 217–47 passim; relations with Lipsky and the Z.O.A., 217–47 passim
Brandeis Group (Brandeisists), 184–95, 204, 208, 215–47 passim
Brown, David, 201
Bryan, William Jennings, 65–66
Bublik, Gedalya, 81, 171
Bund (General Jewish Workers' Union in Russia and Poland), 15, 16
Butterfield, Herbert, 6

Cadre party, 122, 131, 182, 275
Caplan, Ephraim, 81, 133, 243
Cohen, Ben, 105
Conference of Reform rabbis, 25
Conservative Judaism, 26, 29, 33, 37–40, 44, 59, 90–94, 253, 260, 274. See also Jewish Theological Seminary
Coralnik, Abraham, 197, 209, 231, 235, 241–42, 247

Daughters of Zion Association, 51
De Haas, Jacob, 34, 35, 53, 95, 96, 118; Brandeis's aide in the Z.O.A., 105, 107–11, 139, 142–45 *passim*; opposition to the Z.O.A. leadership, 192, 217, 220–21, 237, 243, 244
Deinard, Shmuel, 27
Democratic party, 251
Denial of the Galuth, 43, 71
Diaspora nationalism, 20–23, 118, 132, 140, 151, 165, 168, 174, 185, 195, 197, 221, 235–36, 246
Du Bois, W.E.B., 83
Duverger, Maurice, 122, 131, 182, 216, 257, 274, 275

Einstein, Albert, 167, 172
Etzioni, Amitai, 52n

Fels, Mrs. Joseph, 54
Fishman, Jacob, 81, 120, 153, 244
Flescner, Bernard, 105, 106, 139, 146, 148, 164, 173, 193, 239
Ford, Henry, 165–66
Frank, Leo M., 58
Frankfurter, Felix, 54, 71, 105, 114, 127; dispute with W.Z.O., 139, 140, 145, 148, 173, 174; concept of leadership, 275
Friedberger, David, 242–45 *passim*
Friedenwald, Harry, 26, 31, 32, 53, 105, 223; and the American Jewish Congress, 89–92 *passim*; president of the F.A.Z., 36, 37, 39, 41, 45, 47
Friedlaender, Israel, 37, 39, 47, 89–94 *passim*, 112–13, 118
Friedman, Elisha, 54, 113–16 *passim*

Gans, Howard, 54, 131
Garfield, James Abram, 254
Gegenwartsarbeit, 141, 145, 152, 165, 195, 197

Gemeinschaft, 28
Gesellschaft, 28
Gewerkschaften, 255
Goldberg, Abraham, 43, 81, 106, 109, 127, 133, 154–56, 209–10, 215–16, 219, 235
Goldberg, Israel, 51, 80, 213, 242
Goldman, Solomon, 186
Goldstein, Israel, 242
Gottheil, Gustav, 31
Gottheil, Richard, 34, 35, 41, 53, 70, 89, 113
Grebler, Leo, 249–50
Gouldner, Alvin, 268

Haber, Julius, 24
Hadassah, 51, 112, 180, 196, 204–6, 218, 227–28
Handlin, Oscar, 57, 251
Hapgood, Norman, 64
Harding, Warren Gamaliel, 171
Harrison, William Henry, 254
Hebrew Union College, 256
Heller, James, 242, 245
Heller, Max, 32, 226
Herzl, Theodor, 18, 34, 35, 36
Higham, John, 40, 60, 71, 230
Hirsch, Solomon, 254
Hofstadter, Richard, 57
Horowich, Bernard, 189–90
House, Col. Edward M., 65

Insulation from observability, 96
International Territorialist Organization (I.T.O.), 37–39 *passim*

Jasin, Joseph, 37
Jewish Agency for Palestine, 140, 141, 193, 198, 201–3 *passim*, 207, 211, 213–14, 225, 227, 232, 236–40 *passim*
Jewish Colonial Trust, 50
Jewish Kehillah of New York, 46
Jewish National Fund, 50, 161. *See also Keren Kayemet*

Jewish Theological Seminary, 33, 37–40 *passim*, 59, 93. See also Conservative Judaism
Joint Distribution Committee (J.D.C.), 79, 121, 124, 129, 131, 140, 183, 200–202

Kadushin, Max, 253
Kallen, Horace, 71, 86
Kaplan, Mordecai, 40, 189, 234–35
Keren Hayesod, 161–94 *passim*, 205, 221, 257–58
Keren Kayemet, 50, 161. See also Jewish National Fund
Kesselman, Robert, 142
Kirstein, Louis, 54
Knights of Zion, 27–29 *passim*, 54
Klein, Philip, 26
Kuhn, Loeb and Company, 56, 208

La Follette, Robert, 62
Lamport, Samuel, 89
Landsmanschaften, 25, 27–29 *passim*, 44, 255
Lane, Robert, 251
Leadership: deviant, 4, 231, 232; direct, 273–74, 276; from the periphery, 32, 55, 56, 59; of accommodation, 60, 131; indirect, 273–74, 276
League of Nations, 151
Legitimation of authority, 271–72
Lehman, Irving, 93, 132, 232
Lenski, Gerhard, 267
Leschinsky, Jacob, 8
Levin, Shmarya, 99, 136, 144
Lewin, Kurt, 55, 253–54
Lindheim, Irma, 204
Lindheim, Norvin, 194, 216–17, 219, 220, 222, 225
Lipsky, Louis: active in the F.A.Z., 35, 42, 43, 45–47 *passim*; chairman of F.A.Z., 50, 64, 67, 89; under Brandeis's leadership, 105, 106, 108–9, 113, 119, 120; and

Lipsky, Louis (*cont.*)
the dispute between Brandeis and Weizmann, 148, 153–56; president of the Z.O.A., 195, 198–200, 207–8, 212, 214–16; struggle with Brandeis's group, 217–47 *passim*
Lodge, Henry Cabot, 62, 70
Lowell, Lawrence A., 69

Mack, Julian, 54, 114; active in the Zionist Organization, 71, 89–90, 92, 136; and the Brandeisists, 194–95, 217, 219, 223, 242–47 *passim*; president of the Z.O.A. and the dispute with the W.Z.O., 105–7 *passim*, 116–17, 131, 132, 139, 140, 168–69, 173–74 *passim*; relations with the A.J.C., 116–17, 132, 187, 242
Magnes, Judah Leon: active in the F.A.Z., 37, 39, 41, 45–47 *passim*, 53; against an American Jewish Congress, 85, 89, 91, 94, 95; pacifism, 112, 113
Marginal culture, 252, 267
Marginal group, 264
Marginal man, 30, 32, 61, 264, 266
Margoshes, Shmuel, 207–8, 212, 218
Marshall, Louis: Jewish leader, 61, 75, 113, 139, 214, 270; relations with Brandeis and associates, 64, 92, 95, 114, 115, 117, 130–31, 194; relations with Weizmann, Lipsky, and associates, 187–88, 201, 203, 232–33
Mason, Alpheus T., 54, 61, 150
Mass party, 122, 131, 274, 276
Mayer, Gabriel, 36
McClure, Archibald, 77
Melamed, Samuel M., 181, 211
Merton. Robert K., 4n, 96
Meyer, Eugene, 54, 113, 114
Michels, Robert, 107, 114n

Mitchell, Max, 64
Mohl, Robert, 142
Mond, Sir Alfred, 146, 232–33
Morgenstern, Julian, 256
Morgenthau, Henry, Sr., 65–66
Morrison, Isidor, 42
Mosca, Gaetano, 47, 49n, 268–73 passim
Mossinsohn, Ben-Zion, 143
Mowry, George, 57
Myrdal, Gunnar, 60, 82–83

Neumann, Emanuel, 107, 144, 158, 199–200, 202, 242
New York Times, 95, 228

Oppenheimer, Franz, 21
Order of B'nai B'rith, 32
Orthodox Jewish Congregational Union of America, 26
Orthodox Judaism, 12, 14, 16, 26, 32, 33

Pacifists, 112, 113
Palestine Development Association, 185
Palestine Development Committee, 160, 161
Palestine Development Council (P.D.C.), 184, 186, 190, 191, 194
Palestine Development Leagues, 191
Palestine Economic Corporation (P.E.C.), 194
Palestine Restoration Fund, 117, 121, 123
Pam, Hugo, 186
Parsons, Talcott, 268
Philipson, David, 165, 166, 254
Philo-Semitism, 13
Pittsburgh Program, 126–27
Progressive movement, 56–60 passim, 125, 244. See also American Progressives

Provisional Zionist Committee (P.Z.C.), 53, 68, 79, 96–97, 99–101, 103

Ratnoff, Nathan, 242, 245
Reading, Lord Rufus Daniel Isaacs, 146
Red Scare, 118, 129
Reference group, 9, 264–67 passim; normative and comparative, 264, 264n
Reform Judaism, 13, 31–34 passim, 38, 40, 59, 177–78, 192, 250. See also Union of American Hebrew Congregations
Relative deprivation, 9
Republican party, 56, 251
Richards, Bernard, 82, 83, 103, 139
Role relations, 4, 4n, 5, 32
Roosevelt, Theodore, 85
Rosenblatt, Bernard, 50–51, 103, 113, 178
Rosensohn, Samuel, 194, 219
Rosenwald, Julius, 79
Rothschild, Baron James de, 146
Roucek, Joseph, 92
Rubinow, Max, 140, 143

Sachs, Alexander, 159
Samuel, Maurice, 199, 211–12, 229–30, 235
Sanders, Leon, 89
Schechter, Solomon, 41
Schiff, Jacob, 56–57, 61, 64, 69–70, 82, 84–86, 94, 114–17, 132, 275
Schur, William, 27
Schweitzer, Peter, 106
Secularism, 14, 16, 17, 77, 114, 253
Seff, Joseph, 35
Seligman, James, 56
Selznick, Philip, 268
Shelvin, Bernard, 81, 105, 152, 154
Sherman, Bezalel, 55–56, 249
Silver, Abba Hillel, 178, 186, 191, 245
Sklare, Marshall, 16

Social Gospel, 34, 226, 244
Social Zionism, 51, 126
Socialism, 13, 15–17, 33, 38, 41, 44, 48, 112, 255, 265
Sokolov, Nahum, 66, 146, 148
Spiro, Melford, 5
Status inconsistency, 58n, 267
Status-set, 4, 4n, 5, 96, 263, 268
Stonequist, Everett V., 30, 61, 258
Straus, Nathan, 118, 183, 193, 232
Straus, Mrs. Nathan, 118
Straus, Oscar S., 65, 85, 254
Straus, Samuel, 45
Steffens, Lincoln, 10
Sulzberger, Cyrus, 36–39 *passim*
Sulzberger, Mayer, 95
Szold, Henrietta, 37, 53, 91, 105, 204, 218
Szold, Robert, 105, 106, 194, 217, 224–25, 243–46 *passim*

Taft, William Howard, 70
Temple Emanuel in New York, 30, 75
Tulin, Abraham, 229

Union of American Hebrew Congregations, 38. *See also* Reform Judaism
United Palestine Appeal (U.P.A.), 194–95, 199–200, 212, 213, 226, 231, 236, 257–58
United Zionists, 25–28 *passim*
Untermeyer, Samuel, 183, 187, 194, 228

Ussishkin, Menachem, 143, 174

Warburg, Felix, 61, 130, 187, 201, 203, 214, 232–33, 239–41, 270
Ware, Caroline F., 55
Washington, Booker T., 83
Watson, Tom, 58
Weber, Max, 269
Weizmann, Chaim: the dispute with Brandeis and associates, 133, 135–38, 140–41, 149, 158, 161–62, 167–76 *passim*, 270; relations with A.J.C. and Z.O.A. leaders after 1921, 190, 198, 201, 208, 211, 227, 256
Wilson, Woodrow, 62–66 *passim*, 68, 70, 125, 129
Wirth, Louis, 231–32
Wise, Stephen S.: in the F.A.Z., 31, 32, 34, 36, 47, 53; relations with A.J.C. leaders, 66, 70, 75, 83; president of the P.Z.C., 96–97, 104, 105, 109, 110, 113; the dispute with Weizmann and the W.Z.O., 136, 139, 141, 174–75; relations with the Brandeis group and with Lipsky and the Z.O.A., 185–86, 199, 219, 223, 225–26, 228–29, 242
Wolf, Simon, 65–66, 254

Zeeland Program, 150
Zion Associations, 51, 196, 257
Zionist Commission for Palestine, 136–37, 142, 143
Zolotkoff, Leon, 27